Southern Cr D0357328

Credit: *Abby Brown Ayers*

Southern Crossing

A History of the American South, 1877–1906

EDWARD L. AYERS

New York   Oxford
OXFORD UNIVERSITY PRESS
1998

Oxford University Press

Oxford   New York   Toronto
Delhi   Bombay   Calcutta   Madras   Karachi
Kuala Lumpur   Singapore   Hong Kong   Tokyo
Nairobi   Dar es Salaam   Cape Town
Melbourne   Auckland   Madrid

and associated companies in
Berlin   Ibadan

Copyright © 1995 by Edward L. Ayers

Published by Oxford University Press, Inc.,
200 Madison Avenue, New York, New York 10016

Oxford is a registered trademark of Oxford University Press

All rights reserved. No part of this publication may be reproduced,
stored in a retrieval system, or transmitted, in any form or by any means,
electronic, mechanical, photocopying, recording,
or otherwise, without the prior permission of Oxford University Press.

Library of Congress Cataloging-in-Publication Data
Ayers, Edward L., 1953–
Southern crossing : a history of the American South, 1877–1906 /
Edward L. Ayers.
p. cm.
Abridgement of the author's Promise of the New South.
Includes bibliographical references (p.   ) and index.
ISBN 0-19-508690-2 (cl).—ISBN 0-19-508689-9 (pbk.)
1. Southern States—History—1865–1950.
2. Southern States—Civilization—19th century.
I. Ayers, Edward L., 1953–
Promise of the New South. II. Title.
F215.A943   1995 975'.041—dc20   94-9755

2 4 6 8 9 7 5 3
Printed in the United States of America
on acid-free paper

For Nathaniel and Hannah

Preface

The American South saw remarkable changes in the years between the end of Reconstruction in 1877 and the Atlanta race riot of 1906. The landscape was transformed by the beginnings of large-scale industry, the emergence of small-town life, the spread of general stores, the sudden dominance of the railroad, and the decline of the countryside. Southern politics were redefined by segregation, disfranchisement, the Populist revolt, and the beginnings of progressivism. Southern culture was reconfigured by blues, jazz, gospel, and country music, the stirring of modern literature, the spread of popular sports and amusements, and the birth of new religious dominations.

Although the story we tell about the South in these years is usually a straightforward one of poverty, injustice, and backwardness, to leave it at that is to leave out much that made the South what it was. Things were seldom as simple as they appeared to later generations, for Southerners of every rank confronted the dilemmas brought by new opportunities and constraints. Many kinds of power operated in the South, some built on coercion and others built on persuasion, some consented to and some challenged, some private and some public. This book explores these various kinds of power and their complicated consequences in the South.

Each chapter of the book offers a variation on a common theme. In one area of life after another, we see the currents of modern life running powerful and deep in the New South. Rather than simply pulling the South into the national mainstream, however, those currents created a complex series of backlashes, countercurrents, and unexpected outcomes. Many of the aspects of Southern life that appeared the most old-fashioned grew out of the dislocation and innovation of the New South. These apparent continuities were not merely products of inertia, continuity, folk culture, or backwardness, but often of Southerners' interaction with the outside world and with one another. This book is about the constant and multileveled interplay between inside and outside, old and new; it is about the conflicts between generations, between town and country, between rich and poor; it is about the ambivalence with which Southerners confronted the sudden changes in their society.

As much as I could, I have told these stories through the voices of Southerners themselves. One intention of this strategy is to make the narrative more immediate and engaging, to get us as close as we can to the texture of this place and time. Each voice, moreover, is intended to add nuance and complication to the larger story the chapter is telling. The story is sometimes discontinuous, as chapters move from one topic to another without much warning. This strategy is supposed to remind us that history is not seamless; everyone and everything will not fit in one plot; a society of twenty million people does not fit into one fable. Rather than try to hide that uncomfortable fact with the accustomed voice of the omniscient narrator, I have sought to call attention to the many, often contradictory, things that were going on in the South at the same time.

This book is a shorter version of *The Promise of the New South: Life after Reconstruction.* I have replaced the elaborate documentation of that book with an essay on sources. I have also cut a considerable amount of state-level political history and other topics peculiar to limited parts of the South, while keeping as much material as I could on everyday life, race relations, women, Populism, and culture. The book has also been reorganized considerably, concentrated more by topic. The goal remains the same as in the original narrative: to offer a glimpse into a society undergoing what so many societies in the world have undergone, the sudden confrontation with the promises, costs, and consequences of modern life.

I would like to thank the readers of the original version of this book who kindly shared their impressions with me. Their letters and conversations about its strengths and weaknesses went a long way toward shaping this abridgement. I am also grateful to reviewers and confeence panel members whose thoughtful and generous comments helped me see the book more clearly. Thanks, finally, to Lottie McCauley and Kathleen Miller for their expert help on the index.

Charlottesville   E.L.A.
Spring 1994

Contents

Part III   Cultural Life

Southern Crossing

Chapter 1

Junction

The Southern landscape of 1880 bore the signs of the preceding twenty years. Symmetrical rows of slave cabins had been knocked into a jumble of tenant shacks. Fields grew wild because it did not pay to farm them. Children came upon bones and rusting weapons when they played in the woods. Former slaveowners and their sons decided which tenants would farm the best land and which tenants would have to move on. Confederate veterans at the court house or the general store bore empty sleeves and blank stares. Black people bitterly recalled the broken promises of land from the Yankees and broken promises of help from their former masters and mistresses. Everyone labored under the burdens of the depression that had hobbled the 1870s. Men talked of the bloodshed that had brought Reconstruction to an end a few years before.

Signs of a new South appeared as well, shoved up against the signs of the old. Merchants seemed to be putting up stores of precut lumber at every crossroads. Hundreds of new towns proudly displayed raw red-brick buildings and at least a block or two of wooden sidewalks. Investors began to put money into sawmills, textile factories, and coal mines. Young people of both races set out for places where they could make a better living. Railroads connected the landscape, cutting into clay banks, running across long sandy and swampy stretches, winding their way through wet mountain forests. Enthusiastic young editors talked of a "New South."

Shifting borders surrounded this South. Southern accents echoed into Indiana, Illinois, and Ohio; Northerners moved across the Kentucky and Arkansas lines; immigrants came to Texas, Louisiana, and Mississippi; Southern farmers produced for Northern markets up the coastline or across the river. Despite these porous boundaries, it seemed clear to most people that the South included the eleven states of the former Confederacy, that Kentucky was a Southern state in spite of its Civil War experience, and that the Southern mountains harbored a distinct, but distinctly Southern, region. West Texas and the southern tip of Florida, by contrast, seemed empty and disconnected from the South's history of slavery and war.

Soil, rivers, and climate determined whether counties would flourish or decline, whether railroads and manufacturing would arrive, whether people would come or leave. New technologies and techniques offered sudden hope to areas that had been passed over for centuries, while districts that had long been at the center of the South's political and economic power lapsed into decay. Southerners abandoned old homes and took up new ones within the region, well aware of the different possibilities a hundred miles could make.

Vast plains stretched all along the South's coast from Virginia to Texas, from the Atlantic to the Gulf of Mexico. Tall pines, slow rivers, and swamps dominated the landscape. Above the falls on the rivers, the Piedmont's rolling hills and quick waters promised healthy agriculture and vibrant manufacturing. North of the Piedmont, the mountains and valleys of the Blue Ridge, the Cumberlands, and the Alleghenies enfolded a complex landscape of swelling peaks, narrow hollows, and fertile valleys; the Ozarks of Arkansas, far away from the other highlands, resembled them in most respects. The central plateau of Kentucky and Tennessee claimed farms good for livestock but unsuited for cotton.

To the south of the Piedmont, a dark, narrow crescent called the Black Belt cut across from South Carolina up through Mississippi. The home of the antebellum South's most lucrative plantations, the Black Belt declined in the New South. The Mississippi River bisected the South from the tip of Kentucky, down between Arkansas and Tennessee, between Louisiana and Mississippi to the port of New Orleans. Rich soils and good transportation along the river's shores beckoned farmers of both races to build levees and clear the heavy growth of hardwoods. Sparsely settled rolling uplands covered much of Arkansas, Louisiana, and Texas, offering cheap lands for enterprising farmers to grow cotton. Southerners converged on the Western prairies at the frontier of the South; by the turn of the century the district had a high proportion of its land in cotton.

Great disparities marked the nine subregions of the New South. Both coastal plains contained thousands of square miles of lightly populated land, while the rural districts of the Piedmont and central plateau seemed crowded. Black Southerners made up over two-thirds of the people in the Black Belt but accounted for only about a tenth of those in the mountains and on the Western prairies. New settlers of both races rushed to the Atlantic and Gulf plains, the mountains, and the prairies; blacks shunned the Piedmont and the central plateau, while whites turned away from the Black Belt and the river counties. Thousands of new farms grew up along the southern and western edges of the region even as tenancy entangled the older districts.

Quickly evolving systems of commerce heightened differences among places and people even as they tied them together. Although railroads, stores, and towns came into sudden prominence throughout the South, each place had its own local chronology. Any given year would find some places in a buoyant mood as a railroad approached or a new mill opened, while others, bypassed by the machinery of the new order, fell into decay. The arrival of a railroad could trigger many consequences: rapid population growth or population decline, a more diversified economy or greater specialization, the growth of a city or the death of small towns.

Only a few events in the New South temporarily focused people on concerns beyond their localities. Political changes provided major landmarks that defined the period. The New South era began in the mid- and late 1870s when the biracial and reformist experiment of Reconstruction ended and the conservative white Democrats took power throughout the Southern states. Then, in the early 1890s, the largest political revolt in American history, Populism, redrew the political boundaries of the South and the nation. Business cycles, too, created common experiences across the South. The 1880s saw town and industrial growth in the South but steady economic pressure on farmers. The 1890s began with a terrible depression that lasted through half the decade, followed by a decade of relative prosperity. Within these broad patterns, the people of the New South lived lives of great variation and contrast.

Under Reconstruction, Republicans had hoped to form an alliance that would include influential whites as well as former slaves. Some party leaders stressed land redistribution while others emphasized the vote; some called for federal aid to education and others demanded civil rights. For a while, the party managed to hold together its alliance of for ner slaves, former Unionists, and former Northerners, all dedicated to economic prosperity and equal rights for all Southerners. But the difficulty of binding together a coalition across lines of race and class constantly wore at the Republicans in the South; voters and leaders began to defect in the face of enticement, animosity, violence, and defeat. The Northern wing of the party turned away from its Southern compatriots as it became clear that Reconstruction was unpopular in the North and unlikely to succeed in the South without protection and aid from outside.

Conservative Democrats "redeemed" one state after another, as the Democrats called it, driving Republican governments from power. Conservative governments opposed to Reconstruction took over in Virginia in 1869,

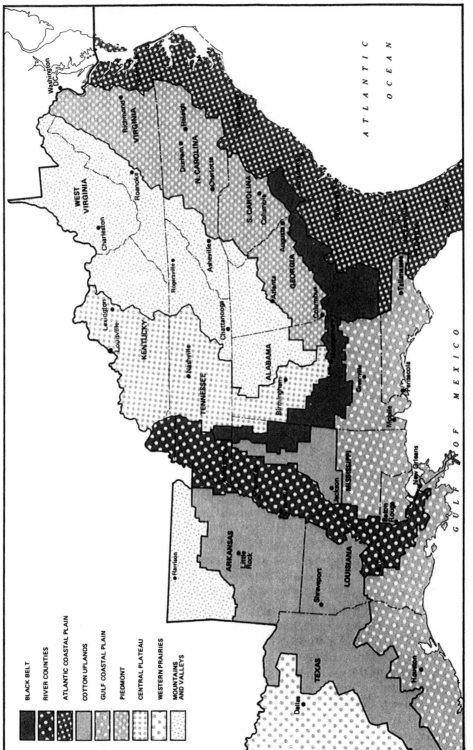

The subregions of the New South.

in North Carolina in 1870, and in Georgia in 1871. Democrats regained dominance in Texas in 1873, in Alabama and Arkansas in 1874, and in South Carolina and Mississippi in 1876. Reconstruction's final gasp came in 1877, when Congress declared victory for the Democrats in contested elections in Louisiana and Florida.

Redemption did not descend in a sudden rush of Democratic glory, but arrived slowly, tentatively, awkwardly. Some counties remained in Republican hands long after Democrats won neighboring counties, years after their state government came under Democratic control. Some conservative Democrats compromised with their opponents, reaching out for black voters, trying to pull opposition leaders into their ranks, offering appeals to Republican businessmen. In other counties, the Redeemers took power through brute force, intimidating and assaulting Republican officeholders and voters with random violence and the aid of the Ku Klux Klan.

Many of the Redeemer Democrats bore impressive pedigrees and could claim distinguished service in the Confederacy. In counties and states across the South white veterans with education and property stepped forward to seize the power they considered rightfully theirs. Under Democratic rule, they promised, political bloodshed would cease, race relations would calm, the economy would flourish, and honor in government would prevail.

The Democratic Redeemers defined themselves, in large part, by what they were not. Unlike the Republicans, the Redeemers were not interested in a biracial coalition. The Democrats would not seriously consider black needs, would not invert the racial hierarchy by allowing blacks to hold offices for which whites longed. Unlike the Republicans, too, the Redeemers would not use the state government as an active agent of change. Democrats scoffed not only at Republican support for railroads and other business, but also at Republican initiatives in schools, orphanages, prisons, and asylums. Democrats assured landowning farmers that the party would roll back taxes. The Democrats saw themselves as the proponents of common sense, honesty, and caution where the Republicans offered foolishness, corruption, and impetuosity. The Democrats explained away their own violence and fraud, both of which soon dwarfed that of Reconstruction, as fighting fire with fire. Democratic policies encouraged economic growth not through active aid, as the Republicans had done, but through low taxes on railroads and on farmland, with few restrictions on business and few demands on government.

Watched over by friendly Democratic regimes, railroad companies worked feverishly in the New South. From the end of Reconstruction to the end of the century the South built railroads faster than the nation as a whole. Different lines raced from one subregion to another, competing for key territories; by 1890, nine of every ten Southerners lived in a railroad county. The construction of a railroad touched people all up and down the track. "From New Orleans to Meridian was a beehive of activity. Literally thousands of

people were employed," a Mississippian recalled. "For the first time there
was a big market for what people could raise in this area." "I believe the
people as a general thing are in better circumstances now than they have
been in several years," Joe Vick wrote from Texas back to his aunt in Virginia; "one cause of it I reacon is because there is a Rail Road building right
through this neighborhood and nearly every body has got afew dollars out
of it."

The railroad crews lived in rough camps. "We have not as orderly a set
of men as may be imagined on the work," a young man wrote to his parents
with considerable understatement. "They all carry pistols and yesterday there
were three men shot in one camp." But the money was good. "Monday was
pay day amongst the railroad workmen between here and Eureka," an Arkansas paper noted, "and several thousand dollars were passed into the
hands of the laborers."

Charley White, a young section hand on a Texas railroad, discovered
the dangers of mixing ready money with the bawdy life of the railroad camp.
Along with his compatriots, White visited "Miss Minnie's," a whorehouse
along the line. He found "too much going on. Killing folks, and beating up,
and slashing with knives." The attractions were considerable, though:
"There was lots of women there. All kinds. Some old, some young, some
half-naked, some dressed nice—just any type you wanted." One beckoned
Charley to her room, but White was scared. The brother of one of the hands
who had been loitering around the bunkhouse was "half eat up" with syphilis, terrible sores covering his entire body. "Some of the other men had it
too, but they wasn't as bad off as he was." White decided to settle down; he
met a nice young woman, "quit the railroad and got me a job working at a
sawmill."

Working on a train was extraordinarily dangerous. The record of acci-
dents on one small line for one year gives some idea of the damage the
railroad could inflict: "hand crushed, collision, killed, collision, foot struck,
hip hurt, struck by #24, leg run over while switching and injury resulted in
death, cut on head, finger cracked, thumb cracked and finger broken, struck
by bridge and killed, leg broken, fall from train sustaining injuries resulting
in death, found injured by side of road, run over and killed, skull fractured,
death resulted, son of Rev. J. W. Miller killed, shoulder blade broken, run
into No. 7 on middle track, hand crushed, negro boy run over and head cut
off, leg run over necessitating amputation, wreck caused by broken wheel,
killed." Yet the railroad was surrounded by an aura of glamour throughout
the New South era. "All that they had said was true, and much more. People
were crowded and seemed to be excited," the son of a poor farmer recalled
of his first trip to the "Big Terminal" in Atlanta. "Hundreds of people, many
of them hurrying, were pushing against each other, pages were yelling
names, a big Negro was calling stations for departing trains; train bells ringing, steam escaping with strange and frightening sounds. . . . The strange

lights, the queer smell of things, and the soft, heavenly feel of the velvet that covered the seats on the train, held us older children spellbound.''

Towns that finally saw the railroad reach them could barely contain themselves. A small town in the Ozark Mountains of Arkansas exulted: "Harrison Is a Railroad Town At Last. The Construction Train Laid Yesterday the Steel Which Puts us in Touch With the World," proclaimed the headline of the local paper. The editor reported that 2000 people thronged the streets, cannons boomed, flags waved. The ice company expanded its electrical capacity, the town fathers ordered the bandstand painted, local merchants began a new iron and stone building, the Bradshaw Saloon received new fixtures, and the hotel even put in bathrooms.

In places lucky enough to have a railroad, the station often became the most prominent feature of the landscape. Opelousas, Louisiana, got passenger service, and "the landing place of the road is crowded every evening by the people of the town. No one ever thinks of taking a walk in any other direction from that leading to the railroad tracks." The editor of the local paper thought he could discern "a very great change" in the town's citizens. "They are rapidly casting aside their old rustic country ways and are becoming metropolitan-like in appearance and deportment."

When the railroads found themselves and their passengers inconvenienced by the old-fashioned way of keeping time—every town in the country basing its own calculations on the passing of the sun and the turning of local clocks—it became clear that time would have to be made uniform if the ever-growing rail system was to operate efficiently and safely. In 1883 the railroads took it upon themselves to divide the country into four time zones and the railroad became the arbiter of time as of so much else in the nation and in the South. "We consulted the clock [only] when we had to catch a train, the clock's strongest ally in clamping down on the human race and holding it in a fixed and rigid rhythm," a South Carolina man recalled. The train, everyone came to realize, lived according to a schedule that suited the system, the mechanism. The locomotive passed through nearly a thousand Southern counties but it belonged to none of them.

Throughout the 1870s and early 1880s Southern railroad companies experimented with ways to accommodate themselves to the different widths of track between North and South; some used cars with especially wide wheels that could operate on either the North's narrow gauge or the South's three-inch wider gauge, some used cars with adjustable axles, some used hoists to lift car bodies while the trucks underneath were changed. All these methods proved cumbersome and expensive, and so in 1885 the major railroads agreed to standardize nearly 13,000 miles of track of eccentric gauge. the great bulk of which lay in the South. The move was all made on one day: Sunday, May 30, 1886. Frantic work crews shoved thousands of miles of rail three inches closer together on that day. The integration and improvement never ceased: steel replaced iron, spur lines reached into ever more remote areas, new companies pushed aside those who got in the way of the system.

While some general stores had grown up at junctions on Southern railroads in the 1850s, the clientele and impact of those stores had remained small. Slaves could purchase very little on their own, and small farmers, who spent most of their energy producing for their household or local market, had little currency and little need for credit. Most of the things small farmers could not import or make themselves—shoes, harnesses, plows, hinges, nails—were crafted by local artisans, slave and free. Farm women usually made their families' clothes, sometimes with store-bought gingham, but more often with homespun; slave women and mistresses did the same work for plantation slaves. Infrequent purchases from local stores usually involved staples such as salt, molasses, and coffee. Planters, whose business depended on trade in international commodity and financial markets, often dealt with factors in New York or London. The factor made purchases abroad on behalf of his clients and shipped goods directly to the plantation.

The situation changed after emancipation, with the rapid emergence of country stores in the late 1860s and early 1870s. National laws written during the Civil War put most banks in the North and left stores to dispense the vast majority of credit in the Southern countryside. With cash scarce, Southern legislators created lien laws that allowed the use of unplanted crops as collateral for loans to get cotton and corn into the ground. Because the few Southern banks had little incentive to lend either to small farmers or to rural stores, stores operated on credit dispensed by wholesalers, who in turn obtained credit from manufacturers or town banks. The stores increasingly stood at the center of the rural economy.

Stores sped the reorientation of plantation-belt economic life. Many freedpeople, at the demand of their landlords, concentrated on growing cotton and abandoned their gardens; they turned to stores for everything they needed. Other freedpeople, working for wages and having some say over how they would spend their money, also turned to the store, eagerly purchasing symbols of their independence. Many planters used plantation stores to wring extra profit from their tenants, marking up goods substantially and doling out credit to keep tenants on the farm throughout the season. Independent merchants established stores as well, though, competing for the business of the freedpeople and white farmers. Both planters and merchants took a lien on the unplanted crop of their customers as security for the loan of goods and supplies. The lien proved a powerful political and economic weapon for those who wielded it.

Farms outside plantation areas had been growing more cash crops even before the Civil War, as railroads proliferated and high cotton prices beckoned. The war had temporarily halted cotton sales but they accelerated in the decade after Appomattox. In the first years after the war, pent-up world demand raised the price of cotton. Northern manufacturers and commission houses sent agents to drum up business in the South; they met eager clients behind the counters. Hundreds of new stores emerged to loan money, market crops, and make profits from the rapidly spreading cotton economy.

"Have you all felt the affects of the low price of cotton," a son wrote his father fifteen years into the post-Reconstruction South. "It nearly ruined us. I did not get my house build. The farmers are very blue here. But getting ready to plant cotton again." Asked how it was that Southern farmers fell into this cycle of futility, J. Pope Brown, a cotton farmer himself, answered the question impatiently: "That was by necessity, almost. You can not go into all of that. We were poor, had nothing to go on, had no collateral, and we just had to plant the crop that would bring money right away. We did not have time to wait." In the immediate postwar years farmers could count on cotton when they could count on nothing else; it was easily grown by a farm family, nonperishable, in demand, seemingly profitable, and easy to get credit for. The fertilizer brought by the railroads extended the growing season in the upcountry and reduced the risks of growing cotton in places beyond the plantation areas. By the 1880s, cotton production had spread to thousands of new farms, into the upcountry of Georgia, Alabama, and South Carolina as well as onto the Texas and Arkansas frontier. Through all the twists and turns of Southern politics, through all the fluctuations of the volatile American economy, Southerners of both races grew more cotton.

The farmers who pondered the problem of low cotton prices faced certain insurmountable facts throughout the New South era. "There is one thing I want to impress upon you," insisted a farmer testifying before a federal commission studying the problem. "Cotton is the thing to get credit on in this country. Ten acres of cotton will give you more credit than 50 acres of corn. . . . You can always sell cotton. You leave home with a wagon load of cotton and you will go home that night with money in your pocket; you load up your wagon with wheat or corn and come here with 100 bushels, and I doubt some days whether you could sell it." Unlike grain or vegetables, cotton would always be worth *something*. Cotton required no expensive machinery, no elaborate ditching or irrigation, no vast labor force, no arcane knowledge. From the viewpoint of the individual farmer, especially one with little capital to risk in experimenting with some new crop, cotton made sense.

Precisely because more farmers became adept at raising more cotton at the same time as countries on the other side of the world greatly increased their production, the South soon grew far too much of the commodity for the region's own good. One farmer explained the cruel cycle. "When the fellow would come up at the end of the year with six short bales of cotton and a mule, the cotton farmer would say to him, 'Why did you not make more cotton? Here is a man that got ten bales.' He went back home and put in to make ten bales, and at the end of the year he had ten bales, and when he came to the farmer the latter said, 'Why did you not make more? Here is a man that made twelve bales, and here is another who made fifteen bales.' " After the farmer had struggled to make as much cotton as he could, he suddenly heard a new set of directions. " 'You fool, you have made too much; you have overdone the thing.' And he was doing what they told him to do all the time. We got in that fix and we did not know what to do. I was one of those fellows." A good farmer had always been one who could make the land yield more. "The trouble about it was we started out making it at 20 cents, and then it went to 15, and then to 10, and when we learned to make it at 10 it went to 8, and when we thought we had learned to make it at 8 it went to 6, and when we had learned how to make it at 6 it went to 4."

After sharecropping and preaching for years, Charley White and his wife Lucille got a chance to buy 27 acres in Texas for $350. "The house wasn't much more than a shack," White recalled, but his wife never complained and the children were too young to care. "Lucille and me always had worked hard, both of us. We hadn't ever minded work. But looked like when we got some land that belonged to us it just set us on fire. We didn't seems to get half as tired, or if we did we didn't notice it. One day when we was cleaning up a field Lucille said, 'You know, Charley, even the rocks look pretty.' " The ambition that drove Charley and Lucille White drove many blacks in the New South.

The cashbook of Daniel Trotter, a black farmer from Natchitoches Parish, Louisiana, showed how a black family pieced together enough for a farm. In 1899, his wife sold eggs, one or two dozen at a time, earning $5.30; she also contributed $7.80 from her sewing of dresses and jeans. The family sold four pigs and made $70.22 picking cotton. Meanwhile, Trotter made even more "cash money" by "fixing miller machinery," "fixing water clock," "bell clock," and guns. Some of this money the family spent on such things as stockings, a mattress, paint, coats, onion sets, "arsh potatoes," "wrighting paper," stamps, "bluin," "sweet oil," sardines, pills, black pepper, a round file, bread, candy, shot, and ginger snaps, revealing that they enjoyed a standard of life above that of most black farmers. By the end of the year Trotter noted that his family's savings totaled $175 in "Green Back" and $33 in silver. In 1900, the Trotters bought a "plantation" for an undisclosed sum. Trotter recorded his labor and his accounting in a little booklet put out by a patent medicine company. As if to mock his ambition, a cartoon opposite his meticulous figures showed a familiar scene from the advertising of the day: a well-dressed white man looks down at a black child and says, "My, what a nice fat little boy!" and the child replies, "Golly, boss, that ain't no fat; dat's nuffin but M. A. Simmons' Liver Medicine. We can't git along widout in dis country."

While white landowners, especially absentee ones, might sell remote or poor lands to blacks, prospective black landowners faced a disheartening situation with regard to land in the Black Belt. "We air in veary bad condishion here," F. M. Gilmore, a black man from Arkansas, wrote the African Colonization Society. "Land Lords has got us Bound To Do Just as they Say or git off of his Land, and we air Compeled to Do so. . . . and they say it is not entend from the begaining for a Dam negro to have. But, a small peace of Land in the South, an it is only 6 feet by 4 wide 4 ft deep." A black man, according to the whites Gilmore dealt with, "has no bisness with money by no means whatever. an ef He git Corn bread and fat meet and $12.00 . . . per year that is A plenty for ever head of A Negro."

"The best sign for the Negroes of our land," a sympathetic white woman observed, "is that they are fast separating into classes, a fact to which their white fellow-citizens often fail to attach the importance it deserves." Black Southerners increasingly differed among themselves in quite self-conscious ways. "Few modern groups show a greater internal differentiation of social conditions than the Negro American, and the failure to realize this is the cause of much confusion," W. E. B. DuBois pointed out. "The forward movement of a social group is not the compact march of an army, where the distance covered is practically the same for all, but is rather the straggling of a crowd, where some of whom hasten, some linger, some turn back, some reach far-off goals before others even start, and yet the crowd moves on."

Southern trains were divided into two cars, a "smoking" car for men and a "ladies' " car for families and non-smoking men as well as for women. Custom had it that blacks would ride in the smoking car, but as a white women's suffragist from Ohio on her first visit to the South related, these cars offered only nauseating conditions: "All Southern trains run a compartment car for nigers, and men spit on floor in all cars so it is dreadful. We always go in looking for clean floor and seat—sure enough I wish I had on short skirts in such dirty cars."

A growing number of black men and women shunned the spitting, cursing, and drinking they too often confronted in the "smoking" car. Unfortunately, they found a different kind of trouble when they attempted to move to better conditions. One well-dressed black man, asked by the conductor to leave the ladies' car after the train crossed the state line between Tennessee and Georgia, refused. Even after three young white men ordered him to move, he declined. The three whites assaulted him. When the conductor returned to get tickets, the black man sought the official's protection. The conductor told the white assailants to calm down and ordered the man whom they had beaten to go to the smoking car. "The negro's face was covered with blood," the Atlanta *Constitution* related. "His silk hat was mashed, and he was scared." He got off at the next station, many miles before his destination.

"Self-respecting colored people would not go into the coach set apart for them" before laws forced them to do so, Mary Church Terrell recalled. In the late 1860s, her father bought a first-class ticket for himself and his young daughter. Mary, five years old, enjoyed the trip until the white conductor came by while her father had stepped into the smoker. "As he pulled me roughly out of the seat, he turned to the man sitting across the aisle and said, 'Whose little nigger is this?' The man told him who my father was and advised him to let me alone. Seeing the conductor was about to remove me from the car, one of my father's white friends went into the smoker to tell him what was happening." Mary's father insisted, successfully, that their ticket entitled them to first-class accommodations. When they reached home, the girl tried to discover what she had done wrong. "I hadn't mussed my hair; it was brushed back and was perfectly smooth. I hadn't lost either one of the two pieces of blue ribbon which tied the little braids on each side of my head. I hadn't soiled my dress a single bit. I was sitting up 'straight and proper.' " Her mother could only respond that "sometimes conductors on railroad trains were unkind and treated good little girls very badly."

The railroad companies did not want to be bothered with policing Southern race relations and considered the division of coaches into black and white compartments an irksome and unnecessary expense. Despite the railroad companies' resistance, though, growing tensions about race and gender, anger at the railroads, and political maneuvering pushed toward the separation of the races. In the late 1880s and early 1890s, the railroads became the scenes of the first statewide segregation laws throughout the South.

New villages emerged in every corner of the South, "buried in bends of the rivers, hidden behind mountains, perched on rises of ground beside bayous, and strung along thousands of miles of virtually impassable roads." These places served as the stages where much of the history of the New South was played out. Every subregion of the South witnessed the emergence and evolution of villages, hamlets of fewer than 2500 people.

Villages beginning with a single store, church, or school quickly grew into larger settlements. The number of villages in the South doubled between 1870 and 1880, then doubled again by 1900, to over 2000 villages containing 1.2 million people. The South's larger towns and cities also took off in the 1880s—the rate of urban growth nearly doubling the national average—and continued strong for generations. By 1910, more than 7 million Southerners lived in a town or city. The cities of the New South stood not as isolated islands in a vast rural sea but rather as the center of trade and ambition for dozens of smaller towns and cities. Overlapping and interlocking systems embraced virtually every village and town in the South. Influence, fashion, and capital moved down through these systems, while crops, migrants, and profits worked their way up. From their very beginning, the villages, towns, and cities of the New South worked as parts of complicated and interdependent networks.

Southern boosters of the early 1880s told everyone who would listen that their region had entered upon the initial stages of a profound and beneficial transformation. While the depression-plagued 1870s had seen only the spottiest and most halting kind of industrial development in the South, in the eighties capital, wages, and value of product all more than doubled. A host of journalists made names for themselves and their publications by justifying, cheering, defending, and aiding these starts at a new industrial South.

But there was a problem: many Southerners detested those who were willing to purchase Northern good will and capital by renouncing the actions and beliefs of their fathers. "I ask in Heaven's name, is it essential that a southern man must eat dirt or wallow therein, denounce his ancestry or ridicule their foibles, or otherwise degrade himself to prove his newborn loyalty and devotion to the new order of things?" a letter writer asked after one editorial urged the South to let go of the past and join the national mainstream.

It was left to Henry Grady, the young and buoyant editor of the Atlanta *Constitution,* to construct a rationale that allowed the South to have it both ways, to be proudly Southern and yet partake of the new industrial bounty. Grady, a member of the generation that had come of age since Appomattox—he was thirty-six in 1886, when he became nationally famous—seemed to embody the South's new industrial growth and optimism. The son of a merchant, a graduate of the University of Georgia and the beneficiary of a year of postgraduate work at the University of Virginia, a correspondent for Northern papers, a champion of diversified agriculture and the "cooperation" of the races, the attractive and personable Grady rose quickly in the late seventies and early eighties. He became a privileged investor in Atlanta and a major figure in Georgia politics, giving him more than a rhetorical stake in the South and his city. He faced a difficult choice in 1886 when he got off the train in New York to make a speech before the New England Society of New York, where no Southerner had ever spoken before. Asked what he was going to say, Grady replied, "The Lord only knows. I have thought of a thousand things to say, five hundred of which if I say they will murder me when I get back home, and the other five hundred of which will get me murdered at the banquet."

In his speech, Grady serenely exaggerated the changes that had come to the South in the preceding few years in politics, in race relations, in industrial and agricultural growth. He praised Abraham Lincoln as "the typical American" and joked that his fellow speaker William T. Sherman was "considered an able man in our parts, though some people think he is a kind of careless man about fire." But the dominant theme of his speech was that the New South had built itself out of devastation without surrendering its self-respect. "As she stands upright, full-statured and equal among the people of the earth, breathing the keen air and looking out upon the expanded horizon, she understands that her emancipation came because through the inscrutable wisdom of God her honest purpose was crossed, and her brave armies were beaten." Grady pushed his point, to make sure he was misunderstood neither by the North or the South: "The South has nothing for which to apologize. . . . The South has nothing to take back." Yet he "was glad that the omniscient God held the balance of battle in His Almighty hand and that human slavery was swept forever from American soil, the American Union was saved from the wreck of war." The portly audience cheered through its tears, and those counting on Southern industry breathed a little easier.

To many people, Southern industry seemed more of a charade than an actuality. After enduring twenty years of exaggerated claims in the *Manufacturer's Record,* even a Southern trade paper could stand the puffery no longer: "If all the saw mills, cotton mills, tobacco factories, new towns, and other enterprises and undertakings which it has heralded to its advertisers and 'subscribers' as having been started up in the various states of the South, had really been erected and put into operation," the *Southern Lumberman* sneered in 1908, "there wouldn't be surface room for them to stand on, water enough under the earth to supply their boilers, nor room enough in the sky for the smoke from their chimneys." Reality looked nothing like this.

Federal banking policy, railroad freight rates, absentee ownership, reliance on outside expertise, high interest rates, cautious state governments, lack of industrial experience—all these hindered the growth of Southern industry. New Southern enterprises had to compete with long-established Northern counterparts for capital, a share of the market, and skilled technicians. In these ways, much of the broad economic development that industrial growth brought to the North in the nineteenth century did not occur in the South.

Yet every measure of industrial growth raced ahead in the New South, the rates of change consistently outstripping national averages. The increase in value added compared favorably with the other industrializing economies of the nineteenth century. Productivity actually grew faster in the South than it had in New England during its industrial revolution fifty years earlier.

Southerners poured enormous amounts of sweat and ambition, along with the relatively little money they had, into the products the world market would buy. They rushed to fill the only gaps in the national and international economies they could find: cheap iron, cheap cloth, cheap coal, cheap lumber, turpentine, sugar, and tobacco products. At the same time, new manufactured goods from the North and abroad flooded the South, undermining small firms who had produced for the local markets. Like other backward economies vying with established industrial nations, the South turned out the few products the more fortunate industrial nations or the less fortunate non-industrialized nations were willing to purchase. Like other backward economies, too, the South endured low wages, absentee ownership, and little control over national policy. The changes these industries brought were remarkable, nevertheless, deep and widespread.

Communities in Virginia, the Carolinas, and Georgia watched as huge crowds of local blacks gathered at railroad stations to await transportation to the Mississippi Delta, the Louisiana rice or sugar fields, or the turpentine camps of the piney woods. "At the depot an interesting spectacle presented itself in the huge mass of luggage piled on the platform," a New Bern, North Carolina, newspaper reported in 1889. "Old meat boxes, various other boxes, barrels, trunks of all shapes and sizes, were piled ten feet high on the platform. The train could not accommodate all who wanted to go." "The negro exodus now *amounts to a stampede*," David Schenck of Greensboro wrote in his diary in January of 1890. "*Nineteen passenger coaches filled to the doors*, nine cars filled with baggage, *1,400 negroes*, all pulled by a twelve wheeled consolidated engine. . . . I judge that between 5 and 10,000 have passed in the last fortnight, on their way to Mississippi, Arkansas, and Louisiana."

Observers expressed widely varying opinions about just what all this movement among Southern blacks foretold. Some worried. "The disposition among the colored people to migrate now is strong, and is increasing," a white Southerner wrote in 1889. "In nearly all communities there are Negroes of whom none knows the coming, or the going, or even the real names. The Negro is restive, the white apprehensive, and both are growing more and more suspicious. Such a status is already half hostile even before an overt act is committed." Others fumed. "Our young negro men are becoming tramps, and moving about over the country in gangs to get the most remunerative work," one white testified to the Industrial Commission. Only the "older men, with families" were willing to stay at one place any length of time.

The states of the Upper South—Virginia, Kentucky, Tennessee, and North Carolina—saw the greatest relative loss of black natives. In those states blacks tended to move in a northerly direction, while those in the Lower South tended to move to states directly to their west. Indiana, Illinois, Ohio, Pennsylvania, New York, Massachusetts, and New Jersey received substantial numbers of black Southerners around the turn of the century; the migrants totaled about 141,000 in the two decades after 1880. And many more whites than blacks fled the South. While the thirteen Southern states saw a net loss of 537,000 blacks between 1880 and 1910, the loss of whites totaled 1,243,000 in those same decades. After 1900, when land in Texas and Louisiana became harder to get, Southern whites began to move to California and other parts of the Far West, places relatively few blacks had the means to go. All along, the South lost white population to every other part of the union.

By the 1880s many Southern planters, and especially their children, were leaving the plantations. "What was once the single occupation of the Southern gentleman," one observer noted, had become "the last that he would voluntarily assume." Philip Alexander Bruce, himself the scion of an antebellum planting family, coolly portrayed the decay of the plantation and its dominant class. "The steady emigration of the members of the new generation" had decimated a planting class economically buffeted for decades, especially in the older Southern states of the Atlantic seaboard, Bruce wrote. "When the survivors of the large planters passed away, as there were few of their sons willing to succeed them in the old homes, the estates were sold, and the proceeds divided among the scattered children." Agriculture now offered "no career, as formerly, to energetic and ambitious young men entering into active life." The only thing that had "prevented a complete disruption of the large plantation system in every neighbourhood," Bruce pointed out, was "the inability in some places to secure purchasers." Although ordinary whites (and, he might have added, blacks) were buying up some of the land, "a vast extent of Southern soil is temporarily lapsing into wilderness" for want of people with money to purchase it.

One scene haunted white observers of the South: "Most of the ancestral homes have been abandoned by their owners for a residence in the cities," a traveler to the Black Belt wrote, "the white-columned porticos of the favorite colonial architecture now mouldering in decay, the wide and once hospitable front halls resounding only to the rough banter and quarrels of negro tenants and their children." A planter from Georgia, when asked what became of white children growing up in the rural South, answered that "most of them drift away from the farm. Some go to towns and hunt jobs, and things like that. . . . If a boy has any move in him he wants something better."

Northerners considered Southerners as lazy and inefficient in the New South as they had been in the Old. Ella Harrison was disgusted when she went down to Mississippi to campaign for woman's suffrage. "What they need is more independence and thrift—some northern snap—but you've no idea how pokey—slow—every one is," she wrote her father. "The niger and white man were both lazy before the war—niger to get a rest had to idle when master was not round, and Master had to idle to maintain his dignity. Now both are helpless." The only hope for the South seemed to be for such people to finish their blighted lives and make room for a new generation. "When they die, and the future fellow who lives in this naturally rich land, gets 'grit,' 'gumpshun,' and 'get' into him then the natural opportunities of this part may become known." In the meantime, "death and education has much to do to redeem this south-land."

To some white Southerners, the region faced greater danger from the triumph of Yankee values than from Southern laziness or imperiousness. A student newspaper at the University of Virginia put it bluntly: "It is very sad to see the old freedom from mean mercenary motives passing away, and instead, growing up in the breasts of our fellow Southerners, the sordid, cold blooded, commercial money idea that has always been the marked characteristic of other sections of the country." Henry Waring Ball of Mississippi observed that his young nephew had "gone to work. He asked his mother to let him help a little chum of his to deliver papers, and brought home in real triumph a nickel as the result of his first venture. He is very faithful and industrious at it, and says his chum will give him 25 cents a week for helping him." Such evidence of enterprise might have heartened other families, but not this one. "We laugh over it, but if it is an indication of his character, it is not a laughing matter. Few boys at 7 years would voluntarily hunt up work and become money makers—even at 25 cents a week. I know it would horrify either one of his grandfathers, beyond all measure, but times change, and we with them, alas!"

Young people, on the other hand, could be perturbed by their elders' lassitude. " 'Come day, go day, God send Sunday' is more the motto of the free and go-easy life of the Boyds," S. D. Boyd, Jr., of Virginia complained in his diary. His parents and grandparents had not been "reared up to hard work. They had their slaves, their servants etc, were not accustomed to it in their youth, and hence cannot understand hard business. They take things easy, love *to talk, to eat* and *to sleep* but it does not come natural to them to come down to hard work." The Boyds were, their son observed, "a Procrastinating People . . . a people who do not feel altogether the great *business importance of keeping an engagement.*"

James Eleazar of South Carolina was twelve years old before he discovered that the South had lost the Civil War: "And it was one of the saddest awakenings I ever had. For hours on end I had listened to Grandpa tell of whipping the lard out of the Yankees on a dozen battlefields. Despite their odds in every battle, the matchless Lee and Jackson had cut the enemy's ranks to pieces." The tales Eleazar's grandfather told, though, somehow never extended all the way to Gettysburg and Appomattox. "It was when I got to that point in our history book that I discovered the bewildering fact that the South had lost that war." The boy was "depressed for days and felt that we should go back and finish the thing right."

Veterans of the Civil War worried that their sons and grandsons would misunderstand—or worse, forget—the struggles of their elders. All around them older men could sense a growing indifference of the young to the central events in their fathers' lives. A Texas man wrote to his state representative to enlist his help in telling "the sons of Confederates and the public generally" about the Lost Cause. "I know, however, the hard and faithful pull that is necessary to ever arouse the public mind sufficiently to come together and listen quietly and gently to the quivering voice of the old ex-Confederate Soldier. It's going to be very hard to impress this generation to ever see that we were loyal to the Constitution of the U.S. and unless the old Confederates take hold and at once the truest, best, and most patriotic people on earth will be handed down to the history of our country as traitors. And the coming generation will be in a condition to believe it too."

Sometimes, after a favorite war story failed to win the attention and respect he thought it deserved, Mel Barrett's father would lose his patience. " 'Ah,' Pa would say, 'You children simply don't understand.' And he would get up, leave the house, and go visit with Loyd Smith to whom he could talk with the assurance that, at least, Loyd would know about what he was talking." Other young men felt anger at the shadow the Civil War threw over their lives. "We were and are disinherited," Walter Hines Page's thinly disguised autobiographical protagonist exploded in *The Southerner*, "we who had no more to do with the Civil War than with the Punic Wars and no more to do with slavery than with the Inquisition, and yet we suffer the consequences of slavery and war."

"I have met women, since we came here, capable, shrewd, and alive with energy," Rebecca Harding Davis remarked with some surprise in 1887. "They manage plantations and shops; they raise stock, hold office, publish newspapers. Indeed, while Northern women have been clamoring for their rights, Southern women have found their way into more careers than they. They keep up with all the questions of the day." White women in the South often belied the stereotypes of languid Southern womanhood. They worked in many of the region's shops, farms, and businesses, often assuming control after the death of a husband, brother, or father. Southern women had taken over such roles in large numbers during the Civil War and its aftermath. More important, though, were the challenges and opportunities facing the new generation. A disproportionate number of women in much of the countryside, especially in the Atlantic seaboard states, meant that some would never find husbands. The decline of plantation life meant they could not follow the time-tested ways of establishing themselves. The ferment of the New South meant that many found new chances at independence.

Young women seemed to live faster, more impetuously, than their elders. Carrie Hall wrote to her daughter with a mild warning: "Dearie, it sounds a little strange to me to hear a young lady speak of 'painting the town red.' It is not a very elegant expression." Theresa Green Perkins of Franklin, Tennessee, confided to her journal that her granddaughter was always on the move: "Her '*set*' go *somewhere* to dance every Friday night, at one or the other of their homes."

Younger women had more serious concerns as well. Thousands, black and white, joined women's clubs and reform organizations; many thousands more worked to establish their economic independence. Though women could not vote in the late nineteenth century, a Southern woman recalled, "they sat in on the speaking and were as interested as the men." It would not be long before women sought to influence politics directly.

David Schenck was appalled by an article in the *Central Presbyterian* in 1889, the product of a professor at Union Theological Seminary in New York. The professor "uttered more words of infidelity, in a brief sentence than I have ever read. He says that the account, in the Bible, 'of the creation, the fall of man and the deluge' is a poem, 'a simple, pure, chaste poem but only a poem.' " The full inspiration of the Bible, the professor asserted, "has been exploded in Germany and England and only remains in America where 'ignoramuses snort at Higher Criticism.' " Schenck admitted that his "faith was shocked and I know many a weaker Christian will find his faith trembling if not tumbling down when he reads it."

Ministers sometimes risked discussing such matters in church. An Alabama newspaper praised a new Baptist minister because his style is "positive, urgent, convincing. There is no uncertainty hanging about his conclusions. They are orthodox, clear-cut and logical." On the other hand, members of some congregations believed their ministers were in over their heads. Oliver Bond described with disgust a sermon he heard in Bamberg, South Carolina. "Brother Elkins entered the ring tonight against 'SPECULATIVE SKEPTICISM.' It is a good thing speculative skepticism couldn't hit back, else the preacher would have been knocked out of the pulpit."

The national literary market of the late nineteenth century pushed Southern writers. American magazines proliferated: *Lippincott's, Scribner's, Harper's Monthly Magazine, Atlantic Monthly*. These journals made a conscious attempt to represent the entire country; even editors with strong Republican sentiments bent over backward to give Southern writers a place. The growing numbers of educated people in the nation created a steady and growing thirst for fresh reading material, while the lack of an international copyright law encouraged American authors to write magazine stories rather than books. The popularity of public readings also created a natural outlet for speakers who could recreate the dialects of regions genteel audiences could only read about. Those writers who could dramatize their own stories were in special demand.

"A foreigner studying our current literature, without knowledge of our history, and judging our civilization by our fiction, would undoubtedly conclude that the South was the seat of intellectual empire in America, and the African the chief romantic element of our population," a Northern man observed in 1888. "It may be noted that a few months ago every one of our great popular monthlies presented a 'Southern story' as one of its most prominent features; and during the past year nearly two-thirds of the stories and sketches furnished to newspapers by various syndicates have been of this character." Fiction was one of the few Southern products that could hold its own in the national marketplace.

A prominent Methodist minister described a scene on the Macon and Brunswick Railroad in the late 1870s, where a lumber crew rode home after delivering a raft of timber. "We saw a very black negro and a fair-haired youth drinking out of the same black-bottle. They sat promiscuously and drank, smoked, laughed, sang, whistled, and danced together. One young fellow knew the potent notes and they sang 'fa, so, la' while he beat time. . . . He sings a sort of wild tenor we used to hear at camp-meeting. . . . Perhaps we ought to be ashamed. . . , but we did enjoy their songs." Black and white Southerners continually influenced one another, every day and in every facet of life.

Black Southerners made the railroad their own in their music. The earliest student of black folk songs discovered that guitar players prided themselves on their ability to evoke the train. "The train is made to whistle by a prolonged and consecutive striking of the strings, while the bell rings with the striking of a single string. . . . And when 'she blows for the station,' the exclamations may be heard, 'Lawd, God, she's a-runnin' now!' or, 'Sho' God railroadin'!'" A lyric from a version of "John Henry," the product of black railroad construction crews in West Virginia, dramatized the pull of the wages and the prestige associated with such steady and high-paying work: "Where did you get that pretty little dress?/That hat you wear so fine?/Got my dress from a railroad man,/Hat from a man in the mine." "When the blues began, the countryside was quiet," one student of the blues has written. "Loudest of the sounds to break the stillness was the roar of the steam train as it traced its way through the lowlands, leaving a smudge of smoke against the blue sky. A brief moment of excitement as it passed, a shrill whistle, dipping and wailing like a blues and it would be gone."

Part I

DAILY LIFE

Chapter 2

Country and Town

The trips farm families made to town in the New South brought mixed feelings. "Precariously perched on top of a bale of cotton," Arthur Hudson recalled of his town visits in Mississippi, "well wrapped in quilts, on a frosty morning I could smell the exciting train smoke" two miles outside of town. "Threading the crowded square and glimpsing the sights of the store windows; stopping at Loewenberg's or Pott's or Jackson's store, where I warmed by the red-hot cannon-ball stove while the merchant sampled my father's cotton," the boy loved this time of year. Sometimes, the stores' clerks or even the merchant himself would "start the day off right for me by giving me a dime, or a stick of striped candy, or an orange yellow as gold, or an apple red as blood."

Town children saw things differently. For them "these beings I regarded as from another planet would begin arriving at the county seat (for them Clarksville was a metropolis) soon after sunup." The springless wagons, pulled by mules, rattled into town with the country families. "The little girls whose petticoats were never of a length with their frocks; the little boys whose misfit 'store pants' were cut of material as uncongenial as buckram to the human form; the misses in muslin dresses of the diluted raspberry color known in the south as 'nigger pink,' would be shooed to the ground." They were followed by "already-weary mothers wearing hats on which reposed entire flimsy gardens and orchards, or else pathetically alighted, stuffed birds!" The fathers set off to do business, and the mothers herded their children down the town's main street "for bouts of window-shopping, in which stoical hearts and vacant imaginations were replenished" with the renewed discovery of "how prolifically objects were manufactured—how many things existed to be bought by *somebody!*" The distance between country life and town life seemed to widen every year in the New South.

If things worked as they should in the rural South, a farmer was supposed to be able to work his way up the "agricultural ladder" from landless laborer, to sharecropper, to renter, to landowner. By proving his mettle as a diligent, dependable worker, and by learning through experience the way to handle a farm, a young man might win the confidence of his employer, some other local farmer, or a merchant. Once he did, he could sharecrop, taking responsibility for the labor on a piece of land and drawing credit at the local store for the crop he put into the ground. Through hard work and hard saving, he might be able to accumulate enough money to buy a mule and then rent a farm on his own. A renter paid a fixed rate for a farm and provided his own work animals and tools; what he chose to grow on that farm was his business and the profits (or loss) he made were his alone. Renting thus marked a significant advance over sharecropping and offered a way for the landless to make enough money to buy a farm of their own.

A family-owned farm, in turn, offered a way of life from which most sharecroppers and renters were precluded. Owner-operated farms produced far more corn, wheat, oats, sorghum, vegetables, and fruits than farms operated by tenants, who channeled their energies into cotton or tobacco. The pace of life on a family farm was relatively varied and interesting, with a year-long series of things to think about and plan for. Many of the chores—chopping cotton, pulling fodder, plowing, peeling fruit—might be tedious and exhausting, but each did not last more than a few weeks. In the meantime, the family ate well, met many people on a basis of equality, saw at least a little cash, and led a generally respectable life. Sharecroppers and renters, on the other hand, found themselves deprived of much of this diversity and diversion; they had only the money crop and perhaps a small garden. Their lives became not only poorer but more barren. The market more completely dominated their lives; the price of cotton, the rates of credit, the availability of land and labor affected them with a brutal force.

The merchant stood at the center of the rural economy. At the beginning of his dealings with a farmer, a merchant secured credit with a lien on the crop the farmer was borrowing to plant; once his crop fell under the lien, the farmer could deal with no other merchant and money produced by the crop's sale went first to repay the debt. If the crop returned as much cash as the farmer and merchant had anticipated, everything worked out. Should the crop bring less than expected—and in the New South era, this happened with increasing frequency—the farmer might well end the year in debt to the merchant. The following season, once again alive with hopes for higher cotton or tobacco prices, the scene might be reenacted—and again for a third year, depending on the merchant's reading of the farmer's character and the prospect for crops. When debt accumulated to a certain point, known only to the merchant, every other consideration had to be set aside; the next year's loan would have to be secured with a mortgage on the farmer's land, mule, and other possessions. If the debt continued to grow, the merchant could foreclose and take ownership of the homestead.

Farmers did not lose their land to merchants in the style of the melo-dramas so popular on the stage of the turn of the century. The merchant, rather than a worldly and oily villain, was as often as not a local boy with the same country ways as the farmer himself. While distressing scenes of sheriff's sales on the courthouse steps did take place, with everything a family owned auctioned off to pay their debts to the merchant, the more common process was less public if no less terrifying to debtors. Merchants might approach a farmer on the verge of losing his farm and offer to negotiate an assignment of deed, avoiding an appearance on the public square and an auction that would be painful for all concerned. If the farmer agreed to turn over his homestead to the merchant, the account would be closed.

Merchants did not foreclose as quickly or as often as the law permitted. Some carried a farmer in the belief that the farmer would eventually pay out, or because the farmer's guaranteed patronage had advantages, or be-cause a farm was so marginal that it was not worth the anger and perhaps loss of business from the farmer's friends and family that might result from foreclosure. Many merchants carried farm families for a while out of simple friendship or compassion.

Merchants have long been blamed for the South's debilitating addiction to cotton, for they served as crucial links in the chain that tied isolated farms to the commerce of the world. The stores dispensed the credit that permitted the rapid and thorough commercialization of areas previously on the mar-gins of commercial agriculture. Without merchants, Southern farmers would have been free of debt and free of the merchants' insistence that they grow cotton. They also would have been excluded from commercial agriculture, on the other hand, and there is little indication that most Southerners wanted to avoid the market. None of them would have wished for the de-bilitating poverty that became their fate, but few wished to be left, alone within the nation, with material standards below those of their grandparents. Only the merchant could provide the credit and the goods to change those standards to something approximating other Americans'.

The patterns of landholding and tenancy in the South varied enormously from one subregion to another, as the quality of the land, access to rail lines, length of settlement, and types of major crops exerted their effects. The Black Belt and the Delta, for example, encouraged renting, the Western prairie bred sharecropping, and the coastal plains fostered land ownership. Among whites, the percentage of owners ranged from nearly 70 percent in both coastal plains to just over one-half in the main cotton-producing regions; about 45 percent of blacks owned land along the coasts and in the mountains, but only 8 percent in the Black Belt managed to attain that status. High rates of white landowning and black landowning tended to coincide, because both races had the best luck where unimproved land remained available and where cotton was relatively unimportant.

In the parts of the Upper South where climate and soil provided congenial circumstances for livestock and food crops, farmers took advantage of the opportunities. The lush farms of the bluegrass region of Kentucky, the Shenandoah Valley of Virginia, the Holston Valley of Tennessee, and other favored areas produced horses, mules, wheat, fruit, and vegetables. The rice and sugar industries of Louisiana showed what Southern agriculture could do if prices repaid the investment. Landholders, capitalists, immigrants, laborers, and large planters rushed into new areas when opportunities beckoned. Railroads and newspapers, networks of merchandising and shipment, government research and capital development allowed these regions of the South to grow almost immediately when someone discovered a way to make the land pay.

Nearly half the counties of the New South, in fact, had only a tenuous connection with cotton. They were lucky. The greater the percentage of a county's farm production devoted to cotton, the greater the chances it would be plagued with a whole series of related problems such as more tenancy among both races, fewer livestock, less grain, and fewer farms operated by their owners. Many of the stores that operated in the Cotton Belt were plantation stores run by or for the owner, carrying a narrower and less appealing line of goods than the independent stores in non-cotton areas. As a result, the areas of the South most intensely devoted to cash crops witnessed the least attractive side of producing for the market.

The general pattern of agricultural work displayed innumerable permutations. A wage laborer might receive payment based on the length of time he worked or the size of the ground he tilled or the amount of cotton he picked. A landowner might contract an individual to sharecrop, or an entire family might be party to the contract. A tenant might bring most of his tools and supplies with him or he might come empty-handed; rent might be paid in cash or crops. A cropper might contract for a fourth, a third, or half of the crop. Sometimes categories mixed, as when sharecroppers worked for wages during slack times or when renters sharecropped a piece of land on which they grew corn. A large landowner might well have renters, croppers, and laborers at work on the same plantation. It was not uncommon for renters to hire day laborers, or even to put sharecroppers on part of the land they rented. Some landlords allowed tenants to graze animals on land for which the tenants had not contracted; others deducted for garden plots or wood rights. These patterns varied enormously over both space and time, with local custom, local opportunities, and local labor markets shaping the arrangements. This variability always held out the hope for the landless that things might be better elsewhere, even on the next plantation.

The threat and promise of moving constantly worked throughout the Southern countryside. Farm owners tended to stay on the farms they built up, but more than half of the region's share tenants lived for a year or less on each farm they worked. Farm laborers moved even more frequently, often seasonally, to wherever work could be found. Race cut across these patterns of mobility in surprising ways: white share tenants were the most mobile of rural Southerners and black landowners the least likely to move.

Southerners with families, like other mobile Americans, usually moved relatively short distances. Not only were these families likely to stay among familiar surroundings, but economic considerations also tended to hold them in relatively small orbits. The only way to win credit on anything but the most exorbitant terms was to establish a reputation as a reliable and hard-working farmer. Ambitious croppers and renters constantly sought out better farms or better terms but found themselves tethered to a locality where they were known. To pack up and leave the area was to sacrifice any good name or good will a family had managed to build. By the same token, to pack up and leave was also a way to escape a bad name or ill will. The tenants most likely to leave were those most heavily in debt.

Many black farmers moved west, especially to the Mississippi Delta. As late as the 1880s black laborers still worked to clear the Delta of its canebrakes and cypress. Rail lines drove deep into rich land that had never been farmed before. Workers strung miles of barbed wire around the perimeters of new plantations made feasible by the levees, completed in 1886, that reduced the danger of rampant flooding. The business conglomerates and wealthy individuals who owned this newly broken land hired resident managers to oversee every detail of the plantations' business and "riders" to travel constantly across their expanse to monitor the work of the hands. Plantation stores provided the only access those hands had to food and other commodities, for every acre of land and every tool belonged to the management. The work paid well, however, and black workers rushed to the Delta, an area that experienced one of the highest rates of population growth of any part of the South. It did not take long to spread news of a place where cotton grew as "high as a man on horseback" and so thick that a good hand could pick five hundred pounds in a day.

Despite all the people leaving older communities for places such as the Delta, large parts of the rural South rapidly became overcrowded. In the 1890s the rate of natural increase in the South was more than double that of the Northeast and much higher than any other part of the country. Only the oldest

Black Belt regions of the deep South, the marginal lands of Texas, and the plateau of central Tennessee saw a decrease in rural dwellers. The largest families in the nation could be found throughout the South, the largest proportions of kin living near one another.

The rural South became caught in a demographic and economic vise. Growing numbers of people tried to make a living on the land, but the crop they grew paid an ever-declining return precisely because so many more people were growing it. Even the best farmers faced a cruel fact: "Their sons can not always be kept on the farm. A young man comes up and the father is not able to give him a number of acres of land and a couple of mules as he used to do," a Georgia man explained, "and he does not like the idea of starting out with nothing, and if he has got a little education he will go to town and hire out at almost anything in the town." The average size of Southern farms shrank every year as parents divided old farms for their children and as sons turned to the only alternative to going to town or moving away: starting out as a tenant on someone else's land.

Tenant families, on the other hand, had rational reasons to raise more children. While landowning families might postpone marriage or restrict their number of children in an effort to keep land intact, tenants found that the incentives ran in the opposite direction. Large families, by pooling their labor, might have better chances at making a tenant farm pay. Young children could step in to help the family as adolescents left. The potential rewards for restricting family size, on the other hand, seemed small, since many parents could not afford to educate their children in any case. Tragically, too, women bore so many children because so many died in their infancy.

Women found exceedingly few opportunities to earn money in the country-side. "Vic is struggling to support herself. Mother and child and works very hard—cooks, washes, irons, keeps the house clean and neat, sews and embroiders," Lucy Mitchell wrote a friend in 1894, "but it tells on her thin and anxious face." "Vic" performed virtually all the work available to an uneducated single white woman in a farming community. While white women certainly ran farms using hired help, and certainly worked hard in the garden, the barn, and even in the fields, few apparently attempted to do all the work a farm required. It made far more sense to sell the farm and move to town, where chances for a respectable life might be found in a shop or a mill.

A widowed, abandoned, or single rural black woman, on the other hand, had probably been working "like a man" for her adult life and might move into renting or sharecropping as a matter of course. "I have a woman that will take your . . . farm . . . she is a good farmer. She have two boys and two girls all able to work they can cotton a full one horse farm they want to rent that place I recomend them to be all right," Jerry Heath wrote Mary Camak in 1896. "They want that mule want you to furnish them but not exceeding

$50. . . . she has been making from 8 to 10 bales of cotton. . . . her husband is dead but I recmend her and her children to be all right." With the labor of a relatively large family, a black woman could earn even more than a subsistence. A contemporary black observer described one Georgia home headed by a widow with nine children: "On the inside of the house and all around it, everything is kept extremely clean. From the appearance of the fireplace one might think that it is whitewashed three or four times each week." The family received two magazines and three newspapers, including the Atlanta *Independent,* a black newspaper.

Even for rural black women within male-headed families (as nearly nine in ten were), the distinction between men's work and women's work was not as marked as in white households. White landlords, and many black husbands, expected black women to work regularly in the fields as well as to perform whatever domestic labor they had time left for; black women did "a man's share in the field, and a woman's part at home." At contract negotiation time, both cropper and landlord figured the labor of the household's women into their calculations: the harder the women worked, the more land the family could crop. In 1900 over half of all black households in the Cotton Belt had at least one daughter sixteen or younger working in the fields as a laborer.

The mothers and daughters in a landowning farm family, black or white, worked in a variety of tasks and carried on a number of activities generally not available to women in cropping families. They could tend a garden, can vegetables and fruit, help with livestock, grow flowers and maintain a yard, work at the church, visit sick neighbors, and spend time playing with their children. Although these women, like their less fortunate counterparts, might work in the fields at those times when every hand was crucial, at hoeing or picking time, the cash crop was not their responsibility. All the jobs women performed were valued, but they remained distinct and distinctly ancillary to that of the main activity of the men, producing a crop for money.

Women's labor provided important insulation from the vicissitudes of debt and price; self-sufficiency came from the work of women as well as from diversified crops planted by their husbands. When all else failed, the foresight and care of a mother could save a family from the worst consequences of hard times. One male commentator stated approvingly that "women are naturally cautious and afraid of debt." Partly to avoid that debt, many women found a local market for butter, eggs, milk, and honey, a market that produced a sure, if small, profit. The money they earned in this way often made the difference between getting by and getting ahead. In Arthur Hudson's family in Mississippi, for example, "most of the little luxuries, new furniture, and household ornaments my mother managed to purchase with her butter-and-egg money."

Some women, especially black women, made additional money as midwives. "Didn't hardly anybody have a doctor when a woman had a baby,"

A Louisiana farm family. (Louisiana State University at Shreveport Archives)

Charley White recalled. "They'd come for Mama and she'd go, and generally be gone all night. They'd pay her any way they could. Potatoes, corn, maybe a gallon of cane syrup." When White's mother received a chicken or turkey, she would usually "take them to the store to trade for sugar or salt or something, but once in a while she'd let us eat one. That was really a day, when we could have an egg Mama fried nice and tender with yellow all soft and gooey."

Women lived most of their lives within the confines of the neighborhood, and so it was women who suffered most from isolation or bad neighbors. "A farmer acquaintance of my parents came to our house one day. He wanted Papa to recommend him to Mr. Henderson, from whom he wanted land to *crop on* the next year. Mamma directed him to where Papa was at work," G. L. Vaughan recalled. At the same time, however, Vaughan's mother sent two of her children "to warn Mr. Henderson of the kind of man it was who wished to rent from him. Mamma beat Papa to rendering a recommendation." Her "recommendation" had nothing to do with farming: "She said, 'Now, if they move here, they will be closest to us. When he gits drunk, and runs her off, she will come here for protection. No tellin' how Johnny [Vaughan] will git into it with him, if he does.' The guy stayed all night with us." He did not get to rent the land, though.

Every rural community expected to have a schoolteacher somewhere not too far away. Turnover was great—the average white teacher stayed at a school about three years, a black teacher two and a half. Leading families worked to make sure that someone stood at the front of the often ramshackle schoolhouse for at least ten or twelve weeks, often in July and August, when the crops needed less attention. "To be a country school teacher in those days meant to live a life just a cut above that of the hired hand, the only difference being what one did during the day," a South Carolina man recalled. The teacher "boarded around" among the families who had children in the school, "taking pot luck and subject to the hazards peculiar to each house: dirt, bed-bugs and other vermin, leaky roofs, musty bedclothes, and poor folks' food."

Things were not much better in school itself. Teachers often furnished all supplies at their own expense and served as their own custodians. Many schools had no wells or even privies. In the late summer the schoolroom was miserable, as "barefoot youngsters have to stifle in ill-ventilated cabins while the mercury rises to ninety-eight or a hundred degrees." The student body varied greatly from one day to the next, as the weather conspired with farm work, playing hooky, and illness. The students might vary in age by a decade and in height by several feet. Teachers often had to establish dominion over some of the larger boys. "We have hard times with the boys at school. They are so bad," a schoolgirl from Mississippi wrote her cousin.

Despite such problems with discipline, teaching became a preserve of women. White women had constituted only about a quarter of teachers from the antebellum years through the 1870s, but their numbers doubled in the 1880s while the number of white men declined. Women accounted for a majority of white teachers by the late 1880s and by 1900 the proportion of women in the South's schools was about the same as in the North. "We want more lady teachers in the county," an east Tennessee newspaper announced. "Past experience proves very conclusively that they are quite or more successful than the gentlemen." Teaching became one of the few jobs in which women enjoyed an advantage, though it was not always a young woman's first choice. In the 1880s, Southern states began creating "normal" schools, schools dedicated to educating teachers. Those schools produced an evergrowing number of college-educated women. Their influence in the South was to be great, though teachers' pay remained at appallingly low levels.

The schools vied with stores and churches as the center of rural communities. Spelling bees and debates were among the most popular entertainments in the Southern countryside. Both activities combined a display of book learning with a long-standing Southern admiration for oral presentation and love of any kind of contest. Winners of a school's spelling bee might go on the road, challenging the winner of another school, followed by supporters from home who would cheer her or him on. A program at the end of each school year attracted many local people, whether they had children in the school or not. The teacher's performance for the entire year was often judged by how good a display the students made in their recitations, plays, and music. The show might go on for five or six hours, with members of the audience quizzing the scholars to see how much they had learned. The renewal of the teacher's contract often depended on their responses.

The hard lives of rural doctors, too, made clear how isolated and dangerous rural life seemed. While people in town could easily find a doctor, those out in the country faced harrowing difficulties in locating a physician when one of the frequent tragedies of rural life hit: "a barefoot boy was snake-bitten, an aged citizen was stricken with apoplexy, an ax glanced off a piece of stovewood and gashed a leg, a mule caused a brain concussion with a close and well-aimed kick, or a baby was smothering to death with hives or croup." Riders from the country frequently raced to the homes and stores of merchants in the middle of the night to use their telephone to call the doctor, who would have a long and slow ride to the farmhouse where the suffering mother, father, or child lay, waiting.

For as long as people could remember, much of the South had been open range. Families who owned cows or pigs simply marked them, allowed them to fend for themselves, and then rounded them up when it came time for slaughter. But new laws, enacted throughout the New South era, which required owners to fence their livestock made it virtually impossible for the landless to keep animals. Political battles raged for decades over these laws. Landed farmers and town dwellers not wishing to have animals encroach on their land sponsored the laws. Poorer farmers and farmers in less densely populated areas argued instead that it was fairer and cheaper to fence crops rather than livestock.

Each side of the conflict over the stock law received eloquent statement in an Opelousas, Louisiana, newspaper. "Humanity to poor dumb brutes demands it. There is no longer any range for cattle, horses, or hogs," a reader signing himself "A Sufferer" argued. "They roam or wander up and down our long, dry, hot and barren lanes, with great poles, or boards, tied to their head, (the ropes or chains eating into the flesh to the very bone) to prevent their going over fences which they are compelled to do, or starve for both food and water." Not only animals but also hard-working farmers faced hardship from the law: "In one night, a few old cows, horses, or hogs, not worth twenty-five dollars, will destroy the labor of a whole year. . . . and hard working families are left to starve, with no recourse for relief, either by law or justice." Driven by such logic, the community enacted the law. But another kind of logic soon came to prevail when the town became "so overgrown with grass that it was demonstrated beyond a doubt that to maintain a stock law in Opelousas was out of the question. It is repealed now, but we are afraid too late for the poor people, many of them having been forced to sell their stock for want of means to maintain them." Across the South, one county after another shifted responsibility to those who owned animals, not land. The growing population density, commercial development, and intensive farming of the New South left little room for those who did not have the means to buy into the new order.

Black landholders seemed to contradict the downward spiral of tenantry experienced by so many whites. Despite the enormous odds facing them, nearly 200,000 black farmers managed to buy their own land. Indeed, the growth of black land ownership was one of the most remarkable facets of life in the New South. The proportions of black farmers who owned land were greatest in the Upper South, along the coastal regions, and in the trans-Mississippi states. Very few blacks owned land in the Black Belt that cut across the region. Black landowning was greatest, in other words, where concentration on cotton was lowest and where blacks made up a relatively small part of the population. Blacks owned farms where land was cheap, where railroads had not arrived, and where stores were few; they got the "backbone and spare ribs" that white farmers did not value.

Landownership hardly guaranteed an easy life, of course, or even financial independence. Black farmers and their families often had to rent from neighboring planters additional land for cash crops or to work off the farm to bring in enough money to keep their place; black landholding may have been so much higher in predominantly white counties in part because wage-paying jobs for blacks were more plentiful there. Those black landowners who had to rent additional land found themselves ensnared in familiar obligations: "The whole family, wife and children, may have to go out daily to work on the land of the large planter," one black observer noted, "abandoning altogether the small farm except to give it such attention as a little chopping in the early morning, late in the evenings or on holidays."

A white native of a predominantly black area found the fruits of black ambition remarkable. "The changes have been enormous, and struck the writer with peculiar force after an absence of several years from his old home." Many blacks had left, and of those who had stayed "not one is at the old home." Furthermore, "material accumulation has gone steadily forward," even though "for a time the prejudice against their owning anything more [than their clothes] was bitter among the whites." Despite the prejudice, "first a cow was bought, then an old horse or lame mule. Now they have as substantial vehicles and as good animals as their old white masters." The blacks used to walk in crowds to church; now they rode in wagons and buggies. "In their houses, too, they have beds instead of bunks, varnished tables, painted chairs. Many have sewing machines; a few have a piano or an organ."

Landowning blacks sought in every way they could to be self-sufficient and free from the snares that caught their less fortunate neighbors. They tended to have larger families, with more people to work the farm. Older children remained unmarried longer, staying on the farm of their parents in return for security and a share of the farm later on. The adult women among black landowners were far more likely to devote their labor to house-keeping alone than were women among the landless; their gardening, sewing, cooking, laundering, and child care could improve the quality of the family's life and reduce their dependence on people outside. Rural blacks could also succeed too well; a black teacher reported sardonically that he had heard of a black man "building a nice house but the whites advised him to not paint it, so he took their advice, which conduced to his personal safety or security, and he is yet living in his unpainted house."

Absentee landownership increasingly troubled the New South. The absence of the landowners had a profound impact on the countryside. As owners turned the land over to tenants, the owners' priorities changed. No longer did it seem to make sense to save a large part of the land in woodlands or pastures or orchards, none of which could return a profit. Better to clear the land to make space for another tenant for more cotton. No longer did it make sense to keep up the house, for it was "just tenants" who would live there, tenants notorious for their hard use of a place.

Landholders recognized the implications of their abandonment. One Mississippi farmer left his place for "a nice little town, to carry his family there, so they might have school facilities and social advantages they could not have in the country." A friend told him what would happen: "Yes, it is several miles out there, and you are getting to be 40 or 50 years old now, and you are perhaps going for the first year twice a week out to your place, the next year once a week, and the following year once in every two weeks, and finally it will be abandoned to the labor on the place, and it will never look like the same place again." The men who heard this story asked, "All the white people left?" and the answer came back, "Yes: and they are doing it in thousands and thousands of instances."

By the early twentieth century, when Ray Stannard Baker was "following the color line" on a journalistic tour of the South, it seemed to him that "the movement of white owners from the land to nearby towns was increasing every year." The process, beginning in the hard times of the preceding thirty years, accelerated when cotton began to bring a bit more. "White planters can now afford to live in town where they can have the comforts and conveniences, where the servant question is not impossibly difficult, and where there are good schools for the children," Baker wrote. "Another potent reason for the movement is the growing fear of whites, and especially the women and children, at living alone on great farms where white neighbors are distant." Parts of the rural South thus saw a kind of "white flight," as the migration of some fueled the migration of others.

Those planters who left the rural districts often held onto their land. Not only were prices low and buyers few, but planter families seemed just as reluctant to sell their land as they were to live on it. The plantation ideal still had its pull in the South, and well-to-do town and city men apparently enjoyed owning farmland. "After a while I came to feel a reasonable confidence in assuming that almost any prominent merchant, banker, lawyer, or politician whom I met in the towns owned a plantation in the country," Baker observed. They augmented their investments in land with investments in stores, in cotton and cottonseed oil mills, in stocks and bonds, in lumbering, in cotton futures. They had moved to town.

The village and town population of the South grew by five million people between 1880 and 1910. The growth came fastest in the 1880s, slowed in the 1890s, and then accelerated again in the first decade of the new century. Villages, settled places with populations under 2500, accounted for about a quarter of that increase. Thousands of new villages came into being between 1880 and 1910 and hundreds more passed over the 2500 line into official "urban" status. In 1900, about one of every six Southerners—in some subregions, one of every four—lived in a village, town, or city.

The great majority of the South's smaller towns were built for the same reasons: to bring commodities together in central locations to be purchased by wholesalers, stored, sometimes repacked, and shipped. Towns grew up around the railroad depots that made all these practices feasible and profitable, whether the commodity was cotton, tobacco, lumber, or fruit. In turn, other people came to these consolidation points to sell goods to the farmers, loan them money, educate some of their children, fix their implements, build them new buildings, furnish them occasional legal and illegal entertainment, maintain the county's courts and offices, and provide the services of lawyers and doctors and undertakers. For a county to have all these services provided within its own borders, where they had not been provided only a few years earlier, marked a dramatic change.

Every subregion contained its landmark cities. The Atlantic coastal plain claimed the ports of Norfolk, Charleston, Savannah, and Jacksonville; the Gulf plain had the ports of Mobile, New Orleans, and Houston. The Piedmont could boast Richmond and Raleigh, plus some of the fastest growing cities of the South—Charlotte, Winston-Salem, Columbia, Augusta, and Atlanta—along with many smaller but flourishing towns. The cities within the recesses of the mountains, Knoxville and Asheville, developed steadily, but Roanoke, Chattanooga, and Birmingham, on the edge of the highlands, grew more impressively. The central plateau looked to Louisville and Nashville, while the river counties focused on Memphis. The Black Belt had Macon, Columbus, and Montgomery; the cotton uplands had Jackson, Little Rock, and Shreveport. On the Western prairies, Dallas and Fort Worth grew at an especially rapid pace.

In the 1880s smaller towns and cities by the dozen laid rails and bought streetcars that tied neighborhoods together, that allowed people to travel across town without bothering with an expensive and troublesome horse and carriage, and that served as proof of municipal improvement. The larger cities of the South built new electric street railways before any other cities in America. Cities growing quickly with little infrastructure to replace or dismantle rushed to adopt the clean and quiet streetcars. Montgomery won the honor of having the nation's first all-electric system in 1886, but Richmond and Atlanta followed later in the same year and Nashville the next.

Electric lights arrived even faster and in more places than street railways. In 1880, when Nashville staged an exposition, the city had to import the entire technology of electric lights from New York; within fifteen years, electricity illuminated Southern towns a fraction of Nashville's size. "Greenville is too large and a city of too much importance to be satisfied with a few street lamps," fumed the editor of the Alabama "city" of 3000. "These lamps were well enough when the town was a village, but she has out grown that several years ago, and these smoky oil lamps now look as much out of place as would a pair of boy's pants on a six foot man." By 1902 the South registered nearly 600 electric light and power stations, an average of about 46 per state.

Like electric lights, telephones arrived in the urban South almost as soon as the technology permitted and spread quickly thereafter. Introduced in the late 1870s, telephone networks appeared in five Southern cities by 1880. In the 1880s telephones rapidly spread throughout the larger cities and by the 1890s had become widely available even in small towns. "What do you think, citizens, of being able to talk every mother's son in Opelousas to death by simply ringing him up?" the town's newspaper asked buoyantly in 1895.

Towns prided themselves on their new water works and sewers. Some major cities established water systems in the 1870s; water works appeared in virtually all large places in the 1880s and in the 1890s in every smaller city and town that could find the means. When a new water system came to Salisbury, North Carolina, in the late eighties, Hope Chamberlain recalled, "some of the younger married folks put in bathrooms. We girls called them 'The Bath-Tub Aristocracy.' " Those "aristocrats" mentioned their new conveniences as often as possible, deeply irritating those "who had not yet graduated from the class with the tin-tub-on-the-back-fence, to be brought in with cold water and warm, in pails, for the semi-weekly rite."

Up-to-date town homes boasted central gables, towers and turrets, large porches, bay windows, and huge chimneys; those who could not afford this expensive panoply of wood and masonry merely tacked some gingerbread on more traditional styles, gimcrackery widely available from new Southern mill works and from Sears, Roebuck. The men financing new suburbs built houses in this elaborate style and people were anxious to buy. Downtown spoke a language quite different from this warm and embracing domestic

Union Station, Atlanta, 1890. (Atlanta Historical Society)

architecture. Commercial districts boasted cast iron, plate glass, and "a smooth skin of evenly-shaded, razor-edge pressed brick." Everything worked for an aura of confident modernity. Atlanta proudly claimed the South's first skyscrapers: the Equitable Building of 1892 and the English-American Building of 1897.

Cities rapidly became more differentiated by function and style, by class and race. Technological innovations seldom penetrated poor urban neighborhoods, which occupied the lowest, wettest, and least healthy areas. Huge expanses of major cities remained dependent on cisterns and private wells, and in those places people did not have access to pure water for decades. Moreover, "horses and mules, the main source of transportation, produced enormous quantities of manure, and with their hooves and wagon wheels pounded it into the brick and crushed stone pavement, where it was then soaked with thousands of gallons of urine each day," a chronicler of Nashville has evocatively written. "This, joined by the garbage, privy fumes, and the contributions of assorted dogs, chickens, and hogs, created an abominable stench on hot summer days. Dead animals were left in the streets for days before being dragged by the city scavenger to the river to be dumped." Tuberculosis, diarrhea, pneumonia, typhoid, and diphtheria flourished in such circumstances.

People from every level of rural society left the countryside for towns and cities. "The towns are being recruited by those too poor to be able to live in the country, as well as by those too rich to be willing to live there," a reporter for the *Outlook* discovered. As a result, the South's towns and cities were "centers of both wealth and poverty." The poor fled from the countryside while "the most capable business men, lawyers, doctors, and preachers are practically all leaving the country for the town and city," a Vanderbilt professor observed early in the new century.

Young business leaders tended to work their way into the new order in a local store close to home in their teens and early twenties and then set out in search of better chances. Most arrived from nearby rural counties in their mid-twenties and worked in a business in the city long enough to learn its ways and accumulate some capital. Then they either became partners in that business or opened another in the same line. Eventually they broadened their investments into real estate, banks, or other businesses.

These changes in the business community translated into a certain amount of confusion in the social world. To Southerners accustomed to worrying about pedigree and lineages, the ability of recent arrivals to win their way into exclusive parlors and clubs made for some discomfort and aristocratic sniffing. One lady from Atlanta felt compelled in 1939 to insert an "explanatory note" in her correspondence for 1891 to explain to her descendants exactly why it was that she had associated with some of the people she had in the New South era. The author of these descriptions wanted her family to know "how utterly mixed-up was the social life in those days." She did allow for the fact that she "was very young then, 18, and had seen so little of the world that I, as you see, took these creatures seriously."

Failure and ambition led people to move often. The working people of the South traveled up and down the coast as the labor market demanded or moved from one town to another along a railroad line. In general, the more prestigious a white man's occupation, the less likely he was to move; the wealthiest merchants and professionals were comfortably ensconced and moved only to enjoy the possibilities of the elaborate new houses being built in exclusive new areas. Small businessmen, on the other hand, moved often, as did clerks, bookkeepers, and traveling salesmen. These white-collar men moved farther out on the street railways that led to the newer residential areas, but they stayed in their new suburban homes no longer than they had stayed in their older residences. Within ten years, most had moved again, even farther away from the central city.

Blacks, though about as geographically mobile as whites, did not move in the same directions. While whites pushed away from the city center, blacks migrated to neighborhoods downtown. Increasing residential segregation accompanied the emergence of more modern cities, with their sharply defined business districts and streetcar suburbs. The newer a Southern city, the more likely it was to be consistently segregated by race; the faster a Southern city grew, the faster it became segregated. By the mid-1890s, the vast majority of blocks in Atlanta, Richmond, and Montgomery were either all-white or all-black, the pattern violated mainly by white widows, grocers, and unskilled laborers too poor to live elsewhere.

Yet towns and cities offered black Southerners what they could not find in the country. "The motives that carried my mother and father from the country into the little town of Pendleton were more than good," William Pickens recalled of his youth in South Carolina, "they were sacred. Having lived nearer town for a year, they learned that the houses, the wages and the schools of the village were superior to those of the country." Picken's family jumped at the chance when a white hotelkeeper offered to pay off their debts and bring them to town, the father to be a man of all work and the mother a cook. In rural districts "the landowner would not tolerate a tenant who put his children to school in the farming seasons" and the youngsters in Pickens's family could go to school only six weeks a year. In town, they received six months of school. Moreover, their mother could better care for her younger children when she worked as a cook and laundry woman instead of a field hand. Although the family received small wages, they picked up their pay every week and binding debt did not pile up. The Pickens family fled the countryside for the town "as one instinctively moves from a greater toward a lesser pain."

Young blacks left the farms for village, town, and city far more frequently than their elders; larger and faster-growing places had especially large proportions of young blacks. This meant not only that the countryside became the refuge for the oldest and poorest black people, but also that towns and cities contained those blacks in the early stages of family formation and of working lives, those most likely to move often, look out for new opportunities, resist indignities and join new organizations, adopt new forms of music and dress, commit crimes or be accused of crimes. An enormous divide separated young blacks from their elders: the young had been born in freedom, had never known slavery. The youthfulness of so many recent arrivals affected the tone of black life and of race relations in Southern cities, lending vibrancy and energy to the black community and creating an uneasiness in whites who watched from a distance.

The emergence of towns differentiated the black community in another important way: it separated men from women, husbands from wives, and parents from children. Even the economic structure of small villages made it difficult for black families to remain together. While women could almost always find jobs as domestics in even the smallest place (and a large majority of young urban black women worked outside their homes), the limited economic base of a village offered little for men. In fact, black men often found their greatest opportunities to make a decent wage in jobs that were either seasonal or involved moving a considerable distance from their homes—

harvesting or working in railroad or lumber camps—situations in which women had difficulty finding work or raising children.

Partly as a result of such conditions, the number of female-headed households rose in the villages, towns, and cities of the New South; 25 to 30 percent of all urban black households between 1880 and 1915 had only a mother present—a percentage double that of rural black families—and the percentage appears about the same in smaller towns. Two-parent black families had been able to hold together under the buffeting of slavery and war, and most even managed to stand up to the postbellum world as well; but a high and increasing number found the combination of relentless poverty, cruelly opposed opportunities, and short life expectancies more than their marriages could bear.

A letter from Alice Simpson of Jackson, Mississippi, to her mother still living in the country offers a rare glimpse into the anguish black people faced in their family lives. "Mother I dont work now like I uster times is hard here and money scarce," Simpson wrote in the midst of the worst depression of the century. "This is the hardest time I ever seen since I have been here nearly (24) twenty four years what you ask for I will send it to you week after next." She had to tell her mother that "Brother is not here but his two children is here yet he dont give them nothing I sent him word in a letter and told him he aught to send you something and I havent heard from him since times is so hard here until no one cant hardly make a living." She ended the letter on a tone of futility tempered by faith: "I think about you night and day I dont get on my knees but what I dont ask the Lord to strength you in your old days I would like very much to see you but times is so hard."

Despite all the odds against them, many urban blacks steadily accumulated property. Black businesses selling goods to the growing black communities sometimes did quite well, especially if whites failed to compete for the business. In every Southern city a black business district grew up and businessmen became one of the most powerful groups in black society.

Blacks of all occupations created a wide range of organizations for themselves. Women led many missionary societies and benevolent groups established by the churches. In the United Daughters of Ham, Sisters of Zion, and Ladies Benevolent Society, church women organized to carry out more effectively some of the duties black women had traditionally embraced: caring for the poor, orphaned, young, grieving, and lost. Women of all levels of wealth and prestige worked in these organizations, united by faith and determination. Black women initiated and sustained these groups in towns and cities across the South; they created a precedent and a pool of experienced talent for other kinds of organizations. Sewing circles, literary clubs, and reform groups without connections to churches developed in larger towns and cities, as black women sought out new avenues of usefulness and self-improvement.

The black women's clubs made a self-conscious attempt to bridge the growing class barriers among urban blacks, out of benevolence and out of self-protection. The National Association of Colored Women, founded in 1896, provided an umbrella organization to unite clubs from every part of the country. Its motto was "Lifting As We Climb," its goal to come "into closer touch with the masses of our women." The president of the association, Mary Church Terrell, admitted that "even though we wish to shun them, and hold ourselves entirely aloof from them, we cannot escape the consequences of their acts." Not only duty but self-preservation as well "demand that we go down among the lowly, the illiterate, and even the vicious to whom we are bound by the ties of sex and race, and put forth every possible effort to uplift and claim them." The Women's Mutual Improvement Club of Knoxville provided food and clothing for 97 families; the club in Selma paid the tuition of several children of widowed mothers.

Black men, while active in some of the same church organizations as women, also created separate fraternal groups and business leagues. Major cities contained hundreds of Colored Masons, Colored Odd Fellows, and Sons of Temperance; one contemporary estimated that half of all black men in Nashville belonged to such an order. Blacks formed their own military companies, volunteer fire companies, baseball teams, debating societies, and trade unions.

A black man "may arise in the morning in a house which a black man built and which he himself owns, it has been painted and papered by black men; the furniture was probably bought at a white store, but not necessarily, and if it was it was brought to the house by a colored drayman," W. E. B. DuBois wrote of Atlanta. "He starts to work walking to the car with a colored neighbor and sitting in a part of the car surrounded by colored people; in most cases he works for white men but not in all"—and even if his employer was white his fellow workmen were black. "Once a week he reads a colored paper; he is insured in a colored insurance company; he patronized a colored school with colored teachers, and a colored church with a colored preacher; he gets his amusements at places frequented and usually run by colored people; he is buried by a colored undertaker in a colored grave yard."

This black world had emerged in the three decades since emancipation. At the end of the Civil War, Richmond's black newspaper proudly reminded its readers in 1890, the black man "had no lawyers, doctors, theologians, scientists, authors, editors, druggists, inventors, businessmen, accredited representatives to foreign countries, members of Congress, legislators, commonwealth attorneys, sheriffs. He has them now." In new cities, such as Durham, leading blacks tended to be businessmen who had made their money with the city, while in older places, such as New Orleans and Charleston, an older elite of mulattoes and antebellum free blacks shared power somewhat reluctantly with the new men. Ministers, teachers, doctors, lawyers, and businessmen tended to take the leading roles.

Despite the possibilities that relatively well-to-do blacks found and created for themselves in Southern towns and cities, ambitious black people confronted heightened frustrations. The black writer Sutton E. Griggs conveyed the almost maddening limitations and contradictions an educated black man faced, as the protagonist of his 1899 novel cast about Richmond for a way to make a living: "It is true that there were positions around by the thousands which he could fill, but his color debarred him. He would have made an excellent drummer, salesman, clerk, cashier, government official (county, city, state, or national), telegraph operator, conductor, or any thing of such a nature. But the color of his skin shut the doors so tight that he could not even peep in." The vast bulk of urban black men worked as laborers, draymen, and porters, with smaller numbers in various cities engaged in carpentry, barbering, stonecutting, and railroad work. A tiny professional elite perched precariously on top. The list of jobs for which Griggs's tormented hero longed were precisely the positions that offered the greatest opportunities for young white men of some education. Those jobs almost never went to blacks.

In the 1880s white working women became more numerous and visible in Southern cities, holding jobs as dressmakers, milliners, and seamstresses. Sewing offered advantages especially important to women: working on their own time, in their own homes, without supervision. Since mothers could sew when children were at school or napping, women of all ages worked in the sewing trade. By contrast, women under the age of twenty-four predominated in the other jobs of urban women: domestic service, mill operation, and school teaching. To the extent they could, it seems, most white women reserved work outside the home for the years before marriage. Women of all ages worked in a scattering of other jobs, ranging from art and music teachers to hotel keepers and nurses to clerks and stenographers.

The Southern city proved preferable to the countryside for single, widowed, or divorced women, who otherwise faced bleak prospects in the New South. Even a woman with a skill, though, could find herself in desperate straits in a city. Those with children had few places to turn for help. City governments offered only a harsh and demeaning kind of public aid, while unions and fraternal orders took care only of their own. Confronting the challenge, more fortunate white city women exerted impressive efforts at helping women and children experiencing hard times. Such organizations seemed natural outgrowths of their work in their own homes, neighborhoods, and churches. For thousands of women and children, women's benevolent work stood among the most important social institutions in the New

South. Some women's clubs built hospitals and colleges, planted trees or established garbage collection, fought alcohol and raised money for nurseries, opened settlement houses and schools for young black women.

Interlocking networks of railroads, towns, and villages exerted influence throughout the South, drawing people out of the countryside, channeling their energies in new directions. Towns saw the accumulation of capital and of men eager to use it. Towns attracted people, especially women and blacks, who had no secure place in the rural districts. The towns displayed new technologies, lured visitors from outside the locality, fostered reform, bred conflict. Even apparently isolated villages, so backward and small, reoriented life in the counties where they grew, concentrating merchants and banks, offering schools and churches, bridging the gap between rural and urban life, dislocating class and race relations. Much that was new about the New South began in these raw places. The countryside could only watch as its power and attractiveness declined with every passing year.

Chapter 3

Store and Mill

Trains steadily pushed their way into the corners of the South, their cars stacked with boxes. Some crates were bound for farmers direct from Sears, Roebuck or Montgomery Ward, others headed for country stores, small towns, or booming cities. Bulky machinery, carriages, and tools accounted for much cargo, as did canned goods, prepared foods, and tropical fruits. Bicycles and musical instruments carried tags showing their far-flung destinations. Mail cars brought magazines and newspapers. Parcels contained fashions from New York or patterns from Butterick, shoes from Massachusetts or suits from Philadelphia. No matter its contents, each box carried more than an inert product. It brought an implicit message: this is the new way of the world.

Each box brought another message as well: the South is behind the times, the consumer of other people's ideas and products. New commodities became increasingly important in the South but they remained incongruous, dislocated. The presence of the new things testified to the South's integration into the national economy, but the distant origins of those goods testified to the South's enduring provinciality.

The number of stores in the South mounted with each passing year, even through the depressions of the 1870s and 1890s. By the turn of the century, the South contained about 144 stores per county. In all but the most isolated places people lived within reach of several stores, which steadily proliferated:

stores tended to concentrate near one another along the railroads in the more recently settled parts of the South while they remained more dispersed in the older counties back east. The stores served as small cogs in a large and complex machinery of trade. Markets converged in even the most solitary country store, which traded in everything from the eggs grown by a local farmwife to cast-iron stoves manufactured in Massachusetts to harnesses tanned in St. Louis.

City-based wholesale firms dealt with town and rural stores through "drummers," essential to the expanding mercantile business of the South and highly visible throughout the region. "I do not think I traveled an hour by railway, while in the Southern states, without the company of at least one of these men, nor stopped at any railroad hotel without meeting one," observed a traveling reporter for the *Atlantic Monthly* in 1882. The great majority of salesmen were in their twenties and made careers out of being obliging and friendly.

One young drummer, Arch Trawick, recalled what it was like to get such a job: "I am traveling on the railroad. I buy a new suit; have grown a full set of whiskers, very imposing. I have a derby hat, a white vest, an ascot tie and patent leather shoes; carry a neatly folded umbrella, ride the bus from the depot to the hotel, 25 cents round trip, the hotel porter handles my bags. I am now a full fledged Commercial Traveler." Trawick remembered four decades later that "in the late 90s the wholesale grocery drummer was tops. He had a good job. The clerks in the retail store, the folks around town generally wished that sometime they too might have a job like that. Of course we didn't quite class up with the 'boot and shoe' men, or the serious looking fellows that sold 'dry goods and notions.' " Those men traveled in true style, unhurried, with impressive sets of trunks, suites in the hotel, and free five-cent cigars for their customers. "They didn't talk much at dinner time, they were reserved and thoughtful. We always addressed them as 'Mr.' "

Wholesale drummers had plenty of opportunities to see their customers at first hand and judge their character and credit worthiness. They had a way, too, to see behind appearances: the books of R. G. Dun and Bradstreet. Those volumes, available only to subscribers, listed a credit rating for every store in the country. The company's representatives came to town, visited stores, talked with people who knew of important information—marital difficulties, drinking problems, a propensity to gamble, a rich father-in-law, a spendthrift son—and sent a report to headquarters. All the tangible and intangible evidence, sifted and reduced, emerged in the books as a letter and a number. Credit was not the only part of wholesaling that became standardized. Central offices assigned territory and determined what lines salesmen would carry. Division managers kept a stern eye on salesmen, deducting unapproved expenses from their pay and making sure every town stayed in "satisfactory shape."

A revolution in advertising accompanied corporate standardization of business, and a peculiarly Southern industry, tobacco, launched some of the earliest mass advertising campaigns in the country. Packages of cigarettes contained cards with alluring color pictures of beautiful actresses (an inordinate portion of them dressed in tights), baseball players, horses, and other illustrations designed to appeal to male tastes. Other businesses had to find other media. Henry Belk, who built a chain of stores through the Carolinas, once arranged for a man dressed as a farmer to lead a "large-uddered" cow through the streets of Charlotte bearing a sign proclaiming the good value of Belk's shoes and the punch line, "THIS IS NO BULL."

It was an unfortunate Southern newspaper in the nineties that did not bear an advertisement for Royal Baking Powder in a prominent upper corner of one page, another in the middle of Ayer's Sarsaparilla, and columns full of patent medicine testimonials. Advertisements often disguised themselves as brief, sensational news articles; one, for example, echoed a common theme of Southern papers when it began, "The Race Question is unsettled. But it is settled that Hood's Sarsaparilla leads all remedies." Advertising changed rapidly in the New South. Representatives in the North procured national advertising, which grew ever flashier and more sophisticated. Holidays, especially Christmas, quickly became commercialized in city and town papers; lithographed Santas beamed out from special supplements that urged parents to give presents instead of allowing Christmas to be the time of raucous noise-making it had been in their youth.

New South commerce received another push toward nationalization when mail-order houses came on the scene. A survey of the registered mail that passed through the post office of tiny Bywy, Mississippi, in the last two decades of the nineteenth century showed that local citizens were "much addicted to shopping by mail." Their favorite firms included Montgomery Ward; Sears, Roebuck and Company; J. Lynn; E. Butterick; E. V. Roddin; J. H. Whitney; World Manufacturing Company; Chicago Household Guest; National Remedy; National Medicine; Ladies Hair Emporium; Peruvian Catarrh; and the Persian Perfumery companies, all from New York and Chicago. Judging from the testimonials the Sears, Roebuck company published in their 1897 catalog, a goodly portion of its clientele lived in the South; of the 70 enthusiastic endorsements in the buggy and carriage section, for example, 23 came from Southern states.

At first, local merchants helped customers place orders with the mail-order companies. Merchants often ran the post office and loaned money, after all, and so it was only natural that people would order from their stores in the days before rural free delivery began in the late 1890s. It was not long, though, before farmers and merchants began a long battle over the mail-order business; farmers saw the trade as a way to bypass overpriced local stores, but storekeepers saw it as shortsighted and disloyal to the community. "Who sympathized with you when your little girl was sick? Was it your home merchant, or was it Sears and Roebuck?'' asked one Ozark newspaper. "When you want to raise money for the church or for some needy person in town do you write to the Fair Store in Chicago or do you go to your home merchant? How much do Seegle Cooper and Co. give toward keeping up the sidewalks of the town or paying the minister's salary?''

Mail order offered an autonomy and anonymity which poor people valued as much as the lower prices. "Just generally, if you were black, you were not supposed to have either time or money, and if you did, you ought not to show it," Mamie Fields of South Carolina recalled. "Some of them did think colored people oughtn't to have a certain nice thing, even if they had money enough to buy it. Our people used to send off for certain items. That way, too, the crackers . . . wouldn't know what you had in your house. Better that way." When cotton prices rose in the late nineties, agents of the mail-order companies traveled through the Mississippi Delta, displaying catalogs to black workers and taking cash orders. Local planters did not approve, but an ever-growing tide of orders left the South throughout the first half of the twentieth century.

Women sometimes took advantage of stores and mail-order companies as a chance to expand their sphere. A woman living in an isolated community in southern Mississippi noted in her diary that "a Mrs. Montana called to solicit orders for a new corset for which she is canvassing, it is manufactured especially for weak backs, I suppose." Although we do not know whether anyone responded, an Arkansas newspaper carried an ad that offered a wonderful commercial opportunity: "Wanted at once, two good hustlers, either sex, to introduce and sell Lightning Vermin Destroyer." A North Carolina woman wrote to a female relative to observe, somewhat concerned, that "Cousin Em began clerking some time ago. What will you girls do with these women who will *clerk*? Home boys leaving and home girls filling all their places." Women helped run many general stores, aiding fathers or husbands, making the stores more congenial for female customers.

Southern stores ran a wide gamut. Some were crude boxes set amidst cotton fields, many miles of rutted road from the nearest railroad station, while others presented imposing brick, cast iron, and plate-glass façades to the best streets of growing towns. Most Southerners experienced something in between, something that came to be seen as an archetype, a universal presence in the rural and small-town South. These buildings became, for many Southerners, a window to the world beyond their localities.

Octave Thanet gives us the best contemporary description of a country store, though her account is written with the sort of knowing condescension people educated in the ways of consumption tend to take toward less sophisticated folk. Upon entering the store in her plantation district of Arkansas, the visitor confronted a tiny cubicle that served as the post office; next to it could be found "the grocery, a little mixed, to be sure, with the crockery, and with a very choice assortment of tinware and colored glass, among which a few bright blue owl jugs are conspicuous. Opposite is the dry goods department, and overhead dangles the millinery shop, in boxes and out." A "large shoe case" serves as "the stationer's stand, the jeweler's, and haberdasher's. At Christmas it is also the toy shop. Our jewelry is of the highest order of gilt plate and colored stones." Not everything was gimcrackery, for the store had to meet fundamental needs as well as transient desires: a door opened into a side building, "where great cypress blocks are the chief furniture of the meat market. Here the pigs and sheep and beeves are dealt out; here, too, are the saddles, the horse 'gear,' the guns, the furniture, and the stoves."

Stores served as more than mere warehouses, as Thomas D. Clark recalled. "They were places where boys bought Barlow knives, copper-toed shoes and jeans britches, and as gangling adolescents with dark threats of beards showing on their chins, their first razors and long trousers. Here girls bought their first dolls, Hoyt's cologne, fancy garter buckles, fine calico dresses and their first corsets." Most of life's material needs could be met in the store, from diapers and toys to wedding rings and dresses to morphine and camphor to coffin handles and shrouds. Hidden in "plain little cardboard boxes" were contraceptive devices, acquired discreetly.

Account books from these stores reveal bold and subtle contrasts. At one extreme, here is what "Len," a tenant listed in the account book of Walter B. Myrick of Satla, North Carolina, bought during the first six months of 1898, for a total of $88.51:

> January: 1 qt. oil/1 lb. sugar/8 lbs. flour/1 gal. salt/2 oz. pepper
>
> February: 1 plug tobacco/1 lb. flour/1 dozen pills/1 lb. meal/1 gal. salt/ 2 lbs. flour/1 lb. meal/1 lb. meat
>
> March: 1 pr. shoes/2 lbs. sugar/4 lbs. flour/7 lb. flour/one-half gal. molasses/1 gal. Irish potatoes/12 lbs. flour/one-half gal. molasses/one-half plug tobacco/1 lb. flour/1 plug tobacco
>
> April: 1 plug tobacco/50 cents cash/one-half gal. molasses/1 bottle medicine/shoe tacks/1 gal. molasses/leather/1 plug tobacco/paid Dr. Burbage/50 cents cash/1 plug tobacco/1 pr. overalls
>
> May: $3 cash/snuff/5 lbs. flour/one-half gal. molasses/50 cents cash/2 lbs. sugar/1 plug tobacco
>
> June: 4 lbs. side meat/one-half gal. molasses/61 lbs. guano/15 cents cash/ 6 lbs. meat/goods at Picots/3 lbs. sugar/medicine/one-half plug tobacco/3 lbs. sugar/snuff/6 lbs. flour/25 cents cash/1 lb. meal/4 lbs. meat

This farmer relied on the store for his sustenance: hardly a week passed that Len did not come to the store for meal, meat, flour, molasses, or sugar. The store provided for the sole doctor's visit, as well as for one bottle each of vague "pills" and "medicine." Len had to come to the store for every cent of cash he wanted, every stamp, every pinch of snuff, every half plug of tobacco. Even when he bought something at another store—"Picots"—it was added to this main account.

To purchase the smallest of items tenants often had to receive permission from their landlord, who might hold the lien on their crop and thus the final say over how they spent their money. "For an hour every Saturday morning a farm owner's time was taken up with writing orders to the storekeeper for a tenant who wanted a new pair of brogan shoes, or for a smiling Negro girl who came up to the back door and asked if she could buy five yards of calico and a batch of bright-red ribbon to make a new spring dress," Thomas D. Clark has written. "On Saturdays the roads were literally filled with customers bearing tiny little slips of paper." On those slips, farmers noted whether the purchase was for their own family or for tenants, so the merchant would know what quality to deal out. One farmer stipulated that a shirt for his tenant should be only "good enough for a darkey to wear."

Not every store presented so bleak a picture. G. W. Willard ran a general store at Kendrick's Creek in the beautiful Holston Valley in the mountains of East Tennessee. His clientele were farmers who generally owned their land. They lived a long way from the etchings, bric-a-brac, and rugs of Richmond or Atlanta, but also a great distance from the lot of sharecroppers. Here, for example, is the tally for January 1890:

broom	candy	cards	comb	eggs (21)
axe	indigo	locks (3)	axle grease	mattock
cash	pants	nails (11)	bolts	pin
forks (3)	shot	leather (3)	tobacco (10)	glass dish
ginger	rivets	cloves	matches (3)	oil can
powder spoons	butter (9)	brass kettle	oil (11)	shoes (2)
shears	coffee (13)	cutters (2)	blacking (2)	thread (8)
cigars	stamps (4)	hat (2)	domestic (4)	sugar (8)
box	lamp (2)	vest	hickory	gingham (2)
soda (3)	cake soap	salt	file (3)	hamburg
overalls	wicks	ink	jeans (5)	flour (3)
plaid (4)	plow point	curry comb	hoe	plow point
oats	buttons pills	Arabine	tacks	
plow line (4)	plow standard			

The most notable improvements over the sharecropper's purchases are in food; the presence of spices, soda, butter, eggs, coffee, and even candy bespeaks a more interesting diet than "Len" enjoyed. The relative absence of meat, flour, and meal reveals that these farmers had their own smoke houses, corn cribs, and wheat fields. Furthermore, their farms and animals received better care than those of tenants, as the curry comb, oats, broom, shears, axe, rivets, plow gear, files, and mattock suggest. These people's homes— with their lamps, brass kettles, forks and spoons, cigars, and glass dishes— offered far more comfort than any sharecropper's. Finally, their hats, vests, buttons, plaid, gingham, blacking, cake soap, and perhaps even "Arabine"— used to make jams and preserves—assured that no one would mistake them for a mere landless cropper in appearance.

The density of trade and variety of goods in a village or small town was far greater than in an isolated country store. A rough and conservative estimate from the account book of Bromley and Martin's store in Waynesboro, Tennessee (pop. 357), shows that the firm sold approximately 33,600 items in the two and a half years between January 1890 and June 1893. In New Bern, North Carolina, a considerably larger town, a druggist's account book records what town folk bought in July and August of 1892:

> cigars (8), beef juice (6), toilet paper (5), malted milk (12), nail brush, Cascara cordial (2), vaseline (4), tooth powder (2), orange toothpick, tooth brush (5), Cuticura Soap (2), Velvet Skin Soap (3), Putz Pomade (2), toilet powder (3), Fountain Syrup (2), nipple, rose water, chamois, insect powder (2), Curley Cream, Nolder's Soap, Cook's Medium, Horse Power, Payson's Ink, shaving soap, tooth paste, moth balls, Hacker's Tar Soap, chewing gum, Ayer's Hair Vigor, Licorice Powder, journal, sachet, Brown Saltzer, bird seed, cologne, Pear's Soap, and C.C. Soap.

These purchases are a far cry from those of Kendrick's Creek, whose residents bought nothing of recent invention during that month in 1890. New Bern residents purchased not generic "cake soap," but a whole range of heavily advertised soaps with name brands as well as nail brushes, toilet powder, rose water, shaving soap, pomade, hair vigor, cologne, tooth paste, tooth brushes, and tooth powder. They bought not merely "candy," but malted milk, cordial, fountain syrup, chewing gum, and licorice powder. They indulged in the new luxury of toilet paper.

As the number of stores mushroomed, so did competition and failure. About a third of all general stores disappeared within any given five-year period. "There are too many people trying to get a living in small one-horse stores," one merchant commented; "in a town where there should not be more than two or three general stores there are a dozen. There is not enough business for all at a reasonable profit." It did not take a large amount of capital to start a store: somewhere between $500 and $2000 sufficed for most businesses. Once it became established, a store offered a return of about 15 percent a year—not a phenomenal rate, but considerably better than the vast majority of farmers could manage.

Markups were considerable in the stores, interest rates high. One merchant testifying before a federal commission freely admitted that farmers had a hard time because of the interest rates that merchants charged. "I can not see any chance for them, unless they change the process of farming or get easier money because they pay too much per cent," he argued. The farmers had to pay high rates—25 percent in his store—to cover the risks created by poor farmers, whom he called "cheap men." "We generally put a pretty good margin on cheap men because we have to take chances on them," he explained. His goal was to clear 10 percent, and in order to make that profit he had to charge high interests to cover the "leakage." "You see, we take all the risk. You take the good percent of them, we have nothing for collateral except the crop, and if they should fail and anything turns up that they do not make a crop, it is a clear loss, and so you see we have to figure for the whole crowd to pay for it." In his view, Southern agriculture faltered because good farmers had to subsidize the bad and the unfortunate.

Other merchants had other explanations for their high prices and rates. Some complained that railroad freight charges discriminated against small places and drove up prices. Others argued that by allowing a farmer credit on an unharvested, even unplanted crop, merchants assumed a risk that had to be covered with reasonable rates of interest and a lien on the crop. Merchants protested that they knew cotton prices had been low and were getting lower, but as only cotton could be stored indefinitely, transported safely, and would meet a sure market, they would accept only cotton or cash in payment of farmers' debts. Merchants maintained that wholesalers and banks charged high interest, which local merchants had to pass along. And they pointed out that farmers always turned to merchants when farm families needed medicine or shoes for school and had no money, yet became angry and hard to find when it came time to settle accounts.

Customers, on the other hand, charged that merchants were merely hiding their greed behind such excuses. Everyone knew merchants squeezed every drop of profit that could be had from every minor purchase. Everyone knew merchants' ledgers often hid shady bookkeeping, always to the merchant's benefit. Everyone knew storekeepers made a good living without getting their hands dirty. Everyone knew merchants were cozy with traveling representatives from big wholesale houses and thereby benefited from good deals they did not pass on. Everyone knew the merchants had become landlords by foreclosing on lands of unlucky neighbors and friends. Everyone knew that the men behind the counter appeared friendly and warm while the credit bill grew, but revealed another face when settling time arrived.

Both the protests of the farmers and the rejoinders of the merchants were true; the store held out new pleasures and comforts, but it pushed the harsher aspects of trade deep into rural life. People viewed the stores nostalgically because the stores had provided them as youngsters their first concrete glimpse of the world outside, because of their association with Christmas, courting, and raising children. People hated the store because it seemed to take all that they earned and still held them in debt. After a year of sixteen-hour days, of sweating and crying children in the fields, women rushing from crop to kitchen and back, men worrying over every change in the weather, promises and wishes delayed, the storekeeper's ledger too often decreed that the family had nothing or less than nothing to show.

Merchandise worked its way into unexpected corners of life. In the spirit of self-sufficiency and subsistence, people used every part of the goods commerce brought. "Dad bought the flour in cloth sacks from Bloxom," Etta Oberseider remembered of her childhood on Virginia's Eastern Shore, "and we emptied the sacks into the barrel. Mother made all of the younger children's nightgowns and many slips from these flour sacks. It was not unusual to see the baby asleep in his crib with the words 'The Best in the World' printed on his little nightgown." Advertising slogans worked their way into everyday language as well. Edna Turpin wrote to a former student to tell of a difficult evening with "three old maids, the Misses Noel," who insisted that their visitors taste various things, from cod liver oil to tomatoes. Turpin became uncomfortable, "But the dear old souls seem so anxious for you to enjoy their dainties (?!) that I verily believe they could inveigle me into making a meal on *Rough on Rats*." "Rough on Rats," as its colloquial name suggests, was a widely advertised vermin poison, familiar to everyone who read a Southern newspaper.

The images and language of modern merchandising appeared in apparently incongruous places. Beginning in the 1880s and 1890s, people who lived in the Kentucky mountains began to decorate their interior walls with pictures from newspapers, catalogs, and magazines. Mixing red pepper and rat poison with boiled flour-and-water paste to keep mice from devouring the paper, combining dried roots of sweet anise and arrowroot for a sweet smell, people applied the pictures with great care and formality. Only straight lines and square corners appeared correct. Illustrations were chosen with care for each room; pictures of food appeared near the stove and table, clothes near the adults' bedroom, toys for the children's. Youngsters often learned their numbers and alphabet from the paper on the walls, messages from a distant world.

Food and its preparation changed quickly in the New South era. One wholesaler told the story of a rural grandmother who visited her family in Nashville for the first time, took one look at the urban family's almost empty larder, and burst into tears. Not knowing about the bounty available at grocery stores, the elderly woman feared the family would starve to death before winter ended. Kitchens contained other novelties as well. The cooking stove, uncommon in the South before the Civil War, proliferated with the spread of railroads and stores. By 1900, most Southern families owned a stove. "Poor indeed is the family in our country that does not have a cook-stove and a sewing machine," Octave Thanet reported from Arkansas. "Last year, the agent for an expensive range sold half a dozen eighty-dollar ranges to sundry farmers and tenants and renters.''

Not only did stoves make hot water readily available and permit women to do their laundry indoors, but stoves also made baking much easier than with a brick oven or coals. The widespread appearance of baking powder and cheap flour pushed biscuits into serious competition with corn bread. By the nineties, farmers could sell the corn they raised and then buy manufactured flour, and they increasingly did so. The sharecropper "has acquired a taste for flour, of late years, and flour is expensive compared with corn meal from his own corn, which he brings to the mill Saturday afternoons, and has ground for a primitive toll of a sixth of the meal," Thanet noted. "He has also taken to 'store truck'; that is, canned vegetables, meats, and fruit."

The South discovered other, subsequently popular, foods at the restaurant counters in the stores. "Piles of cracked bowls and assortments of tarnished knives, forks and tablespoons" sat beside "bottles of pepper sauce, catsup and vinegar" on a "long, greasy counter" before the grocery shelves. Oysters, canned meat, sausages, and cheese cut from a large wheel attracted many hungry customers, but the most popular of the new foods were the sardines "packed in cottonseed oil, seasoned with pepper sauce and eaten with salty cracker." This treat could be washed down with a new Southern invention, Coca-Cola.

Coca-Cola was a product of the growing network of Southern stores. In his Atlanta backyard in 1886, Dr. John Styth Pemberton mixed melted sugar and water with various extracts and oils in a brass kettle over an open fire, trying to find a headache elixir that would also taste good. The concoction contained caffeine and small amounts of two ingredients widely believed to invigorate: coca leaves and cola nuts. Pemberton and his three partners decided to sell the drink at the soda fountains growing up in drug stores across Georgia and the South. Those fountains were seasonal affairs, dispensing their drinks only during the warm months, replaced with displays of other goods in the winter. The liberal use of rebates and premiums encouraged store owners to sell the drink, while salesmen distributed signs, posters, billboards, calendars, bookmarks, paperweights, blotters, trays, and Japanese fans, many of them featuring attractive young women enjoying Coca-Cola.

When he could not obtain enough bottled fruit soda for a workers' picnic on a nearby plantation, a Vicksburg druggist decided to bottle the Coca-Cola that country and town folk enjoyed at his fountain. Three years later, two men in Georgia replaced the unwieldy wire, cork, and rubber stopper (the loud popping sound it made gave the drink the nickname of "soda pop") with a cork and seal. Within a few years a Georgia Baptist Association felt compelled to warn that "there is a beverage known as coca cola; nearly everybody indulges in this drink; we are told that the more you drink the more you want to drink. We fear great harm will grow out of this sooner or later, to our young people in particular." The next few decades would see this product of provincial Southerners sold all over the world, one of the most visible symbols of the entire nation.

New innovations such as Coca-Cola pulled more people to Southern stores more often. Communities grew up around stores just as they did around schools and churches. Of these, ironically, the store proved most common and perhaps most cohesive; while many families might not have children in school or attend church, everyone patronized the local store. Yet, by putting on display things made and sold in greater abundance elsewhere, the store indirectly and inadvertently pushed people away from the very community it helped create. Mail-order catalogues and national advertising brought tidings of a feast with its origins and full richness far away. Each new generation experienced a mounting desire to escape communities that had not seemed so backward only a generation earlier.

For all the changes it witnessed, the South as a whole remained a backwater. Judged by its own past, the region had moved an enormous distance in a generation. Judged by the standards of Pasadena, Buffalo, or Toledo, the South's patterns of consumption were laughable. "I used to wonder what became of the unsuccessful adventures in fashions of head gear or wraps, but now I understand," Octave Thanet wryly observed from Arkansas. "They have gone South!" She recounted how a planter visiting St. Louis was sold "an uncommonly cheap lot" of hats "in perfect condition." Back in Arkansas, the planter distributed the hats through his store. "Thus we observe a fashion of our own. Last winter, all the women and children, black and white, blossomed out like a tulip bed with bright-hued toboggan caps, which they wore, defying age, looks, or weather, late into the spring."

As a fictional character journeyed from Broom Corn Bottom, Arkansas, to New York, wearing hand-me-downs from a wealthy and well-traveled lady of her county, she made a terrible discovery. Although the dress she wore came from New York—surely a sign of good taste—"it had begun to go out of fashion at the first town where the train stopped, and it had grown worse at every station until she got off the cars, and now, while she trod the city of its birth, she felt it shrink into the past with every step she took." The importation of style seemed awkward, too. Orra Langhorne noticed a group of mothers and daughters, loaded down with "boxes and bundles" and enjoying "the recently completed railroad which had at last given them easy access to the busy world from which they had been so long removed." They wore "ill-assorted millinery and overtrimmed dresses, laboriously made in the vain effort to adopt the New York fashion plates to the backwoods of Virginia." The railroad carried the commodity of fashion as surely as it carried flour and cotton, though fashion often seemed more perishable.

In the week before Christmas the freight register of Athens, Georgia, marked the arrival of some unusual items among the prosaic tools, meat, and guano.

Even in the depression year of 1893, the Seaboard Air Line brought, as in a children's story, boxes of toys, raisins, oranges, candy, nuts, and apples. Most children could expect no toys in their stockings, but "there were continual squeals as we emptied our stockings and examined the contents. For each child there would be rosy red apples, sticks of striped candy; a few raisins, what joy, raisins!—only at Christmas; then a few nuts, and the crowning glory a big golden orange," Caroline Coleman remembered. She considered the children of the twentieth century underprivileged, "never to know the joy of having just one orange a year—the Christmas orange— ambrosia and nectar couldn't compare with its taste." The oranges were shared, one by one, by the entire family, mothers saving the peeling to cook something special later on.

Some families would not know such luxury. G. L. Vaughan remembered the Christmas when he and his five brothers and sisters eagerly awoke only to find their stockings empty. Their father had set out on Christmas Eve morning with a "meal sack—to carry gifts in—folded, under one arm, and walked all day, and returned at dark with long face, and the meal sack still empty." The year before, the sack had been full, but now "he was out of money, and tried to buy candy and apples for us six young Georgia Crackers, on credit. Negotiations fell flat. He said nothing, and we asked no questions."

An observer from the more prosperous North found Christmas in the South a time of "infinite pathos," even in good times. At a holiday celebration at a schoolhouse in Arkansas, Octave Thanet thought the children "so happy over their toys that it gives the beholder a softened pang. Watching them; knowing their narrow lives; picturing the cabin left behind in the lonely clearing, where the wind whistles through the broken windows, and, outside, the lean kine are vainly nibbling at the cotton stalks, I feel the weight of the immemorial tragedy on my holiday mood." Not the children: "one boy is winding a Waterbury watch, and his whole being is flooded with content; another is quite as happy over a pair of rubber boots; and little Johnnie Kargiss would not exchange that clumsy pocket knife for anything on the tree." The love of things endured. In an Alabama cemetery, James Agee discovered in the 1930s, kin decorated women's graves with "the prettiest or the oldest and most valued piece of china: on one, a blue glass butter dish whose cover is a setting hen; on another, an intricate milk-colored glass basket; on others, ten-cent-store candy dishes and iridescent vases." On the children's graves, toys rested: "small autos, locomotives and fire engines of red and blue metal; tea sets for dolls, and tin kettles the size of thimbles."

Partly because of the lure of such things, people of both races and genders sought manufacturing jobs that would pay cash. In 1880, a mass of small workshops employed about three-quarters of all Southern manufacturing wage earners. Beginning in the 1880s, however, the key Southern industries began to take shape. Over the next two decades, entrepreneurs established factories in a broad arc through much of the Piedmont. This area made an impressive showing in tobacco, furniture, and building supplies, using modern methods and local capital to build growing enterprises of national importance, turning High Point, Durham, and Winston into important small cities. The coastal plains stretching from Virginia into east Texas offered work at sawmills, in turpentine camps, and in phosphate mines. Lumber mills employed men, too, in Arkansas, west Tennessee, and western Kentucky. People in north Alabama, north Georgia, and east Tennessee earned wages in the coal and iron fields, transforming the bustling young cities of Chattanooga and Birmingham. People in eastern Kentucky, West Virginia, and southwest Virginia could look to the expanding coal mines of the mountains.

Nevertheless, Southern manufacturing did not fit what we recognize as the general pattern of industrial development that transformed other Western countries in the nineteenth century. While the cigarette, furniture, and textile industries made impressive strides in the New South, most Southern industrial workers labored in forests and mines rather than in factories. Those extractive industries became increasingly dominant throughout the New South era, outstripping the growth of more heavily mechanized enterprises. Southern industry created relatively few salaried clerks and other officials and failed to fuel the widespread economic development of the sort experienced in the Midwest at the same time.

Given these very real limitations, many contemporaries and subsequent scholars have seen the Southern economy as essentially "colonial," producing raw products for distant markets where the profitable finishing and use of the products took place. Some have ascribed the South's colonial position to the actions of the federal government, to the unfair policies of major corporations, to the selling-out of the region by its own political and business leaders, to the machinations of Northern capitalists, to the resistance of powerful planters. These critics stress, with good reason, the conscious decisions that shaped the industrial experience of the South and look for those to blame for the region's lack of long-term development.

It is misleading, though, to stop there. Whether or not Southern industry in the aggregate measured up to standards achieved elsewhere under more favorable circumstances, it touched the lives of a million people. Whether or not Southern industry measured up to the claims of the region's boosters—and it did not—it shaped the histories of hundreds of counties. The impact of industry in the New South needs to be measured in people's experience, not merely in numbers, not merely by debunking inflated rhetoric.

Textile mills could be built anywhere where there was power to run the machinery—and the Piedmont from Virginia through Alabama offered dozens of rivers and streams with an adequate flow of water. After the 1890s, when the production of the Southern coal fields made steam power feasible, textile mills could be located over an even broader area. A textile mill required far less capitalization than heavier industries and most labor in a textile factory required little experience and little physical strength; even children would do for some jobs. The competition with other regions and countries was less harsh in textiles than in other industries, because mills could specialize in particular weaves or grades that other mills were not producing.

The Southern textile industry steadily spread. The 10,000 textile hands in the South of 1870 (the same number as in 1850 and 1860) grew to 98,000 by 1900. In 1870, the South held only 8 percent of the nation's textile workers; by 1900, 32 percent. Each of the Carolinas contained a third of the region's mills, Georgia, one-fifth. The mills varied widely in size: in 1900, the average mill in South Carolina employed 377 workers, in Georgia 270, and in North Carolina 171; the regional average was 243. The larger mills tended to be located in or near cities and large towns, not in isolated enclaves.

The South's textile mills boasted the latest and most sophisticated machinery. By the 1890s electric lights illuminated some mills during the night shifts; automatic sprinklers and humidifiers appeared in the more advanced factories. Southern manufacturers were among the first to adopt the latest in manufacturing equipment as well, including a new revolving card in the 1880s and an automatic loom in the 1890s.

This rapid proliferation of up-to-date textile mills inspired much of New South boosterism. Here was evidence, in county after county, state after state, that factories could prosper in the South. Here was an industry that used expensive and sophisticated machinery to manufacture products that could hold their own with those produced in Great Britain or Massachusetts. Here were products sought in China, India, and Latin America, for the South supplied 60 percent of all the American cloth sent abroad at the turn of the century. Here were factories that paid a profit early on and kept on paying for decades. Here were factories that tapped the South's great cotton crop at the source, that saved the expense of transporting the bulky fiber thousands of miles. Here were factories that prospered even during the depression of the 1890s, while virtually every other business in the country—including New England textile factories—suffered.

Perhaps most important for the South's perception of itself, the textile mills were built with local capital and employed local people. Until after the turn of the century, Northern capital played only a small role in building the Southern factories. The Northern capital that did arrive came through the companies that also supplied the machinery and marketing of the Southern crop. Every property holder in and around the towns that built textile mills could reasonably expect to profit from the mill's arrival.

People caught in the excitement of mill-building spoke often of the benefits the mills' working people would enjoy. The argument took different shapes depending on the context. Sometimes the mills were healthy because they would employ "white women and children who could find no other work equally well-adapted to their strength, and producing as large a return for their labor"; sometimes the mills were good because they brought the erstwhile rural folk "together in groups, where they are subject to elevating social influences, encouraged them to seek education, and improved them in every conceivable respect, as future husbands and wives, sons and daughters, parents and children." The town people saw the operatives from the very beginning as people unlike themselves, as helpless women, benighted rustics, or failed farmers. For some, that perception of the workers fed a desire to minister to them, to help bring them into the fold of the progressive New South; for others, perhaps most, that sense of otherness bred only pity or contempt.

Near the turn of the century a writer for the *Outlook* visited a mill town near Augusta. He asked several mill families why they had come there. "The reasons given for leaving their rural homes were widely various: 'because we lost our "plantation" '; 'because my wife was lonely'; 'because the darkeys came in.' " The pervasive decline of Southern rural life created a sense of dissatisfaction and desperation among white farming families that made it easier for mill operators to find a work force. The demographic pressure on the land, the decline of cotton prices, the growing proportion of women to men in the older regions, the mobility of blacks, the disaffection of the young for rural life—all these dislocations made it easier to undergo the powerful dislocation of leaving home to work in a textile mill.

Some people were obviously more willing to leave than others. Widows with children found the mills a place where they could keep their families together and live without dependence on others. Any family with several young daughters at home might find the mills attractive, for the labor of those daughters was worth far more in a factory than in the countryside. Single young men, on the other hand, found opportunities that paid at least as well as the textile mills; at least until the turn of the century, a farm hand made as much as a spinner in a mill and a hard worker could make considerably more money cutting logs or working on a railroad. Those young men who stayed on at a mill through their mid-twenties, however, often remained for the rest of their working lives and rose in the company hierarchy. Women, who moved in and out of the mill as they had children, generally stayed in the lower-paying jobs.

While some parents would do anything to keep the children out of the mills and in school, others saw nothing wrong with children learning to work early on in life, contributing to the family income and being where they could be watched. Employers differed as well; some were anxious to have the cheap labor of children, while others would have happily replaced them with other, more dependable and less controversial, workers. In any case, a quarter of all male mill workers at the turn of the century were fifteen or under and over a third of females were that young; most workers of both genders were in their late teens or early twenties.

This laboring force was unique among Southern industries, both within the Piedmont and within the South as a whole, for the conspicuous presence of women and children and for the predominance of whites. Whereas the workers in virtually every other major industry in the South were nearly balanced between the races, the machine rooms of the cotton mills rapidly became the preserve of whites only. Mill owners would not allow blacks to work alongside the white women and girls who made up the bulk of the work force. Black men were permitted to work only at outside loading and unloading and in the suffocating rooms where they opened bales for processing. Black women found no work at all.

This labor force held many attractions to mill management. By employing the entire family, the employer received not only inexpensive labor but also considerable sway over that labor. Unlike a single man, a family had a difficult time leaving; while workers who moved from mill to mill during those frequent times when there was not enough labor to go around inflated turnover figures, most mills enjoyed a stable core of families. The famous "mill village" setting increased that stability, for the company provided the school, the church, the recreation, and the store as well as the work.

These villages exhibited a broad range of conditions and elicited a broad range of reactions. The workers' evaluation of the results of their move from the countryside varied just as widely as the reasons they had left in the first place: "Some declared they had improved their conditions; others that they had ruined what good fortunes they had had." At first, one mill owner commented, workers seemed "supremely happy and contented" as they enjoyed the water pumps and nearby churches and schools unavailable in most farm communities. Yet "by and by the novelty wears away. Things once longed for and regarded as unattainable become commonplace." As one mill worker put it, "They's more money at the mill, but a better livin' on the farm. Unless a man's mighty sorry he can raise good somethin' t'eat on the land, while he has more spendin' money in the mill—and he spends it too. All he does at either one is jus' about break even."

The typical village combined urban crowding with the kerosene lamps, hand pumps, meddlesome livestock, flies, and mud of the countryside. The factory itself, filled with choking fibers and loud machines, was little better. The typical mill looked something like the one described in a novel of the time: "a low, one-story structure of half-burnt bricks" next to "a squatty low-browed engine room" with a "black, soggy exhaust-pipe stuck out of a hole in its side."

Because not enough families or young women were willing to work in the textile factories, owners experienced recurring labor shortages, especially around the turn of the century. During those times, a steady stream of transient workers flowed into and out of the mill villages, moving to find higher wages, a better house, or merely a new setting. "This mill will be o.k. if we ever get enough weavers to run everything without depending on floating 'bum' labor," a manager for a North Carolina mill wrote his mother in 1897. "Whenever I see a strong, robust country girl, I am almost on my knees in my effort to try to get her to go to the mill to learn to weave." While the mills of the 1880s and 1890s managed to get most of their workers from nearby rural areas, by 1900 mill recruiters often had to search 250 miles afield. Some ran trains into the mountains to persuade families to come to the mill villages. Other mills sent agents into their competitors' towns to entice experienced hands to move, partly by "getting them dissatisfied" with their present lot.

The mill villages, while often separated from neighboring towns by different school systems and churches, were not self-contained paternalistic enclaves. Not only did "floaters" move from village to village, but even the long-term workers seldom had a personal relationship, positive or negative, with the mill owner. The kind of men who had the money to invest in mills had no interest in living in mill villages. "I was so impressed with the uninviting surroundings, lack of educational facilities and civilized society, etc.," remarked one South Carolina man who was considering buying a small mill, "that I decided that I would not move my family down there for the whole outfit as a gift."

Groups of investors owned most mills and merely paid a superintendent to keep an eye on things. Those superintendents lived in the villages themselves and sent their children to school with the operative children. Chosen for their character and the respect they held among the workers as well as for their ability to keep things in order and to turn a profit, the superintendents often found themselves caught between employer and employee. Of the workers' class and background, but acting as the agent of absentee owners, the superintendent "only demanded of the operatives what the president demanded of him," a mill pastor pointed out. In turn, "the president demanded what the directors demanded of him; the directors demanded what the stockholders demanded of them. The stockholders demanded large dividends and there is where the driving began and there is where the responsibility rests." As in so much of the South, distant forces seemed to power the machinery, while people struggled in their face-to-face encounters to make the best of hard situations.

The Appalachian countryside began to change well before the arrival of the coal companies brought wholesale changes. By the 1880s, in even the most isolated hollows the stereotypical log cabin had begun to give way to frame houses; by 1900, nine out of ten new mountain homes were built from milled lumber. At the end of a rail line through some of the most rugged terrain in the mountains, Charles Dudley Warner came upon a blast furnace and its supporting array of structures: "a big company store, rows of tenement houses, heaps of slag and refuse ore, interlacing tracks, raw embankments, denuded hillsides, and blackened landscape."

Such furnaces and mines touched communities many miles away. Although the residents of the Hollybush community in Kentucky, for example, were half a day's wagon ride from any such industry, they began to feel industry's effects early on. They learned that the stores in the mining towns would pay cash for produce; farmers, able to count on a reliable market for the first time, began to clear more fields and plant more crops. Others, hearing that the mines and the railroads needed timber, cut logs and sold them to the companies. Some of these men, seeing all that the new coal towns had to offer, began to work in the mines and send money back home; others moved their families. All the while, the mounting pressure on the land brought about by high fertility rates and relatively small amounts of farm land increased the incentive to leave the farm for "public work."

The coal was an open secret. The mountaineers did not have to read the brochures put out by their state governments to learn of the mineral possibilities of their land. It was not so much that the large commercial coal companies "discovered" the mineral as that they possessed the desire and the industrial wherewithal to mine it on a new scale. After the depression of the early 1890s, the great industries of the Midwest began to shift to Southern coal, especially after the United Mine Workers managed to establish collective bargaining in the Northern fields. Southern coal was of a higher quality than the Midwestern mines', yet less expensive because of the South's topography, lower freight costs, and labor rates. As a result of these advantages, the 40,000 tons of coal West Virginia sent to the Great Lakes in 1898 grew into six million tons fifteen years later.

The Southern Appalachians saw enormous population movement around the turn of the century. The mountains pulled in thousands of workers and their families, and parts of this subregion, famous in folklore for isolated cabins, in fact exhibited some of the highest population densities in rural America. Although West Virginia's miners officially lived in rural places, they lived among urban conditions. "It was smoky, sooty, and grimy," one miner recalled of his coal town. "The constant puff of railway locomotives, the crash and grind of engines, cars, and trains, night and day, produced an atmosphere similar to that surrounding one of the great steel centers like Homestead, Youngstown, or Pittsburgh."

The new arrivals did not stop once they arrived in the mountains; miners were among the most geographically mobile of American workers. The miners moved a great deal among different employers but tended to stay in one industry and one region. "It was easy," recalled one miner, "all you needed was a pair of gloves, overalls and experience and you could get hired anywhere."

A surprisingly large proportion of the new arrivals were black men. Black

Young black couples in southwest Virginia. (University of Virginia Special Collections)

recruiters held out free transportation, high wages, and company housing as they traveled to churches, bars, and streetcorners. These recruiters were selling what every black American male wanted: "a man's chance in the world." West Virginia, unlike other Southern states, did not disfranchise blacks and did not legislate an extensive set of Jim Crow laws. The recruiters traveled not only to the cities of neighboring states but also to the coal mines of Alabama, where experienced black miners received a train ticket and $25 to move to West Virginia. As with all other instances of black labor recruiting, the business was dangerous: "If the law caught you with a bunch of tickets, you were gone."

The degree of segregation these black miners faced varied from place to place, depending on the size of the company town, the size of the black population, and the predispositions of the white miners. During the coal boom of the turn of the century the companies' need for miners led them to make concessions to blacks they would not make in more depressed times. Generally, black miners lived in houses identical to the houses occupied by white miners, but in separate areas. Miners of both races worked together and received the same payment for their labor; their wives shopped at the same store and their children went to the same school. In some places and times, blacks and whites even attended political rallies and religious revivals together. While this situation would take a turn for the worse in a few decades, for a number of years blacks found some of their best opportunities in the Southern coal fields. Many managed to work in the mines and, with the hard work of their wives and children, also maintain farms in Virginia or even North Carolina.

During good times, workers did not voice much complaint about the company housing, the company store, the company school. Indeed, workers viewed the mining towns as a part of the deal employers had to offer if they were to attract workers from nearby competitors. The coal towns went up in sparsely populated areas, after all, and everything had to be built from scratch. The average company town contained only a few hundred people, not enough to attract merchants. Thus, the coal operators had little choice but to establish stores for their employees, and a flagrantly unfair store would repel far more workers than it could keep through debt. The stores apparently held few miners in long-term debt, though they did issue scrip as an advance before payday.

On the other hand, the company store and houses also provided means by which virtually all the wages the miners received came back to the company through purchases or rents. During good times, the high wages and relative freedom of the mines assuaged the distrust and anger inevitable when all economic power was concentrated in the hands of the company; during hard times, though, when the coal operators had to depend on these ancillary forms of business for any profit they might make, the potential for unfairness and conflict quickly rose to the surface.

Every major industry and every major city depended on coal to drive the huge engines of modern life. Yet it is a notorious fact that the counties producing this coal became some of the poorest in the nation. While the textile company towns were owned by Southern capital and tied to nearby towns and cities, outside capital owned and operated the coal towns. The development that did attend the Southern coal industry occurred hundreds of miles away: in Roanoke, where the Norfolk and Western was headquartered; in Newport News and Norfolk, where the coal dug out of the West Virginia mines was loaded on to ships bound for New England and abroad; in Huntington and Charleston, which the coal companies used as bases; even in Boston, Providence, and New Haven, where the coal went to fuel factories. The coal fields themselves, for all the buying and selling, all the population influx and railroad building, saw mainly hard work and hard times.

Lumbering, more than any other industry, captures the full scope of economic change in the New South, its limitations as well as its impact. In the early 1880s, Northern timber companies, aware that the white pine reserves of their own region would be largely exhausted in fifteen years, sent "cruisers" to locate the most promising stands of long-leaf pine in the Southern states with public lands: Alabama, Arkansas, Florida, Louisiana, and Mississippi. One of the men reported back from Florida in 1882 that "the woods are full of Michigan men bent on the same errand as myself." Special trains brought Northern investors down to look over the government land. Between 1881 and 1888, nearly five and a half million acres of public timber land were sold in the five states.

As the public and private lands of the South came into the hands of timber companies, railroad companies, coal companies, phosphate companies, iron companies, and speculative companies, the pace and scope of Southern lumbering greatly accelerated. Sawmills appeared every five miles or so alongside the railroads spreading across the South. In 1870 the South accounted for only 11 percent of the nation's production of lumber, but by 1910 the South turned out 45 percent of that total—even though huge logging firms had emerged in the Pacific Northwest. The South's increased share came at the expense of the Northeast and the Great Lakes states. The biggest sawmills in the United States stood in Louisiana, Texas, and Mississippi. In 1900, nearly one out of five Southern wage earners in manufacturing worked for the lumber industry. While some of these were farmers who labored for the lumber mills only part of the year, as the years passed it became more common for workers to live with their families in towns built around the milling operation.

A large commercial sawmill needed 50 to 70 men. Aside from the superintendent, foreman, and bookkeeper, the mill demanded workers experienced at specialized jobs. Every mill required a sawyer to run the mill, a filer to keep the blades sharp, log jackers to position the logs on the moving carriage, edgers to square up the planks, off bearers to carry the planks to stackers, and "dust monkeys"—young boys who kept the space beneath the whirling blade free from sawdust. Whites held the supervisory jobs and many of the skilled ones, but blacks might well work their way up to an important position in the mill or in the logging crews made up of 18 to 30 additional men.

Danger lurked everywhere around the timber industry, which had an accident rate seven times that of the national manufacturing average. The greatest risks grew out of situations over which the worker had little control. Not only did limbs fly in every direction when a felled tree struck the ground, but the perils multiplied as the operation became more mechanized. When the Southern industry adopted steam skidders in the early 1890s, lumbermen faced a whole new set of dangers. Steel cables, often a thousand or more feet long, were attached to four or five logs and then pulled to the rail siding as the skidder revolved and hauled in the cables. Not only did the man hooking the cables risk getting caught between the steel and the lumber, but a cable that broke or pulled loose endangered everyone in the vicinity; the flying steel could easily decapitate a man or sever his arm.

As the railroads pushed through the enormous pine lands of the South, lumber companies established one instant town after another. Everything

Lumber railroad, Mobile County, Alabama, 1895. (Armitstead Collection, University of South Alabama Archives)

revolved around one purpose: to cut and mill as much lumber as workers in the town could effectively reach. It was well worth the investment, for a series of spur tracks branching off along three or four miles of the main rail line could penetrate about 20,000 acres of land and supply 30 million board feet of lumber, employing hundreds of workers for over a decade. A large commissary housed the company office, a doctor's office, a post office, and a general store. These buildings immediately became the center of the community.

The lumber camps were rough places. "We are in the woods," one mill superintendent wrote to a friend. "No church. No school. No society but thank *God* for one thing. I with Gesina's and one old ladies help (*Who by the way is a Baptist*) have partially remedied one of these defects." He had established a Sunday school, "and I am proud and happy to say that every Sabbath afternoon we have all the children and all the ladies singing, hearing lessons, etc. But I am sorry to say I am the only man so far." A logger from Arkansas saw things from a different perspective. Ormie Twiford frequently caught the train to the "Red Light" in a nearby town. He commented one evening that "Misses Lilly and Maud, two scarlet ladies who stay at our hotel, came into my room this evening where I sat reading, and putting on my pistols and belts played 'cowboys.' They looked romantic thus accoutered."

It was easy to close out a milling operation, even a company town. Workers dismantled the mill and buildings and loaded them on railroad cars to move to the next holding. Some houses might be abandoned or sold to workers who chose to remain behind. The merchants who had cast their lot with the towns sometimes tried to make it without the mill, but they almost never succeeded. The cut-over land was sold cheap and poorer families rushed to take a chance on making farming pay. Towns vanished. A visitor to a Louisiana lumber town described the scene only six months after the mill had cut its last log: "The big sawmill that for twenty years had been the pulsing heart of this town, was already sagging on its foundations, its boilers dead, its deck stripped of all removable machinery." The hotel, bank, and stores stood empty; grass grew in the streets.

The powerful skidders, which had so speeded the timbering process, destroyed the next generation of trees. The huge logs dragged across the land uprooted or crushed smaller growth; only coarse wiregrass remained. Twenty-five years later, the areas where skidders had worked still stood out for their unnatural barrenness. An amateur ornithologist in the mountains of North Carolina watched as golden eagles, bald eagles, peregrine falcons, and other species native to the region disappeared. "Floating sawdust swirled in eddies on the surface and the water was black as soot," one mountain novelist wrote. "Here and there the white belly of a fish lay upturned to the sun, for the cruel, deadly work of civilization had already begun." The language was melodramatic but hardly hyperbolic. Only extreme words could capture the hope and misgivings sweeping through the New South as railroads, stores, mines, towns, and crop liens spread.

Part II

PUBLIC LIFE

Chapter 4

Election News

Political passions ran high in the New South. The Civil War loomed over the two-party system of the United States, for people could not forget that the Republicans had been the party of Abraham Lincoln and of black freedom, that the Democrats had been the party of Copperheads and secessionists. Moreover, the American economy experienced unprecedented acceleration and unprecedented collapse, bred growing class differences and geographic complexity. Caught between a bloody recent past and a threatening future, voters felt they were playing for high stakes.

Politics mattered enormously to most Southern men. Casting one's lot with the Democrats, the Republicans, or one of the many independent candidates of the 1880s often defined a man's friends, business dealings, and even marriage prospects. In many Southern states, eight of every ten eligible men—black and white—voted in the early 1880s. In others, Redemption had driven many black voters away from the polls not to return; in those states, only about six in ten men voted. In Georgia and South Carolina, where Democrats enacted restrictive laws, only about four men in ten cast a ballot. Politics varied greatly from district to district as well, with the percentage of men who voted varying as much as 30 percentage points among districts in the same state.

Throughout the era, no matter the current political climate, most of a politician's work involved getting and keeping jobs for oneself and one's "friends." Patronage was the great constant of Southern politics. "A party that don't go in for everything in sight," the editor of a major Southern newspaper has a fictional character say, "won't be able long to get nothing. Party workers has got to see something to work for, and when there is anything good to be passed round, a party has got to do its best to get it for its own supporters, or it won't have supporters enough long to carry local or any other sort of elections." Or as a Virginia politician put it in a letter to his party's state chairman, "the fodder should go to the working ox."

The two major parties of Gilded Age America were machines within machines, elaborate interlocking combinations of local, county, state, and national organizations. It was by no means clear which level of party was most important. While the national leaders articulated party policy on the tariff and currency, state leaders maneuvered dozens of diverse county leaders into position on gubernatorial and senatorial seats, county leaders controlled access to most political positions, and local leaders turned out the vote. Complex negotiations flowed up and down this hierarchy, as men at each level sought to make sure their efforts won appreciation and reward. Throughout the 1880s and 1890s, even as civil service reforms began, virtually all of the hundreds of thousands of government positions in the United States were filled through the party mechanisms. Party loyalty was the basis on which everything else stood. All a party member needed to know, a neophyte learned, was "the name of our son-of-a-bitch."

Any party's well-being began with getting out the vote, and that job required large numbers of men willing to devote their time and personal connections to the task. A Democratic Canvass Book published in 1885 for use in Virginia gives some idea of the labor demanded: "Enter in this Book, commencing with the first page, the names of *fifty qualified voters* who live within the limits of the Sub-district, and intend to vote for the Democratic candidates," the book's instructions began. "On the day of election five leaders will take charge of these ten voters each, to see that they vote." The "chief of fifty" would make sure the workers at the lower level did their job, by checking off the names of those who came to the polls. Such grassroots workers had an intimate knowledge of their territory, as handwritten questions on the inside of the book revealed. Not only was the worker to find out the number of registered Democrats and Republicans, but he should learn "how many doubtful voters will probably vote Democratic." Such party workers pushed, sometimes to unlikely extremes, to get every vote they could into their column. A registrar in a closely divided North Carolina township wrote to a party official with a pressing question: "Let me know if it is lawful for anyone who has partly lost his mind to register and vote."

No group was better able to serve politics than the lawyers who worked in the heart of every county, town, and city. The correspondence of state leaders bulged with stationery bearing the letterheads of lawyers from across the state. Lawyers dealt with each other at district as well as local courts, developing the sort of acquaintanceships beyond the borders of their counties that few people in the New South enjoyed. Lawyers had more free time than many, made a living out of talking and public speaking, and were anxious to attract public attention. Moreover, young lawyers frequently needed the business afforded by a position such as public prosecutor, which allowed an attorney to get to know counterparts and judges throughout a circuit. If he did a good job in an important case, or even if he were merely flamboyant and entertaining, a prosecutor could attract an important following among the men who loitered around Southern courthouses.

To work near the courthouses and railroad junctions of the South was a great advantage to town men. In critical elections speedy communications could give one party or faction a significant advantage over another. "I am at the office before breakfast to answer yours of yesterday in the hope of mailing it by first train this morning," a Raleigh politician wrote to his superior. These town men also enjoyed the aid of modern office methods. "We are ruled by the type-writer and the mimeograph—and the phonograph-audiophone," a party worker complained in 1892 after an opponent for a state supreme court position used these new weapons to create the impression that he possessed great popularity. One local leader suggested to a party official in Virginia that a "personal" letter-writing campaign would help persuade the leading 49 men of his county to come around, "if you have the time and an abundance of stenographers and type writers."

It seemed to many Southerners that political machines ran the show, that politics was a closed game. In most of the region, only white men were considered for office and only white men of education had a chance for anything more than a county office. The great majority of those county positions were held by the Democrats, nominations coming out of a Democratic convention that put forward only one candidate for each post. Those conventions, in turn, were run by local politicos. Noting that two-thirds of the white voters had been removed from jury rolls in his county, one furious farmer raged: "We would like to know to what clique we must belong, and whom we must allow to do our thinking. To whom must we pull off our hats, and whose boots must we lick to be counted worthy to serve on the jury?"

For good reason, Democrats continually worried about apathetic or disenchanted voters. While "some men seem to think it would not be so bad to go to perdition if they might hold some office when they get there," one newspaper joked, others could not care less. "There are entirely too many white men in this town who seem not to care whether one party or the other carries the day," a Durham newspaper complained. To many people, politics seemed a cheap shortcut, a way to avoid real work while making things harder for everyone else. One upcountry Georgia paper used the familiar language of the Bible to convey popular disgust and distrust of the breed:

The politician is my shepard, I shall not want. He leadeth me into the saloon
for my vote's sake. He filleth my pockets with five-cent cigars and my beer glass
runneth over. He inquireth concerning the health of my family even unto the
fourth generation. Yea, though I walk thro the mud and rain to vote for him,
and shout myself hoarse, when he is elected he straightway forgetteth me. Yea,
though I meet him in his own office he knoweth me not. Surely the wool has
been pulled over my eyes all the days of my life.

Politics garnered great attention in the New South, even among those who
decided not to vote. Politics was not necessarily a simple matter of choosing
sides between Democrats versus Republicans, farmers versus industrialists,
white versus black. Politics had all kinds of shadings and implications, all
kinds of risks and rewards.

Redemption failed to eliminate the opponents the Democrats had faced under Reconstruction. The Republicans carried considerable strength into and
throughout the 1880s. After the party's sharp losses between 1872 and 1876,
when the share of Southern counties won in presidential elections by the
Republicans declined from 45 to only 21 percent, the party began slowly to
gain ground again. In the congressional races of the mid-1880s the party
made its best showing on the Atlantic plain of Virginia and North Carolina,
winning 44 percent of all elections in those counties. The Republicans ran
nearly as well in the counties along the lower Mississippi River—in Louisiana
and Mississippi—and in the mountains of Tennessee, Kentucky, and West
Virginia. The Republicans also won at least a quarter of the counties in the
Piedmont of Virginia and North Carolina and in the cotton uplands of Arkansas.

The mountain Republicans remained strong in the 1880s, dominated
by powerful leaders who played to local Unionist loyalties and who effectively deployed patronage positions and pensions. The upland Republicans
portrayed themselves as the champions of the common white man, as heirs
to the Unionist legacy. The Republicans assailed the antiquated ideology
that had bound the lowland Democrats before the Civil War and that
bound them still. "They taught their children that it was a disgrace to
work," one Tennessee paper charged. "They had the utmost contempt for
poor working white men, and regarded them as no better than slaves. The
idea of equalizing themselves socially with the common classes was repul-
sive to their 'royal' minds, and such a thing as honoring a common 'self
made' man with a public trust was a thing not even thought of." Not
much had changed. Mountain Republicans were frustrated that so many
white men in the South voted against their own best interests, blindly following the corrupt Democrats when the Republicans represented a real
alternative.

Black Republicans remained powerful in the early 1880s as well. Democrats bolstered Republican strength in some districts when they gerrymandered lines so that black population would be concentrated; by sacrificing one district the Democrats could help ensure the stability of the Democratic party in several neighboring areas. Mississippi had its "shoestring" third district that ran through the black counties along the river; Virginia's fourth district embraced much of the Southside; and South Carolina's seventh district wrapped around black counties. North Carolina was the clearest example of such politics, where the "Black Second" repeatedly elected a black congressman. Each heavily black district returned substantial Republican majorities and sent black representatives to the national House of Representatives throughout the 1880s.

Black Southerners inherited a tradition of voting Republican and only Republican; to cast a Republican ballot was to attack the enemy, the Southern white who kept the black man down. When Booker T. Washington arrived in Alabama in 1882 to create the Tuskegee Institute he received a quick lesson in black politics from an elderly freedman. "You can read de newspaper and most of us can't," Washington was lectured, "but dar is one thing dat we knows dat you don't, and dat is how to vote down here; And we wants you to vote as we does." The method was simple and unerring: "We watches de white man; de nearer it gets to 'lection time de more we watches de white man. We watches him till we find out which way he gwine vote. After we find out which way he gwine'r vote, den we votes 'zactly de other way; den we knows we's right." Such blacks made it an article of pride and race solidarity that they stick together, that they vote Republican no matter the rewards of voting for a white Democrat.

But the rewards for voting for some other candidate tempted blacks to turn away from the party of Lincoln. In 1885, a black political leader in Nashville announced to the Democrats that "if the Democratic party prove a better friend to the Negro than the Republican party, the vote of the Negro will certainly divide and go with you, increasing as the friendly relation increases." Or as another put it, "I offer my vote to the highest bidder, not for money, but the greatest measure of justice." The editor of a black Tennessee newspaper observed that men of his race had no true white friends, regardless of party: "Every time when the Negro sticks his head up for office he is slaughtered by those with whom he affiliates, and for whom he always works and votes." In such an atmosphere, many black men decided they had little to lose by associating with the Democrats. They hoped that a divided black vote might make both sides take black demands and needs more seriously.

Their loss of faith in the Republicans and in politics in general made individual blacks more susceptible to Democrats who held out rewards or who threatened retribution. Democrats enjoyed the influences over blacks of "employer on the laborer, of the creditor on the debtor, of the rich on the poor, of the humane and charitable on the friendless or affected," one white observer noted. All these instruments of power could be brought to bear on a sharecropper, worker, or customer on election day. Whites often resorted to outright bullying. The Yankees had insisted on giving the blacks the vote despite common sense and justice, the reasoning went, and so anything white Southerners did in self-defense was fair enough.

It usually took far more than bullying, though, to gain the votes of disaffected or apolitical blacks. Politicians of both races tried to buy all the votes they could among voters of both races. "We don't propose to throw away money in barbecues and drinking," wrote one North Carolina county leader in 1880, "but to purchase directly the votes at the polls." "We must spend money among the colored people—we must get votes from them to counteract, and off-set votes we will certainly lose from other sources," another worker cautioned eight years later. "Am buying Negro votes," yet another reported. "Go on with your real or seeming confidence," urged a Democratic leader in that state, "but don't forget to impress trusty men with the gravity of affairs and try in some way to get it to be discreetly understood that every ironclad Democrat must vote *one* Negro through. . . . It ought to be worked so as not to call too much attention to it." A joke in a South Carolina newspaper showed the cynicism with which whites viewed the black franchise:

STRAWBER: Thomas Jefferson, I just heard that you sold your vote for two dollars at the last election. Aren't you ashamed of yourself?
THOMAS JEFFERSON: Well, sah, dat's all I could get.

"The right of suffrage is fast becoming an article of merchandise," the New Orleans *Republican* complained, "and is placed upon the market with about the same eagerness that the fruit vender betrays in the disposal of his fruit. One thing is certain, that there is a very large portion of voters in this State who never vote unless they succeed in getting some mercenary consideration for their votes." That "very large portion of the voters" willing to sell their vote included whites as well as blacks, though the transaction among whites might be sealed by a mere slap on the back and a swig from a common bottle.

Despite the open contempt with which they discussed Republicans, many Southern Democrats cut deals with the opposition. In arrangements known as "fusion" the Democrats remained comfortably ensconced in their white man's party while striking bargains of convenience with black opponents, ceding some offices to black Republicans. As a result, white Democrats could hold office in heavily black districts and black politicians could benefit from white protection and support. Yet fusion could be dangerous to white Democrats. The Republicans extracted promises of elective and appointed offices, of patronage, and of financial help, playing one group of ambitious Democrats against the other. In this way, the Republicans managed to keep

In line to vote, Caddo Parish Courthouse, Louisiana, 1894. (Louisiana State University at Shreveport Archives)

a few local offices in their hands and to keep their party alive with hopes for better days ahead.

It is not surprising that such deals infuriated the whites who found themselves left out. The deals also worried bystanders who feared that fusion would undermine not only Democratic power but white hegemony in general. Fusion dissolved party boundaries and thereby tended to make black voters free agents in a market where their votes were valuable commodities. Even if the Republican party had always been repugnant to white Democrats, it nevertheless had served to control black political activity; in the face of concerted black voting, deals could be struck with Republican leaders that served to contain black political power. Without the control of the Republicans, black voters became more volatile and therefore more dangerous. "The tendency toward fusion and the breaking up of party lines has made possible a very dangerous evil, which is constantly increasing," a student of Southern politics warned in 1885. "It is that thousands of the Negroes have become a mercenary element in local and State politics." Thoughtful people of both races worried that corrupt politics polluted the rest of the society.

The battle over the prohibition of alcohol focused much of the energy and anxiety of the New South. In one Southern state after another, fights over prohibition pulled people into political debate who had been excluded or aloof from ordinary politics; women, religious folk, and self-consciously respectable blacks eagerly entered the prohibition battle. Some of the largest cities as well as some of the most isolated counties of the region divided over liquor, and the major political parties maneuvered as best they could to capture new votes and avoid massive defections.

Because most of its campaigns were waged on the local level, the political importance of the prohibition issue has been masked. The reasons for prohibition sentiment were not hard to find. Liquor, by all accounts, took a heavy toll in the New South. Alcohol became much easier to get as the number of towns and stores proliferated in the region. Enterprising bar owners set up shop in any town they could, importing nude pictures to hang behind the bar and permitting loud, obscene language.

Entire communities, women and men, black and white, divided on the issue. Town boosters who wanted as much business for their town as it could get warned against prohibition. "Here's our humble opinion: Once this town goes dry, the ruin of Opelousas will follow as sure as the wreck succeeds the storm." Neighboring towns will take the business, the town's Democratic paper warned, and "will soon cause Opelousas to shrivel up and crumble into nothingness, and ere many years the crack of the herder's whip will be the only sound to disturb the vast solitude of the cow pasture occupying the scene of Opelousas' present bustle and activity."

Left to their own devices, state legislators would have done nothing, but they sometimes bowed to the petitions and letters that arrived and to the threat prohibitionists posed to local Democratic stability. Such equivocation led both the defenders and attackers of prohibition to grow impatient with the two major parties. There was a widespread belief among whites that blacks provided the swing votes on prohibition in many communities and states, and as a result black votes and influence went at an uncomfortable premium.

Indeed, blacks enjoyed their greatest political activity and visibility of the entire New South era in the prohibition movement. In Mississippi in the early 1880s, just a few years after a wave of violence and intimidation had killed Reconstruction, all the major prohibition rallies made a point of announcing that "everybody regardless of color, . . . is cordially invited to attend." County organizing committees and delegations to state meetings often included members of both races; blacks held important posts and sat on the speakers' platform. In Atlanta, black voters were "courted, bribed, feted, and marched to the polls by both wets and drys"; when the dry forces narrowly won, they gave a great deal of the credit to black voters. A group of white prohibitionists cheered a large group of black supporters for thirty minutes at a rally, and the Young Men's Prohibition Club handed out awards of $285 and satin banners handmade by white women to the black organizations that had proven most helpful in the campaign.

Although based in separate organizations, black and white opponents of liquor associated publicly, spoke from the same platform, celebrated together, and warmly talked of each other in their newspapers. Such collegiality was partly the result of necessity, since white prohibitionists needed black votes if the cause were to triumph, but it also grew out of faith. People who took Christianity seriously recognized a certain form of equality among all believers, a recognition that, given the right conditions, could lead to a healthy conviction of fellow feeling and tolerance. The class basis of prohibition also encouraged racial cooperation; the businessmen, ministers, professionals, and their wives who formed the nucleus of the white movement could recognize in their black counterparts aspirations and values similar to their own. In all these ways, the prohibitionists forged relatively open and democratic—if temporary—racial coalitions.

Women of both races found an elevated role in the prohibition movement. The prohibition crusade saw the Women's Christian Temperance Union give Southern women their first widespread opportunity to organize independently for a political cause. While Southern women increasingly organized for other reasons as well, it was prohibition that first mobilized many women and gave them a sense of their power to persuade the men with the votes. The WCTU was "the generous liberator, the joyous iconoclast, the discoverer, the developer of Southern women," a Mississippi reformer remembered. Frances Willard toured the South in the 1880s and inspired women throughout the region to form their own local organizations. In villages, towns, and cities across the South, women came together in one another's homes, in churches, and in convention halls to discuss how they could best fight alcohol.

Prohibition raised great hopes, hopes of dissolving constrictions of race and gender as well as other divisions that kept the South from being what it could be. "Let us make a great pile of all the unreasonable race prejudices, all political animosities, all sectional bitterness, and partisan hate, all narrowing and belittling views of public questions," an anti-liquor white minister in Atlanta preached in the wake of his crusade's success. Such a dream was a politician's nightmare, for it would destroy the very conflicts on which most Southern politics subsisted. Prohibition did not rise and fall like the insurgent political movements that developed before, during, after the anti-liquor crusade; prohibition resembled guerrilla rather than frontal warfare and as a result it proved almost impossible for politicians to defeat decisively.

Men spent money and blood largely to get an office, not to do anything in particular once in office. The Redeemers in the state legislatures were largely anonymous party functionaries. One or two sessions in the state legislature marked the highest political achievement of most Democratic politicians; afterward, they returned home where they served as judges, officials in the court house, or lawyers who spent a good part of their time talking politics.

Election to the state legislature might occasionally serve as a stepping-stone
to higher office; most United States senators began their political careers as
state legislators. Yet the inconveniences and costs of holding the office were
considerable, too, for a term in the state legislature took a man away from
his business. As a result, the state legislatures gathered relative novices who
held positions of state-level power only for a short time.

The delegates' brevity of tenure and the shallowness of their experience
did not mean that the legislatures were particularly democratic bodies. The
representatives who went to the state capitals could be counted on to carry
out the desires of the local party leaders. The legislators were not themselves
the biggest planters, the richest lawyers, the wealthiest businessmen; more
than likely, they were young men on the make sent to win whatever they
could for the county, pick up some experience, keep taxes down, and stay
out of trouble. As a result, the legislatures of the New South wavered with
the prevailing political winds, subject to the dictates of a few powerful or
persuasive men. In a time and place when any governmental action was
viewed with suspicion and hostility, politicians took a risk if they did anything
at all. So most did nothing. A legislator who called attention to problems
that needed solving appeared to be a troublemaker who put his own vanity
above the good of the party and of white taxpayers. Most were all too happy
just to go along.

Temptation and persuasion began to beckon as soon as new legislators
arrived in the state capital. The big hotels, with their cut glass and rich wood,
harbored nonstop politicking. Candidates for appointive offices, especially
judgeships, openly courted supporters with well-stocked bars in comfortable
suites; the men who wanted to lease convicts made the rounds among the
legislators, as did those who wanted to squelch some crackpot bill about
regulating insurance companies or railroads. "Fancy women were employed
to attract a few legislators and keep them until after the vote was cast in the
House," Josephus Daniels recalled of a key vote on a railroad commission
in North Carolina. "If there was any string the railroad officials did not pull
to carry their point, it was one that they did not know existed." Ben Tillman
described how quickly and easily the compromises began in such an intoxi-
cating setting, even for a good-hearted farmer. "He enters the State House
a farmer; he emerges from it in one session a politician. . . . The contact with
General This and Judge That and Colonel Something Else, who have shaken
him by the hand and made much of him, had debauched him. He likes this
being a somebody; and his first resolution, offered and passed in his own
mind, is that he will remain something if he can."

It was hard to predict what a legislature might do in any given session.
Most Democratic voters, especially farmers, sought to keep government
small, inactive, and cheap; on the other hand, many powerful interests, especially men with money to invest, sought to use government to aid railroads
and industry. Some isolated voices called for the state to take better care of

schoolchildren, criminals, the insane, the poor, disabled veterans; sometimes
it did. Depending on the condition of the economy, events in Washington,
the strength of dissident organizations, or the determination of an energetic
representative, the actions of Southern state legislatures jumped erratically
from one pole to the other, sometimes in the same session.

Planters and landowning farmers won considerable attention early in
the Redeemer years. The rural majority had felt neglected by the Republican
legislatures of the late 1860s and early 1870s, which struggled to rebuild
railroads and attract investment capital, experimented with laws that would
help tenants and croppers, and raised taxes on land. When the first Redeemer regimes took over, powerful landholding farmers and planters made
their demands clear, and the new Democratic legislatures eagerly wrote into
law a series of bills designed to help planters control their laborers: vagrancy
acts, tougher punishments for petty theft and trading in stolen goods, limits
on interest rates. In most states, landlords won the right to the first lien on
a tenant's crop; if a tenant owed a crop to the landlord and a debt to a local
merchant, the landlord received his share first. Legislatures in the seventies
also proved friendly to other demands of well-to-do farmers for agricultural
colleges, departments of agriculture, geologic surveys, and state fairs. Most
of this legislation met little opposition, either because it hurt no other organized interest or because interests that might have fought against the
changes—merchants, for example—had little voice in government. Planters
got what they wanted early on in the New South years and asked little of the
government afterward except that it keep taxes low and blacks in their place.

In their rush to dissociate themselves from the spending of the Republicans, Democrats restricted state support for private enterprise; according
to the new constitutions they wrote, there could be no direct subsidies, no
use of state credit, no bond issues to help railroads or anyone else. Within
these constraints, Southern Democrats did what they could to entice capital
to their states and counties. Some states with large amounts of relatively
empty land, Florida and Texas in particular, gave millions of acres to railroads as incentives to open new areas for development. Other states offered
tax breaks, foregoing immediate additions to the state coffers in the hopes
of greater rewards when the new industries got off the ground. Nevertheless,
compared with the days of Reconstruction—indeed, the days before the Civil
War—Southern legislatures did relatively little to aid investment in their
states.

The state governments of the South created a regressive tax structure
and taxed citizens at a rate lower than the national average. The South did
not differ from the rest of the country nearly as much, on the other hand,
in the ways it spent its money. Southern states disbursed state funds on various governmental functions in the same proportions as states elsewhere,
with slightly less on administration and slightly more, surprisingly, on courts,
prisons, and education. Southern expenditures, as a percentage of income,

actually stood above the national average. Moreover, with the passage of the 1880s the Redeemers spent more as the tax base increased and as they repudiated or retired state debts accumulated during the antebellum years and wartime. Taxes edged up, with tax-paying farmers receiving little for their money.

Farmers and other debtors viewed the nation's currency situation with alarm, for prices steadily fell and many blamed a shortage of currency for the decline. Early in the Redeemers' years in power, "Greenbackers" demanded that the federal government create enough money for the growing needs of the nation, not limiting the amount of currency to the availability of precious metals. Opponents viewed the Greenback plan as economic suicide, one that would drive the United States out of the gold-based economy of the civilized world. The debate soon took on overtones of class conflict, as Greenbackers labeled their opposition "the 'money power,' the 'bloated bondholders,' the 'Wall Street sharks,' the 'moneycrats,' the 'bugs,' the 'mere vermin' who consumed profits belonging to the producer." Gold advocates, for their part, considered Greenbackism not only foolish and ill-informed, but a form of communism.

Southern Democrats, eager to please farmers as well as businessmen, vacillated. They supported a gradual expansion of the currency, but refused to adopt the Greenbackers' policies. Disgruntled farmers promptly abandoned the new Redeemer regimes. Men running for Congress under the Greenback banner pulled in tens of thousands of votes in Alabama, North Carolina, Arkansas, Kentucky, Mississippi, and Texas. As early as the late 1870s, farmers began to speak bitterly of Democratic "ring rule," of town cliques.

The Democrats squirmed under the problems of state finances. Enormous debts hung over most Southern states, debts that had accumulated since the antebellum years and that had been augmented by generous postwar deals handed out by state governments, Democrat and Republican, desperate to rebuild the South. While business feared debt repudiation would further erode the South's credit and lessen profits on investments in state-supported bonds, many taxpayers, especially farmers, insisted that something be done. The Democrats promised to repudiate as much of the debt as they could, to cut interest payments on what they could not repudiate, and to lower taxes. In the late 1870s and early 1880s they did just that, usually with little challenge.

In some states, conservative Funders—often bondholders or lawyers for bondholders—dug in their heels against readjustment. "This contest is a struggle between ill-disguised communism and conservatism," warned one Democratic paper in Tennessee, while a Republican paper in the same state called on "business men of all parties to take warning. Communism, socialism, agrarianism, nihilism and diabolism are on the increase in America."

Virginia experienced the deepest and most protracted battle over the debt of any state. Fury against the Funders in Virginia rose as more of the state's money went to pay interest on the debt and less went to pay for essential state services; people became furious in 1879, when a million and a half dollars were diverted from the school fund.

A new party arose in Virginia which embodied the worst fears of the Conservative Democrats. The rebellious party was led by an influential capitalist and ex-Confederate general, William Mahone, who united poor blacks and white farmers in a large-scale revolt against the Democrats. The party's policy was advertised by its name: the "Readjusters." They won control of the Virginia legislature in 1879, sent Mahone to the legislature, won the patronage and endorsement of President Arthur, handed West Virginia a third of the debt, rearranged taxes so that farmers paid less and corporations paid more, and increased support for education at every level and for both races.

Throughout the South, opponents of the Redeemers took heart and attempted to overthrow their adversaries, adversaries who had been in power only a few years themselves and, it seemed, might be toppled with the right strategy. The early 1880s witnessed many attempts at cooperation and fusion among Republicans and independents. Those coalitions were bolstered not only by voters from the Greenback party, not only by people angered at the handling of the debt, but also by voters dismayed at the lack of progressive leadership the Democrats offered and the lack of the vital two-party system the South had enjoyed before the Civil War. The smoldering resentments arising out of the economic depression of the late seventies fed the discontent. The Democrats, in turn, warned that the South would return to the chaos and degradation of Reconstruction if independents continued their flirtations with the Republican party. The years between 1880 and 1884 marked the high point of independent voting in the South, when between 30 and 46 percent of the voters in Alabama, Arkansas, Florida, Georgia, Mississippi, and Texas cast their ballot for independent candidates for Congress.

In 1882, a writer for the *Atlantic Monthly* discovered that "there was everywhere a sense of hollowness, of the unreality of the issues and grounds of dispute between the parties; a half-suppressed cry—sometimes agonizing in its intensity—for 'new issues,' for some development or combination. . . . They were 'waiting for a chance,' to use an expression which one constantly hears from them." When asked, " 'What shall you try to do? What will be the basis or aim of the new movement in your State?' " the answer nearly always was, " 'Don't know; we shall go in for anything, for a new deal. That we're bound to have.' " Voters seemed ready to recast Southern politics, to vote for men other than the Democrats, to define a new party.

Yet only Virginia under Mahone was able to put together a broad coalition that effectively wielded statewide power for even a short time. The fault lines in the other coalitions, lines of race, subregion, and doubt, widened under Democratic charges of disloyalty to race and region. Established Republicans were reluctant to share offices with erstwhile Democrats, and the Republican administrations in Washington reconsidered the wisdom of handing out patronage to independents who were no more able to claim a victory than the regular Republicans had been. No other anti-Democratic leader in the South possessed the connections and the acumen of William Mahone. The task of forging a new coalition overwhelmed everyone else who tried, and no other insurgent party came up with an issue that bridged the class and racial divides of the New South. The Democrats did not hesitate to return to the methods they had used to gain power in the seventies. Wielding fraud, bribery, and intimidation, they gave their opposition little time or space in which to develop a coherent and long-lived party.

Many Democrats hoped that the election of Grover Cleveland in 1884 would help resolve some of the conflict and tension in Southern politics. "Everywhere there were celebrations with horns and whistles, guns and pistols, bells and chimes, pots and pans, skyrockets and firecrackers, along with every conceivable noisemaker anyone could pick up," Sue Ellen McDowall recalled. White Southern Democrats felt in 1884 what they had not felt for a quarter of a century: that the federal government was finally theirs, that their political fate rested not in the hands of a Republican administration that could neglect and abuse white Southerners while handing out coveted patronage jobs to blacks. Grover Cleveland's election offered white Democrats, as one of them put it, an "escape from captivity and humiliation." They had finally found "an opportunity for the display of the patriotism which really exists," a chance for the Southern states to "feel that the Union is really restored."

The excitement did not last long. Southern Democrats soon discovered that having their man in the White House made them the object of heightened expectations and sharper criticism. Only two years after Cleveland's victory, on the eve of the off-year election of 1886, a local party leader from North Carolina described a bleak situation to the party's senator in Washington. "Unless there is some way to get them out there are hundreds of people that have been voting the democratic ticket are going to stay home. . . . You can hear them saying, 'it don't make one cent of difference which party is in, it is only for the benefit of the few, that taxes are just as high as before, that the Internal Revenue is going on in the old way, and there is no difference, and dont intend to vote again,' etc." Even Democratic party workers found that President Cleveland often allowed Republicans to keep the jobs that they had held under earlier administrations. Redeemer rule in the 1880s turned out to be not so glorious after all.

To make matters worse, a generational rift threatened to divide the Democratic party. Many of the Confederate heroes were passing from the scene;

before Jefferson Davis died in 1889, he had witnessed the deaths of his vice president, three-quarters of his cabinet, and three-quarters of the signers of the Confederate Constitution. By 1888 three-quarters of Southern voters were too young to have voted for or against Davis in 1861. Now men of the new generation were ready for their chance. "The old men have never quite recovered from the blow," a middle-aged man told a visitor in Charlottesville's train station in 1887. "Some of them even yet fancy that the old issues are still alive. But it is the men who were children in '65 that have their hands on the lever now." State legislators tended to be relatively young, only in their thirties when writing laws for their states.

But even as young men ran the show at the lower levels of politics, at the very top older men hung on to their power, battling among themselves. The Democratic organizations continued to shuffle the most prestigious positions among their old warhorses. The congressmen and senators elected by the Southern Democrats in the 1880s were undistinguished in intellect or vision, significant for their role in their states' political machines but without commanding national presence. Most Southern senators served term after term in Washington without doing anything of note in the national arena. Spending most of their energy controlling patronage back home, they were brokers, deal-makers, organization men. Southerners never won serious consideration for either party's presidential or vice-presidential slots, seldom served as leaders in either House or Senate, rarely won seats on the Supreme Court.

In Washington, Southern representatives and senators offered little help to the South. The bounty of the federal government flowed to the North, especially in the disbursement of pensions for Union veterans of the Civil War. Attorneys and agents encouraged veterans to file claims, whether valid or fraudulent; over 10,000 a month arrived in Washington in the 1880s and even more in the 1890s. The Republican party cashed in on the bonanza by running the corrupt Pension Bureau and by offering to expedite claims for potential Republican voters. In special Friday-night sessions, the Republican House approved pension claims by the dozens with non-incriminating voice votes. The South paid in far more to the national treasury than it received, with the region running an annual deficit of $9 per capita.

The Republicans had a strong interest in building up the federal revenues that funded such spending. The greatest source of that income, well over half, came from customs duties. The Republicans argued that a tariff with high duties would protect American industry, much of which was concentrated in Republican strongholds. The Democrats charged in response that Southerners would be injured at every turn: when they bought imported goods at higher prices, when they paid higher prices for American manufactured goods, when they tried to sell their agricultural commodities to countries angry at American protectionism. It only added insult to injury when most of the money raised by higher import duties was handed out, in the form of pensions, to Northern communities already profiting from protected industry. The Democrats saw the fight against the tariff as one of their greatest contributions to the welfare of their region.

In contrast to other industrializing nations in the late nineteenth century, then, the United States did not witness a political marriage between industrialists and agrarian interests. The Civil War and Reconstruction created instead a two-party system that was in large part a two-region system, the Republicans representing the most powerful interests in the North, the Democrats representing the most powerful interests in the South. In such an arrangement, the South could not hope to win much from the federal government. Southern planters, industrialists, farmers, artisans, merchants, professionals—all found themselves in one party, their divergent interests papered over by white unity. The Democrats' half-hearted measures fed the political confusion of the 1880s and 1890s. Party leaders could claim with some justice to be the best friends the farmers had in Washington; farmers could claim with equal justice that such distant and passive friendliness, no matter how polite, was useless.

The Republicans in Congress tried their best to keep the Democrats off-balance and on the defensive. As soon as the Republicans won control of both houses of Congress and the presidency in 1888 they began to look for ways to break the Democratic hold on the South. The Republicans had long resented the fact that the South, despite its defeat in the Civil War and despite Reconstruction, was still overrepresented in the national legislature. Some Southern states liberally counted voting-age citizens when determining their representation in Congress, but then used stringent registration laws or poll taxes to prevent many of those citizens from voting. As a result, one vote in a congressional election in Georgia or South Carolina carried the same weight as five votes in Oregon, four votes in New Hampshire, or three votes in Wisconsin.

Threats, bribery, bloodshed, and deceit suffocated the Republican party in the South. When the party won control on the national level in 1888, it finally found itself in a position to draft legislation to promote fair elections in the South. Many ideas were put forward, but the bill that finally emerged bore the name of Henry Cabot Lodge of Massachusetts, a well-known supporter of federal supervision. By the terms of his bill, one hundred voters within a congressional district or a city of 20,000 who believed there had been fraud in an election could petition the federal circuit courts to appoint a board to determine the validity of the charges. Despite its relative weakness and its application to places outside the South, the proposed law pitted the South once again against the North, igniting the hottest sectional conflict in Congress since the end of Reconstruction.

White Democrats who vehemently opposed the mild Lodge bill knew what they were doing. The bill threatened to undermine the way politics worked in the South. Although the Democrats regularly won most elections in the South, there were hundreds of counties where at least one hundred angry Republicans might petition for the federal inspection of a contested election. The inquiries of federal boards, whether Republican or Democrat, would advertise to the nation the many sins perpetrated in the name of the Democratic party in places throughout the South. Democratic representatives and senators would have to spend much time and political capital squelching or controlling investigations. Perhaps most frightening, third parties might be emboldened to make a run at the Democrats, knowing they could appeal to national tribunals in the face of Democratic fraud or violence. The Lodge bill threatened to strip away the illusion of unanimity and harmony Southern Democrats tried so hard to create at home and in the state capitals.

By the end of the 1880s Southerners on both the outside and the inside of the major parties expressed serious misgivings about the drift of politics. Outsiders had become disgusted with the favoritism, fraud, and insensitivity of officeholders. In turn, officeholders were alarmed by the shallow loyalty of voters, their willingness to sell their votes to competitors, and their receptivity to new parties and programs. In this environment, many people from all over the political spectrum began to think it might be time to reform the Southern electoral system. In the 1880s Democrats in several Southern states began to devise ways to cripple any opposition party. Some made more positions appointive; others enacted more restrictive registration laws; some piled on poll taxes; some turned to the secret ballot to discriminate against the illiterate.

Political life in the New South was a complicated and contradictory affair. Southern men of both races cared passionately about the success of their candidates at every level. The majority of eligible voters went to the polls in the early 1880s, casting ballots for Republicans, prohibitionists, independents, and Greenbackers as well as various kinds of Democrats. Yet the men in whom voters invested so much passion and even blood did relatively little once they got into office. The national government took more from the South than it gave back; state governments permitted the rich to get richer and the poor to get poorer; local governments barely kept the machinery running. All politicians seemed able to do effectively was circumscribe the lives of black Southerners.

Chapter 5

In Black and White

Every human emotion became entangled in Southern race relations. Booker T. Washington claimed to find "at least one white man who believed implicitly in one Negro, and one Negro who believed implicitly in one white man" wherever he traveled in the South. Yet even when human sympathy and friendship drew people together, the rituals of Southern race relations constrained and distorted the feelings. "There was a part of me in which it did not matter at all that they were black," Harry Crews remembered of his childhood friends, "but there was another part of me in which it had to matter because it mattered to the world I lived in." When Crews referred to a respected black man as "Mr. Jones," Crews's aunt quickly corrected him. "No, son. Robert Jones is a nigger. You don't say 'mister' when you speak of a nigger. You don't say 'Mr. Jones,' you say 'nigger Jones.'" Children soon learned the lesson.

White rituals of black naming conveyed various shades of deference, condescension, affection, and respect, and tried to maintain the illusion of personal relationships where none existed. Blacks called white men they did not know "mister," "cap'n," or "boss." Black men attached "Mr." to a white acquaintance's first name; the first name of white women was accompanied by "Miss." Whites never addressed black men they did not know as "mister," but rather as "boy," "Jack," or "George"; black women were never called "Mrs.," but rather "aunt" or their first name. A black person, regardless of age or gender, was referred to in white newspaper accounts as

Whites and blacks on Florida store steps. (Florida State Archives)

simply a "negro," as in "two men and two women were killed, and four Negroes." According to custom, the two races did not shake hands, walk together, or fraternize in public. Black men removed their hats in public places reserved for whites, while whites did not remove their hats even in black homes. Whites "even segregated the days of the week," Mamie Garvin Fields recalled of growing up in South Carolina. White people stayed away from town on Saturday afternoons, setting aside that time for blacks from the countryside to shop and meet. "Those white folks didn't want you to come to town in the weekday at all. . . . Really, certain whites didn't like to think you had leisure to do anything but pick cotton and work in the field."

Some blacks, especially in towns and cities, refused to follow the etiquette. A Louisiana newspaper complained that "the younger generation of negro bucks and wenches have lost that wholesome respect for the white man, without which two races, the one inferior, cannot live in peace and harmony together. . . . Is it not every day manifest when your house-girl informs you that Miss Johnson (your cook) says dinner is ready; that Mr. Jones (your butler) will hitch up the buggy in a minute as he is busy talking to a lady (your washerwoman) at the gate. If you address one of the younger generation with the 'uncle' or 'auntie' the older ones delighted in the chances are you will hear 'I aint yah uncle, doggone you.' "

On the other hand, many whites and blacks managed to create humane relationships even in the face of the general distrust and dislike. Kindness toward elderly or worthy blacks was taken as a symbol of good character among whites. At the Belk store in Monroe, North Carolina, one of the jobs of a young clerk named John Parker was to help women coming into the store. One day, William Henry Belk recalled, when "an old colored woman came along and stopped in front of the store, John went out and helped her out of her buggy and held the umbrella over her until she got out of the rain. It was a nice thing to do, and it was just like John to do a thing like that." Another clerk "made some remark about it—not bad, but in a sort of teasing way." Belk's brother, the boss, heard the comment "and he didn't like it. He spoke up right quick. He knew that John wanted to be a lawyer when he grew up. 'Don't let him tease you, John,' " the employer said. " 'When he's still clerking you'll be on the Supreme Court, son, and I mean the United States Supreme Court.' "

Stories of white aid to blacks did not happen only in white folklore. Charley White recalled one white man with real affection. White's mother, left alone with three children when abandoned by her husband, supported the family through farm labor, midwifery, and washing. Moving from one farm to the next, they eventually settled on the farm of Prayter Windham. Charley was sick the day they arrived, and Windham brought his young daughter with him. "This is my daughter Tish," the landlord said. "We heard you had a sick boy, and Mrs. Windham sent him this chicken broth." When Charley recovered, Windham recognized that the boy was interested in learning about farming "and he took to teaching me the right way to do things. . . . And seemed like he'd be as tickled as me when I could do it right." When Windham went out on circuit with the court, he put Charley, then about seventeen years old, in the room next to his wife and ten year-old daughter. A gun rested under his bed. "Nothing ever happened," White recalled, "But if somebody had tried to come in there I'd a shot him, sure as I lived." Although White's mother soon died and the youngster went to live with relatives, when he first got married White returned to Windham's farm to start out.

Rural race relations often seemed marked by such personal ties, patronizing as well as helpful. The diary of Clive Metcalfe, a young white planter surrounded almost entirely by black people in the Delta region of Mississippi in the 1890s, has about it some of the air of the antebellum plantation. Metcalfe took upon himself much of the authority of the planter under slavery. "Caught a negro girl stealing clothes from one of my darkeys, and I gave her a good whipping," he wrote in 1890. A few weeks later, he blandly noted that he went coon hunting, "Did not see a coon. Came home and whipped Harrison for feeding the dogs on the gallery." Like the planters of the Old South, Metcalfe mixed his violence with what he took to be paternalistic concern. Metcalfe intervened in a domestic fight. "Came home last night, found that Powell had given his wife a good whipping. Had to go over and settle it for them." On the Fourth of July the next year the planter and a friend "gave the darkies a dinner in the Cold Springs yard, which went off very nicely. There was quite four hundred darkies there."

Another holiday showed the continuity that marked some facets of race relations. For generations, black Southerners had celebrated Christmas as a time of white gift-giving and ritualized freedom. While the practice faded in the highly mobile New South, vestiges of the tradition remained on some plantations. Clive Metcalfe dreaded the season, partly because black share-croppers moved from one farm to another then ("like a lot of sheep," he spat), and partly because black folk on his place always seemed to be "begging a little something for Xmas. It is just awful to be bothered to death by the black faces from morning until night." The next year, in a softer mood, Metcalfe noted that "the darkies are shooting Xmas guns and having lots of fun." Gifts flowed in the other direction as well: a white widow from Mississippi noted in her diary in 1890 that "our colored tenants Bob Rollins and Sam Houston each sent us this evening a nice piece of fresh pork." William Pickens, who grew up in Pendleton, South Carolina, recalled that "the black folks used to say that 'there is no law for Christmas.' And so the young Negro men, in a good-natured spree, would catch the lone policeman, who was always more a joke than a terror, and lock him in the calaboose to stay a part of Christmas Day, while one of the black men with star and club would strut about the town and play officer." Pickens, himself black, thought that this carnival-like inversion of the early 1890s would, in 1911, when he wrote, "summon the militia from the four quarters of almost any state and be heralded an ugly insurrection."

Black people turned to whites when they felt they had no other choice. Adelaide Brown, a black woman living in Savannah, wrote to Mary Camak asking for help as Christmas approached in 1896. "Miss Mary My Dear friend," she began, "I am out on the waves of the world by my self no body to help me at all. Joe has quit me and took up with another woman compleat so I thought I would write you to let you know my troubles. Sometimes I field like I haven got a friend on earth." Brown had been ill "for quite a while" and was still sick. "The white people who I am working with has been very kind to me, but I have got to the place wherein I can hardly go or come when I was throude out of doors by Joe these white people taken me in they help me to meet my Groses bill and I tryes to meet my house rent the best I can." Brown wanted to borrow eight or ten dollars. "I make $14 dolars a month if I live . . . I will . . . surely pay you back soon." Brown was writing to Camak "because you is able if you only will. you all are the only people I have. My mother is dead and if she was living she woulden be able to do this favor." Remember, Brown closed, "you are lendeding to the Lord."

Few laws circumscribed day-to-day rural race relations. Rural roads, country stores, and cotton gins were not segregated; hunters and fishermen respected rules of fair play, regardless of race. Corn shuckings saw black and white men working around the same fire and black and white women cooking over the same food, though members of the two races went to separate tables when it came time to eat. In the diary of Nannie Stillwell Jackson, a white Arkansas woman of moderate means, it is difficult to determine whether the people she describes are white or black. Jackson tells, with affection and gratitude, of the visits and gifts black friends brought her during an illness. She trades with her black neighbors, writes and receives letters for them, sews for them; a black midwife tends to her baby. The best of Southern race relations appeared in such scenes, where individuals developed personal respect for one another beyond the reach of hateful laws. The conditions of the New South, though, often worked against people of good will.

In a quest to channel the relations between the races, white Southerners enacted one law after another to proscribe contact among blacks and whites. Some things about the relations between the races had been established quickly after emancipation. Schools, poor houses, orphanages, and hospitals, founded to help people who had once been slaves, were usually separated by race at their inception. Cities segregated cemeteries and parks; counties segregated court houses. Churches quickly broke into different congregations for blacks and whites. Hotels served one race only; blacks could see plays only from the balcony or separate seats; restaurants served one race or served them in different rooms or from separate windows. In 1885, a Memphis newspaper described how thoroughly the races were separated: "The colored people make no effort to obtrude themselves upon the whites in the public schools, their churches, their fairs, their Sunday-schools, their picnics, their social parties, hotels or banquets. They prefer their own preachers, teachers, schools, picnics, hotels and social gatherings." In the countryside as well as in town, blacks and whites associated with members of their own race except in those situations when interracial association could not be avoided: work, commerce, politics, travel.

Even if the general boundaries of race relations had been drawn early on, though, many decisions had yet to be made by the 1880s. The notion of a completely circumscribed world of white and black had not yet become entrenched; the use of the word "segregation" to describe systematic racial separation did not begin until the early twentieth century. Although most whites seem to have welcomed segregation in general, others saw no need to complicate the business of everyday life with additional distinctions between the races, no need to antagonize friendly and respectable blacks, no need to spend money on separate facilities, no need to risk bringing down Northern interference. Although many blacks fought against the new laws with boycotts, lawsuits, and formal complaints, others saw no use in fighting the whites who had all the power on their side, no use in antagonizing white benefactors or white enemies, no use in going places they were not welcome. The segregation begun in the decade following the end of the Civil War did not spread inexorably and evenly across the face of the South. The 1880s saw much uncertainty and much bargaining, many forays and retreats.

Most of the debates about race relations focused on the railroads of the New South. While some blacks resisted their exclusion from white-owned hotels and restaurants, they could usually find, and often preferred, accommodations in black-run businesses. Travel was a different story, for members of both races had no choice but to use the same railroads. As the number of railroads proliferated in the 1880s, as the number of stations quickly mounted, as dozens of counties got on a line for the first time, as previously isolated areas found themselves connected to towns and cities with different kinds of black people and different kinds of race relations, segregation became a matter of statewide attention. Prior to the eighties, localities could strike their own compromises in race relations, try their own experiments, tolerate their own ambiguities. But tough decisions forced themselves on the state legislatures of the South after the railroads came. The result was the first wave of segregation laws that affected virtually the entire South in anything like a uniform way, as nine Southern states enacted railroad segregation laws in the years between 1887 and 1891.

By all accounts, the railroads of the 1880s were contested terrain. Trains ran cars of two classes; in the first-class car rode women and men who did not use tobacco, while in the second-class car rode men who chewed or smoked, men unaccompanied by women, and people who could not afford a first-class ticket. To travel in the second-class car was to travel with people, overwhelmingly men, who behaved very differently from those in the car ahead. The floors were thick with spit and tobacco juice, the air thick with smoke and vulgarities. The second-class car had hard seats, low ceilings, and no water; frequently, it was merely a part of the baggage car set off by a partition. The second-class car ran right behind the engine and was often invaded by smoke and soot. The cars saw more crowding of strangers than in any other place in the New South. "The cars were jammed, all the way over here, with the dirtiest, nastiest set I ever rode with," a Louisiana man complained about a trip to Texas.

A first-class, or parlor, car contained a diverse group of travelers, but their behavior tended to be more genteel than those in the smoking car. "It was the ordinary car of a Southern railroad," Ellen Glasgow wrote, with "the usual examples of Southern passengers. Across the aisle a slender mother was holding a crying baby, two small children huddling beside her." "A mulatto of the new era" sat nearby, while "further off there were several men returning from business trips, and across from them sat a pretty girl, asleep, her hand resting on a gilded cage containing a startled canary. At intervals she was aroused by the flitting figure of a small boy on the way to the cooler of iced water. From the rear of the car came the amiable drawl of the conductor as he discussed the affairs of the State with a local drummer, whose feet rested upon a square leather case." The seats were covered with soft plush fabric, the floor covered with carpet.

Strangely enough, the scenes of racial contention and conflict on the trains focused on the placid first-class cars rather than on the boisterous cars ahead. Sutton Griggs, a black Virginia novelist, gave a compelling account of the random violence that hovered around blacks who rode in the parlor cars. A young black man on his way to Louisiana to become president of a small black college had traveled all the way from Richmond without incident. Absorbed in a newspaper as the car crossed the line into Louisiana, he did not notice the car gradually filling at each stop. "A white lady entered, and not at once seeing a vacant seat, paused a few seconds to look about for one. She soon espied an unoccupied seat. She proceeded to it, but her slight difficulty had been noted by the white passengers." Before the black man knew what was happening, he found himself surrounded by a group of angry whites. " 'Get out of this coach. We don't allow niggers in first-class coaches.' " The black passenger resisted moving, only to be thrown off the train altogether. "Covered from head to foot with red clay, the president-elect of Cadeville College walked down to the next station, two miles away."

This sort of clash was hardly confined to fiction. Andrew Springs, a young black man on the way from North Carolina to Fisk University in Nashville in 1891, told a friend back home about his experiences. "I came very near being locked up by the police at Chattanooga. I wanted some water. I went in to the White Waiting [room] and got it as they didn't have any for Cuffy to drink. Just time I got the water here come the police just like I were killing some one and said You get out of here you black rascal put that cup down. I got a notion to knock your head off." As so often happened, the black man refused to accept such treatment without protest. "I told him I were no rascal neither were I black. I were very near as white as he was. Great Scott he started for me. . . . he didn't strike tho, but had me started to the lock up." Springs, like many blacks harassed on the railroad, used the law to stop his persecution. "I told him I had my ticket and it was the duty of the R.R. Co. to furnish water for both white [and] black." The officer let him go. The young man then took the dangerous, and atypical, step of threatening the officer: "I told him if ever I catch him in North Carolina I would fix him."

Aggressive single young men were not the only ones who threatened, intentionally and unintentionally, the tenuous racial situation on the railroad. In 1889, Emanuel Love, a leader of the First African Baptist Church of Savannah, was asked by an agent of the East Tennessee, Virginia, and Georgia Railroad to travel over the road to a convention in Indianapolis, assuring Love that he and his entourage could have first-class accommodations the entire way. Love assumed the delegation would have a car to themselves so they would not antagonize white first-class passengers who might be on board. As the train pulled out and the pastor walked through the car greeting the other delegates, he soon noticed that there were indeed whites in the first-class car, and they began to whisper among themselves and to the white conductor. A black railway workman warned the delegation that trouble was ahead, but there was little they could do; someone had already telegraphed news of the black effrontery to the next stop. There, at least fifty white men, carrying pistols, clubs, and pieces of iron, pushed their way into the car and assaulted the "well dressed" delegates. Some sought to defend themselves, while most fled. One who could do neither was Mrs. Janie Garnet, a graduate of Atlanta University and a schoolteacher, who screamed in fear. One of the white men put a cocked pistol to her breast and said, "You G-d d—d heffer, if you don't hush your mouth and get out of here, I will blow your G-d d—d brains out." The delegation was treated for their broken bones and bruises and made their way, presumably in a separate car, to Indianapolis. Accounts of the violence directed at blacks often spoke of well-dressed clergymen and well-dressed women as the objects of white anger.

Whites also experienced racial discomfiture that did not necessarily result in violence or even overt conflict. In 1889, a Tennessee newspaper related in a light tone a story that captured some of the risks of the "parlor car." At Nashville, "a bright, good-looking colored girl (or rather an almost white colored girl)" boarded the train. A "flashily-dressed white gentleman, usually known as the 'car masher,'" began an elaborate flirtation with the girl, whom he assumed to be white. She "very modestly" accepted his attentions, "slightly blushing probably out of compassion for the fellow's mistake, but which he evidently took as an indication of a surrender to his charms." He bought his "'lady friend' a lunch, and the two sat for half an hour enjoying their supper tete-a-tete, . . . every passenger on the train enjoying the situation. The girl was entirely innocent of any intention to entrap or deceive the fellow, but he was the victim of his own inordinate conceit and folly." He eventually found out his mistake after she had reached her destination. "He was probably the maddest man in the State when he found it all out. He was mad at the girl, mad at the passengers and doubtless wanted to kick himself all the way home." The account ended, significantly, with the information that "none enjoyed the episode more than the ladies on the train."

If the situation had been reversed, if some "almost white" black man had been flirting with a white girl, deceiving her, eating with her, what then? Such a scene would have invoked the sense of pollution whites associated with blacks, no matter how clean, how well dressed, how well mannered they might be. As a New Orleans newspaper argued in 1890, when the state was considering the segregation of its railroad cars, "one is thrown in much closer communication in the car with one's travelling companions than in the theatre or restaurant," which were already segregated. In the railroad car, the article related in suggestive language, whites and blacks would be "crowded together, squeezed close to each other in the same seats, using the same conveniences, and to all intents and purposes in social intercourse." The lesson was clear: "A man that would be horrified at the idea of his wife or daughter seated by the side of a burly negro in the parlor of a hotel or at a restaurant cannot see her occupying a crowded seat in a car next to a negro without the same feeling of disgust." Any man "who believes that the white race should be kept pure from African taint will vote against that commingling of the races inevitable in a 'mixed car' and which must have bad results." A white woman or girl who let herself fall into easy and equal relations with a black man in such an anomalous place as the parlor car would risk her reputation.

The sexual charge that might be created among strangers temporarily placed in intimate surroundings, many whites worried, could not be tolerated in a racially integrated car. In the late nineteenth century, sexual relations did not have to end in intercourse or even physical contact to be considered intimate and dangerous to a woman's reputation and self-respect. In fact, the history of segregation shows a clear connection to gender: the more closely linked to sexuality, the more likely was a place to be segregated. At one extreme was the private home, where the intimacies of the parlor, the dining table, and the bedroom were never shared with blacks as equals; it was no accident that blacks were proscribed from entering a white home through its front door. Exclusive hotels, restaurants, and darkened theaters, which mimicked the quiet and privacy of the home, also saw virtually no racial mixing. Schools, where children of both genders associated in terms of intimacy and equality, saw early and consistent segregation. Places where people of only one gender associated with one another, though, tended to have relaxed racial barriers. The kitchen and nursery of a home, which "should" have been off-limits to blacks for white taboos to have remained consistent, in fact saw black women participating in the most private life of white families. Part of the lowered boundary, of course, grew out of the necessity whites perceived to use black labor, but blacks were permitted in the heart of the home because those rooms saw the interaction only of white women and black women. Male preserves, for their part, were often barely segregated at all: bars, race tracks, and boxing rings were notorious, and exciting, for the presence of blacks among whites. Some houses of prostitution profited directly from the sexual attraction black women held for some white men.

The railroad would not have been such a problem, then, had blacks not been seeking first-class accommodations where women as well as men traveled, where blacks appeared not as dirty workers but as well-dressed and attractive ladies and gentlemen. When the Arkansas legislature was debating the need for a separate car in 1891, some whites argued that whites should not be forced to sit next to dirty blacks; other whites argued instead that the worst blacks were those who were educated and relatively well-to-do and who insisted on imposing themselves on the white people. A young black legislator, John Gray Lucas, a recent graduate of Boston University, confronted the white lawmakers with their inconsistency: "Is it true, as charged, that we use less of soap and God's pure water than other people. . . . Or is it the constant growth of a more refined, intelligent, and I might say a more perfumed class, that grow more and more obnoxious as they more nearly approximate to our white friends' habits and plane of life?"

With every year in the 1880s, more blacks fought their way to white standards of "respectability." Black literacy, black wealth, black businesses, black higher education, and black landowning all increased substantially. When whites discussed segregating the railroads, respectable blacks responded in fury and disbelief. "Is it not enough that the two races are hopelessly separated in nearly all the higher relations of life already?" an open letter from seven black clergymen and teachers from Orangeburg, South Carolina, asked in 1889. "Are you not content with separate places of public entertainment, separate places of public amusement, separate places of public instruction, and even separate places of public worship? Why, in the name of common sense, of common humanity, of the common high-bred sensitiveness of every decent person of color, should you wish to force further unnatural separation even upon the thoroughfares of daily travel?"

A Northern traveler in the South observed that "a few colored men are inclined to insist upon enjoying whatever right belongs to them under the law, because they believe that any concessions on the part of the black people, or surrender of their legal rights, would invite and produce new injuries and oppressions." Educated and assertive blacks, especially those of the younger generation, chafed at every restriction against them and looked for opportunities to exercise their legal rights to attack the very assumptions and presumptions of segregation. A black Georgia newspaper reflected this aggressive mentality: "When a conductor orders a colored passenger from a first class car it's a bluff, and if the passenger goes to the forward or smoking car, that ends it; should he refuse, it ends it also, for the trainman will reflect seriously before he lays on violent hands, for he knows that such a rash proceeding makes him amenable to the law."

Mary Church, sixteen years old, boarded a train by herself only to be ushered to a Jim Crow car. She protested to the conductor that she had bought a first-class ticket. " 'This is first class enough for you,' he replied sarcastically, 'and you just stay where you are,' with a look calculated to freeze the very marrow of my bones." Having heard about "awful tragedies which had overtaken colored girls who had been obliged to travel alone on these cars at night," Church decided to get off the train. The conductor refused to let her pass, wanting to know where she was going. " 'I am getting off here,' I replied, 'to wire my father that you are forcing me to ride all night in a Jim Crow car. He will sue the railroad for compelling his daughter who has a first class ticket to ride in a second class car.' " The conductor relented.

Blacks resorted to the law in increasing numbers in the 1880s, taking railroads and railroad employees to court to press for equal accommodations. Blacks actually won several of these cases, even in Southern courts. These rulings reflected the growing consensus of the nation's appellate and federal courts, Northern and Southern, that equal accommodations had to be provided for those who paid equal amounts for their tickets. Those rulings also stipulated that the railroads could provide separate accommodations for any groups of passengers, as long as the facilities were equal and as long as separation was consistently enforced and publicized before passengers boarded the train. The railroad's case would be strengthened if it could show that separation encouraged "peace, order, convenience, and comfort" by adjusting to dominant customs in the area through which the railroad passed. In the 1880s, black Southerners were able to use this body of law to win more equitable treatment on the railroads of the region, to force the railroads to provide them equal facilities. "There is a plain rule of justice, which ought to be recognized and enforced, viz: that every man is entitled to what he pays for," a defender of the rights of black passengers in 1890 argued. "If there be on the part of the whites an unwillingness to occupy the same cars and to sit in the same seats with the blacks, let them be separate; only let equally good cars be provided for both, if both pay for them." In 1887 and 1889, the new Interstate Commerce Commission ruled that trains crossing state lines had to "give one passenger as good accommodations as another for the same price, but they are not compelled to permit a passenger to take any car or any seat that may please his fancy." The "equality of accommodations" must be "real and not delusive." The federal government simultaneously stressed equality and sanctioned segregation, giving with one hand and taking away with the other.

In the 1880s, then, blacks confronted a dangerous and uncertain situation every time they bought a first-class ticket to ride on a Southern railroad. Each road had its own customs and policy, and the events on the train might depend on the proclivity of the conductor or, worse, the mood and make-up of the white passengers who happened to be on board. Although the courts upheld the rights of several blacks who had the means to take their cases to court, there was no telling how many blacks suffered discrimination, intimidation, and violence in the meantime. Some railroads sought to avoid the problems simply by refusing to sell blacks first-class tickets; the L & N resorted to this policy until blacks threatened to boycott, then it allowed black women to travel first-class, then reversed itself again two months later when whites protested. At least one railroad in Alabama, operating in the piney woods along the coast, sought to avoid the potentially costly conflicts by running its own separate and identical car for blacks as early as 1882. "The rule is made for the protection of the blacks as much as for anything else in a part of the country in which they might be subjected to drunken men's insults," a Mobile paper argued.

If other railroads had followed the example of this Alabama company, rail segregation might have remained in the uncertain realm of custom and private business decisions that guided so much else in Southern race relations. Other railroads, however, especially those in parts of the South where blacks did not make up a large part of the clientele, were reluctant to go to the considerable expense and trouble of running twice the number of cars. The railroads, unenthusiastic about passenger traffic in any case because, as the L & N's president put it, "You can't make a g- d—cent out of it," wanted neither to police Southern race relations and then be sued for it nor to run extra cars. It was clear that white Southerners could not count on the railroads to take matters in hand. Some whites came to blame the railroads for the problem, for it seemed to them that the corporations as usual were putting profits ahead of the welfare of the region.

The earliest railroad segregation laws carried an ambiguous message. They took racial division and conflict for granted but placed the blame and the burden of dispelling that conflict on the railroads. Laws demanding separate cars seemed a compromise between white sensibilities and black rights, and, to whites, the only one who seemed to lose was the railroad who had to pay the cost. Blacks, on the other hand, clearly did not see a separate car as an equitable solution to the violence they suffered on the trains.

Two blacks in New Orleans, furious at the turn of events, decided to make a test case of a new law in Louisiana. They sought the help of a white Northern lawyer long dedicated to black rights, Albion Tourgée, who responded enthusiastically. "Submission to such outrages," he wrote, tends "only to their multiplication and exaggeration. It is by constant resistance to oppression that the race must ultimately win equality of right." Accordingly, they enlisted a man named Homer Adolph Plessy, seven-eighths white, to board the East Louisiana Railroad and refuse to leave the white car even though officials had been notified earlier of his status as a black. He was arrested, and his case tried in Louisiana in late 1892. "The roads are not in favor of the separate car law, owing to the expense entailed," a lawyer looking into the matter reported, "but they fear to array themselves against it." It took four more years for the United States Supreme Court to hear the Plessy case, by which time segregation had been written into the laws of every Southern state except the Carolinas and Virginia. The years in between saw the political map of the South redrawn.

The timing of the first wave of segregation law is explained, then, by the growing ambition, attainments, and assertiveness of blacks, by the striking expansion and importance of the railroad system in the 1880s, by a widespread distrust and dislike for the railroad corporations, by the course of legal cases at the state and circuit level, and by the example each state set for others. Most white officials who held power in these years played their role in the creation of statewide segregation; it was the product of no particular class, of no wave of hysteria or displaced frustration, no rising tide of abstract racism, no new ideas about race. Like everything else in the New South, segregation grew out of concrete situations, out of technological, demographic, economic, and political changes that had unforeseen and often unintended social consequences.

Railroad segregation was not a throwback to old-fashioned racism; indeed, segregation became, to whites, a badge of sophisticated, modern, managed race relations. John Andrew Rice recalled an incident from his youth in South Carolina in 1892. He visited Columbia, then "an awkward overgrown village, like a country boy come to town all dressed up on a Saturday night." Despite the rawness of the state capital, "the main entrance to the town was the depot, and here was something new, something that marked the town as different from the country and the country depots at Lynchburg and Darlington and Varnville: two doors to two waiting rooms and on these two doors arresting signs, 'White' and 'Colored.' " Soon those signs *would* be in Lynchburg, Darlington, and Varnville as well, for state law would demand it. The railroads took a piece of the city with them wherever they went. The railroad cars and waiting rooms were marked by the same anonymity that was coming to characterize the towns and cities of the South, the same diversity within confined spaces, the same display of class by clothing and demeanor, the same crowding of men and women, the same crowding of different races. In fact, the railroads were even more "modern" than cities themselves, detached from their settings, transitory, volatile.

After 1891, only Virginia and the Carolinas did not have statewide railroad segregation laws. The same forces working in the rest of the South worked in those states as well, of course, but having failed to put railroad segregation laws on the books in the late eighties and early nineties, they found that the political events of the next few years prevented them from joining their neighboring states. It was not until the late nineties that these states could implement their version of the law, just when the other Southern states began to enact even more kinds of segregation designed to enclose yet more of the machinery of the new age.

In the same years that statewide railroad segregation peaked, the South embarked on the constitutional disfranchisement of black voters. Southern disfranchisement, scattered and isolated with the poll tax and election legerdemain of Georgia, South Carolina, and Florida in the 1860s and 1870s, appeared to be moving into the current of the national mainstream with the adoption of secret ballots in Tennessee in 1888 and 1889; many Northern states were doing the same. In 1889, too, North Carolina's legislature tightened registration laws by requiring greater accuracy and detail on age, place of birth, and occupation, requirements that could restrict the vote in ways that sympathetic reformers in the North might appreciate.

The course of Southern voting restriction suddenly veered off in a uniquely Southern direction in Mississippi in 1890. For over a decade, legislators from outside Mississippi's Black Belt had attempted to organize support for a new constitution that would give their counties a more equitable role in state affairs. Rings composed of a few white Democrats in the heavily black counties exploited the inflated representation created by their large black populations, manipulating the votes in their counties, controlling the state government, and ignoring the needs of the majority of Mississippi whites. These despicable politicians, an editor speaking for white hill-country farmers charged, "disregarded the rights of the blacks, incurred useless and extravagant expenditures, raised the taxes, plunged the State into debt, and actually dominated the will of the white people through the instrumentality of the stolen negro vote."

The Black Belt delegates and the state leaders they elected resisted any change throughout the 1880s, but suddenly changed their position in 1889. United States Senator James Z. George, a prominent Redeemer and leading politician of the state, predicted that the 1890 census would "show that the black population of Mississippi will exceed that of the whites [by] nearly one-half million." Moreover, the Republicans controlled not only the White House but also both houses of Congress. The Republican ascendency in Washington had produced "an exciting of sectional passions and sectional prejudices." With "all the departments of the government in unfriendly hands," George warned, the "check on bad legislation" offered in the past by a Democratic-controlled House had disappeared. It seemed "almost certain" that the Republican majority would "pass a law taking the federal elections from the control of the state."

Recent events at home showed just how volatile the situation had in fact become. In Mississippi in 1889 and 1890 the Republicans became emboldened by the state of affairs in Washington. With firm control of the federal government won in their national victory of 1888, the Republicans prepared to contest three of Mississippi's seven recent congressional elections. Blacks in fusion arrangements demanded a greater share of the offices. Some blacks even refused to pay their taxes until guaranteed their right to vote. Moreover, the Republican party established a newspaper in Jackson and applauded as Mississippi Republicans who had kept the faith saw their loyalty rewarded by appointments to desirable federal posts. Some 40 Republicans, including 32 blacks, took federal civil service examinations for positions ranging from copyist to meteorological clerk. A convention of Mississippi blacks offered a state fusion ticket with the Democrats; when they were denied, they nominated candidates for all state offices, the first time the state Republican party had run a complete ticket since Redemption. Black leaders from 40 counties met in 1889, in what some whites feared as the "largest colored convention" ever held in Mississippi, to denounce the "violent and criminal suppression of the black vote." The convention called for federal intervention to "break up lawlessness and ballot-box stuffing." Clearly, the political situation in Mississippi was anything but settled.

The prospect facing the Democrats was one of perpetual turmoil, violence, dispute, factionalism, and growing opposition if they could not find some way to purge the black vote without bringing down on themselves the Republican-controlled power of the federal government. Many white Mississippians had grown weary of the constant fraud and violence they used to check black aspiration. "The old men of the present generation can't afford to die and leave the election to their children and grandchildren, with shot guns in their hands, a lie in their mouths and perjury on their lips in order to defeat the negroes," one Mississippian passionately argued. A constitutional convention could break this cycle by doing away with the need for force altogether. The Democrats pushed through a convention to be held in 1890. The object of overt threats, most local Republican organizations did not put candidates in the field; one man brave enough to canvass his district as a Republican candidate was assassinated. Of the 134 delegates, all but four were Democrats; the one Republican was the only black man at the convention.

It soon became clear that no one had a workable idea of how to disfranchise blacks without either disfranchising whites in the process or obviously violating the Fifteenth Amendment and losing federal representation. Delegates from white counties wanted no educational or property requirements, while black-county delegates favored such requirements. "Impose a property test, weigh true manhood against dirty dollars, and for the black problem you will have a white one which will revolutionize the state," ran one warning. An educational or literacy test was no more acceptable to poorer whites. The Black Belt delegates, rich and educated, looked on the compromises they had to make with disgust. "To avoid the disfranchisement of a lot of white ignoramuses we can't have an educational qualification," one Black Belt judge moaned, "and to pander to the prejudices of those who have no property we cannot have a property qualification."

Ironically, the property and educational requirements won the endorsement of the sole black delegate to the convention, Isaiah T. Montgomery. Montgomery, the former slave of Jefferson Davis's brother, had become a well-to-do planter after the war and founded the all-black town of Mound Bayou. Montgomery sought to deflect the pain inflicted by the convention from at least some blacks by calling for strict adherence to an educational or property qualification. Political conflict and bloodshed could be reduced, he hoped, even as some educated and propertied blacks—up to a third of all black voters—would be able to vote and exert some political influence. As black progress continued, Montgomery felt sure, an increasing percentage of Mississippi blacks would win the right to cast a ballot. "I have stood by, consenting and assisting to strike down the rights and liberties of 123,000 free men," Montgomery told the convention. "It is a fearful sacrifice laid upon the burning altar of liberty. Many of these men I know personally; their hearts are true as steel." Montgomery wanted to tell these men "that the sacrifice has been made to restore confidence, the great missing link between the races; to restore honesty and purity to the ballot box and to confer the boon of political liberty upon the Commonwealth of Mississippi." Whites, Montgomery insisted, must repay black acquiescence by working to settle racial problems "upon the enduring basis of Truth, Justice and Equality." The disfranchisement law promised safety if it promised nothing else: "It is the ship. All else is an open, raging, tempestuous sea."

The bill was an unsound ship, however, its timbers rotten and its sails poorly patched. The 35-member committee on the franchise listened to the ideas of each of its members and then spent weeks assembling those ideas into an acceptable plan. The white counties were granted a majority in the House while the black counties controlled the Senate. As for the franchise itself, the convention decided to erect a series of supposedly color-blind obstacles designed to let white voters pass while stopping blacks. Voters had to be registered by state-appointed officers (so that blacks could not use local or federal power to appoint black or Republican registrars), and only registered voters could hold any office. A potential voter had to prove he had lived in the state for at least two years and at least one year in his election district—a direct result of "the disposition of young negroes . . . to change their homes or precincts every year." A man presenting himself to vote could not have been convicted of any of a certain range of stereotypically "negro" crimes; arson, bigamy, and petty theft precluded a man from voting, but not murder, rape, or grand larceny, for blacks were supposedly "given rather to furtive offenses than to the robust crimes of the whites." He also had to be on record as having paid all taxes, including a poll tax of two dollars, for the last two years. Each of these provisions, Mississippians knew from the experience of other states Southern and otherwise, would remove an appreciable number of black voters.

The convention was not satisfied, though, until it had tacked on one final and novel provision: the so-called understanding clause. An aspiring voter had either to be able to read any section of the state constitution or to understand that section when it was read to him "or give a reasonable interpretation thereof." The idea, of course, was that illiterate whites could understand the constitution to the satisfaction of the white registrar while even a literate black man would find it difficult to persuade the official of his understanding. Even illiterate whites supposedly possessed "the aptitude of free government" as an automatic product of their racial heritage, while "if every negro in Mississippi was a graduate of Harvard, and had been elected as class orator . . . he would not be as well fitted to exercise the right of suffrage as the Anglo-Saxon farm laborer."

To their credit, many white Mississippians rejected such rationalizations as the nonsense they were. Only one newspaper in the entire state endorsed the understanding clause before its passage, and that was the newspaper that enjoyed the printing patronage of the convention. More common was this sort of denunciation: "It is evident that the clamor of demagogueism is riding the convention with whip and spur," the Raymond *Gazette* fumed. "The people of Mississippi who are sick and tired of ballot box frauds, perjury and all their attendant demoralization, and the people of the entire nation, are looking on and expecting something higher and more manly than this from a Convention of Mississippi's picked statesmen." "Every State suffers more or less from corrupt practices at elections," one paper bitterly observed, "but it was reserved for the State of Mississippi to make its very Constitution the instrument and shield of fraud."

But it was too late to turn back. The convention decided it would be "unnecessary and inexpedient" to allow Mississippi's voters to decide whether they wanted to live under such a constitution. Delegates dared not risk a vote once they saw what kind of popular reception greeted the new document. Mississippi's Democratic papers, full of ridicule and disgust during the convention, fell into line as soon as the work had been done.

Sexual relations between the races changed along with other kinds of relationships. In general, interracial sex and marriage came to be far more opposed by both blacks and whites as the decades passed. Whites thought black people were widely infected with venereal disease; that fear discouraged white men who might otherwise have pursued black women. For their part, black women and men strengthened their resistance to the callous abuse of black women by white men as soon as slavery ended. By moving into their own homes and out of the quarters, black families reduced the access white men had to black women. One white man testified before a national commission that there was less intercourse between white men and black women than before the war, not only because of syphilis "but because the negro will not let them have it. The negro buck will go down and will stay right around them." This retired planter from Mississippi told the investigators that "if a woman comes into a store, and there is a white man standing around, there will be a half a dozen colored men in front of the store waiting for her."

Interracial sex by no means ended, though the sexual contact between the races seems to have shifted from plantations to the less well-defined terrain of stores and towns where white men felt freer to proposition black women. "In the towns, where the white population, unlike that of the country, is so largely a floating one, and where the opportunities for a single act of intimacy between white men and negro women, entirely unacquainted with each other and passing at once out of each other's knowledge, are so numerous," Virginian Philip A. Bruce wrote in a London periodical in 1900, "the intercourse is more frequent, as the danger of exposure is very small." In such places, white men harassed black women. "The way in which many respectable, intelligent colored girls are hounded by white men of the baser sort does much to create bitterness among the negroes," a Hampton Institute professor said. Indeed, a black pastor wrote from Alabama, "if one of our men look at a white woman very hard and she complains he is lynched for it; white men on the high ways and in their stores and on the trains will insult our women and we are powerless to resent it as it would only be an invitation for our lives to be taken. The South is a pretty good organized mob and will remain so until bursted by the Federal Government."

For their part, Southern whites were convinced that it was blacks who were dangerous, who bred the violence that hung over the South. Virtually every issue of every Southern newspaper contained an account of black wrongdoing; if no episode from nearby could be found, episodes were imported from as far away as necessary; black crimes perpetrated in the North were especially attractive. Black men were thought to be inclined toward certain kinds of crimes, crimes of passion rather than crimes of cunning. "The longer I am here, the more I dread and fear the nigger," a white woman from Massachusetts wrote to a relative from her new home in Louisiana. "They have no regard for their own lives, and seem to have no feeling. Consequently if they have some fancied wrong to avenge, the first thing they think of is to kill. You rarely hear of them fighting fist fights. It is always a razor or knife or revolver."

Whites believed that such men were responsible for a rising tide of crime in the South in the late 1880s and early 1890s. One state after another passed laws in the early 1890s and again in the early 1900s to check black mobility; they piled on restrictions against vagrancy, contract evasion, and labor agents. Black men moving from one place to another, with no white boss to speak up for them or pay their bail, found themselves at the mercy of local police and courts. Planters, railroads, or other employers facing labor shortages were all too happy to purchase, merely by paying a small fine and court costs, the labor of black men convicted of petty crimes. County officials were eager to arrest black men moving through a county, whether for vagrancy or some other trumped-up charge, when they knew they could make money for the county and themselves by farming the prisoners out. The white men who hired convict labor had no incentive to treat the convicts with anything other than enough care to keep them alive and working. County officials looked the other way when mistreatment and even death resulted.

In the decades after emancipation the prison populations of the Southern states had burgeoned with black men convicted of property crimes; the hard times of the 1870s had seen the numbers surge as desperate men resorted to theft and as landowners prosecuted mercilessly, even when guilt was in doubt or the object of the theft low in value. From 1866 on, every Southern government had struggled to find a way to deal with this new prison population, for spending money on black criminals was at the bottom of every white taxpayer's list of priorities. As a result, one state after another turned to the leasing of convicts to private businesses. For a small fee, a railroad builder, a planter, or a mine owner could use the labor of state convicts with little financial risk and with no labor troubles.

It is not surprising that such a system bred inhumane travesties. In some of the most forbidding landscapes of the New South terrible scenes of inhumanity were played out: mass sickness, brutal whippings, discarded bodies, near-starvation, rape. Time after time, word leaked out about what was happening in the camps in the swamps or the piney woods; time after time, investigations lamely concluded that something would have to be done; time after time, the deaths and exploitation went on. Some of the wealthiest capitalists in the South became convict lessees, and some men with little capital but good political connections became rich off the franchise in the state's felons. The convict camps became places not only of profit, but also of political patronage, places where party workers with little ability could be posted with a shotgun, a ledgerbook, or even a doctor's bag. Critics repeatedly raised their voices against this crime committed by the state, but it went on for decades, while thousands died.

Southern whites tolerated such barbarities partly because they were persuaded that black crime was out of control. White papers began to speak of "bad niggers" who held white law in contempt, who feared no white man, who longed for revenge against all whites, who held it as a matter of pride that no white boss qualified their freedom. These black men, considering the courts the "white man's law," accorded sheriffs and judges no respect. Whites heard rumors that black criminals were held up as heroes by the black community, championed for their bravery against persistent white injustice. Whites in the cities and the countryside were certain that black crime was rapidly escalating. In the late 1880s, arrests and prison terms for black men began to mount, along with white rhetoric, anxiety, and violence.

The New South was a notoriously violent place. Homicide rates among both blacks and whites were the highest in the country, among the highest in the world. Lethal weapons seemed everywhere. Guns as well as life were cheap: two or three dollars would buy a pistol known in the trade as a "nigger killer," or one of its major competitors, the "owl-head" or the "American Bulldog." In a memoir about a Presbyterian picnic, one man recalled that "each young gentleman desired to have a pistol, a jack knife, and a pair of brass knucks," all of which were considered "the proper accoutrements of the young blades of the day." One young man working at a cotton compress on the border between the Carolinas wrote a friend for a favor. "I want you to get me a gun if you know where you can get a good one, and send it to me. This is a tough place up here. I am simply afraid to go out at night without one. They shoot about one hundred times every night."

In the turbulent South of the 1880s and early 1890s, when politics and economic turmoil constantly threw people into conflict, such weaponry and violence could easily spark interracial bloodshed. Most of that violence was directed by whites against blacks, whether in barroom shootings, political assassinations, labor disputes, or because of some real or imaginary breach of the racial code. When blacks did turn against whites, they risked terrible retribution from other whites. That, in itself, was nothing new: black men, in both the antebellum and postbellum years, had been taken from jail and hanged, tortured, and burned by mobs of white men because a legal execution seemed too good for such criminals. Events of this sort had happened throughout Reconstruction, in high numbers.

The visibility and ferocity of lynching seemed to assume new proportions in the 1880s and 1890s. One peak of lynching appears to have occurred in the early 1880s and another in the years around 1890. Newspaper and magazine articles proliferated both in defense and in denunciation of lynching; a steady stream of more thoughtful articles and books emerged throughout the first decades of the twentieth century which tried to discover the origins and solutions to lynching.

Lynchings were far more likely to occur in some regions of the South than in others, and those patterns call into question easy assumptions about the forces behind lynching. No simple political argument will work. Although North Carolina witnessed the greatest amount of racial conflict in the political realm of any Southern state, including a brutal white supremacy campaign and riot, the heavily black part of the state registered a remarkably low rate of lynching. Although white South Carolina under a race-baiting governor was given every permission to hate, the state fell far below the regional average in the number of black men lynched. Although white Virginia felt compelled to hold a disfranchisement convention, it recorded one of the lowest lynching rates in the South. Kentucky, on the other hand, near the border of the North and with a relatively diversified economy, saw a remarkably high rate of lynching. Even West Virginia, dominated by Republicans, reached the regional average in black lynching. Clearly, something other than the political environment triggered the bloodshed.

Two subregions witnessed especially high rates of lynchings: the Gulf Plain stretching from Florida to Texas, and the cotton uplands of Mississippi, Louisiana, Arkansas, and Texas. While both of these subregions had a high proportion of blacks in their populations, they were by no means the regions with the highest black proportion. Neither did they register a particularly high level of voting against the Democratic regime.

What they did share was a particular demography. These subregions had an extremely low rural population density, often only half that of states in the East. In the last two decades of the nineteenth century they experienced tremendous rates of black population increase. While the average county in the South saw its black population grow by 48 percent between 1880 and 1910, counties in Florida's Gulf Plain grew by 131 percent, Alabama's grew by 119 percent, Mississippi's by 91 percent, and Texas's by 71 percent. The only state whose Gulf Plain area had a relatively low lynching rate, close to that of the region as a whole, was Louisiana's, which did not see great black population change. The subregions with the second and third highest rates of lynching—the cotton uplands and, surprisingly, the mountains of Appalachia—also combined a relatively low population density and high rates of black population growth.

The counties most likely to witness lynchings had scattered farms where many black newcomers and strangers lived and worked. Those counties were also likely to have few towns, weak law enforcement, poor communication with the outside, and high levels of transiency among both races. Such a setting fostered the fear and insecurity that fed lynching at the same time it removed the few checks that helped dissuade would-be lynchers elsewhere. Lynching served as a method of law enforcement in sparsely populated places where white people felt especially insecure. Whites dreaded the idea that black criminals could get away with harming or insulting a white person without being punished, worried that the lack of retribution would encourage others to raise their hand against isolated whites on remote plantations, farms, or roads.

The sporadic violence of lynching was a way for white people to reconcile weak governments with a demand for an impossibly high level of racial mastery, a way to terrorize blacks into acquiescence by brutally killing those who intentionally or accidentally stepped over some invisible and shifting line of permissible behavior. The brutality was not generated by crowding and friction; places such as the Black Belt and the Piedmont, with high population densities, saw relatively low rates of lynching. In such places, black people were more likely to know at least a few whites as neighbors or employers. They were also able to turn to black friends and allies should they be pursued by a lynch mob.

Lynchings tended to flourish where whites were surrounded by what they called "strange niggers," blacks with no white to vouch for them, blacks with no reputation in the neighborhood, blacks without even other blacks to aid them. Lynching seemed both more necessary and more feasible in places such as the Gulf Plain, the cotton uplands, and the mountains. In those places most blacks and whites did not know one another, much less share ties of several generations. The black population often moved from one year to the next in search of jobs at lumber camps and large plantations. "The salvation of the negro in this country depends upon drawing the social lines tighter, tighter all the while, North and South," the president of a black college in Alabama warned an Emancipation Day audience in 1901. "The moment they become slack the white man becomes brutal—the negro goes down forever."

Local black leaders, for their own purposes, readily joined whites in blaming vagrant blacks for any crime in the neighborhood. "There never was a respectable colored man lynched in the south, except in a case of murder," a black minister from Montgomery wrote even as he denounced lynching. "I speak from my own experience when I say that in the lynchings I have known about, the victims were always men in the community no one could say a good word for. They came out from the slums at night, like the

"The Lynching of Henry Smith. The Torture. Burning his feet with a red-hot iron."
From R. W. Shufeldt, The Negro: A Menace to Civilization, 1906.

raccoon, and stole back again." Local blacks had every reason for displacing white anger, for finding some stranger who could bear the brunt of white men determined to wreak vengeance.

Although most lynchings were inflicted in response to alleged murder, most of the rhetoric and justification focused intently on the so-called "one crime" or "usual crime": the sexual assault of white women by blacks. That assault sometimes involved rape, while at other times a mere look or word was enough to justify death. Black reformers such as Ida B. Wells argued repeatedly that even the accusation of rape made up only a fraction of the reasons giving for lynching. Just as repeatedly, whites argued that violations of white womanhood were the crimes that unleashed the lynching beast. Whites opposed to lynching, Northern and Southern, apparently felt compelled to acquiesce to this argument.

Whites assumed that black men lusted after white women, but there was a widespread suspicion that it was more than lust that drove black men into the alleged assaults. "I think there can be no doubt that a considerable amount of crime on the part of colored men against white men and women is due to a spirit of getting even," a white Southerner observed. "Not getting even with any particular individual, but just an indefinite getting even with white race." Whites could not help but realize that black people chafed under their many injustices. It did not seem far-fetched to whites that furious black men would attack the most vulnerable among the more privileged race. One woman who had grown up in the countryside of middle Tennessee recalled that white girls were taught to sew, but not cook, "because we were never allowed to enter the kitchen. There was a prohibition because the Negro men on the place that didn't have families were fed in the kitchen." This woman told the younger white woman interviewing her in 1952 that "you can't remember and maybe can't understand the horror that had grown up of any contact with a Negro man."

Just as white girls and women were raised to fear strange black men, so were black boys and men taught to avoid any situation where they might be falsely accused. For generations, young black men learned early in their lives that they could at any time be grabbed by a white mob—whether for murder, looking at a white woman the wrong way, or merely being "smart"—and dragged into the woods or a public street to be tortured, burned, mutilated. It was a poisoned atmosphere, one that permeated life far beyond those counties where a lynching had actually taken place, one that pervaded all the dealings each race had with the other.

Juxtapositions of the modern and the archaic constantly jarred the New South, as Mell Barrett, a young white boy, discovered when he spent a nickel to hear his first Edison talking machine at a country picnic in 1896. "With the tubes in my ears, the Pitchman was now adjusting the needle on the machine. . . . My excitement increased, my heart was pounding so I could hardly hold the tubes in my ears with my shaking hands." At first, he thought he was listening to a recording of a convention of some sort. " 'All Right Men. Bring Them Out. Let's Hear What They Have to Say,' were the first words I understood coming from a talking machine." The young boy listened to two men confess to a rape, then beg for mercy. "The sounds of shuffling feet, swearing men, rattle of chains, falling wood, brush, and fagots, then a voice—shrill, strident, angry, called out, 'Who will apply the torch?' 'I will,' came a chorus of high-pitched, angry voices." Barrett could hear "the crackle of flames as it ate its way into the dry tender," and the victims asking God to forgive their tormentors. The crowd fell quiet; only the sound of the flames remained.

"My eyes and mouth were dry. I tried to wet my lips, but my tongue, too, was parched. Perspiration dripped from my hands. I stood immobile, unable to move. Now the voice of the Pitchman saying, 'That's all gentlemen—who's next?' " As Barrett took the tubes from his ears, the next man asked, " 'What's the matter, Son—sick?' " The Pitchman, "sensing what my trouble was, said, 'Too much cake, too much lemonade. You know how boys are at a picnic.' "

Chapter 6

Alliances

As Southern legislatures wrestled with the politics of race a challenge of a different sort began to shake the political system. The challenge came from an unexpected quarter: the countryside. Southern farmers decided that public policy and private enterprise favored almost everyone in America other than themselves. Even though they produced more goods, paid more taxes, and cast more votes than any other group of Gilded Age Americans, farmers' voices often seemed to go unheard. Farmers felt abused by both of the major parties and exploited by every level of business from national corporations to local storekeepers.

Soon after the Civil War farmers launched crusades to correct some of the wrongs that had developed in rural life during the turmoil of the war and Reconstruction. The Patrons of Husbandry—popularly known as "the Grange"—made a strong impression on the rural South even before Redemption, pulling in nearly a quarter of a million members at its peak in the mid-1870s. In states across the region, farmers eagerly joined this national organization in the hope that it could help them deal with the problems of chronic debt and rural decline; by 1875, over 180,000 Grangers had enlisted in Southern states. The Grange, envisioning a unified agrarian interest arrayed against merchants and railroads, sought out large planters to lead its fight. In several states, prominent Grangers were also prominent Redeemers. It is not surprising that many smaller farmers distrusted the organization as a mere adjunct to the Democrats.

Some Grangers, however, opposed the Democrats even before Redemption. As a result of Greenbackers' influence in the 1870s, the Grange sometimes fostered radicalism as well as conservatism. These Grangers and Greenbackers blamed the farmers' distress on the nation's money system, which seemed rigged against all farmers. To avoid established commercial networks as much as possible, the Grange sponsored cooperative buying and selling in the organization's own stores, gins, warehouses, and brickyards. Local chapters in the South rushed to establish a broad range of cooperative activities, even as the national leadership, worried about the political and economic dangers of too many independent cooperative enterprises, discouraged the proliferation of the stores and other businesses. The leadership placed its emphasis instead on creating agricultural colleges, on attracting immigrants and industries to the South, on crop diversification, and on creating a richer home life for farm families. Farmers needed immediate help, however, and these long-range goals attracted few members. The depression and the political conflicts of the 1870s buffeted the movement, which emerged from the decade weakened and without direction. Yet the Grange had planted the seeds for what were soon to become its numerous competitors.

The largest and most active offshoot of the Grange appeared in 1882 in Arkansas, where farmers had migrated to make a new start only to find their ambition undermined by the familiar crop lien and merchants; the group called itself the Agricultural Wheel. The Wheel assembled its philosophy from the French physiocrats, the Bible, and other diverse sources. The Arkansas order felt secrecy and the exclusion of townsmen absolutely necessary. The experience of the Grange showed that inviting merchants into meetings reduced the gathering to a "Babel"; in fact, no local of the Wheel was permitted within any incorporated town. At the same time the Wheel began, another order called the Brothers of Freedom (an allusion to the Sons of Liberty of the American Revolution) emerged in Arkansas. Its purpose was much the same as the Wheel, with similar origins among the Greenbackers and the Grangers. The two organizations joined forces in 1885 under the name of the Wheel, claiming 1,105 locals in four states.

Over the next few years, the newly expanded Agricultural Wheel grew in both activities and size. The order attempted to purchase farming implements directly from the manufacturer, using the bargaining power of its large membership as a powerful inducement. Leaders urged locals to adopt the cooperative techniques of the Grange and distributed guidelines about how they could start their own cooperative enterprises. The farmers erected stores worth tens of thousands of dollars in Arkansas and Tennessee. Plow companies agreed to sell their products at reduced rates to the Wheel, and members received reductions of 40 to 50 percent on wagons and buggies, reapers and mowers. The order even sponsored an innovative plan to allow tobacco growers to control the storage and marketing of their crop, holding the product from the market until they could dictate better terms.

The Wheel made it clear that legislators would have to help if the politicians hoped to win the farmers' votes. The Wheelers adopted the Greenbacker critique of the postbellum political economy, calling on the federal government to issue money so that farmers could transact their business in cash, and urging the reduction of government spending, a graduated income tax, and the opening of government lands to homesteaders. The Wheel agitated for the government of Arkansas to regulate its railroads, telegraph, and telephone lines, keep trains from running on Sunday, make railroad corporations reimburse farmers for the stock their trains killed, and ban the employment of armed men by corporations. By 1887, the order claimed half a million members.

Throughout the early 1880s, organizers for the Noble and Holy Order of the Knights of Labor were also busily organizing locals throughout the South. Blacks as well as whites, women as well as men, enlisted in the order. The message of the Knights was as multifaceted as its membership. Lectures and newspapers preached a fiery and powerful mixture of the Declaration of Independence, the Bible, and artisanal pride. The organization openly opposed the concentrations of power and monopolies that dominated large parts of the nation's economy. By 1886 the Southern Knights claimed 50,000 members in ten Southern states. The order agitated for bureaus of labor statistics, consumers' cooperatives, the eight-hour day, the abolition of convict labor, greenbacks, child labor laws, and equal pay for women doing the same work as men.

Twenty-two times in the mid-1880s, Southern workers marching under the Knights of Labor banner struck to gain better wages, hours, and working conditions. Textile mill workers near Augusta, sugarcane workers in Louisiana, miners and foundry workers in Alabama and Virginia, lumber workers in Florida, Alabama, and Mississippi, dock hands in Newport News and Wilmington, cotton compress workers in Richmond, fish cannery workers in Mississippi—all struck with the support of their local Knights of Labor organization. Knights also supported boycotts in cities across the South, opposing the local products of convict or nonunion labor. The initial success of several of these struggles helped bolster the rolls of Knights locals throughout the region.

Yet another reform group appeared in the South in the early and mid-1880s. Like the others, this new organization, the Farmers' Alliance, spoke of voluntary cooperation so that working Americans could free themselves from a demeaning dependence on the men who handled the money in Gilded Age America. The Alliance, too, used the rhetoric of America's founding documents and the Bible. Its vision grew until it offered help to black as well as white Southerners, offered something to women as well as men, offered connections with other organizations working toward a reorientation of American society.

The founders of the Farmers' Alliance, like their counterparts in the Wheel, the Brothers of Freedom, and the Knights of Labor, constructed their organization from materials at hand: the ritual and secrecy of fraternal lodges, the discipline of Protestant churches, the monetary policies of the Greenbackers, the agrarian pride of the Grange, and the educational tactics of neighborhood schools. Like other voluntary associations, including the Knights of Labor and the Women's Christian Temperance Union, the Farmers' Alliance spread its message through lecturers who traveled from one place to another and through newspapers sympathetic to the cause. By 1883, the Alliance in Texas had 26 lecturers busily establishing locals in 11 counties in the central and eastern parts of the state as well as in the western counties where the order began. The first constitution of the Alliance opened membership to anyone of either gender over sixteen years of age who believed in a supreme being and who was "a farmer, farm laborer, a country school teacher, a country physician, or a minister of the gospel." Many of the lecturers had been rural doctors or preachers, and the Alliance's first subsidized newspaper began its life as a Sunday school magazine published out of the editor's farm house. Over 500 local "suballiances"—assemblies focused on rural neighborhoods—had been founded in Texas by the summer of 1885, and six months later more than 1,650 came into being. By the summer of 1886, the Alliance claimed over 100,000 members in the state of its birth.

The new order overwhelmed what remained of the Grange, an order now marked as old-fashioned by its elaborate ritual, internal ranking of members, stiffly nonpolitical orientation, and the strictly cash transactions of its cooperative stores. The Knights of Labor, strong in Texas, sought to join forces with the Alliance; after some deliberation, the farmers enthusiastically united with the Knights in the struggle against what both saw as control of the country by monopolies. When the Knights became locked in a bitter fight with Jay Gould—the nation's most notorious "robber baron"—in 1886, members of the Alliance donated money and food to the strikers and held meetings of solidarity. One county alliance announced that "we sympathize deeply in the misfortunes of the Knights of Labor in their struggle to feed and clothe their families, and ask them to meet us at the ballot box and help overthrow all monopolies." Coalitions between farmers and laborers emerged in over 20 Texas counties; 10,000 Knights and Alliancemen marched through Dallas. Gould brutally crushed the Knights, but the Alliance continued to gather strength and members.

In 1886 the Alliance held a convention in Cleburne, Texas, and enumerated 17 reforms necessary to save the country, demands that echoed the goals of the Knights, the Greenbackers, the Wheel, and other dissatisfied

groups. This broad program provided the foundation for the Alliance's phenomenal growth through the rest of the South in the next few years. Most
important for the Alliance's future was the call first articulated by the Greenbackers for a flexible currency in which the money supply would keep pace
with increases in the population and business transactions, checking the decline in prices of the products farmers raised. To this end, the "Cleburne
Demands" called for the unlimited coinage of gold and silver. There were
also calls for the state's recognition of unions and cooperative stores, the
establishment of a national bureau of labor statistics, a better mechanics lien
law, statutes requiring workers be paid on time and with cash instead of scrip,
the abolition of convict leasing, and a national conference of all labor organizations. The Cleburne convention demanded, too, that railroad property
be fairly taxed and that an interstate commerce commission prevent unfair
combinations. Finally, it called for the taxation of all land held for speculative purposes, the immediate opening to settlers of all land forfeited by railroad companies, the removal of fences around public school lands, the end
of futures markets for all agricultural products, and a stop to the speculation
in American land by aliens.

A new leader, Charles W. Macune, stepped forward to give the movement cohesion and force. Thirty-five years old, born in Wisconsin, an orphan
at ten, acquainted with both medicine and law, Macune had lived in California and Kansas before moving to Milam County, Texas. There, working
as a doctor, he joined the Alliance and was chosen as one of the three Milam
County delegates to the convention at Cleburne. Impressed with Macune's
performance during the heated debates at Cleburne, his colleagues elected
him chairman of the executive committee of the Farmers' Alliance. In this
role, Macune managed to reconcile divergent groups. At the order's next
annual convention, in Waco in 1887, Macune proposed the expansion of
the Farmers' Alliance throughout "the cotton belt of the nation." Only the
federal government had the power to right the enormous wrongs that af-
flicted the nation's farmers, he argued, and only a national movement could
take the government in that direction. At Waco, the Texas Alliance joined
with the Farmers' Union in Louisiana, the Agricultural Wheel in Arkansas,
and a similar group called the Great Agricultural Relief in Mississippi.

At Waco, too, the newly expanded Alliance launched into a critical debate over the political involvement of the organization. Many farmers were
leery of involving the Alliance in politics. Some feared the effect political
partisanship might have on the broad reforming mission of the Alliance,
while others worried that the Alliance might undermine the strength of the
Democratic party in the South. Nevertheless, it soon became clear that many
other farmers welcomed a bold stand and saw in the Alliance their first real
opportunity to fight back against the powers of the nation and the New
South. "Political parties in this country can and will take care of themselves,"
a North Carolina leader told a gathering in 1887. "We want the farmers to

Charles W. Macune, from The Arena, *April 1892.*

take care of themselves." Macune put the matter even more bluntly: "Plainly, we will not consent to give indefinite support to men who are. . . . unfriendly to our interests. . . . If this be party treason, make the most of it." The leaders of the Alliance decided to allow each suballiance to make its own decisions about whom it would support in local elections; they would not try to steer the national organization through the dangerous shoals of state and national politics. The Waco Convention of 1887 enthusiastically adopted Macune's plan, unanimously reaffirmed the Cleburne principles, and voted funds for speakers to carry the word throughout the South. Seven lecturers went out to Tennessee, six each to Mississippi and Alabama, five to Missouri, three to Arkansas, and others to Georgia, the Carolinas, Florida, Kentucky, and Kansas.

Farmers rushed into the Farmers' Alliance in numbers that surprised everyone. "In spite of all opposing influences that could be brought to bear in Wake County, I met the farmers in public meetings twenty-seven times, and twenty-seven times they organized," one lecturer wrote back to headquarters from North Carolina. "The farmers seem like unto ripe fruit—you can gather them by a gentle shake of the bush." Soon, 21 lecturers were traversing North Carolina, and the state leader claimed that he could use five times that many. In Mississippi, lecturer S. O. Daws took only six months to organize 30 counties and establish a state Alliance; in Alabama, farmers were so anxious to belong to the Alliance that they organized themselves and then pleaded with the central office to send a lecturer to make them official. In Georgia, it took only three years for the Alliance to organize 134 of the state's 137 counties; in Tennessee, 92 of 96 counties established branches of the Farmers' Alliance; in West Virginia, 41 of 54 counties joined. Each year marked new high points. In 1887 the Farmers' Alliance had expanded into Louisiana, Mississippi, Tennessee, and Kentucky. By 1888, the Alliance had pushed farther east, into what were to be some of its strongholds in the nineties: Alabama, Georgia, and North Carolina. In 1889, the Farmers' Alliance claimed 662,000 members in the Southern states; a year later, 852,000.

Alliance organizers had the greatest success in areas settled mostly after the Civil War. These places, whether on the Texas and Arkansas frontier, in the wiregrass of Alabama, Florida, and Georgia, or in the hill country of Mississippi, had experienced rapid growth of population and the rapid emergence of commercial agriculture in the preceding ten or fifteen years. The Alliance met little resistance in these counties. On the one hand, there were few established old families who could use their names, their power, and their patronage to channel politics into safe areas; on the other, there were fewer rural churches, schools, newspapers, and neighbors than in the older counties to soften the hard life of the farmer. The towns, railroads, and stores in these counties also were of recent construction, products of men the farmers had watched prosper at their expense. The farmers who lived in these counties had good reason to believe that by joining together they could bring change.

Older counties that had seen a substantial increase in cotton production in recent years also proved receptive to the Alliance. Here, too, in North Carolina, South Carolina, and Georgia, the Alliance offered a reasonable response to the problems that faced the farmer, a response that built upon language, techniques, and ideas with which farmers were already quite familiar. The Farmers' Alliance made sense to many farming communities that had struggled with town growth, fence laws, increased tenancy, and growing indebtedness. The Alliance appealed to the most depressed agricultural counties in Texas, Virginia, and North Carolina, regardless of their major crop, where farmers of all ranks saw their future eroded. In these places, larger landowners were more involved in the Alliance than their counterparts in more prosperous areas.

The Alliance was dominated neither by tenants nor by the wealthiest planters but by the landowning majority. Landowners had the most to lose and the most to gain from the sorts of reforms the Alliance championed. The Alliance appealed to landed farmers who wished to have something to pass on to their sons, to young men desperate not to lose their inheritance. The order also proved attractive to professional men who had cast their lot with the rural South and watched in anger as the fortunes of the countryside faded. Tenants had less room for maneuvering, less room for mistakes. They could not afford to antagonize a conservative landlord, to pay dues out of cash they did not have, to stand up to those people with connections and money. While tenants were free to join the Farmers' Alliance, most did not. Landowners set the tone and agenda of the rapidly growing order.

Throughout the South, many well-known men lent their prestige and power to the new movement, allowing it to grow where it might not otherwise have flourished. In five states, the Alliance joined forces with men who already had become powerful spokesmen for dissatisfied farmers. Leonidas L. Polk of North Carolina, Benjamin Tillman of South Carolina, Reuben Kolb of Alabama, Frank Burkitt of Mississippi, and Tom Watson of Georgia brought great ability and influence to the farmers' movement in the early years. Seeking to use the state government to help the farmers, all these men had won large followings before the Alliance had achieved much visibility in their states and all five had grown disgruntled with the Democratic status quo. Their presence and power channeled the evolution of the Alliance.

The careers of these men bore striking similarities. All had come from privileged backgrounds, had eagerly adopted the much-touted New South strategy of diversified farming, and had enjoyed better fortunes than most of their neighbors. All five turned against the Democratic party only when they became convinced that it would not help the countryside. In the eyes of the Democratic leaders of the 1880s, all five were mavericks, troublemakers. All five spoke with real anger about the farmers' lot, and all posed real challenges to the established politicians of their states. To the most radical members of the Alliance several of these leaders seemed parasites on the farmers' movement or perverters of its deepest ideals. Yet in the late 1880s it had not yet become clear which strategies would dominate the Farmers' Alliance, which strategies offered farmers the best chance to regain their central position in state politics. Many farmers turned to one or another of these five men for their strong roots in their states and large personal followings, for their experience fighting the established powers.

In the late 1880s, while the Alliance itself was deciding fundamental questions of policy and strategy, it seemed only natural that these established leaders would be the ones to lead the new movement. The next few years

Leonidas L. Polk, from The Arena, *April 1892.*

would see the relationship between the Alliance rank and file and these ambitious men become more complicated. Polk, Kolb, and Watson identified deeply with the policies of the Alliance leadership and sought to further their ends; others, such as Tillman, John Buchanan of Tennessee, and James Hogg of Texas, came to reject key parts of the Alliance program and bore a strained association with the order.

The Farmers' Alliance, it is clear, did not merely arise as a unified, original, coherent movement spreading from Texas to the East. As the Farmers' Alliance washed over the South, it flowed into channels already cut by men dissatisfied with the Democratic order, by independent political movements, by local farmer organizations, by planter clubs and the Grange. As a result, the Alliance was always more diverse than it seemed in its official pronouncements. The farmers did not always find it easy to determine who spoke with the real voice of rural interests, whether it was the exciting Alliance sweeping in from Texas or the man who had stood up to the legislatures and the railroads before the Alliance arrived on the scene. Both the Alliance and the settings it confronted were complex and constantly changing.

The Alliance was built of local suballiances, formed in tiny rural communities, their memberships numbering in the tens. Those suballiances developed in different ways, sometimes growing up indigenously when a local farmer heard or read about the Alliance, sometimes converting from a somnambulant Grange or farming club, sometimes beginning when an Allianceman moved into a new neighborhood. As the Alliance became better established in a state, lecturers went out and formed new suballiances. These lecturers worked full-time, carrying Alliance literature to sell to eager new recruits and collecting dues from those who signed up. The lecturers received a commission—sometimes as much as five dollars—for each suballiance they formed. "This system of Lecturing is the only one, which I see," a new lecturer in Virginia was told by his superior, "that can be made effective against the tremendous money and boodle campaign that will be conducted by those who oppose us."

Most of the lecturers were obscure men, country editors or ministers taking on this new job for a while to see where it might lead. Others were flamboyant types who thrived on the attention they won every time they stood before a new audience. One of the earliest lecturers in North Carolina, for example, was James Buckner "Buck" Barry. In his late sixties when he went on the lecture trail, with his long beard, hair down to his shoulders, and buckskin suit, Barry, as he was the first to admit, put "no brakes on my small amount of brains or tongue." As he traveled from one rural community to another in 1887, he asked the farmers who came to see him, "Is slavery so sweet that you are willing to puppy down and lick the boot that kicks you?" Barry left a wide stream of suballiances in his wake.

Newspapers played a critical role as well. Alliance newspapers could keep isolated suballiances informed on recent developments and readers focused on the issues the state and national leadership deemed most appropriate at particular junctures. Alliance newspapers could keep the fires of reform burning after the members of the suballiance had long heard all that each of the other members had to say. Papers continually emerged during the heyday of the Alliance and totaled perhaps a thousand in 1890; Texas and Alabama each generated a hundred Alliance papers.

Because word of the Alliance spread in several ways, lecturers often found that news of the organization preceded them. Sometimes letters mentioned the Alliance in brief snippets. Amanda Boyd of Starkville, Mississippi, received two letters from relatives that told her of the movement in Texas. In 1887 her nephew wrote: "Dear aunt as I never hear from you I thought that I would write to you this leaves all well. times is hard here and we alliance folks are doing all we can to better them. we have had some bad weather. I will send you the childrens pictures." A couple of weeks later Amanda Boyd received an exhortation from her niece in Tanglewood urging her to nudge the men she knew toward the Alliance. "I want you to write to me in your next whether the farmers are organized in your State or not—nearly every Farmer in this state belongs to the farmer's Alliance and they express themselves hopeful of Sucksess Alph says tell Mr Rickey if he does not belong to some farmers club to join and help in the great struggle for Freedom."

Much of the business of the local suballiances was dedicated to encouraging the sense of unity and common purpose. Like fraternal lodges, the suballiances sometimes held secret meetings, with elaborate protective measures. "I have just received the new Pass-word," the secretary of a county alliance in North Carolina wrote. "The door-word is changed. The room word is *not* changed. Tomorrow I will send you the 'prefix' to the Door-word and Room-word. The envelope in which I shall send it will contain nothing except the 'prefix' and it will be without date or signature." Likewise, prospective members had to meet the standards of the group—not always a sure thing. The minutes of the Jefferson Alliance in Jackson County in Georgia's Piedmont noted that "the committee on the caracter of J. M. Hill made a favorable report, and he was balloted for their being 2 black balls the president declared that J. M. Hill was rejected and notifyed the Sect. to inform the Sect of the county Alliance as the law directs." Even after a person had become a member, the local suballiance kept a close eye on him. The president of the Jefferson Alliance was told to correspond with the judiciary committee of the state alliance "as to the advisability of Brother W. J. Whitehead selling medison all so Brother W. J. Davenport selling books." Members often moved away and wanted to take with them certificates attesting to their good character. At least eight times in late 1889 and early 1890, the Jefferson Alliance issued these "dimits" for members moving on.

Such practices were familiar to Southerners because churches used the same methods. In fact, the local alliances often resembled congregations of an evangelical church. "The lodge was open in the usual way—prayer by the chaplain," the Jefferson Alliance secretary noted in 1889. Like the churches, members of local Alliances sought to help one another in times of need. The order might offer neighborly concern: "Bro. W. L. Webb was reported sick and the pres requested the members to visit him." Or they might offer critical support. When "Bro Jesse Williams was reported sick and in need of assistance," the Jefferson Alliance formed a committee "to look after him and if he needed his crop worked out they were instructed to hire hands and work it out and the Pres was authorized to draw his warrant on the Treasurer for the pay." Such help might make the difference between keeping and losing a farm.

Like churches, too, local alliances sometimes sought to adjudicate conflicts among their members. Two men were appointed by the Jefferson Alliance to confer with the Galilee Alliance, "and ask a like commity be appointed to join said Jeffson Alliance committie in adjusting the trouble between Bros. Kisler and Glenn." Like the churches, the alliances listened to testimony of conversion and faith, urging the speakers on. The minutes of the Gillespie County Alliance in Texas observed that "Bro. Jennings received permission to exercise his vocal organ for thirty minutes which he did to the edification and logical information of all. All a man needs is a chance and he will be another Cicero." Like the churches, as well, those in charge sometimes had to take measures to make sure that the meetings stayed focused on the matters at hand. The Jamestown Alliance of North Carolina resolved "that any young man or Lady . . . caught sparkin[g] in time of bus[iness] be fined to sweep and have water for the next meeting."

Despite dangers of inappropriate sparking, the Alliance's openness to women provided one of the organization's greatest sources of strength. A fourth of all members were women—in some suballiances, as many as half were female—and they played an important role in the movement's growth. Women who embodied and articulated the traditional female attributes of Christianity, devotion to family, and attention to the home added a critical dimension to the Alliance, just as they did to temperance and the Knights of Labor. These various reform movements, in fact, tended to interlock. "I am going to work for prohibition, the Alliance and for Jesus as long as I live," one woman proclaimed. Women in the Alliance were anxious to take on active roles. "The Alliance has come to redeem woman from her enslaved condition," a female member from Texas put it. "She is admitted into the organization as the equal of her brother, and the ostracism which has impeded her intellectual progress in the past is not met with."

Women in the Alliance enjoyed all the benefits of membership: they could vote on applicants, take part in all the business of the order, and learn all its secret passwords and signals. Some held local offices, some gave addresses, some ran business affairs, and some wrote for Alliance papers. A history of the young movement written in 1891 bore an effusive dedication "To the Wives, Mothers and Daughters of the Farmers and Laborers of America, Whose Heroic Devotion and Patient Fortitude Helped to Establish American Liberty, and Who Now, As in the Past, are Nobly Aiding in the Second Struggle for Independence." The letterhead of Fanny Leak, secretary of the Texas State Alliance, proclaimed, "Get in Your Women and give them Something to Do!" She wrote to a "Dear Sister" in the movement that "such women as wave the Alliance banner, *will* like the Spartan mothers *urge* their loved ones on and on, until our nation of toilers is once more free from the grip of the money power."

Women's support often took somewhat less Spartan forms. J. H. Sailor from Mana, North Carolina, described how women rejuvenated a long Alliance meeting in his neighborhood. In language that sounds like a rustic translation of a biblical feast, Sailor told of a welcome scene: "Up the road came about a dozen or two of the women with baskets buckets and large dish pans and the Brethren said fix the table and they moved the benches back and brought in three large tables and the good Sisters comenced fixin the table and when it was done there was on it Beef Mutton Fried Chicken Baked chicken Turkey all kinds of pies all kind of pickels all kinds of cakes." Sailor claimed he "never enjoyed a better dinner in my life. I ate so much Turkey I felt like gobling the ballance of the week." Such events furthered one of the main objects of the Alliance: securing among farmers the "intimate social relations and acquaintances with each other" called for in official literature, intimacy without which no amount of speech making and platform hammering could succeed.

Women's role in the Alliance, however, could also be problematic for the order. One Mississippi Allianceman wrote to the organization's newspaper to ask, "We have a sister in our Alliance that talks too much. What shall be done about it? . . . It was never intended that ladies should take that course in the Alliances." Some women used the Alliance meetings to suggest to men that they should not have been so willing to go along with the established political parties in the first place. "Why," asked one female assistant lecturer in North Carolina, "is it that the farmer and laboring class generally, have got no self-will or resolution of their own? . . . as a general rule they have been ever ready to link their destinies with any political aspirant who can get up and deliver a flowery address of misrepresentation." Or as another woman put it, a bit more bluntly, "Some men can't see beyond their nose." Not every man was willing to accept criticism, and some suggested that women be still. One Tennessee Alliancewoman described these opponents of women's voices as "those old drones, who think women only fit to cook, wash, scrub and wait on men, [and] values them only a little higher than the animals he works."

Much more than gender, race presented a recurring source of conflict for the Farmers' Alliance. The farmers' organizations of the New South had to wrestle with a set of problems about race different from those confronted by the planter-dominated Grange, the town-based prohibitionists, the industry-based Knights, the desperate Republicans, or the nervous Democrats. Despite gains in black landholding and increasing white tenantry, most blacks remained tenants and most whites remained landowners. Thus it was that people of the two races generally had antagonistic economic interests, interests that the Agricultural Wheel, the Brothers of Freedom, and ultimately the Farmers' Alliance struggled to contain.

In its early days the Alliance showed little sympathy for rural blacks and used its increasing power to force any organization that wanted to join with the Alliance to adopt its whites-only requirement; both the Wheel and the Florida Farmers' Union gave up black chapters when they fused with the

Alliance. The Knights of Labor, with their large black membership and egalitarian ideology, were not so easily absorbed. Black Knights charged that the
Alliance offered black farmers nothing but "oppression and death." White
Alliance landlords, fearing the organization of black sharecroppers and laborers, would not hire black day laborers if at all possible.

Despite the outright hostility against black farmers shown by members
of the white Farmers' Alliance, blacks recognized in the program of the
Alliance the potential for their own advancement. As they had in the Knights
of Labor, black farmers took it upon themselves to organize their own locals
and then work to win a place in the larger, white-dominated organization.
As early as 1886, when the Farmers' Alliance was just beginning its sweep
through Texas, several groups of blacks formed their own alliances. One
group, calling itself the "Grand State Colored Farmers' Alliance," invited
white Alliance leaders to speak and asked for cooperation with the larger
organization. Another black Texas organization, under the leadership of a
white Allianceman, dispatched lecturers into Louisiana as early as 1887 and
offered to send information to anyone who wanted to "organize Alliances
of this kind among the negro farmers in any part of the South." A third
black Alliance began in Houston County, Texas, at the end of 1886. Although its president and all its delegates were black men, this organization
appointed a white Baptist minister, Richard Manning Humphrey, as its "General Superintendent." It was on the minister's farm, in fact, that the first
meeting of the new order convened. Humphrey had attended Furman College back in his native South Carolina, fought for the Confederacy, and, like
other leaders of the Alliance, taught school and preached as well as farmed
in several states before he arrived in Texas. There, he ministered to several
black churches while living as a farmer.

This Colored Alliance soon attracted a large number of black farmers
and laborers in Texas and named itself the Colored Farmers' National Alliance. In 1888 and 1889, lecturers of both races set out to create new
branches in the nearby Southern states. In 1890, after the merger of his
group with one of the other major black alliances in Texas, the Reverend
Humphrey claimed 1,200,000 members for the organization. Some state
leaders were white, but those in Georgia, Louisiana, and Mississippi were
black. Branches of the Colored Alliance used all the strategies of the white
alliances, including the establishment of their own exchanges in Norfolk,
Charleston, Mobile, New Orleans, and Houston. White Alliancemen were not
quite sure what to think about the Colored Alliance. Leonidas Polk cautioned in the *Progressive Farmer* that "we think the negroes had better let the
Alliance alone," but added, "yet he that is not against us ought to be for
us."

The existence of black Alliancemen was not particularly troubling to
whites either inside or outside the order in the late 1880s. After all, Southern
blacks and whites enrolled in other parallel organizations, such as the major

religious denominations and Masons. Many whites imagined that the Colored Alliance would actually help race relations in the South by teaching black Alliancemen "to love their country and their homes . . . to labor more earnestly for the education of themselves and their children, especially in agricultural pursuits . . . To be more obedient to the civil law, and withdraw their attention from political partisanship." The problem was that black farmers saw different meanings in such phrases; they saw the organization of the Colored Alliance as a chance to show their love for their country, homes, and family by taking a stand against those who kept them down.

In 1889 black farmers in the Mississippi Delta sought to use the Colored Farmers' Alliance to gain immediate help. The Delta was especially volatile because of the large influx of single, young, black male workers in the 1880s. A black organizer with the prescient name of Oliver Cromwell traveled among these men in Leflore County, urging them to trade with the Farmers' Alliance store thirty miles south, in a town called Durant on the Illinois Central Railroad. Cromwell apparently made trips between Leflore and Durant, filling the black Alliancemen's orders. It did not take long for white Leflore County merchants and planters to learn what was happening, for every transaction with the Alliance store cut into their own profits and their control over the black customers. The white merchants and planters sought to persuade their black clients that Cromwell was taking advantage of them, but to no avail; the white men then turned to familiar patterns of intimidation, sending Cromwell a letter emblazoned with a skull and crossbones. Instead of being cowed, 75 black Alliancemen marched into a village in Leflore County "regular military style" and delivered a letter to the white antagonists vowing their support for Cromwell and signing the letter "Three Thousand Armed Men." The whites sent their wives and daughters away and gathered arms.

"The white people all along the line of the Illinois Central Railroad and in every county of the delta are actively preparing for an anticipated general attack by the blacks," a black newspaper from Kansas related in the fall of 1889. "Prominent men with whom interviews have been had are seriously considering the outbreak and arms are being bought on both sides." White leaders shut down black newspapers and halted black excursion trains. Reports circulated that Alliance stores had made guns available to black Alliancemen, albeit "as a regular commercial transaction," and planters resolved to blockade the Alliance store to prevent any further such commerce. The sheriff in Leflore County wired for troops and used a white posse of two hundred to track down troublesome blacks. While the whites who took part said little about what happened in the manhunts deep in the woods and swamps of the Delta, reports had it that 25 black men were killed.

Throughout the South, hearing of such terror, Alliancemen of both races wondered what kind of relationship the black alliance would bear to its white counterpart. "I will give as my experience with the Col. Alliance

that you need not expect to organize the Negro to-day and expect him to
vote with us tomorrow," a white state leader of the Colored Alliance advised
the president of the white Alliance, "but first organize them because their
interest and ours as farmers and laborers are the same and *teach them*. They
will then if called on vote with us for our good and theirs." In the late 1880s
those who believed in the Alliance could only hope that the organization
could discover some way to pull together the black and white farmers of the
region before their multitude of enemies pulled them apart.

Many people found it difficult to maintain their dedication to the Alliance.
In February 1890 a resolution appeared before the Jefferson Alliance to
reduce its quarterly dues from 25 to 15 cents; the next month the secretary
was requested to report the names of delinquent members; the next month
the secretary "was instructed to notify the finance committee to appear at
the next meeting with their report or answer to a charge of neglect of duty."
Money was not the only problem. In June the suballiance appointed a committee of three to "ascertain if possible the Brother who informed the editor
of the Jackson Herald as to the action of the county Alliance at the last
county meeting." By October a Brother Brooks asked for a dimit "and gave
for a reason that he could not express himself on a subject without fear it
would be divulged outside the alliance. After some discussion on the importance of keeping the secrets of the alliance Bro. Brooks withdrew the application."

A rare account by a rank-and-file member of one of the organizations
that fed into the Farmers' Alliance described the inertia that always threatened. "Along in the spring, a man came through organizing an order called
the Brothers of Freedom," Waymon Hogue recalled of his youth in Arkansas.
Hogue and his brother Sam joined, "as did almost every other farmer. We
held our meetings in the schoolhouse and met every Saturday afternoon."
Unlike the Grange and agricultural clubs, the Brothers did not discuss improved farming techniques; instead, the order sought to organize in opposition to the town people. "The merchant, although necessary, was looked
upon as a common enemy, and under the miserable system of business and
farming which prevailed, the people had some grounds for complaint."
Meetings became dull; the members "soon grew tired of lambasting the
merchant and other people who wore store clothes, and we began holding
our secret and business meetings once a month." The order held meetings
on Saturday nights open to everyone. "Women and children attended, and
our programs consisted of readings, recitations, speeches and debates." The
Brothers of Freedom, like their Farmers' Alliance counterparts throughout
the South, found it impossible to sustain the fire of the early days without
some specific measure on which to focus their energies. Meetings of Alliances throughout the South turned to social activities—picnics, barbecues,
and singings—to keep their units going.

Even as many members were losing interest in the Alliance, others were deciding that the organization was just beginning to live up to its potential. The Alliance was fortunate to find an outlet for the young order's energy in early 1889. For many years farmers had wrapped their bales of cotton in jute bagging to protect it during shipment to market. In 1888 a combination of jute manufacturers announced that they were raising the price on their product from 7 up to 14 cents per yard. The new Alliances across the South rushed into action. The Jefferson Alliance noted in May 1889 that "the Brethren ingaged in a very lively discussion of the exchange allso the proprity of using cotton cloth for covering of cotton bailes? which was very interesting and instructive." Two weeks later the Jackson County farmers endorsed the actions of the state and national Alliances at Birmingham "in refusing to contract with any parties for the manufacture of jute bagging." Across the South, state alliances struck deals with textile manufacturers to provide bagging made of cotton instead of jute. Alliancemen paraded in clothes made of cloth bagging, and an Atlanta woman noted in her diary that "immense crowds visited Piedmont Park to-day. Two weddings took place. The bridal parties being attired in cotton bagging. The object of which was to demonstrate to the world that the Alliancemen had abandoned jute to bind their cotton in, and were wedded to cotton for that purpose." The jute trust soon collapsed, and the next year Alliancemen were able to get their jute bagging for only five cents per yard.

Many Alliance members took the success of the jute boycott as evidence of the potential power of united farmers. At the same time, they took the continuing failures of state and local cooperative stores—a considerable number of which closed their doors a year or two after opening—as examples of the way the economic system was rigged against farmers. Banks would not loan to the cooperatives, while non-Alliance merchants and wholesalers colluded against them. The Greenback portion of the Alliance creed became all the more compelling, the edge of the movement's ideology sharper. Alliancemen became more committed to the movement in 1890 than ever before. They believed that the cooperatives had failed not because small men led them but because the commercial system of the United States would not allow them to succeed. The entire financial structure of the country needed to be revamped if the people who fed and clothed everyone were going to survive.

It was in the context of these contradictory currents that the Farmers' Alliance moved into the political arena. At the same time the Alliance had been organizing in the South, in 1888 and 1889, it had also been sending lecturers to states north and west of Texas. The Alliance had enjoyed great success in Kansas and the Dakotas and had won considerable numbers in Colorado, California, and other Western states, where lecturers addressed groups that had begun under the aegis of a separate Northern Alliance. In 1889 the organization hoped to double its membership at a convention in

St. Louis by merging their Southern order with the Northern Alliance, the Knights of Labor, and other farmers' organizations. The failure of many exchanges had persuaded leaders of the Alliance that only national legislation could begin to right the wrongs that held down the farmer. The creation of a truly national organization, with more fully articulated political goals, seemed an essential step in securing for the farmers the power they needed.

The leaders of the much smaller Northern Alliance decided in St. Louis that they were unwilling to lose the identity of their organization in a merger with the Southern Alliance. The Alliances of Kansas and the Dakotas, however, did choose to unite with the Southerners, as did the Knights of Labor, immediately bringing a new political dimension to the Alliance. Many of these new members had been more deeply involved in the Greenback party than most Southerners and had long questioned the inviolability of the two-party system. Ready to break with the Democrats and Republicans, they helped push the Alliance toward a more radical political stance.

In St. Louis, too, the Farmers' Alliance adopted a more national, less Southern, perspective that helped loosen the order from the Democratic party. Leonidas Polk of North Carolina was elected president of the unified Alliance. Although Polk was a Southerner, he was well known for the breadth of his national vision. Polk, an outspoken Unionist who had reluctantly gone with his state and fought for the Confederacy, had called frequently for sectional reconciliation in the years since the war. The election of this magnetic leader helped give the Alliance the coherence and strength it needed as it set out in a more political direction. The platform of the order, reflecting its new, more radical, membership, called for the public ownership of "the means of communication and transportation," the free coinage of silver, and what was to become the cornerstone of the Alliance's efforts over the next few years, the subtreasury plan.

C. W. Macune, the architect of the subtreasury scheme, argued that the period since the Civil War had seen the development of a complex commercial system surrounding agriculture that required far more currency than had its antebellum counterpart. The number of farms, farmers, products, merchants, wholesalers, and consumers had swollen, but the national government had done nothing to expand the money supply. This shortage of currency kept prices low. As a result, when the enormous and continuously expanding cotton crop of the South flooded onto the market in the fall, the farmer found the prices for his commodities lower than he could bear. Cotton prices had fallen in the mid-1880s and showed no sign of recovery at the end of the decade, even as the scarcity of cash in the South kept interest rates and prices for manufactured goods high. Macune offered the subtreasury plan as a more thorough and more precise solution to the problem of agricultural distress than the general inflationary plan of the Greenbackers.

Macune called for the national government to build warehouses—"subtreasuries"—in every county that produced over $500,000 worth of agricultural commodities each year. Eligible crops included the cotton and tobacco most Southerners produced, as well as wheat, corn, oats, barley, rye, rice, wool, and sugar. Farmers could store their crop in the subtreasury to wait for higher prices than those available during the glut created when all farmers sold their produce at the same time. While farmers waited to sell their crops, they could borrow from the government as much as 80 percent of the value of the crops, paying interest at the rate of 2 percent per year and a small fee for grading, storage, and insurance. Under this plan, the Greenback dream of a flexible and expanded currency would become reality; farmers could bypass all the middlemen they believed were taking their profits and holding them in the bondage of the crop lien. Moreover, increased amounts of money would come into circulation, raising farmers' prices and creating general prosperity. In the months after the St. Louis convention, Macune elaborated one dimension of the plan after another in the Alliance's national newspaper, the *National Economist,* published in Washington.

In early 1890, Macune sent lecturers to spread the word to all Alliance members, arranged to have the subtreasury bill submitted to Congress, circulated news of the bill and sample petitions to the suballiances, and encouraged the submission of signed petitions to national headquarters for presentation to Congress. The petitions poured in, with hundreds of thousands of signatures attesting to the need for the national government to take action. Macune, Polk, and R. M. Humphrey of the Colored Alliance testified before the Senate Agricultural Committee. The Knights of Labor, not enthusiastic about this bill that offered little to their working-class constituency, nevertheless contributed their support. Despite all these efforts, and despite a growing sense in Washington that the Farmers' Alliance would soon exert its full weight, the subtreasury bill was buried in committee.

Southern Alliancemen were frustrated by the failure of their bill to get a hearing in Congress but they still did not talk of political revolt. Instead, they worked to pressure their Democratic congressmen and senators to take action, to elect Democrats who would help Southern farmers get what they needed. Many state, county, and local alliances used the "Alliance yardstick" to evaluate candidates in 1890; support for the subtreasury plan usually marked the difference between those who measured up and those who did not, even though the subtreasury was particularly difficult for Democrats to accept. A Republican newspaper from Tennessee savored the situation: "The Democrats are between the devil and deep blue sea on the sub-treasury bill. Their pet subject for declamation has always been the danger of centralization. With inflamed countenances and loose tongues they continually abuse the republicans because, as they assert, the republicans favor centralization." Now the people the Democrats had always counted as the "foundation, the superstructure of that crazy old patch work edifice they call their party, the farmers, have declared for the sub-treasury scheme, a measure that has more centralization in it, smacks more of paternal government than any that has ever been suggested in this country." Indeed, some Alliance members saw matters in just that way. One county alliance published this resolution in a Louisiana paper: "We are opposed to said sub-treasury bill because its tendency towards centralization, it is robbing one man for the benefit of another, and that it is contrary to one of the cardinal principles of the Alliance, 'Equal rights to all and special favors to none.' " An organization built on stringent notions about monopoly and unfair taxation could well have doubts about the subtreasury. Nevertheless, in 1890 the Alliance leadership judged legislators by their willingness to stand up and be counted for the Alliance's most novel and far-reaching reform.

Many Democratic leaders in 1890 refused to adopt the subtreasury, issuing vague assurances to the Alliance instead. In Texas, a group of reform-minded Democrats sought to win Alliance votes by supporting a railroad commission and a 300-pound gubernatorial candidate sympathetic and attractive to the farmers, James S. Hogg. Though Hogg's candidacy and campaign generated much enthusiasm in the countryside, Alliance leaders warned that the Democratic convention had denounced the subtreasury, the true test of Alliance loyalty; radical leader William Lamb began a campaign to break the newly strengthened bonds between the Alliance and the Democrats. The immediate gain of a railroad commission seemed too good to turn down for most farmers, however, and Hogg won. The Alliance now had to fight against a governor that offered the farmers an appealing combination of Democratic loyalty and moderate reform.

The Democrats adopted similar strategies throughout the South. In Tennessee, John P. Buchanan, the president of the state Alliance, received the organization's support for governor but then refused to support the subtreasury because the state Democratic platform had not mentioned the plan. In Georgia, the Democrats elected to the governorship an Allianceman, William J. Northen, even though Northen never gave the subtreasury his unqualified support. In South Carolina, Ben Tillman elbowed his way into power with the votes of many Alliancemen even though he offered no endorsement of the subtreasury.

That these men were seen in 1890 as "Alliance governors" shows just how unsettled the Alliance was during its first confrontation with state politics. The idea of the subtreasury had been publicized for less than a year, after all, and the idea of electing men sympathetic to the rest of the Alliance aims must have seemed more attractive than maintaining strict policies and giving up such heady political influence. The election of governors who belonged to the order would have seemed a mere dream a few years earlier, when Alliance lecturers had first arrived in forlorn Southern counties. The elections at the local level were even more heartening to the Alliance, which elected dozens of legislators in Georgia, Tennessee, North Carolina, and Florida.

There was plenty for the Alliance to be proud of in 1890, and most members looked to the future with high expectations. It seemed that the order had taken control of the Democratic party with a bloodless coup. For those who cared to look, though, the signs of trouble were not hard to find. Throughout the South, the Democrats viewed the Alliance upstarts with barely disguised contempt and distrust. Democratic politicians began plotting revenge almost as soon as the ballots had been counted; as one assured another, "the present craze in Georgia politics will not last and a day for settling old accounts will come and then we can pay our respects to some of the 'Alliance upheavals.' " Little wonder that the Alliance worried about its new emissaries in the Democratic party.

So much depended on what would happen when the men who had been elected with the support of the Alliance took office. The commitment of those dozens of men remained untested and unsure; the temptations to adapt to the Democratic machines were strong and it might be hard to trade the prestige of office for the purity of Alliance doctrine. Getting elected was one thing, exercising power was another. The political drama of the New South shifted to the state capitals. In four states—Alabama, Florida, Georgia, and North Carolina—representatives elected with the aid of the Alliance actually held majorities in the legislatures, and Tennessee Alliancemen constituted nearly half of the representatives. Members of the Alliance anxiously watched the state capitals for the beginning of genuine changes in the tenor of state politics. Democratic stalwarts watched for the same thing, for signs that the farmers' representatives would seize the initiative and force the Democrats to go along or fight back.

The Farmers' Alliance had not turned to unlettered or impoverished farmers to represent them. Yet the men sponsored by the Alliance differed from their Democratic colleagues in several ways. In Georgia, for example, their ranks contained almost no lawyers or businessmen, while nearly three-quarters of the Democrats were one or the other. Only a quarter of the Alliancemen had attended college, while over half of the regular Democrats had done so. Surprisingly, the men elected with the help of the Farmers' Alliance were, on average, a decade older than the Democrats—forty-nine compared with thirty-nine. This meant that the Alliance legislators were far more likely to have served in the Civil War than their non-Alliance counterparts; 60 percent of the farmers' representatives were veterans, compared with only 16 percent of the Democrats. Despite their greater age and military experience, the Alliancemen had much less experience in the legislature; only about one in six had ever served before, while about half the Democrats had been in the legislature in a previous session. In other words, the Democrats tended to be young lawyers, come of age since the Civil War, who had made their way in the new order; the Alliancemen tended to be older farmers and veterans who had played a circumscribed political role before the Alliance swept them into office. The Alliance leaders differed in their wealth and political connections, then, from the rank and file of the organization they putatively represented, and they differed in their age and political experience from the men with whom they had to jostle in the legislature.

Their inexperience showed. "Everything is a mass of confusion to most of them, and would be to any man who has had no experience in this business," reported the Atlanta *Constitution*. There were "the rules of the house, the rules of order and the parliamentary laws that keep a humble man subdued and hemmed in, and he is afraid to move or rise up or stretch himself, or say a word for fear he will break a rule or make a blunder and attract attention and get in the newspapers." The Alliancemen in the legislatures of 1890, with no clear direction on most issues, tended to go along with the rest of the Democrats, whether it came to reelecting a warhorse senator in Georgia, revising the election laws of Tennessee, or abolishing the railroad commission in Florida.

Or writing new segregation laws. Four states—Alabama, Arkansas, Georgia, and Kentucky—wrote their separate-car laws in 1891, while Tennessee, the original leader in the movement, toughened its law that year. Moreover, in the early nineties South Carolina also considered the law. These were the years when the legislators elected under the auspices of the Farmers' Alliance exercised their greatest power, which may seem to suggest that the segregation laws in those states were products of the rising influence of racist and provincial farmers. Yet there is no reason to believe that the representatives of the farmers were any more—or less—inclined to work for racial separation than were other white Southerners. When the Alliancemen arrived in their various state capitals in 1890 and 1891, full of anger at the railroads, they found that segregation was already the trend in other Southern states and in the nation's courts. A segregation law could serve as an easy and concrete way for Alliancemen to express their displeasure with the railroads and to join with other Democrats in a crusade popular among most whites. Just as the Alliancemen left little mark for good on the state legislatures, in other words, neither did they burden their states with racist laws that would otherwise have remained unwritten.

The Alliancemen in the legislatures of 1890 had their reasons for doing so little to change things. The Alliancemen officeholders found they were relatively powerless to solve the immediate problems of the farmer; the states, after all, had no control over currency, over the tariff, or over creating the subtreasury. Moreover, the subtreasury was still a new idea that had yet to be tried in the crucible of widespread debate in suballiances and conventions, and an Allianceman could harbor doubts about the plan and still consider himself a loyal member of the order. Yet the Alliance legislators could have fought back considerably more than they did on questions of state railroad commissions, support for agricultural colleges, land grants, and the like. Inexperience accounted for some of their inaction, and so may have the ambition of which they were often accused—ambition to enter into the

Democratic elect, to hold on to their offices even if the Alliance disappeared. Also, the Democrats handled the Alliance newcomers with the adroitness of practiced politicians, treating Alliance colleagues with gestures of respect, adopting calls for soft money into their platforms, making them feel at home. In all these ways, the influence of the Alliance became weakened, neutralized. For all the talk about "Alliance legislatures," the Alliance in fact had little effect for good or ill in 1890 and 1891.

The years of 1890 and 1891, then, saw the Alliance caught in many different poses. In some communities, the movement was just getting established, its suballiances engaged in the first exciting debates over the best strategies for farmers to help themselves; in others, suballiances, having struggled with failed cooperatives and state exchanges, had already begun to divide or fade away. In places such as Arkansas, the Alliance had already tasted political loss and was fighting for its life; in others, Alliancemen had just forced cocky Democrats either to bow to the subtreasury or to go down in defeat. In some places, such as the Mississippi Delta, black Alliancemen had been killed after organizing; in others, the joining of the white and black Alliances seemed to hold out the best hope for attaining the things farmers of both races needed. It was clear to many inside and outside the movement that the next year or two might well determine the fate of the Farmers' Alliance and, they believed, the nation.

Chapter 7

Populism

The Farmers' Alliance could not avoid the tensions, promises, and dilemmas of the New South. The order somehow had to remain true to its skeptical, ascetic, and self-consciously traditional values even as it constantly improvised new tactics and coalitions. Centrifugal forces threatened to tear the movement apart while leaders at every level tried to hold the ideology and the organization together.

Southern farmers were adamant in their defense of rural life but all too aware of its limitations. They were furious at those who profited unfairly from the new industrial and commercial order but knew that the changes brought undeniable benefits to the South. They were dismayed by the politics of sectionalism but proud of the Confederacy. They were distrustful and contemptuous of black politicians but eager for black votes. They were hopeful about the Alliance but fearful about abandoning the Democrats. Farmers chafed under the Democrats' fence laws, tax rates, and convict leasing but hated the Republicans' tariff, pensions, and force bill. As the stakes rose, the story of the farmers' revolt became the story of these countervailing pressures, of unrelenting danger and vaulting possibility.

Alliancemen knew how the politicians of both parties would reply to the threat of the third party that more and more people mentioned in 1891: "Stick to the grand old party. Don't bolt the convention, or scratch a ticket," an early chronicler of the Alliance mocked in the usual Democratic language. "Don't act independent, you'll be one of the other fellows if you do. Vote 'er straight. Don't kick. Help us this time. If you don't see what you want in our platform, ask for it. Wait till we get there, and we'll show you how 'tis done. Whoop 'em up down in your neighborhood. Use dynamite and lay it on the other party. Use whisky. Vote 'em wherever you find 'em, niggers and all." Other Democrats were annoyed by the Alliance's failure to differentiate between the two major parties: "The people—the tillers of the soil—have not been treated fairly, but it is the Republican party which has wronged them while the Dem. party has championed the people's cause."

Even as Democrats worried and Alliance leaders spoke more militantly and more confidently about the movement's political effects, economic depression eroded the foundations of the order. Cotton prices relentlessly declined in 1890 and 1891 to their lowest price in thirty years and showed every sign of continuing their descent. The depression that was eventually to wreck the entire country had already begun in the South, undermining business as well as farms. The crop lien, the object of so much Alliance energy, brought down farm after farm as desperate merchants pushed for repayment in any form they could get. "Hundreds of men will be turned out of house and home, or forced to become hirelings and tenants in fields that they once owned," wrote a Georgia Alliance editor. "The doors of every courthouse in Georgia are placarded with the announcement of such [sheriffs'] sales." A local Alliancemen wrote that "our county is in a terrible, terrible condition. Out of fifteen hundred customers at one store only fourteen paid out."

Faced with the loss of everything, farmers began to withdraw from the Alliance. Wholesalers pushed the Alliance cooperatives for immediate repayment—and often the cooperatives could not pay. One after another of the cooperatives that had attracted so many farmers into the movement collapsed throughout 1890 and 1891. These failures coincided with the farmers' increasing realization that the Alliance legislatures were not helping them in any significant way. All the talk in the suballiances seemed wasted, all the dues, all the estrangement from skeptical Democrats, all the tension with the storeowners, all the raised hopes. Throughout the South, tens of thousands of farmers left the Alliance in 1891; in Virginia and Tennessee, in North and South Carolina, the membership declined from 10 to 30 percent. In Georgia, one of the strongholds of the movement, two-thirds of the members left in 1891, to be followed by many more the next year. The only states where the order seemed to be gaining strength in 1891 were Alabama and Texas. Women, so important to the early history of the Alliance, faded from public view as political machinations in the all-male electorate replaced the social emphasis of Alliance meetings.

The losses and the gains were hard to gauge, for the decline of the Farmers' Alliance coincided with the movement's increasing political visibility as a third-party threat, its expansion in the Midwest and West, and a tangle of political events in the South. Democrats used the electoral and legislative machinery still in their command to control the state houses and to encourage diverse groups of Alliancemen to split their votes. Increasingly, the powerful press of the Democrats turned against the Alliance. Papers that had praised the organization a few months earlier now smirked at its ideas and leaders. Tom Watson in Georgia and Reuben Kolb in Alabama, in particular, were vilified for their betrayal of white supremacy, common sense, the memory of the Confederacy, good government, progress, and any other virtue Democratic editors could invoke.

During the winter of 1891–92, as everyone waited to see what would happen in a long-anticipated convention of reform groups in St. Louis in February, some of the incongruities and impossibilities began to be resolved. Farmers who thought the Alliance had no business even thinking of a third party rushed back to the Democrats. Farmers who considered the subtreasury unconstitutional, too expensive, or politically dangerous dropped out of the Alliance. Farmers who had joined in the hopes of immediate help in the marketplace left as the cooperatives failed. Politicians who had joined the Alliance in the easy days of the late 1880s, when the order asked little of its members, returned to their old party as the stakes got higher.

Those Alliancemen who remained through all these trials made a stronger commitment to the Alliance. Even as the formal Alliance organization lost members in 1891 and 1892, men who had not joined the original movement found themselves attracted by the possibility of a new political party in the South. Even farmers too independent, poor, cheap, isolated, or cynical to join the Farmers' Alliance could and did become excited by the possibilities of a third party in the South. Farmers who lacked the interest or the means to participate in cooperative stores, weekly meetings, theoretical debates, or mass picnics might be engaged by the different sort of emotions and commitments created by an overtly political party. Even men who had originally seen little appeal in the Alliance might well be disgusted at the way the Democrats bullied the opposition in local elections, legislative halls, and newspaper columns in 1891 and 1892. As the Alliance and the Democrats broke into open warfare, many voting farmers watched with mounting interest and excitement.

Black men, balancing an especially precarious set of aspirations and fears, sought to define their place in the movement as well. The Colored Farmers' Alliance had built a formidable organization in the late 1880s with little help from the white Alliance. In the St. Louis convention of 1889 the black Alliance had met separately, though the white Alliance had officially acknowledged the black order by exchanging visitors to committee meetings. The awkward maneuvers between the races continued at the Ocala, Florida, convention of 1890, where the Colored Alliance again held a separate but simultaneous meeting. The black Alliancemen suggested to the whites that representatives of the two organizations create a confederation "for purposes of mutual protection, cooperation, and assistance." The white leaders eagerly agreed and both sides "heartily endorsed" a pledge to work together for "common citizenship . . . commercial equality and legal justice."

It was hard for black people to know which way to turn in the summer of 1891. Over the last year, the white Alliance had publicly professed its support for the Colored Alliance, had funded some of the white organizers of the movement, and had denounced the race-baiting tactics of the Democrats. This show of support gave black farmers confidence in the Alliance, for the white Republican allies of black voters appeared as ready as always to desert their black compatriots at the first opportunity. On the other hand, the black and white Alliances did not agree on political matters of key importance to blacks, such as the Lodge elections bill and black office-holding. Just as important, black and white Alliancemen tended to occupy antagonistic positions in the Southern economy, the positions of tenant and landowner. Even a group filled with determination to overcome racial barriers as a matter of principle could not have reconciled those conflicts. The white Farmers' Alliance did not have that conviction.

To top it all off, blacks in the Colored Alliance differed deeply among themselves as well. The tensions, internal and external, erupted in the early fall of 1891 when some within the Colored Farmers' Alliance sought to use its newfound strength to tackle the most pressing problem facing its membership. Over the preceding years the amount paid to cotton pickers had declined. R. M. Humphrey, the white general superintendent of the Colored Alliance, suggested that the pickers go on strike on September 6 until planters agreed to pay a dollar a day instead of the prevailing rate of 50 cents. Humphrey claimed that 1,100,000 pickers throughout the South had sworn to strike if called. Other leaders of the Colored Alliance, black men, argued against the plan. In Atlanta, E. S. Richardson, the superintendent in Georgia, argued that "this was not the purpose of our organization; that we were banded together for the purpose of educating ourselves and cooperating with the white people, for the betterment of the colored people, and such a step as this would be fatal." Whites agreed: Leonidas Polk argued that the demand for higher wages was "a great mistake on the part of our colored friends at this time. With cotton selling at 7 and 8 cents, there is not profit in it." The *Progressive Farmer* urged white Alliancemen to leave their cotton unpicked rather than cave in to the black demands.

Many in the Colored Alliance seemed eager to take some concrete action despite these admonitions, and Humphrey allowed his call for a strike to stand, organizing the "Cotton Pickers' League" to lead the effort. A group of black men attempted to begin a strike in East Texas but a planter summarily fired them and announced the conflict "immediately settled." The strike flared up again, though, a week later and several hundred miles away. It was led by Ben Patterson, a thirty-year-old black man from Memphis who

traveled to Lee County, Arkansas, to organize the pickers. He won more than
25 men to his side, several of whom combed the area trying to win more
converts to the cause. When black workers on one plantation got into a fight
with the strikers, two nonstrikers were killed. While a posse went out in
search of Patterson and his allies, a white plantation manager was killed and
strikers burned a cotton gin. Eventually 15 black men died and another six
were imprisoned. The white Alliance immediately sought to dissociate itself
from the strike and distanced itself from R. M. Humphrey. The Colored
Farmers' Alliance fell into sharp decline.

The ideas and tactics of the farmers' movement continually shifted because
they were the products of people in especially unstable circumstances. Landholding farmers occupied an anomalous class position in Gilded Age America. In an era increasingly concerned with appearances, the farmers fell
behind. Farmers, even in their own minds, became identified with makeshift
and awkward clothes, unpolished language, and red necks. One Georgia
farmer chafed at "a lot of city dudes who consider every person born in the
country a stupid ass who was created as a beast of burden to support them
in their gingerbread life."

   Although landowning farmers, like professionals and businessmen, profited directly from their labor and could expect their assets to grow over time,
they were like common laborers in that they worked with their hands out-
doors. By the 1890s the plantation ideal had corroded for a quarter of a
century. Not many young people of education seemed to fix their ambitions
on the countryside. On the other hand, most Southerners, whatever their
class, had ties to a farm of one sort or another. And farmers, the majority
of Americans in 1890, still enjoyed a sense that they held special political
virtue. The farm pushed people away at the same time it drew them back.
The tensions surrounding farm life would have been strong even if crop
prices had been high, even if the government seemed to be trying to help
the people who fed everyone else. Low prices and official disdain made the
tensions and conflicts intolerable.

   The anxieties of rural life appeared in the bitter words about self-
sufficiency that flew around the farmers' movement. Ironically, the belea-
guered farmers often demanded a more active role in the market while
merchants encouraged farmers to withdraw from trade. City and town editors
urged farmers to grow more of what they needed at home rather than spend
all their efforts producing a surplus for market. Even Alliance papers that
reluctantly admitted that such a strategy might make sense in the short run
vehemently denounced the notion that farmers should remain self-sufficient;
self-sufficiency "requires the farmer to step out of the line of progress, to
refuse to avail themselves of the industrial improvements of the nineteenth
century, turn back the wheels of civilization three thousand years, become a
hermit and have nothing to do with the outside world." As another North

Carolina Allianceman put it, "True wisdom does not sanction a retrograde movement . . . to 'hog and hominy.' "

Farmers were not afraid of modern America, but they were angry that national progress seemed to be built on their backs. "None are more ready than the farmer to admit the usefulness" of commerce, a spokesmen for the Alliance argued, "but it is the false system upon which they are based, and the legalized frauds which are practiced upon the public; the excessive charges, extortionate rates of interest and exorbitant profits which the public is compelled to pay into their hands, that they war against." As the president of one state Alliance put it, "Steam and electricity have centralized our government. The National Government alone has power to correct these evils and to it and not elsewhere must we look." Such language was common throughout America in the 1890s; it reflected neither paranoia nor an especially astute grasp of political economy. Indeed, the farmers were so furious because their complaints seemed so obvious, the wrongs so blatant. To them, the Democrats and Republicans were the ones who seemed unable to understand what was happening to the country.

No single idea or policy drove the farmers' movement, only a general insistence that the government pursue actions more equitable for the majority of citizens, become more open in its actions, and be willing to go beyond shibboleths. The two major parties had log-jammed the country's national government, the Alliancemen thought, and any tactic that might break that jam was worth discussing. The movement's multiplicity and flexibility were especially evident in the Alliance portrayal of the nation's financial system. Leaders in Texas and some editors elsewhere in the South supported greenbacks and a throughgoing revision of the nation's money policy in 1892; their advocacy was sophisticated and subtle, but too radical and too ambitious even for most Alliancemen. The subtreasury plan, on the other hand, was important because it served as a sort of bridge between the promises of the abstract and ambitious greenback plan and the immediate problem of the crop in the farmer's field. The plan would address the rural South's most pressing concern without changing the basis of the entire American economy. It seemed increasingly clear, though, that the subtreasury would demand an involvement of the federal government that most Americans—and many farmers—found exorbitant, dangerous, and perhaps unconstitutional. As early as the summer of 1892, therefore, many Alliance newspapers focused their energies on winning a greater proportion of silver in the metallic base of the existing system. The inclusion of silver, its advocates argued, would permit the money supply to expand, prices to rise, and prosperity to return—all without fundamental change or risky experimentation.

The beginning of 1892 confronted the Farmers' Alliance with an extraordinarily complicated set of circumstances. The order was losing members every day and remaining cooperatives faced imminent failure. The two most important leaders, Leonidas Polk and C. W. Macune, fell into open disagreement and distrust over tactics and leadership. The Colored Farmers' Alliance had challenged the basic class and racial relations of the rural South, only to be crushed. Democrats and Republicans who had been cautiously receptive to the movement in years past now denounced the movement as a threat to the white South, the black South, the national economy, the national party system, property, democracy, and freedom.

Yet Alliancemen could find reasons for optimism as the order approached the St. Louis convention in February of 1892. Many farmers who had been resistant to the Alliance before now seemed deeply interested in a third-party effort; perhaps an election year was just what the order needed to bring it new life. The People's Party had coalesced the previous year in Cincinnati and many expected the St. Louis convention to witness the merging of the Farmers' Alliance with the nation's other insurgent groups; Terence V. Powderly of the Knights of Labor was in attendance, as was Frances Willard of the Women's Christian Temperance Union. Everything seemed to depend on the movement of the Southern Alliance into a third party, and Leonidas Polk immediately removed any doubts in his opening remarks to the convention: "The time has arrived for the great West, the great South and the great Northwest, to link their hands and hearts together and march to the ballot box and take possession of the government, restore it to the principles of our fathers, and run it in the interest of the people."

In Washington, the two major parties struggled in an especially tumultuous political arena. The control of Congress won by the Republicans in 1888 had soon proven to be a burden for the party. Labeled by their opponents the "Billion Dollar Congress," Republican lawmakers had enacted virtually everything for which they had campaigned. To the great majority of white Southerners each law was anathema or disappointment: the Lodge "force bill," the highest tariff in American history, increased pensions for Union veterans, a bill that would siphon money from the embarrassingly bloated treasury into black schools in the South, a largely ineffectual compromise on the financial system.

Voters elsewhere in the nation were disappointed with the Republican Congress as well, and the Democrats regained control of the House in 1890. With a Republican President and Senate on one side and a Democratic House on the other, the national government accomplished little as the economic condition of the country deteriorated and dissident parties gathered strength. The Democrats could barely wait for the 1892 presidential election. Grover Cleveland began to plan for another run for the White House and it soon became apparent that he would win his party's nomination. The party made no sign of trying to conciliate the Alliance and its demands.

Most observers looked to Leonidas Polk to win the presidential nomination of the People's Party in 1892. He had gained stature with his strong but moderate leadership of the Farmers' Alliance and had become recognized as a thoughtful proponent of the third-party strategy. Moreover, Polk was virtually unique in his ability to attract both Southern and non-Southern support; despite his role in the Confederacy, Polk had been speaking and working for many years for sectional reconciliation. His experience in Washington as president of the Alliance had brought him into contact with national leaders and national problems. Everything in Leonidas Polk's life seemed to be pointing toward success at Omaha.

Then, in what may well have been the decisive moment in the history of the Southern Alliance and the People's Party, Polk suddenly died on June 11. For months, Polk had taxed his body in his work for the movement that had given him national fame. While those close to him could see the toll his labor was taking, Polk refused to slow down for long. While preparing in Washington to travel to Omaha among trainloads of Confederate veterans, he died of a hemorrhage of the bladder. He was fifty-five years old. The People's Party had lost, as a newspaper observed just before Polk's death, "the one man in the country who can break the Solid South."

Now the People's Party flailed about in an effort to find someone to take Polk's place. Finally, they turned to James Baird Weaver of Iowa, a former Union general and presidential candidate for the Greenbackers. Although the party balanced Weaver with Virginia's James G. Field, a former Confederate, the loss and disappointment were considerable. When Weaver went on the campaign trail, Democrats gleefully set out to disrupt his speeches and intimidate his followers. Jeering, catcalls, and foot-stomping smothered his words, while nightriders and thugs taunted his audience. In Georgia, the situation became more desperate at each stop. Democrats assaulted Weaver and his wife in Macon, throwing rocks, tomatoes, and rotten eggs. "The fact was, Mrs. Weaver was made a regular walking omelet by the southern chivalry of Georgia," one laconic observer noted. Weaver abandoned his tour of the South.

The People's Party—or "Populists," as they came to be called by their opponents and then by themselves—tried to mobilize their forces using the tactics of the Farmers' Alliance. Tom Watson's *People's Party Paper* urged its readers on, conveying an image of the party as a healthy, family-oriented, religious, sane alternative to the bluster of the Democrats. Populists such as Watson spoke in a self-consciously straightforward language that tried to cut through the thick tangle of emotion, memory, self-interest, race pride, and fear that tied white Southern men to the Democrats. Sometimes the voice was intimate, the voice of one friend to another. "Stand by your principles and vote for Sally and the babies," Watson urged in the spring of 1892. "What is 'party' to you?"

The Democrats, though, had tradition and "common sense" on their side. From the viewpoint of regular party men, the Populists were misfits, men who could not hope to win the game if they played by the regular rules of politics. Confronted with the third-party challenge, Democrats suddenly discovered that the perpetually detested Republicans were really not so bad after all—and the Republicans suddenly found a soft spot in their hearts for the Democrats as well. "We are sure there are too many honest Republicans and Democrats to allow this crowd to get there just yet," a Republican up-country Tennessee paper assured its readers about the Populists. To the Democrats and Republicans, the third party (the demeaning label most frequently used by the Populists' opponents) seemed to want something for nothing. Doggerel in the Atlanta *Constitution* put these words in the mouths of the Populists: "Rah for labor! Smash your neighbor! Ring out the old— Ring in the gold and silver, too! Whiskey free for you and me; Milk and honey. Fiat money; Inflammation and damnation." "Poor, pitiful, sinful cranks!" one Democratic paper commented in mock sympathy for the Populists and their lack of sophistication. "Not one of them were ever inside a bank, and know as little as to how they are managed as a hog does about the holy writ of God."

The national elections of 1892 offered real opportunities and real dangers for the Populists. Events in Washington and the South pushed the party ahead—perhaps faster than it was ready to run. Cleveland's nomination at the head of the Democrats despite his well-known advocacy of the gold standard and the national convention's failure to adopt the Farmers' Alliance platform drove many undecided Democrats into the Populist rush. The Republicans' recent billion-dollar Congress and force bill prevented disenchanted Democrats who might have thought of moving into the Republican party from doing so. Meanwhile, the Southern cotton economy continued to decline. On the other hand, the death of Polk left no one at the head of the national Populist organization to give the movement direction. The Farmer's Alliance deteriorated and Populist policies developed no farther. No one came forward with "some better system" than the subtreasury, and yet that idea, without the nourishment provided by a vital Farmers' Alliance organization, seemed to atrophy. One situation offered both opportunity and danger: despite the attrition of the black vote by legal disfranchisement in several Southern states, a majority of Southern blacks still voted in the late 1880s and early 1890s. Neither white Democrats nor white Populists could afford to ignore black voters.

Because the arrogance and greed of white Republicans had eroded the bonds between black voters and the party of Lincoln, in the early 1890s black leaders made it known that they would consider switching their allegiance to a party that would grant them a fairer deal. Moreover, the increase in the numbers of propertied blacks in towns and in the country in the 1880s created voters who might be more independent and who might have influence among their compatriots. All these contingencies made the already heated conflict between Democrats and Populists even hotter. There were many precincts, counties, and congressional districts where black votes might swing the election.

White Populist leaders set the tone of any interracial negotiations. While black voters and leaders could respond in a variety of ways to white invitations or threats, they could not publicly initiate interracial politics. White Democrats, for their part, had already staked out their positions, had already struck their deals; they could not appear to be scared or intimidated into making new public overtures to black voters. Populist leaders, on the other hand, were starting from scratch. They had to make their positions on race known and they often experimented to find a rhetoric and a strategy that would permit them to win black votes without losing white ones. As a result, tactics varied widely. Populist candidates in Alabama, Louisiana, Virginia, North Carolina, and Texas, while using the same behind-the-scenes techniques of winning black votes that the Democrats used, made few public statements about black rights and opportunities. Although influential blacks worked among black voters, attended conventions as delegates, and spoke from the same platforms, the Populist press of those states published few accounts of interracial cooperation and said little about the implications of the third-party crusade for black citizens in the 1892 campaign. It was to no white candidate's interest to profess anything in public that could be construed as racial heresy and to no black leader's interest to heighten racial conflict. It was to everyone's interest to be on the winning side, however, and winning often required clandestine dealing. In most states in 1892 the racial struggle surrounding Populism remained a quiet and desperate sort of hand-to-hand combat.

In Georgia, though, the Populists publicly confronted the political meaning of race in the New South in 1892. Tom Watson was both temperamentally inclined and strategically impelled to articulate what others refused to say. Watson had been elected to Congress in 1890 as an outspoken Alliance man from Georgia's Tenth District, running as the Democratic representative of rural counties against the entrenched power of the Democrats in the cotton-mill city of Augusta. The same savagely honest language that got Watson elected kept him in the forefront of the farmers' movement and on the front page of the state's newspapers. An early convert to the third-party strategy after Ocala, Watson clashed so repeatedly with the Georgia Democratic party that he considered himself, with cause, "the worst abused, worst disparaged, worst 'cussed' man in Georgia." In Washington, Watson became the most active and aggressive Populist legislator in the House, introducing bill after bill to keep the demands of Ocala before the nation. He published a book about the Populist challenge whose subtitle was *Not a Revolt; It Is a Revolution,* a book the Democrats attacked on the floor of Congress with blistering criticism.

So when Tom Watson came back to Georgia to campaign for reelection in the spring of 1892, he was the focus of great attention. Crowds lined the

Tom Watson, from The Arena, *April 1892.*

railroad track beyond the bounds of his district, and when he got home farmers carried him on their shoulders to a stage. An enormously popular speaker and soon sole owner of the *People's Party Paper,* Watson was never at a loss for an opportunity or a desire to make his opinions known. His opponent, James C. C. Black, seemed the embodiment of the town-based Democrats: a lawyer, a Confederate veteran, and a Baptist deacon. He argued that "it is un-American and un-Christian, arraigning one class against another," that he was "a friend of all classes," and that the farmer's economic troubles were "exaggerated." The campaign was brutal. Watson fumed when Populist candidate James Weaver was driven from Georgia by Democratic mobs, and he warned that the intimidation was only a foreshadowing of what was to come in the fall elections. A black Populist and a white Democratic deputy were killed in separate shootouts. Democratic leaders professed that they would prefer to see Black elected than Cleveland, so great a threat did Tom Watson present. Even Cleveland declared himself almost as interested in the Georgia election as in his own.

In the midst of this important campaign, Watson wrestled with the role of race in Southern politics. Both in his speeches and in the columns of his newspaper, Watson discussed what many thought should not be discussed. His appeal to blacks was relatively simple. "There is no reason why the black man should not understand that the law that hurts me, as a farmer, hurts him, as a farmer; that the same law that hurts me, as a cropper, hurts you, as a cropper; that the same law that hurts me, as a mechanic, hurts you, as a mechanic." His guiding idea was that "self interest rules," and that as long as white and black Populists each followed their own—congruent—self-interest, they could work together. As long as blacks were on Watson's side, he would help preserve their vote.

Other Georgia Populists were willing to join him. "Why is it that the Democrats are hallooing negro supremacy so persistently?" a man who signed himself "Hayseeder" wrote to the *People's Party Paper* from Burke County, Georgia. "Are they not citizens of the State, holding the same rights under the law that the white man does? If so, isn't it better to give them representation in the convention [as the Populists did in the Georgia State Convention in 1892], that they may know for whom they are voting, thereby getting them to vote with the white people at home than to ignore them till the day of election and then try to buy or force them to vote, thereby driving them into the Republican party?" The correspondent asked these questions because he was "no politician, but simply an old hayseeder, who was born under a Democratic roof, rocked in a Democratic cradle, sung to sleep with a Democratic lullaby, and have always voted with the Democratic party, but finding, in my humble judgment, that the party had drifted from the landmarks of its founders." Another Populist taunted: "Listen at old false Democracy in his dying hours. See him swell up till his lungs are fit to burst, and stand on his tip-toes and hollow at the top of his voice, 'N-i-g-g-e-r Equality,' until his breath is gone."

Such pronouncements were indeed remarkable in the New South. Just a few months earlier, no white would have thought of saying them. The political exigencies of the Populist revolt put good orthodox white men in the position where the racial injustice of their society suddenly appeared to them as injustice. When it was *their* allies attacked and threatened, *their* voters bullied and bought, *their* morality challenged, suddenly things appeared different than when only white Republicans were implicated. The very fact that such language could surface so quickly in the New South is one more indication of the fluidity of the political world and of race relations. We should not be too quick to write off such statements as self-serving campaign tactics or as the idiosyncratic rantings of isolated men. Populist speakers stood on platforms in front of hundreds of hard-drinking, fired-up white men and said these things, stood on platforms alongside black men and said these things. In the context of 1892, they were brave things to say.

There were other things said on those platforms, though, things that were also a part of the white Populist view of blacks. In the same speech where Watson talked of the self-interest that should unite blacks and whites, he also made very clear what he did not mean. "They say I am an advocate of social equality between the whites and the blacks. THAT IS AN ABSOLUTE FALSEHOOD, and the man who utter[s] it, knows it. I have done no such thing, and you colored men know it as well as the men who formulated the slander." The *People's Party Paper* made a point of including the responses of blacks in the audience as a sort of chorus, showing that black men recognized the wisdom of Watson's words. "It is best for your race and my race that we dwell apart in our private affairs. [Many voices among the colored: 'That's so, boss.'] It is best for you to go to your churches, and I will go to mine; it is best that you send your children to your colored school, and I'll send my children to mine; you invite your colored friends to your home, and I'll invite my friends to mine. [A voice from a colored man: 'Now you're talking sense,' and murmurs of approval all through the audience.]" What Watson did not want blacks to do was to vote Republican "just because you are black. In other words, you ought not to go one way just because the whites went the other, but that each race should study these questions, and try to do the right thing by each other." Watson, in other words, wanted blacks to support Populist economic policies but not to expect anything besides economic unity.

The language of racial fairness appeared adjacent to casual arrogance in the pages of Watson's paper in the summer and fall of 1892. "The Democrats are whooping up the negro. While the interests of white and colored laboring men are identical, the interest of both and the general welfare demands that governmental control should rest in the hands of the more intelligent and better educated race," wrote a man from Wilkes County. Whites sought to play off divisions among blacks, caricaturing urban and educated blacks in the process. "To the colored farmers and laborers of Georgia I appeal. You who suffer as we suffer, who, through cold and heat, rain and shine and all kinds of weather, carry this State Government and its rascally officers in sweat, don't be fooled by those rascally town foppish negroes who are bought by Democratic leaders to catch your vote." In the same issue that contained this appeal to black voters, the *People's Party Paper* lashed out at a Democratic paper that supposedly said that a Populist speaker, while in the minority in a crowd, "did have a majority of the FARMERS AND OF THE NEGROES. Why this slur on the farmers? Why couple them with negroes?"

It should not be surprising that black voters approached the Populists cautiously. Even a black man who joined Watson on the speakers' stand during the heat of the 1892 campaign gave an extremely wary endorsement of the third-party cause. Anthony Wilson, elected to the Georgia legislature in 1882 only to be voted out by white Democrats—including Watson—on the basis of contested election returns, gave black rights greater weight than they had in Watson's speech. "It is right, it is just that we colored men should stand by each other as the white men stand by each other," Wilson began, directly contradicting Watson's appeal that blacks divide their votes, "and I would not give a snap [of] my finger for the colored man that would sell his birth-right, or his State-right. Now, so far as you are concerned, when you come to cast your vote, exercise an intelligent discrimination in casting it for the cause of right and justice—I am not going to say how that should be." Not exactly a rousing call to arms for black Populists, but not words to comfort white Republicans or Democrats, either.

It was dangerous for a black man to say more. One of Watson's most assiduous allies was a young black minister, H. S. Doyle. Despite many threats of assassination, Doyle made 63 speeches for Watson. As the campaign drew to a close, Doyle received threats of a lynching. He went to Watson for help, and Watson sent out a call to gather supporters to help protect his black ally. Two thousand men appeared, heavily armed, after hearing rumors that Watson himself was in danger; they stayed for two nights. Watson announced at the courthouse "that the humblest white or black man that wants to talk our doctrine shall do it, and the man doesn't live who shall touch a hair of his head, without fighting every man in the people's party." "Watson has gone mad," a Democratic paper warned. Although the two thousand would not have rushed to save the black man alone, the event took on a momentum and racial meaning of its own. White men, after all, had rallied to support a leader who had boldly breached the wall between the races.

The Populist overtures to black voters encouraged Democratic candidates to make their own pledges. William J. Northern, a one-time Allianceman who renounced the subtreasury and won the Georgia governorship on the Democratic ticket in 1890, increased his support for black schools and made forthright and repeated denunciations of lynching. As a result, some black leaders, including the respected black minister Henry M. Turner, supported Northern in 1892. The Georgia governor's closest counterpart was James Hogg of Texas, who also denounced lynching and sponsored rewards for the arrest of lynchers. Black leaders in Texas threw their support behind Hogg in 1892.

Black Southerners could not perceive their "self interest" in the single-mindedly economic terms that Tom Watson preached. They had to move cautiously in a time and place where black men and women could be assaulted with little danger of punishment by white authorities, where hundreds of black men were publicly lynched every year, where black tenants had either to vote as their landlord dictated or lose their place, where all political parties were dominated by white men who treated black supporters capriciously and callously. Even speeches that pleaded for black votes were couched in qualified, reluctant, guarded language that insulted at the same time they implored. Black voters faced political choices even more complicated than those faced by white voters. Populist pleas for the black vote mattered, but black voters were also listening to many other voices that urged, cajoled, or ordered them to vote otherwise.

The 1892 elections unleashed tensions and conflicts that had been building for years. Elections were rough and dangerous in the New South anyway, with drunks, braggarts, and bullies enjoying a license to indulge their weaknesses in public. People feared what the impending elections might become. Throughout the South, both sides used proven tactics of getting out the vote, including the liberal application of liquor, bribery, intimidation, ballot stuffing, and the importation of voters over state lines. The regular Democrats held great advantages in this game, with most of the electoral machinery in their control. James D. Weaver finished far out of the running everywhere, tallying about a million votes in the nation compared with over five million votes for each of his opponents. Grover Cleveland became President once again, with most of the votes of the South in his column as usual.

The third party had a greater impact on the state level. The gubernatorial and congressional candidates of the Populists made strong showings in many parts of Texas. The elections in Alabama and Georgia were extremely close, but it was the familiar story: Black Belt counties were counted heavily enough to more than counterbalance white votes elsewhere. A congressional investigator found that "Negroes who had been dead for years and others who had long since left the county" showed up in the Democratic tallies, along with the names of men who had never existed. Tom Watson and his supporters in Georgia watched as the Democrats in his district openly stole the election, counting twice as many votes in Augusta as there were legal voters. Although the Populists had done their best to counter those Democratic increments with added votes of their own in rural counties where they held the ballot boxes, it was clear to them that they had been defrauded of the election. "Who believes it?" Watson asked about the result. "Not the Democratic bosses who stole the ballots. Not the managers who threw out returns. Not the newspapers who have to 'cook' their news with such care. Not even the candidates who received the stolen goods. Nobody believes it. Least of all do we of the People's party."

It was hard in 1892 to know just who voted for the Populists, and historians ever since have been trying to untangle that mystery. Class or race interests, already complex, became even more so when refracted through the political system. Southern politics in the age of Populism, despite the apparent simplicities of black versus white, town versus countryside, and rich versus poor, were extraordinarily intricate. A close look at the way voting returns meshed with economic and demographic conditions may reveal patterns not immediately apparent from correspondence and newspaper accounts.

Since there were not enough town folk to outnumber the angry farmers, the question has to be why some farmers voted for the Populists while others did not. The starting place is clear: in most states, especially those of the lower South where the Populists were strongest, the higher the percentage of blacks in a county, the less likely Populists were to win. The most obvious reason for this pattern is that the possibilities for fraud, intimidation, persuasion, and violence directed at black men were much greater in the Black Belt than elsewhere. Voting returns from the Black Belt cannot be accepted at face value for reasons that congressional inquiries and outraged Populist editorials made all too clear.

A large black presence in a county, though, had effects other than the mere opportunity for manipulation by Democrats. Black Belt counties possessed a social and political order quite different from that of other counties in their states. First of all, many whites in heavily black counties tended to be better off because they owned land that black tenants worked for them; these landlords, who often lived in town and were closely tied to the merchant elite, were too satisfied with the status quo to listen to the Populists. Just as important, poorer white men in heavily black counties had fewer opportunities to build autonomous parties and groups. Those whites were often tenants or customers of richer men, often bound by ties of debt, obligation, or gratitude to the bulwarks of the Democratic party. The poorer whites also tended to belong to the same churches and sometimes to the same families as their wealthier neighbors. There were many social and economic reasons, then, for tenants and small farmers in the Black Belt to shun the Populists.

There were political reasons as well. Despite class differences, whites in the Black Belt often felt compelled to maintain political unity, whether by consensus or by force, against the black majority. Blacks, after all, had held political power fifteen or twenty years earlier in those counties and had struggled to maintain a living Republican party in the years since. Those Republicans were often anxious to cut a deal with the Populists to help dislodge the Democrats; they had the power of numbers and organization among black voters to offer the insurgents, and in dozens of counties such coalitions won in the early 1890s. It did not seem inconceivable that black and white Republicans could regain some of their old power if white Democrats let down their guard, if a version of the force bill were enacted, if the Democrats lost the presidency.

As incongruous as it may appear, too, considerable numbers of black men, with varying degrees of willingness and enthusiasm, voted for the Democrats in Black Belt counties. As white Republicans in the nation, state, and county increasingly banded against their black compatriots, it began to seem that black voters might do just as well to forge political alliances with the powerful whites in their own districts. In the short run, the Democrats had far more to offer blacks than did the third party. A Georgia Populist bitterly complained in the wake of the 1892 elections that though the whites in his county voted for the new party, "the negroes voted with the opposition, with some few exceptions. What the promise to have their names on the jury list did not bring into the fold of the 'dear old Democratic party,' the lavish use of 'red-eye' and money did." A black man might well decide that his appearance on a jury in the next session of his county court, or even hard cash in his pocket, was worth more than a hypothetical subtreasury plan that must have seemed far away.

Although a heavily black electorate strengthened the hands of the Democrats, a heavily white electorate was no guarantee of Populist success. In Kentucky, Tennessee, Virginia, and North Carolina, the Populists did best in counties where blacks made up a considerable part of the population and won virtually no support in the almost entirely white mountain districts. White mountain Republicans, long persuaded that the Democrats were a drag on progress—just as the Populists charged—turned to their own party for relief. The same kind of social and economic ties that bound Democratic whites to one another in the Black Belt bound Republican whites to one another in the mountains. As a result, the Populists won few votes in Appalachia even though white farmers there faced none of the racial constraints on their voting confronted by potential white Populists in the Black Belt.

In Georgia and Alabama, on the other hand, upcountry whites proved to be some of the strongest supporters of the Populists. Most Georgia and Alabama upcountry whites—unlike their counterparts in the upper South—had been neither staunch antebellum Whigs nor wartime Unionists and had not been willing to go over to the Republicans after the war. On the other hand, their interests often conflicted with the Democratic powers in Montgomery and Atlanta as well as with the Democratic rings in their county seats, and throughout the 1870s and 1880s the farmers of the Georgia and Alabama upcountry had experimented with ways to exert their own political voice without deserting to the Republicans. Those regions had been strongholds of independent and Greenback movements and were willing to listen to other dissident voices. They listened to the Populists when they arrived on the scene.

Even the strongest statistical likelihood, of course, could be circumvented by a persuasive speaker, the influence of friends, effective organizing, or a particularly obnoxious Democratic employer. Even the most powerful tendencies could be overridden by a powerful personality, as when Tom Watson led his heavily black Georgia Tenth District into the forefront of the Populist movement. Such leaders were scarce, though, and if the Populist movement as a whole were to succeed it would have to win in counties without cities and without heavy black majorities. An examination of those predominantly white rural counties in the five most successful states for the Populists—Georgia, Alabama, North Carolina, Arkansas, and Texas—reveals a strong pattern. Populist votes tended to increase in counties where the concentration on cotton was strong but where the land was poor or relatively unimproved.

That does not mean that there was a simple or straightforward connection between the misery cotton caused and Populist voting. Populism was strongest in counties where white farmers still owned the land they farmed, not in counties where the crop lien had stripped land from former owners. Populism does not seem to have been a product of particularly isolated or backward rural counties. The presence or absence of railroads made little difference, and the cumulative size of village population counted for little in every state except North Carolina—where Populist votes actually increased as town population increased. Stores did tend to be dispersed in Populist counties, which probably reflected a lack of towns. Populist votes tended to be few where manufacturing was present, though the relationship was weak.

Populism, in other words, grew in counties that had seen the arrival of the new order's railroads, stores, and villages but not its larger towns and mills. The Populists tended to be cotton farmers who worked their own land, though it was land that produced only with reluctance. Living in counties that were predominantly white but had no strong Republican presence, these farmers felt they could, indeed must, break with the Democrats.

The Populists, judging from their words and their backgrounds, wanted a fair shot at making a decent living as it was being defined in the Gilded Age. There is little evidence that Populist voters wanted to return to the "hog and hominy" days of their fathers, abandon railroads, or withdraw from the market. The state with the largest Populist presence of all, Texas, attracted men who took anything but a cautious approach to their economic lives. They had risked everything to move to the farming frontier and were determined that their risks would not be in vain. They were farmers, with all the ideological, social, political, and economic connotations of that word—not small businessmen or petty capitalists—and they wanted a fair place in market relations as producers and as consumers. The Populists' language rang with disdain for monopoly capitalism and monopoly politics, for Populists saw both as recent perversions of a political economy that could have been democratic and equitable. The Populists did not urge that their communities return to the way things used to be. Instead, they insisted that the new order be brought into alignment with the ideals of American democracy and fair capitalism.

Such a vision had radical implications in late nineteenth-century America. Far from being conservative, it sought to change the way the government and the economy operated. The Populist campaign revealed the radical component always latent in mainstream American ideals: a persistent and unmet hunger for vital democracy, a constant chafing at the injustices of large-scale capitalism. Those ideals, usually held in suspension by a relatively widespread prosperity and by a wide and expanding suffrage, could, given the right conditions, coalesce into powerful and trenchant critiques of the status quo. The raw material for such critiques lay all around the farmers, in the messages of Christian equality they heard in their churches, in the messages of the Declaration of Independence they heard at political rallies, in the ideals of just and open market relations they knew from Jefferson and Franklin. Amidst the many injustices of the New South and in the context of the Farmers' Alliance and Populist party, these ideals worked their way to the surface.

A straightforward and interest-driven critique of the jute trust could become, under pressure of debate and study, a critique not only of monopoly, but of the entire way business had evolved. A straightforward critique of the Democrats could become, under pressure, a critique not only of the Bourbons, but of institutionalized parties, politicians, and winner-take-all politics. The farmers' latent notions of justice and equality could, under pressure, even lead into positive reconsiderations of the place of black men in Southern politics.

The Populists, confronting their immediate problems with commonplace notions of justice, found depth and meaning in those notions they had suppressed. The radical implications of their ideals had been dimmed by decades of slavery, war, defeat, resentment, poverty, and injustice. They had been obscured in the North, in the West, and in Washington by greed and arrogance. The enormous influence of big money in the political parties had perverted both democracy and the market. Many thinkers and groups longed for the recovery of the best parts of the American heritage in the Gilded Age, but it was left for the Populists to launch the most powerful crusade for that purpose.

Tom Watson told the Populists in the winter of 1892 that "you stand for the yearning, upward tendency of the middle and lower classes." It was their very ambition that made them "the sworn foes of monopoly—not monopoly in the narrow sense of the word—but monopoly of power, of place, of privilege, of wealth, of progress." Such yearning, the fuel of Populism, burned in the hearts of young tenants and patriarchs of large families, in wary upcountry farmers and planters willing to experiment with new crops, in men who had been passed over by the courthouse clique or whose children were mocked or ignored by the merchant's children. It burned in men who rode from farmhouse to farmhouse to minister in body or spirit to those hurt by a heedless New South. Populism took its power in 1892 from anger and pride. It would not rest with the defeats it suffered in that year.

Signs of hard times became ever more obvious in 1893 and 1894. Strikes erupted in several places, most visibly in the coal mines of Alabama and

Virginia and on the docks of New Orleans. At the end of 1894, a Louisiana paper sadly observed that the year's passing was "regretted by none. It was, without a doubt, the hardest year, financially and otherwise, that people have experienced for a long time." The year 1895 was not to be much better. The countryside, already besieged by the ravages of the Gilded Age, was devastated in the early 1890s. The price of cotton fell relentlessly, reaching a level where it cost more to grow the crop than it was worth.

Watching in 1894 as the Farmers' Alliance collapsed, the Republicans staged a comeback, and Grover Cleveland foundered in the depression, the *Nation* argued that "all danger of the Populists becoming a serious factor in politics in the far Southern States seems to have gone by." The party was indeed waning in most Southern states, never to revive. Though Populists in Alabama, Georgia, and Texas were still gaining strength and numbers in 1893 and 1894, the Democrats escalated their fraud and violence. Reuben Kolb in Alabama and Tom Watson in Georgia lost in 1894 just as they had lost in 1892, with inflated Democratic votes. In Texas, too, a stronger Populist vote proved to no avail.

The only path to power for the Populists in the next elections, therefore, seemed to lie in compromise, in building bridges to other aggrieved groups. Increasingly, silver seemed to exert the greatest attraction to the greatest number. Many historians have portrayed the turn to silver as the perversion of Populism, a cynical or shortsighted attempt by late-arriving politicians to gain power while abandoning everything the Farmers' Alliance had built. In these critics' view, the call for silver embodied little that was good about the Populists, especially their thorough critique of American political economy. The silver appeal was so bland and shapeless, these historians argue, that virtually anyone could, and did, swear allegiance to it. The most influential historian of Populism has argued that the silver crusade was merely a "shadow movement," a weak and derivative caricature of the real spirit of the agrarian crusade.

From the viewpoint of the men who had built the Alliance out of the Greenbacker crusade, such a judgment is fair. Silver attracted many voters who wanted no significant change in America. "It is indeed demoralizing to real, honest silver men," Louisiana's St. Landry *Clarion* moaned, "to see the manner in which the cause is being murdered by spoilsmen, and old political barnacles who see in it a chance to regain a seat around the pop table by hoodwinking the people into believing that the next parish and ward campaign should be fought on a silver line." Any politician might try to use the issue, "Republican, Populite, Mugwump, Sugar Teat, Independent, Democrat; anything, anything, just so he knows enough of the English language to say 'I am for silver.'" Because most Southern Democrats had long been championing silver, the turn toward silver was a turn back toward the old party, even if people had grown to hate the old party.

From the viewpoint of those who felt the Populists had to win political power to retain their credibility in the eyes of American voters, however, silver seemed a means toward further reform. Silver permitted a much shallower commitment both to reform and to an understanding of the nation's financial system than the greenback and subtreasury plans demanded, but silver nevertheless became a vehicle for the same class divisions and even class analysis that the Farmers' Alliance had deployed. The demand for silver was merely the surface manifestation of a far deeper cleavage in America.

The silver issue was extraordinarily volatile; it carried a heavy symbolic burden, the pent-up frustrations and ambitions of the entire postwar era. Precisely because silver seemed so reasonable, so mild a reform, gold supporters' frantic opposition appeared that much more selfish and narrow. Silver, unlike the subtreasury, promised, its advocates claimed, to help all working people and debtors, not merely farmers in counties that produced a large amount of cash crops. Silver, unlike government ownership of the railroads, promised to make the capitalist economy more equitable without risking damage to one of its most important institutions. Silver was something that millions of angry people in America could adopt as the first step toward hope.

Radical Populist leaders thus found themselves in a quandary. In their eyes, the rush to silver was a lemming-like rush to disaster. To abandon all the programs that gave their party its reason for being was to kill the party. These men called for a path down the middle of the Populist road, as the phrase went, fusing neither with Democrats who called for silver nor with Republicans who called for honest elections. The Populists might not be able to win in 1896, but they would live to fight another day, their flag and their cause unsoiled by alliance with erstwhile enemies.

All across the South, leaders wrestled with the complications of the impending election of 1896. While many Southern states had seen the farmers' movement already fade away, in other states the issues and the personalities of Populism were still very much alive. Georgia and Texas Populists proudly marched straight down the middle of the Populist road, while Alabama and North Carolina Populists were prepared to strike fusion arrangements with other parties. The strong personalities of individual men, such as Tom Watson or Marion Butler in North Carolina, swayed some of these decisions. Some of the decisions came by default, when the Populist party in a state was simply not strong enough to stand on its own. Some of these decisions codified cooperation that had already begun between the Populists and Republicans. Most were difficult, constantly affected by new events on the local, state, or national scene. "Like a Kaleidoscope," one Populist wrote, "every turn brings new and unexpected combinations."

Many Democratic leaders felt that no matter who they nominated, they would be unable to defeat the attractive and popular man who would in all likelihood be the Republican nominee: William McKinley of Ohio. Several men who did not belong to administration circles were put forward for the Democratic nomination. William Jennings Bryan of Nebraska was one. Too young at thirty-six to be thoroughly tarred with the brush of Democratic responsibility and failure, Bryan thought he was just what the Democrats needed in 1896: young, energetic, pro-silver, an effective campaigner, a Westerner. His famous "Cross of Gold" speech persuaded his party that Bryan was right.

The debate over fusion that had torn at the Populists throughout the 1890s now turned to the national level. Some Populist party leaders had counted on both the Democrats and the Republicans to put gold men forward, but Bryan's nomination upset that easy plan. Now the Populists had to decide whether to support Bryan and silver or to put their own nominee in the field. The mid-roaders and the fusionists waged a desperate battle at their convention in St. Louis, fighting over the definition and the future of the Populist movement. Delegations from Texas and Georgia led the fight for the purists, while delegations from the East and Midwest pushed for fusion with the Democrats. In an awkward compromise, the Populists nominated Bryan but then nominated Tom Watson for the vice presidency. The entire maneuver had been full of misinformation, withheld knowledge, and lies; none of the principals involved would have permitted the deal had he known of the true course of events.

Things did not get any better as the campaign progressed. For months, the Populists were afraid to notify Bryan officially of his nomination for fear he would decline it. Bryan made a point of ignoring Watson, who suffered a steady barrage of bitter attacks from fusionist Populists, from regular Democrats, from Republicans, and from the press in general. He gave as good as he got, denouncing the Populist leaders who had fathered the bastard ticket of Bryan and Watson. Every state Populist organization seemed to follow a different route through the campaign, a different way to make the best of an impossible situation. While the election was close in many states, McKinley won all the populous states of the North while Bryan won every Southern state except Kentucky and West Virginia, and he lost those two states narrowly. McKinley triumphed by a margin of 600,000 votes.

There was really no bright side to 1896 for the Southern Populists. The momentum built up over the preceding decade dissipated as the movement flew in many directions at once. Even those who believed in the cause with all their hearts could see that the party had suffered a crushing blow with Bryan's defeat and the party's loss of unanimity. "Our party, as a party, does not exist any more," Watson admitted. "Fusion has well nigh killed it. The sentiment is still there, but confidence is gone."

The year of 1896 marked a turning point in Southern politics. A Republican President once again held the White House, espousing doctrines that few white Southerners supported; the Republicans controlled the House, Senate, and presidency for the next fourteen years. The Democrats at home had been badly shaken, discredited by their weakness and by their flagrant injustices at the polls. Many townsmen, manufacturers, and workers lost faith in the old guard Democrats even though they were unwilling to vote for the Populists. The Populists had lost their sense of separate identity but had attained none of their goals. Southern politics churned under the surface.

Chapter 8

≁ ≁ ≁ ≁ ≁ ≁ ≁ ≁ ≁ ≁ ≁ ≁ ≁ ≁

Turning of the Tide

As Populism rose and then fell, other parts of public life in the South witnessed their own contests. Southern women joined compatriots from the rest of the country to agitate for the vote and women's rights. Black Southerners found—or had thrust upon them, depending on their point of view—a new spokesman who gained the attention of the nation. Disfranchisement rushed to a conclusion, marked by cynicism, empty words, and bloodshed. The hope unleashed by Populism seemed long distant. A new kind of reform took its place, well intentioned and productive of good, but not as democratic or as deep as the changes of which many Southerners had dreamed just a few years before.

Young women, far more athletic than their elders had been, were encouraged to take exercise. An article entitled "A Woman's Beauty Partly in Her Own Power" published in, of all places, the *Southern Planter*, told readers that "the day has passed for admiring pale, young women with hour-glass waists, unable to eat more than a few mouthfuls and ready to faint away at a moment's notice. The modern standard and ideal are different, demanding the glow and vigor of health as indispensable requisites to beauty." Some of the accompanying changes proved a bit disconcerting at first. Annie Jester reported from college that she had received her gymnasium outfit and it was "nothing but full loose *bloomers* and blouse or shirtwaist! . . . I dread the idea of putting them on." Prudence Polk of Tennessee remembered the challenge of swimming in the 1890s. Thrilled at the chance to swim in the ocean, "I hurriedly put on my ravishing bathing suit and went in swimming without any stockings. My aunt was in complete distress, saying that I had disgraced the family as a result of my careless immodesty." Fortunately, not many saw and the Polks were far from home.

Bicycles became all the rage among female Southerners bold enough to ride in public, although older people and many religious folk considered the bicycle intrinsically unladylike. One experienced rider offered this advice to girls who wanted to take up the sport without offending: "Sit straight, ride slowly, have the saddle high enough, use short cranks, never, never chew gum, conduct yourself altogether in a ladylike manner and sensible people will not shake their heads in disapproval when you ride." In the mid-1890s, when the bicycle craze hit, women pedaled throughout the South. Ministers bemoaned the innovation, but a New Orleans newspaper thought women were "going to ride a wheel in spite of red-hot sermons. . . . The female on the bicycle is the new woman in the process of evolution." A Virginia paper agreed that the bicycle "may have the effect of more rapidly developing the 'new woman,' by cultivating in her a spirit of independence of action."

Southern white women became "new women" in other ways as well in the 1890s. "Southern women have in the past five years resorted in many states to their constitutional right of petition upon the question of property rights, 'age of consent,' and the licensed liquor laws," Josephine Henry pointed out in her 1894 article, "The New Woman of the New South." "They have pleaded for admission into state universities, and asked for a division of state funds to establish industrial or reform schools for girls. . . . They have asked that women be placed on boards of all public institutions for the benefit of both sexes, and in many cases sought and obtained the county superintendency of public schools." Women helped plan for Southern states' exhibits at the World's Fair in Chicago and at the Atlanta Exposition, where the Woman's Building quickly established itself as the most popular attraction. Women took over the cause of school reform in some states, becoming, in the process, ever more confident of their abilities and their rights. Women's clubs proved to be fertile sources of ferment for all kinds of troublesome issues, ranging from opposition to the South's penal practices and child labor to agitation for votes for woman suffrage.

The debate over woman suffrage in the South began in Mississippi's 1890 constitutional convention, though women had not yet formed a suffrage organization the state. One newspaper used census figures to show that if white women were allowed to vote there the black majority would become a white majority; the paper found it incomprehensible that an "ignorant, besotted, prejudiced, immoral, worthless negro man" should be able to vote when a "refined, educated white woman who owns property, pays taxes, and performs all the duties of citizenship" could not. A lawyer delegate from Meridian introduced a measure that would enfranchise all women who owned, or whose husband owned, at least three hundred dollars' worth of Mississippi real estate. To avoid the distinctly male environment of the polling place, women would have their votes cast by male stand-ins; no females could hold office.

Mississippi men reacted to the idea with a mixture of open contempt and a show of chivalry. Who would want to see "pure, noble, lovely woman" lured from her "beautiful, modest, feminine sphere" and lowered to "the common level of a ward politician"? A persistent strain of self-laceration echoed in their responses, betraying a fear that Mississippi's white men had grown so weak as to need the help of their women in politics. "Are the white men of Mississippi no longer men, that they must ask women to come to their rescue and save them from an inferior class?" one editor asked. "Must men cower behind petticoats and use lovely women as breast-protectors in the future political battles of Mississippi? God forbid." Such a tactic "aims to unsex our ladies, and then place them to man (?) the battlements which the men are unable to defend against negro supremacy." To add the worst insult of all, propertied black women would be permitted to vote while the wives of the state's white poor men would not. The proposal for white female suffrage quickly faded.

Nevertheless, women suffrage leaders began to pay more attention to the South after the debate in Mississippi. Laura Clay of Kentucky, who had been active in her own state in the 1880s, was persuaded by letters from Mississippi that white women elsewhere in the South were ready to be organized. Clay complained at the national convention of the National American Woman Suffrage Association in 1893 that the organization had ignored the South, placing no Southerners on the board of directors and never holding a convention in the region. Soon, a campaign in Clay's home state testified to the power of women in Southern politics and helped put the South on the map of the woman suffrage movement.

In 1893, Madeleine Pollard charged the Honorable W. C. P. Breckinridge, a fifth-term congressman from Kentucky, with breach of promise. Pollard, then twenty-eight years old, declared that she and Breckinridge, fifty-six years old, married, and a Confederate veteran, had for nine years been engaged in an affair. The relationship had supposedly begun soon before she became a student at a Lexington female institute and had been sustained in Cincinnati, New York, and Washington. The young woman charged that Breckinridge had promised to marry her when his wife died, but instead the congressman had secretly married another woman upon his wife's death in 1892. The trial became national front-page news, pushing aside the silver issue and Coxey's Army. Breckinridge, fighting for his political life, pulled no punches: he testified that Pollard had not been a virgin when they first met and that he had been the victim of "a designing school girl." His desperate and unchivalric defense failed, for the jury found Breckinridge guilty and awarded Pollard $15,000 of the $50,000 she had sought.

Breckinridge decided to run for reelection despite his humiliating loss, confident that his male constituency would understand his male weaknesses. Indeed, even though a group of ministers publicly denounced Breckinridge, 2500 men cheered him on in his defiant opening speech. The Women's Christian Temperance Union joined in the attack against the congressman, passing a resolution that condemned the double standard. Breckinridge managed to mobilize at least some women in his behalf, displaying a large floral wreath from the women of his home district testifying to their forgiveness. It was to no avail, as women staged a rally in Lexington in support of an opposing candidate, bringing "thousands upon thousands" of baskets of food and attracting 30,000 people. The conflict soon pitted individual men and women against one another. One woman threatened to take poison if her husband went to a Breckinridge rally; he went anyway and she executed her promise. One man told another that any woman who would attend a Breckinridge rally was no better than a prostitute, not realizing that his listener had taken his wife and daughter to hear Breckinridge speak; he paid with his life for the insult. Newspapers reported that women spurned suitors who supported Breckinridge, and pro-Breckinridge storeowners claimed women boycotted their establishments. Come election day, Breckinridge's opponent won the Democratic primary by 255 votes out of 19,299, the highest total ever recorded in the district. "The Women Defeated Mr. Breckinridge," the state's largest newspaper announced. His political career was over. The woman suffrage movement had been bolstered.

Advocates for female voting organized in the towns and cities of Tennessee, Georgia, and Texas. Questions simmered within the Women's Christian Temperance Union over whether to work for the vote. "We have known for years that, *individually*, nearly every woman in the unions of Atlanta is a suffragist at heart, perhaps not for full suffrage, but for municipal suffrage with an educational qualification, or at least for the liberty to vote against saloons and on school questions," a Georgia woman wrote in 1892. Southern politics were corrupt to the core; seeing the Georgia legislature from the gallery "made a suffragist of nearly every Atlanta W.C.T.U." woman. Warren Candler, a leader in the Georgia prohibition campaign, argued, however, that "W.C.T.U. suffragists have hurt the cause of prohibition in the South more than all other causes in the last several years." The vote for women would unleash the votes of black women and women without children, swamping the good people and postponing prohibition for fifty years. "Besides," the minister concluded, "we believe the whole basis of the womens suffrage movement unscriptural and sinful." For a young woman to join the movement was to risk her marriage prospects; for an older woman to join, one veteran recalled, required "strong purpose and heart" to "brave the caricatures from the artists' pencils and the malicious and undeserved reproach from the pens of editors and literary critics.''

The WCTU provided the forum for similar debates in South Carolina. Women had held a conference in Greenville in 1890 and in subsequent years Virginia Durant Young gave speeches around the state at WCTU meetings. In 1892, the National American Woman Suffrage Association appointed Young secretary for the state and she began to organize the South Carolina Equal Rights Association. Some 60 women joined from 19 towns ranging in size from Chitty and Frogmore to Columbia and Charleston. Young distributed pamphlets, wrote hundreds of personal letters, and sent articles on woman suffrage to South Carolina newspapers. Robert R. Hemphill, a newspaper editor and member of the state senate, amplified Young's efforts; he managed to win 13 colleagues to his side in an attempt to enfranchise women in 1892, but won mainly condescension and ridicule from the state press. Young continued to work throughout the state in 1895, speaking to large audiences and submitting petitions to the legislature.

When South Carolina's constitutional convention gathered in September 1895, suffragists lobbied behind the scenes and gained permission to address the delegates. Governor Ben Tillman dominated the convention in body and in spirit, glowering over the gathering with his one piercing eye. The supporters of female voting argued that white women's votes could aid in the cause of white supremacy. Ben Tillman's estranged brother George supported the vote for women with a property qualification, but the votes lost 121 to 26. Other advocates of female suffrage linked the cause to democracy for all South Carolinians. One of the six black delegates, Thomas E. Miller, called for suffrage for women of both races. Floride Cunningham, from "one of the most cultured and aristocratic of southern families" and one of the "lady commissioners" at the 1893 World's Fair, lambasted the convention. "I deny that the men who compose that body are statesmen, with a very few isolated exceptions; that they are machine politicians who would prostitute humanity for their own selfish ends. Their injustice to the negro is as pronounced as it is to woman." Cunningham wanted everyone who could meet an educational and property qualification to have the vote, including women and blacks. "The reduction of the negro vote in South Carolina is a problem that this constitutional convention has to solve and it is one of grave importance to our supremacy. And I had hoped to see it accomplished without discredit to the race who stood loyally by us during the civil strife, and who still look to us to guide and sympathize with them. ... Truly the moment has come when its women are needed at the polls for its redemption!"

Laura Clay, in national prominence after her victory in Kentucky, went to South Carolina for the convention. "It is because of the awful corruption of politics that we women (who keep the churches going and the preachers from starving, and who don't increase the penitentiary forces) want to come in with mops and brooms and a flood of pure water to cleanse away the corruption," Clay announced. Clay appealed to educated whites, urging them to base the franchise on education and property rather than on race and gender alone. One male opponent responded that to give women the vote would be to instigate the "total downfall of the already tottering domestic fabric"; another, a minister, warned that "there is no such violence of partisanship in the world as the violence of female partisanship. It was the women of the South who fanned the flame of secession, who forced the continuance of the hopeless strife, and who, today . . . are the unrelenting, unforgetting, unforgiving Southerners." Women, far from being evangels of light and forgiveness, would bring even more rancor to Southern politics. The machine politicians ignored the pleas and demands of the suffragists.

Many young Southern white women belied the stereotype of passivity. The clubs they formed, the kindergartens and philanthropic groups they founded, the work they performed, the education they won all marked them as new women. Some went farther, demanding political and legal rights, demanding access to careers of the highest prestige. But the New South left little room for their ambitions. Politicians sneered. Husbands balked. Colleges turned their backs. The white women of the New South quickly discovered the limits of how new the New South would be for them. Desire, determination, and hard work were forced into narrow channels. Despite a renewed campaign in the 1910s, woman suffrage did not come to any Southern state until the passage of the Nineteenth Amendment in 1920. Even then, nine of the eleven states that voted against it were from the South.

Education and towns had offered opportunities for a postwar generation of black Southerners to develop a stronger sense of their own abilities and the injustices they faced, yet they confronted mounting legal and illegal restrictions in every facet of their lives. They struggled to find a way to persuade whites that such restrictions hurt the entire society, to persuade whites to stop the persecution.

The most prominent voice belonged to Booker T. Washington, who leaped to national fame in 1895. He spoke from an impressive platform: Atlanta's Cotton States and International Exposition. Here, in an event symbolized by the phoenix rising from the ashes of defeat, stood the effort of the most successful Southern city of the postwar era to advertise its importance to the nation and the world. The six railroads that intersected in the city of 110,000 people poured money into the impressive undertaking built in Piedmont Park. The federal government appropriated $200,000 for exhibits as imposing as those at the mammoth World's Fair in Chicago two years earlier. A new street railway ran a car every minute from downtown to the fair. The exhibition included buildings dedicated to electricity, transportation, manufacturers, railways, minerals. Opening in September, the fair attracted about 13,000 people a day by November; eventually, the exhibition attracted a million visitors. The national media gave it extensive coverage.

Only two years earlier, Booker T. Washington had been relatively obscure, though he had long been laboring in his rise to the pinnacle of black power. Born in 1856 to a slave woman in Virginia, fathered by a white man whose identity he never knew, Washington had fought his way up from slavery through the means of the Hampton Institute, a black training school established and run by Northern whites. In 1881 Washington had become principal of the Tuskegee Institute, a new black school in Alabama. Washington worked closely with local whites and blacks to build a successful school, winning support from Alabama's legislature, treading a crooked and narrow line between assertion and accommodation. He corresponded with moderate white leaders such as Henry Grady, agreeing with them that racial peace was crucial for Southern economic progress, that economic progress was essential for racial peace.

Washington's philosophy rested on a faith in the training of young black people in practical skills. For the great majority, Washington argued, it was far better to learn how to make bricks or how to cook than it was to learn literature, foreign languages, or philosophy. Washington stressed such a course because it had been his owns means of ascent at Hampton and Tuskegee, because it attracted large sums of money from Northern businessmen, and because it won considerable autonomy from Alabama whites. He did not oppose all higher education for black youths, but he did believe that scarce resources should be concentrated on industrial training. His many black critics argued that without black colleges, there would be no one to teach, no lawyers and doctors, that "industrial" training was in fact training young blacks for menial and outmoded jobs. Booker T. Washington spoke for that large number of Southern blacks who favored gradual, nonconfrontational change. It is thus not surprising that most whites agreed with him.

Washington first attracted the attention of white Atlantans in 1893, when he spoke to the Annual Conference of Christian Workers in the United States and Canada. Although he lectured for only five minutes, he addressed 2000 white listeners. They were heartened with what he had to say. The next year, Atlanta's delegation to the nation's capital in search of federal support for the Exposition requested that Washington join them there along with two black churchmen. At that meeting, Washington spoke last and spoke briefly. He told the congressional committee that "he had urged the negro to acquire property, own his land, drive his own mule hitched to his own wagon, milk his own cow, raise his own crop and keep out of debt, and that when he acquired a home he became fit for a conservative citizen." Both the committee and the white delegation were impressed. Washington and other black leaders worked for a Negro Building, and although the Chicago World's Fair had blocked such requests out of fear of offending the white

South, Atlanta's directors agreed to it. They asked Washington to take charge, but the press of work at Tuskegee prevented him from doing so; instead, he recommended a young black man, whom the directors soon appointed. Washington would speak at the opening exercises, though, along with six white men and one white woman.

Despite the role of black men in winning the federal appropriation and the Negro Building, the black community in Atlanta had misgivings about the Exposition rising in their midst. Convict labor had graded the grounds, after all, and the streetcars carrying visitors to the celebration would be segregated. While blacks who attended the fair could enter all the buildings, they could buy refreshments only in the Negro Building; seated audiences were strictly segregated. A local black newspaper warned that "the Fair is a big fake ... for Negroes have not even a dog's show inside the Exposition gates unless it is in the Negro Building." Blacks from other places had written to the paper asking whether the Fair would repay a trip to Atlanta. "If they wish to feel that they are inferior to other American citizens, if they want to pay double fare on the surface cars and also be insulted, if they want to see on all sides: 'For Whites Only,' or 'No Niggers or dogs allowed,' if they want to be humiliated and have their man and womanhood crushed out, then come." Many blacks boycotted the Exposition.

Ironically, national attention focused on the Negro Building. The national press was more interested in the new modus vivendi of Southern race relations than in the industrial progress the fair had been designed to display. The Negro Building showed that Southern whites recognized that Southern blacks deserved representation and formal recognition, but the building also embodied the new thoroughness of segregation emerging in the South. Blacks insisted that the building be the product of black brains and hands, and it was. Although the planners of the Exposition relegated the Negro Building to a corner of the grounds, more visitors came there than to any other building except the Woman's Building. As if to symbolize the tensions surrounding the Negro Building and the entire black presence at the fair, the entrance to the building bore two large medallions: on one was a mammy, her head tied up in a handkerchief; on the other was Frederick Douglass, symbol of everything Southern whites hated about black assertiveness in the nineteenth century.

A shortage of funds caused the Negro Building to be unfinished when Booker T. Washington arrived on opening day. That was fitting in a way, for race relations were not settled in 1895 in Atlanta or anywhere else in the South. The nation realized that the Atlanta Exposition was to be an important landmark in Southern race relations. Washington's speech was both a sign that whites recognized the millions of blacks in their midst and an attempt by conservative white leaders to encourage Washington's brand of racial progress. Although he had received "not one word of intimation as to what I should say or as to what I should omit," Washington was all too aware that one wrong sentence could destroy, "in a large degree, the success of the Exposition"—as well as his own aspirations and the aspirations of blacks everywhere in America. Washington felt that he had to reassure Southern whites at the same time he reinforced the efforts of Northern white reformers and black leaders who had been struggling for black progress for thirty-five years. He was determined "to say nothing that I did not feel from the bottom of my heart to be true and right."

Washington was not a mere tool of white men. In the 1880s he had publicly attacked the segregation of railroad cars; in the year before his trip to Atlanta he had encouraged blacks to boycott streetcar companies that would separate the races. Washington supported boycotts because such resistance fell in the economic rather than the political realm; it sought to use the leverage of blacks as paying customers to win their fair rights in the marketplace—blacks' best hope for justice, in his eyes. Washington believed in the market as a color-blind arbiter that would eventually award its benefits without concern for race. Black Southerners might as well admit, he thought, that electoral politics offered more danger than promise by 1895. Why not publicly give up that which was already lost, he argued, in order to win goals still within reach? Once black men and women owned their homes, farms, and thriving businesses, once they had their own schools and colleges, once they were willing to divide their votes along lines of economic self-interest, then the vote would return. These were the ideals Washington held as he boarded the train for Atlanta. He hoped he had found the right words to express them.

When he arrived, people thronged the hot city. The opening speeches had been delayed an hour and the crowd had grown restless. At least one white observer felt "a sudden chill" in the crowd when it spotted the black man among those mounting the platform, though he was soon forgotten in the excitement. When it was Washington's turn to speak and former Governor Rufus Bullock announced that "we shall now be favored with an address by a great Southern educator," the crowd broke into loud applause— only to stop abruptly when Washington stood and the white people realized they had been applauding a black man. Bullock added that Washington was "a representative of Negro enterprise and Negro civilization," and the crowd, reassured, renewed its welcome; the black people in attendance, in their segregated section, cheered loudest. Washington began his speech with the late afternoon sun striking him full in the face, but he spoke intently and effectively nevertheless. The audience became increasingly engaged and encouraged by what the black man before them was saying.

Southern blacks and Southern whites should turn to one another in recognition of their mutual needs and interests, he told the audience. Whites as well as blacks should cast down their buckets where they were, cast their lots with one another. That need not involve racial mingling in places where whites did not welcome black people. "In all things that are purely social we can be as separate as the fingers, yet one as the hand in all things essential to mutual progress," Washington assured his listeners. While the white audience roared in relief and approval at the image of the separate fingers, it was the mutual progress of the hand that Washington wanted to stress. The infusion of Northern capital would help black and white alike as the South became more prosperous. The time had come for blacks to put old delusions of office-holding and opera-houses behind them, Washington said, for whites to put old hatreds and recrimination behind them, he implied. White and black should join; North and South should join. When it was all over, ex-Governor Bullock strode across the stage to shake the black man's hand. The editor of the Atlanta *Constitution* announced that Washington's speech "is the beginning of a moral revolution in America." White women threw flowers. Black people cried in the aisles.

The response spread throughout the country as the text of the speech appeared in newspapers. Whites seemed almost universally in favor of what W. E. B. DuBois was later to call the "Atlanta Compromise": the trading of black political activity and integration for black economic progress. Even with the spread of disfranchisement, it was not a fair trade. Politics and integration were concrete concessions with immediate consequences; black economic advancement, on the other hand, was vague, subjective, and gradual. While blacks had indeed been making considerable economic progress, especially in rural landholding and rough industrial wage labor, such progress posed little danger to influential whites. Whites had every reason to applaud Washington's appeal.

Blacks were bound to be more ambivalent. It was wonderful to see a black man win so much adulation, but had Washington given up too much? Segregation was by no means complete in 1895, after all, and thousands of black voters still dared to cast ballots in several Southern states—including Washington's base of Alabama. Was Washington capitulating too easily, easing white consciences too freely? Frederick Douglass had died just the preceding year, and in the wake of Washington's success many people suggested that the mantle of black leadership had passed to the Tuskegee leader. One black man thought the comparison ludicrous, "as unseemly as comparing a pigmy to a giant—a mountain brook leaping over a boulder, to a great, only Niagara." Many other blacks, especially those in the North, agreed, calling Washington "sycophantic," "an instrument in the hands of an organization seeking money gain." One bishop sadly commented that Washington "will have to live a long time to undo the harm he has done our race." Booker T. Washington never won the unanimous support among leading blacks that he won among leading whites.

It soon became common among more assertive black leaders to disdain Washington's compromise. Indeed, as a statement of the desires and intentions of all black Americans, that compromise was grossly misleading. No one other than the white leaders of the Atlanta Exposition ever granted

Washington the role of speaker for his race. In fact, even Washington did not claim to speak for all black Southerners; the Atlanta speech was an attempt to promote himself, his school, and his particular program. He was happy to discourage black politicians, who he thought were doing more harm than good. In his own eyes, he had not surrendered but merely retreated to what he considered the only defensible position on the field.

From that position, behind the trenches and bulwarks of Tuskegee Institute, behind the smoke of his Atlanta speech, Washington built a powerful organization. His war chest filled from the bank accounts of Northern white philanthropists and industrialists, Washington dug in for a long war on white racism. Many of his ends he sought to accomplish through espionage, through infiltrating the ranks of the enemy, through a tight hold on black allies and would-be challengers. He campaigned endlessly in the years after 1895, traveling from one end of the country to the other, giving his Atlanta speech over and over again. Northern black radicals and Southern black leaders of higher education saw Washington as a traitor, giving away too much too easily. What he saw as tactical retreat they saw as surrender.

Yet in towns and cities throughout the South, thousands of blacks had adopted Washington's strategy before they ever heard of him. "We believe education, property and practical religion will give us every right and privilege enjoyed by other citizens," 500 Alabama black men had resolved before Washington's speech, "and therefore, that our interest can be served by bending all our energies to securing them rather than by dwelling on the past or by fault finding and complaining." Washington's rise and fame encouraged such men in their focus on business, property accumulation, and education, even as it assuaged them in their abandonment of politics. A leading black politician, George White of eastern North Carolina, admitted that politics had come to hurt black Southerners. "It is difficult for an illiterate white or colored man to differ in politics without differing in church, business, and everything else." Although a white man might be "kindly disposed" to his black neighbors, "unfortunately politicians have not only dragged the race into politics, but even on the farms and in domestic affairs." From such a perspective, politics was not so much an instrument of democracy as a weapon of those who would set the races against one another. The battles over Booker T. Washington after 1895, then, were arguments among blacks over the best response to an impossible, and deteriorating, situation.

In the year after Washington's speech, as if echoing his bargain on segregation, the United States Supreme Court handed down its famous decision in *Plessy v. Ferguson*. The plaintiffs, a group of black citizens from Louisiana insisting on their right to ride in a first-class car if they paid a first-class fare, argued that the Fourteenth Amendment guaranteed all rights that could be inferred from the Declaration of Independence, that the Constitution was color-blind. Railroads and state governments, therefore, they insisted, could not abridge the freedom of people merely because of their skin color. The lawyers for the state of Louisiana, on the other hand, turned to the growing body of laws throughout the United States, North as well as South, that established a wide precedent for the segregation of railroad cars by race. Separation by race, the defendants argued, was natural, inevitable. Indeed, the Supreme Court ruled that "legislation is powerless to eradicate racial instincts"; its decision in *Plessy* finally legitimated the doctrine of "separate but equal," which had been debated in the South for nearly twenty years. The decision turned less on constitutional principles than on assumptions about the natural course of race relations, the reasonableness of segregation.

The Court voted seven to one against the aspiration of Louisiana's black plaintiffs. The one dissenting voice belonged to Justice John Marshall Harlan of, ironically, Kentucky. Harlan compared the *Plessy* decision to the Dred Scott case of four decades before: the 1896 ruling threatened not only to "stimulate aggressions, more or less brutal and irritating, upon the admitted rights of colored citizens, but will encourage the belief that it is possible, by means of state enactments, to defeat the beneficent purposes" of the Thirteenth and Fourteenth amendments. "The destinies of the two races in this country are indissolubly linked together," Harlan argued, "and the interests of both require that the common government of all shall not permit the seeds of race hate to be planted under the sanction of law." What could plant those seeds more deeply than laws that ruled that "colored citizens are so inferior and degraded that they cannot be allowed to sit in public coaches occupied by white citizens?" To the retort that the coaches were to be equal as well as separate, Harlan replied that "the thin disguise of 'equal' accommodations for passengers in railroad coaches will not mislead anyone, or atone for the wrong this day done." Everyone knew that segregated cars were, almost uniformly, unequal cars. The court's majority looked to the preceding two decades for its validation; Harlan looked to the best part of the nation's ideals.

Most of the country paid little attention when the court announced the *Plessy* decision. Not only did the towering economic and political issues of 1896 preoccupy people, but the law seemed merely to ratify the course of race relations in the years since Reconstruction. The separate but equal doctrine encouraged every level of government in the white South to turn to segregation as a matter of first resort. The doctrine bore the imprimatur of the national government, after all, the patina of fairness, the weight of inevitability. Segregation would have proceeded without *Plessy*, without outright endorsement, but *Plessy* was welcome to those white Southerners who still cared for what the rest of the nation thought, for the validation of federal law. *Plessy* encouraged white progressives as well as white reactionaries to continue the systematic division between the races.

Disfranchisement pushed on relentlessly. South Carolina whites used its constitutional convention of 1895 to add literacy requirements to earlier laws to discourage black voting. Louisiana's revised constitution emerged in 1898 after years of debate and maneuvering in the state's byzantine politics. The document borrowed the literacy and property requirements used in Mississippi and South Carolina but devised what was to become an especially notorious new provision for Southern disfranchisement constitutions. Looking for a more reliable way to exempt poor whites from the restrictions on voting, the Louisiana convention enacted the so-called "grandfather clause." Under its provisions, those who had voted before the beginning of Radical Reconstruction in 1867, or those whose father or grandfather had voted then, could bypass the new requirements by registering during the next three and a half months. Even the men who threw this sop to poorer whites thought the United States Supreme Court would strike the provision down, but it seemed good politics for the short run.

But not everything was settled, not everywhere in the South. Even as other Southern states eviscerated the vote in the 1890s, North Carolina Republican and Populist fusionists constructed intricate and fragile political alliances. Nearly nine of every ten eligible voters in the state cast ballots in 1896, splitting votes among different parties, issues, and men. White Populists helped elect black men in the eastern part of the state and black appointees appeared in remote post offices and county seats. Across the state, black men who had helped sustain the Republican party for decades and had made the victories of 1896 possible received local governmental posts. White critics were outraged at post offices run by black men, where blacks might congregate and where white women had to visit. In such communities, it seemed to whites, the much-bandied "negro domination" had become a reality.

White Democrats began to organize for the 1898 election long before election day, determined to rout the fusionists from power in North Carolina in any way necessary. The Democrats embarked upon a coordinated campaign to push all blacks and their allies from office. Black speakers were misrepresented, black "outrages" fabricated, black assertion exaggerated.

So it was that North Carolina, the Southern state with the highest voter turnout, the most vital black political organization, and the most evenly matched party system in the region throughout the 1880s and 1890s, underwent the most violent convulsion to restore unquestioned and unblemished white power. In the heat of the 1898 campaign, white Democrats did not hesitate to threaten Populist and Republican candidates with death if they refused to withdraw from the race. The crisis grew far beyond the bounds of the usual political violence. Every facet of life seemed touched by racial anger and anxiety, every kind of racial interaction had become tainted by diseased politics.

In Wilmington, the major city of the eastern part of the state, the animosity grew to the breaking point. Whites began to form "Red Shirt" companies to help put down what they saw as black insolence and make sure the coming election removed the humiliating fusion government. A young newspaper editor, Alex Manly—the mulatto son of a former governor of the state—published an editorial in August of 1898 that cut white men to the quick. "Poor white men are careless in the matter of protecting their women, especially on farms," Manly announced, hitting on the one charge guaranteed to drive Southern white men insane with anger. "They are careless of their conduct toward them and our experience among poor white people in the country teaches us that the women of that race are not any more particular in the matter of clandestine meetings with colored men, than are the white men with colored women."

Everything about Manly's statement infuriated white men, from its claims that white men were at fault, to the charge that white women secretly longed for black men, to the implication that Manly himself had firsthand knowledge of white women's secret desire. White men rose to the challenge: "If it does not make every decent man's blood boil, then the manhood is gone, and with it Anglo-Saxon loyalty to the pure and noble white women of our land," responded the *Wilmington Messenger.* "We hope the white men will read again and again that brutal attack . . . and swear upon the altar of their country to wipe out negro rule for all time in this noble old commonwealth." To help ensure that white men did read it "again and again," the Democrats' leading paper in Raleigh printed and distributed 300,000 copies of Manly's editorial.

White women, as usual, were supposed to play silent roles in the unfolding drama of Wilmington. The lines spoken by two of those women have survived, though, and they could hardly be more different. As if on cue, Rebecca Cameron of Washington, D.C., wrote her cousin Alfred Moore Waddell, who was soon to ride the white supremacy campaign into the mayor's seat, to urge him on for the honor of white women. "If the white men can stand negro supremacy we neither can nor will. . . . It has reached the point when blood letting is needed for the health of the commonwealth, and when the depletion commences let it be thorough. Solomon says, 'There is a time to kill.' That time seems to have come so get to work, and don't stop short of a complete clearing of the decks."

Jane Cronly, living in Wilmington itself, watched the events with different emotions. "For the first time in my life I have been ashamed of my state and of the Democratic party in North Carolina," she privately wrote soon after the crisis. The triumphant Democrats, not content with overwhelming victory in the election, insisted that all Republican and fusionist officeholders resign immediately to make room for their newly elected successors. A Democratic committee, trying to keep the hotheads of the party under control, suggested instead that they merely force Alex Manly and his newspaper from Wilmington, announcing to the world that Wilmington's Anglo-Saxon white men were worthy of the name. Manly apparently agreed, but a mix-up in conveying the message prevented the white leaders from hearing of his acquiescence. Furious at what they imagined as his temerity, a white mob—led by many of the professionals and businessmen of the city—marched to Manly's office and set it on fire. A crowd of black men from a nearby cotton compress came into the street, unarmed, and asked, according to a leading white man present, "What have we done, what have we done? I had no answer, they had done nothing." Suddenly, shots echoed from another street, where a similar scene had been enacted. About twelve men, all black, were mowed down. Black leaders, fearing even more bloodshed against innocent blacks, quickly agreed to resign. The entire city government fell into the hands of white Democrats. Black people, despairing, debated whether they should abandon Wilmington, sacrificing their homes and businesses in exchange for the safety of their families. "There was not a shadow of excuse for what occurred," Jane Cronly bitterly concluded in her private memoir.

Thanks to violence and intimidation, North Carolina Democrats were three times as strong in the legislature elected in 1898 as they had been in the 1896 legislature. Whites won most of the local elections as well. The Democrats purged the electorate quickly, passing a constitutional amendment in 1900 that required literacy of all voters except those included under a grandfather clause. "The 'white man's government' is in full blast in this State," a young historian wrote to his advisor at John Hopkins. "If it honestly provided for an intellectual standard for suffrage it would be a good thing." Instead, "it is one more step in the educating of our people that it is right to lie, to steal, and to defy all honesty in order to keep a certain party in power."

Even as white men gunned down black men in Wilmington in 1898, the United States Supreme Court ruled in *Williams v. Mississippi* that poll taxes and literacy tests did not violate the Fifteenth Amendment. The Spanish-American War and its expansionist aftermath fueled a spirit of reconciliation among white men, North and South, and a spirit of disdain for "colored" people. Republican President William McKinley toured the South, to ovations and the strains of "Dixie."

Alabama Democrats had been dreaming of a new constitution throughout the nineties, but the state's tumultuous political situation had kept them from orchestrating a convention. By 1900, the way seemed clear. The disfranchising laws enacted by the convention when it met in 1901 were nothing new: stringent residency requirements, a cumulative poll tax, a literacy or property qualification, a grandfather clause. The Alabama constitutional convention, though, displayed a new kind of complexity in Southern disfranchisement. Inchoate variations among young and old Democrats, among city dwellers and country men, among conservatives and progressives that had worked underneath the surface of Democratic unity now came into visibility. While the South had been fixated on the rise and fall of the Populist crusade, deep changes had been working in the very foundations of Southern political life, within the Democratic party.

From the viewpoint of 1900, the situation of 1890 appeared calm and peaceful, Populism unheard-of, fusion nowhere a statewide threat, tempers relatively low. The decade of the nineties had shattered the carefully tended illusions of white unity and black docility. Many men in political power at the turn of the century had as their formative experiences not the Civil War or even Reconstruction, but Populism and fusion. The average convention delegate at the turn of the century had first been able to vote only after Reconstruction. Those delegates had watched as entire communities became polarized, fragmented, violent; they saw government immobilized when the dominant party devoted all its energies to staying in power. Such delegates seemed determined that subsequent decades would be different.

The voting patterns among the 155 delegates displayed a dizzying array. Without the discipline and ideology of a party arraigned against another party, the delegates reflected what they took to be the concerns of their most important constituents. Thus, delegates from the hill districts voted, as they had back in the days of the early Alliance, for the cheapest government they could get and found that the delegates from the Black Belt counties did the same. Their common identity as farmers, as men who paid taxes on land but could hope for little from government in return, overrode the differences in the political economy of race that had kept the planters in the Democratic party.

Delegates from the cities, on the other hand, who had also been opposed to the Populists, now voted for a more activist government. While the city men had little reason to support the Populists' currency reform, they could certainly see the need for greater control of the railroads, higher limits on state borrowing, and higher taxes to support new and needed services. On some issues, such as the convict lease system and anti-lynching laws, the differences in voting were not so much direct reflections of a delegate's home district as they were of his sense of justice. On other issues, such as railroad reform, most delegates voted to protect and pacify some of the largest businesses in their state and counties. In all these ways, the Alabama Constitutional Convention of 1901, while apparently producing merely one more in a series of disfranchisement constitutions, foreshadowed the course of Southern politics in the first part of the new century. Politics would now be far less focused on the issues of Reconstruction and Redemption.

Virginia held a similar constitutional convention in 1901–2, enacting the usual disfranchising laws. Texas instituted a poll tax and secret ballot law in 1903 and 1905 that seriously cut into the electorate, and in 1908 Georgia tidied up its election laws by adding, in a dispirited referendum, a literacy test and a property qualification to its longstanding poll tax. By the time Georgia acted, every state of the former Confederacy had instituted a poll tax. That tax, the oldest tool of the disfranchisers, also proved to be the most effective of all the laws enacted in the heated legislatures and conventions of the New South. Each kind of law, though, did its share of defeating or discouraging one more kind of voter; by and large, the more restrictions a state piled up, the lower the proportion of eligible men who voted.

By the first decade of the twentieth century the Southern electorate had been transformed from what it had been twenty years earlier. More than two-thirds of adult Southern males had voted in the 1880s, and that proportion had risen to nearly three-quarters of the electorate in the 1890s in states that had not yet restricted the franchise. In the early years of the twentieth century, by contrast, the percentage of voters who cast a ballot for someone other than a Democrat declined to the point of near invisibility in many states. That situation was not to change significantly for generations.

Disfranchisement decreased the electorate even more than its advocates expected. The new laws made it difficult for any kind of transient person to vote; a low proportion of men from the South's growing cities and manufacturing districts went to the polls early in the twentieth century. All across the United States, moreover, competitive party-driven politics faded during these years. Political leaders embarked on less flamboyant means of getting out the vote and reformers agitated for nonpartisan municipal government, the direct election of senators, and corrupt practices acts—all of which eroded party discipline and turnout, all of which had their counterparts in the South.

One widespread innovation of the new politics, widely touted as a reform, became quickly established in the South: the direct primary. Intended to open up the nominating process to candidates outside the dominant rings and cliques, the primary seemed made to order for the white South. Insiders would not have to worry about the party's dissatisfied elements on election day, while outsiders would have a chance to appeal directly to white voters early in the process. The Democrats portrayed the primary as evidence of their devotion to true democratic politics and as a peace-making measure within the party. The Democratic primary would permit vital competition among white men of differing views without risking the involvement of black voters.

To some extent, it did so: in the South as a whole, nearly half of all white men voted in primaries. In two of the least democratic states—Mississippi and Georgia—about two-thirds of the white men voted in Democratic primaries. Disfranchisement, in other words, had not completely killed off white politics. Southern men still found more than enough to argue over, even kill over, in the new politics of the early twentieth century.

Disfranchisement, for one thing, left many former Populists in the electorate. Those who organized and sustained the Alliance and Populism a few years before were not the sort to be purged by the new laws: they were white

farmers who owned land, who could read newspapers and conduct democratic meetings, who would never think of selling their votes. Populism had
not been the party of truly dispossessed and marginal men, after all, but of
angry farmers determined to have a say in the commonwealth in which they
owned a stake. Despite disfranchisement, and despite the rise of cotton
prices and currency levels in the late 1890s, the ideas and spirit of Populism
remained alive in the South long after the death of the party.

Because the Populists were a heterogeneous and complex group themselves, former adherents of the party followed many different paths after its
collapse. Some, such as those in Georgia, continued to vote together with
some effectiveness, following Tom Watson's lead. Others, such as those in
North Carolina, had been intimidated into silence or chose to withdraw from
a political system in which they had lost confidence. In most states, former
Populists looked for new men to stand up for some of the things in which
they believed, looked for new opportunities to pursue their vision of a more
just society. The South after 1900 had no Populists, but had many candidates
who portrayed themselves as—and were perceived as—populist in sympathy
and intention.

The new brand of politician in the post-disfranchised South had to be
flamboyant enough to grab the attention of voters disenchanted with politics,
fiery enough to give voters a reason to register and pay a poll tax months in
advance. He had to have a program to distance himself from the bland
lawyers and party functionaries put forward by the machine. He needed to
set himself apart from the outside-controlled businesses that became even
stronger in the early twentieth-century South than before. He would almost
always find it profitable to play to the fear and anger toward black people
that festered among so many white Southerners despite disfranchisement. In
state after state, a man arose to take advantage of the situation. Jeff Davis in
Arkansas, James K. Vardaman in Mississippi, Andrew Jackson Montague in
Virginia, Braxton Bragg Comer in Alabama, Charles B. Aycock in North Carolina, Hoke Smith in Georgia, Napoleon Broward in Florida, William Goebel
in Kentucky, Coleman Blease in South Carolina—all battled with their Democratic opposition, all cast themselves as reformers.

The men who led the Southern states in the first decade of the twentieth
century were a diverse lot in temperament and image, ranging from the
exhibitionism of Davis, Vardaman, and Broward at one extreme to the busi-
ness-like demeanor of Comer, Aycock, and Montague at the other. What they
had in common was a willingness to use the power of the state government
in more active ways than it had been used before. They shared that willingness partly because the new political environment of disfranchisement and
primaries led influential white people to think that the government would
now be more responsive to their needs and demands without risking black
or Republican influence. Confident that propertied white men held substantial control over the state, influential businessmen and local leaders were

willing, even anxious, to see the government wield power. The many whites who were neither reactionary diehards nor Populist radicals, especially those in towns and cities, now perceived a chance to address some of the problems that most concerned them. The broad, uncoordinated series of reforms called "progressivism" seemed to offer a middle way out.

The most visible progressive reforms began with the regulation of business by state governments. One state after another, one politician after another, turned to the control of corporations as the first priority of the new century. Between 1897 and 1909, virtually every state in the South mandated lower passenger and freight rates. Dozens of new laws, pushed by groups of producers, professional travelers, city boards of trade, and powerful newspapers, helped put teeth in earlier laws. Some states—North Carolina, Georgia, Florida, Alabama, and Texas, in particular—devised especially tight regulations.

Prohibition forces shared most of the ideals of the progressive crusade: control over greedy monopolies and unruly citizens, government intervention, educational campaigns, economic growth. Indeed, prohibition appealed to the broadest array of Southern reformers. Whether they were male or female, religious or secular, urban or rural, leery or supportive of business, educated or uneducated, black or white, Democrat or Republican, all could agree that rooting out liquor and the liquor trust was a prerequisite to any other deep change. As one locality after another enacted local option only to see illegal liquor pouring into their community from nearby towns, prohibition advocates decided that statewide prohibition was essential. They flooded legislatures with petitions, appearing in the galleries, staging parades, dispensing cold water and white ribbons. These progressive reformers were able to do what their Gilded Age predecessors had not: beginning in 1907, they oversaw the enactment of statewide prohibition in one Southern state after another, leading the entire country in what many people thought would be the premier reform of the century. By 1909, one reformer wrote, "the crow can fly from Cape Hatteras in a straight line through North Carolina, Tennessee and Arkansas to the farthest boundary of Oklahoma, and return by way of Mississippi, Alabama and Georgia to the starting point, through prohibition territory."

Despite the successes in reforming business and alcohol, changes in education became the most widely heralded and beneficial of all the reforms of the progressive South. The Southern education campaign had roots deep in the region. Walter Hines Page had helped accelerate the movement in the 1880s with his forthright criticisms of his home state of North Carolina, the most illiterate in the nation. Josephus Daniels, editor of one of the state's leading papers, took up the challenge, and two young graduates of the University of North Carolina in Chapel Hill—Edwin A. Alderman and Charles McIver—began to stage public rallies and organize teachers' institutes around the state in the late 1880s. Meanwhile, the agents of Northern philanthropy lent their aid to Southern education. The Peabody Education Fund supported schools for both blacks and whites, while the Slater Fund put money into black education. J. L. M. Curry, a white Southerner, labored as a representative of these groups to further education in the region. The Hampton Institute, founded in Virginia in 1868, was the focus of much Northern concern and support as it tried to educate young blacks in the ways of artisanal and household labor—the only proper training for blacks, agreed Northern and Southern whites. At the turn of the century, thanks in part to the recent national fame of Hampton graduate and defender Booker T. Washington, many Northern whites eagerly aided Hampton and other vocational schools for blacks.

Even Southern legislatures seemed willing to spend money on education when they would not spend money on anything else—as well they might. The region lagged far behind the rest of the country in literacy and school attendance for both races. The South's high birth rate meant that Southern adults had twice as many children to educate as their Northern counterparts; Southern poverty meant they had about half as much income with which to educate them. Many children attended school only sporadically if they attended at all, and facilities and pay for teachers were dismal. The region had a weak antebellum tradition of public schooling, even for whites. It was only after emancipation that Republicans, blacks, women, and reformers among white Democrats pushed for public schools characteristic of the rest of the nation.

In the first fifteen years of the new century the South instituted longer school years, higher teacher salaries, and thousands of new school buildings. As a result, only half as many Southern children were illiterate on the eve of World War I as in 1900. The widespread adoption of active state support for public schools marked a significant departure for Southern state governments. While state legislatures spent money for whites on longer school years, on lower student-teacher ratios, and on higher salaries for white teachers, those same legislatures allowed salaries for black teachers to decay and class sizes to grow larger. In effect, blacks in the South paid for schools for whites. The more black citizens in a county, the greater the benefits to white students. Pleas for greater equity by blacks and their white allies went unheeded and black schools remained discriminated against for generations.

The crusade against child labor joined regulation, prohibition, and education as key reforms of Southern progressivism. Several states had limited the hours of child labor in the 1880s and 1890s, yet the practice of overworking children was rampant and growing at the turn of the century. Child workers labored in tobacco factories and fish canneries, but textile mills employed the greatest proportion of children: about half of all spinners were under fourteen and nearly nine of ten were under twenty-one. Labor-hungry management was eager for every white hand it could get in the boom years of the 1890s and early 1900s. The advanced machinery adopted by these new mills made child labor especially attractive to management.

The movement to limit child labor took off when an agent for the American Federation of Labor was dispatched to Alabama in 1901 to investigate. She traveled to twenty-five mills and found child labor and its abuses widespread. Trying to establish support for a measure to prevent such labor, she contacted those most likely to respond: women's groups and clergy. One young minister, Edgar Gardner Murphy of Montgomery, took the initiative and began to lobby the legislature. His first efforts at ameliorating the condition of children were slapped down by textile interests, but Murphy organized anew, wider and deeper, turning out pamphlets and establishing national alliances. He carefully avoided attacking the motives of the mill owners even as he exposed the costs of their practices. By 1903, after much negotiation and compromise, the South saw in Alabama the enactment of its first child labor law. A like-minded reformer in North Carolina, Alexander J. McKelway—also a minister in his thirties—joined Murphy the next year to form the National Child Labor Committee to serve as a clearinghouse for local and state efforts.

The Alabama crusade embodied much of what progressive reform was about. Often, reform was not generated from within the political system but was urged on reluctant legislators by organized citizens. It was often triggered and encouraged by people from beyond the borders of the South. It tapped the talents of young, articulate, and self-consciously reformist professionals who appealed to women as well as men. It depended on the creation of a broad network of reform, pulling in other concerned but disinterested people through speaking, literature, and organized clubs. It appealed to an audience beyond the South itself, transcending the kinds of local power that mill owners wielded all too easily. It literally embarrassed the region into action, advertising the South's moral failings before the nation. It was nonpartisan and sought to portray the reform as a purely humanitarian gesture to help the politically voiceless. It dwelt exclusively on the welfare of white people, making much of the degradation of "Anglo-Saxons." It focused its concerns on the welfare of children and their mothers. In all these ways, the child labor reform movement stood as a prototype of progressivism.

As in education reform and prohibition, the intended beneficiaries of child labor reform sometimes resented the efforts of those who would reform on their behalf without their active participation or even consent. While unions had denounced child labor during the National Union of Textile Workers' brief period of power at the turn of the century, workers did not lead the crusade against child labor. When both Carolinas began to struggle with the issue in the first decades of the century, encouraged by a favorable Supreme Court decision, reformers discovered resistance they had not anticipated: the parents of children working in the mills. Children were often eager to go into the mill with their parents, siblings, and friends. What began as play often turned into "helping," which often turned into a full-time job. The job could begin when supervisors needed help on short notice, when families hit by illness or some other misfortune needed the additional money, or when an independent child decided she would rather work than go to school or stay at home to watch younger siblings. The desires of the mills and the needs of the workers conspired to put and keep children in the factories. Both resented the efforts of reformers to enact laws that would limit their choices.

The reformers tended to attack the parents rather than the mill owners and managers. Reformers vilified fathers who allowed their children to support them while loafing around the mill village, even though such men were actually quite rare. Reformers, who valued education above all else, were horrified that white children were kept out of school to earn their small pay. Such childhoods, they argued, could produce only poverty, prostitution, and disease. The same men and women who demanded an end to child labor also demanded compulsory education, paid for by the state. Indeed, one reforming editor told the legislators of South Carolina that "this matter should be considered without reference to what the operatives themselves wish." The progressive reformers thought that their proposals operated on a plane above petty self-interest and should be met the same way. Critics of these plans charged in response that the reformers were replacing government "of the people, by the people, and for the people" with one "of the newspapers, by the school teachers, and for the office-holders." "These people are our people," Governor Coleman Blease of South Carolina protested, "they are our kindred; they are our friends, and in my opinion they should be left alone, and allowed to manage their own children and allowed to manage their own affairs." The mill people rewarded him with their votes and devotion, even as well-meaning people in South Carolina shook their heads. Hindered by opposition on every side, child labor reformers were largely frustrated in their effort to enact effective laws before World War I.

The progressives were hard to pin down. Despite their efforts to regulate business, it is too simple to see the progressives as the inheritors of the Populist spirit of reform. Despite their receptivity to the language and social goals of business, it is too simple to see them as front men for corporate domination. Despite their concern with the downtrodden, it is too simple to see the progressives as champions of the common folk. The progressives saw themselves as mediators, educators, facilitators. They wanted to encourage the forces of progress already active in the South without rocking the boat too much. Such was the cautious style of Southern reform for generations to come.

Part III

CULTURAL LIFE

Chapter 9

Faith

Religious faith and language appeared everywhere in the New South. It permeated public speech as well as private emotion. For many people, religion provided the measure of politics, the power behind law and reform, the reason to reach out to the poor and exploited, a pressure to cross racial boundaries. People viewed everything from courtship to child-rearing to their own deaths in religious terms. Even those filled with doubt or disdain could not escape the images, the assumptions, the power of faith.

People in the New South worshipped in a wide variety of ways. Some counties—especially those on the western edge of the South—might hold only a few Southern Baptist and Southern Methodist congregations, remaining largely innocent of non-Protestants or even Protestant dissidents. Counties in the Piedmont, on the other hand, often contained a wide diversity of other denominations and faiths, ranging from Lutherans to Quakers to Jews. Along the Gulf coast, especially in Louisiana, Catholics predominated over large areas. In the mountains, where Catholics and Jews were rare, a constantly changing array of Baptist congregations flourished and differed heatedly over issues outsiders could barely understand.

Great variability in church membership marked the South. In some rural communities, only about 10 percent of the residents belonged to a church, while in others nearly 60 percent claimed membership. Contrary to the assumptions of many rural churchgoers, a higher percentage of city dwellers belonged to churches than did people in the countryside. It was harder to minister to scattered congregations, harder to keep the church up, harder to pay for a pastor in rural districts. Because it was more rural, then, the South was less churched than the nation as a whole. On the other hand, every Southern state experienced rapid growth in its church population in the New South era, with additions in church membership in every state except Florida and North Carolina outstripping population growth.

Despite their impressive gains, the churches did not enjoy an easy dominion over the South. The leaders and members of the Protestant churches of the South faced obstacles and opponents in every direction. "We have found that good preaching does not fill our church nor save many souls," Joseph Milward of Kentucky wrote in his diary. "Our people are too much in the hands of the world and its mammon." A pious young man wrote from western North Carolina that "Christianity is at low ebb here. People don't go to church as they should, and I am fearful somebody will wake up at the judgment disappointed."

It was hard to keep the churches going. "It is the case nearly everywhere in small communities that a few individuals in each church have all the responsibility to bear, all the money to pay, and all the work to do," an Alabama man complained in his local newspaper. "Hundreds of idle dead-heads sit around complacently from year to year, go out to preaching, get the benefit of the speaker's brains and midnight thoughts, enjoy the social intercourse accorded by church circles and associations, and if they ever think that it takes money to run the thing they never show it by their assistance." Ministers had a hard life; most, it appears, stayed at a church only a year or two before moving on to greener pastures. About half were forced to work other jobs to support themselves. Fewer than a quarter of rural churches had a full-time minister, and over a third of rural ministers served four or more different churches. Even in towns, only about half the churches had full-time, resident preachers.

The black churches confronted all the problems white churches confronted and others besides. Like black political leaders, black church leaders constantly negotiated between the desire of their congregations for autonomy and the need of their churches for money, the demands of assertive young blacks and the caution of more conservative older leaders. Black ministers were central figures in their communities, with a relative importance far greater than that of their white counterparts. "Within his own parish he is practically priest and pope," one observer commented, while W. E. B. DuBois described the black preacher as "a leader, a politician, an orator, a 'boss,' an intriguer, and idealist." A black minister had to be "a horse doctor, weather prophet, must attend the living, bury the dead, tell the farmer when to plant, act as a bondsman for all his people," a white South Carolina Baptist commented.

Some young people resented the conservative influence older ministers held over the black community. "Think of a pastor or pastors, who can neither read nor write, governing, or rather trying to govern large congregations, one-third of whom have been to school and have considerable intelligence," a furious young black man wrote to a black Northern paper from the "sticks" in Arkansas in 1894. These ministers were "continued in their places by old fathers and mothers" who refused to remove the older men even though their preaching was only "a kind of mourn or twang of the voice." Why did their parents work so hard "raising and educating their children if they intend to kill them before they are grown just because they happen to know more than brother John or uncle Harry, who have done what they could, it's true, but are now behind the times in everything"? Congregations split into new churches along generational lines, as young people despaired of removing older pastors.

White church leaders alternately patronized, chastised, and ignored black members of their denominations. White Southerners viewed the black Christians among whom they lived as exotic and mysterious creatures. "As I write the wailing voice of a negro preacher floats over the hills to me," Sarah Huff of Georgia noted in her diary. "He is evidently making some impression on some of the sisters' feelings, and in fact, to judge from the noise it would seem that the whole congregation were united in their effort to make things lively. There they go at it again! worse than ever—jumping, dancing, singing—Pandemonium let loose." Bessie Henderson wrote to her husband off in Washington that he would be shocked to learn that "I went to a negro baptist baptizing in the creek! I never saw anything of the sort and felt a real curiosity." She took their four children, though it was a long, hot walk. "This was a stylish occasion and the preacher, a tall fine looking negro, was dressed in a long black robe fitted at the waist and with a black cap on and looked like a R.C— priest." The fifteen candidates "were dressed in pure white robes and white caps and it was quite picturesque when they entered the water, but the African nature had to assert itself in spite of *robes*. They clapped hands, shrieked, clasped the preacher and were generally idiotic. I am glad to have seen it once."

Most rural communities tried to hold at least one revival a year, often in late summer when the crops had been laid by. The revivals were sponsored by all of the major denominations, with those saved joining any church they preferred. People enjoyed the revivals, partly for the fellowship but also for the preaching. "I do love to hear the old Baptist preach I think they can tell my feelings better than I can tell it myself," Fannie Tilley of North Carolina wrote her cousin after going to a revival. "I think I have enjoyed religion so much better since I joined the Baptist than I ever did before." A teenaged girl exulted, "Oh! we had a glorious meeting last night." Not only was the sermon wonderful, but she along with relatives and neighbors persuaded her brother John and his friend Bud ("we all know what kind of

A black baptizing near Richmond. (Valentine Museum, Richmond)

boys they were") to profess their faith in Jesus. "You never heard such a shouting when they went up as we had. . . . I tell you there was not any quietness there at all and it seemed as if every one had a work to do. Daisy, Lizzie, and myself just walked up those aisles and we could not keep still." John "does not act like the same person."

Educated town whites were bemused and somewhat baffled by white revivals. A group of bicyclists wheeling through North Georgia suddenly found themselves "mixed up with innumerable wagons, buggies, and mounts of indescribable varieties, enveloping us in a choking cloud of dust." They tried riding past, but their vehicles scared the horses and they were forced to wait for an hour at the side of the road. Intrigued by the procession, the cyclists rode to the arbor where 4000 revivalists gathered. When the preacher offered the invitation for the unconverted to come forward, "immediately, a thin, high-pitched voice rose tremulously in an indescribably weird chant, and, after a few wavering notes, it became apparent that this was the special hymn of the occasion." A young man visiting a church suddenly noticed a Mrs. Davis beginning to tremble while the congregation was singing "Rock of Ages." He thought she was having a fit. "Her hat went off and she gave a great shout and sank down again grabbing at my hat as she went. I eluded her grasp and held her down by main force and it took all the strength I had. She murmured things and moved her free arm in the air. At last she sank on my shoulder and told me how she loved me." The next week, he noted laconically in his diary, "we hear that Mrs. Davis was not having a fit she was merely shouting happy. It seems that I kept her from getting happy."

The number of congregations multiplied in response to competing loyalties. "Churches abound in all the small towns," Octave Thanet reported from Arkansas. "They are, one may say, almost too abundant, since they are often scantily supported; the town that might have one church in peace and comfort keeping two or three in discord and leanness." DuBois explained: "Some brother is called to preach. This call is so thunderous, and the confidence that he can 'make a better preach' than the present pastor so obtrusive, till he soon finds that there is little welcome in the sacred rostrum of the old church. He therefore takes his family and his nearest relatives and moves away." In such a way, the number of churches proliferated, often leaving hard feelings on both sides. This process worked among both races, in towns as well as the countryside.

Members of some Protestant denominations viewed others with mild disdain. A well-to-do young woman condescendingly commented that "I was so amused when you asked if Mr. C. was a Baptist—*no indeed* I never would have married him if such had been the case, and I am truly thankful he is an Episcopalian." The Baptists reciprocated. A college student reported that a minister at chapel "read his sermon and did not enjoy it very much. He belongs to the Episcopal Church. They have almost as much 'monkey work' as the Catholics." A female student felt much the same way: "I have just come in from preaching in the chapel. It doesn't seem like service at all," she wrote to her Baptist parents, "as the Episcopalian preacher was here tonight. He was dressed so funny and most of the service, he read."

Members of other Protestant denominations were less suspicious of one another. It was not uncommon for people to attend three or four different churches a month, going to wherever a sermon could be heard. Each church preached the same morality and people could take satisfaction in feeling a part of a larger Protestant Christianity. On the other hand, many people took the theological distinctions among the Baptists, Methodists, and Presbyterians quite seriously. Differences over whether the Bible demanded complete immersion during baptism, or whether or not infants should be baptized, could pit neighbor against neighbor and church against church.

It was hard for others, Southerners or not, to admire such attitudes. "At the turn of the century every third Southerner was an uncompromising and fanatical puritan, as ruthless as Cotton Mather," John Andrew Rice recalled. Corra Harris, in her novel of the New South, described a town where "the saints had gotten the upper hand" and ruined the morals of the place. "If you played cards, you were lost and might as well go the whole hog, gamble and have done with it. If you drank, you were also lost, and might as well get drunk for the same reason." If you danced, "your feet took hold on hell. . . . Righteousness is a terrible thing when a conscientious fool enforces it."

Discipline within the churches declined throughout the late nineteenth and early twentieth century. The number of people censured by their churches for dancing, swearing, adultery, drinking, or any other offense fell with each passing decade. Part of the decline may have resulted from the growing differentiation of the churches: people who disapproved of worldly amusements could and did form their own congregations, while those who held less stringent views could turn to town and city churches where discipline was especially lax. Moreover, the growing number of churches meant that rather than face a committee and censure from one's home church, a person could, by profession of faith, join another. Indeed, membership at another church became, along with simple failure to attend, the most frequent reasons for excommunication. Increased population movement, stronger law enforcement, and growing tolerance for the world among younger members all contributed to the decline of discipline within the churches.

Internal discipline may also have declined because town and city churches, and the statewide organizations they dominated, increasingly turned their energies on the society as a whole. At the same time that church discipline waned, the Protestant churches of the New South extended their work farther than they ever had before in Sunday schools, religious newspapers, and campaigns for prohibition, sponsoring laws to outlaw public swearing, boxing, and dog fights. The South of railroads, stores, and towns, of commercial entertainment and bicycles, threw the world and the Christian into increasing conflict. The churches at the turn of the century went on the offensive, trying to reform what they saw as the greatest threats to their moral standards.

The Southern churches responded with energy and determination. Many women, of both races, found in the church their greatest sanctuary. Women played increasingly important roles on church committees—especially those dedicated to fund-raising—and assumed positions of greater authority. It was women, by and large, who collected millions of dollars for foreign missions (and an increasing number of those missionaries were themselves women), who maintained the church building and the parsonage, who financed and administered help for local people in need. When women who poured such energies into their churches found that men still held on to the positions of leadership, they created organizations within churches, uniting women to do the things men could not or would not attempt, putting control into the hands of the women who did the work.

The aid provided by the churchwomen often focused on women who had been widowed, abandoned, or otherwise severed from the aid provided to men by ethnic, fraternal, or labor societies. Such women had no recourse except a public dole that extracted a heavy price of humiliation and dependency. Middle- and upper-class women directed their energies at providing for these women and their children, a provision that no one else was willing to provide. Far more than the bare help offered by county and municipal governments, churchwomen labored to keep families together and healthy, labored to bring the poor and marginal back into the larger society. White men, too, worked within the churches in the South's own version of the Social Gospel. Churches took stands on temperance, gambling, political corruption, public morality, orphans, and the elderly. They built settlement houses and founded YMCAs, started schools and built playgrounds.

Not everyone within the churches welcomed such efforts. Some charged that if the churches would only live up to their true purpose, saving souls, then there would be no need for reform. "Far be it from me to discourage any efforts along this line of work," one church member wrote, "but what these people need is to be made over again. There is but one power in the world that can do this, and that is the gospel of the Son of God."

The white churches had many reasons for not playing an active role in the South's political battles: a lack of accord on those issues, a long Southern tradition that partisan stands were inappropriate in church, the recognition that wealthy men and women contributed both money and influence to the churches, a loyalty to the Democrats among many ministers. The churches did nothing about the most overt political conflicts of their day and by their actions countenanced the status quo. They were willing to render unto Caesar what Caesar claimed, even as they ministered to some of the victims of the emerging order.

Many of the complexities and tensions surrounding white Southern Protestantism were manifested in the ministry of one man, perhaps the one Southerner whose name was known to the greatest number of people inside and outside the region: Sam Jones. Jones, born in Alabama in 1847, barely missed the Civil War and instead worked alongside his father as an attorney in the late 1860s. Alcohol brought the young man down, and as his father lay on his deathbed Jones promised to abstain the rest of his life. Like so many other men at such junctures, Jones turned to the church for strength as he tried to overcome his weakness. He joined the Southern Methodists and became an itinerant minister in north Georgia. Thin, short, and sallow, with sunken cheeks and a spreading mustache, disheveled and intentionally uncouth, marked by a high voice, casual gestures, and blunt common language, Jones got people's attention. He became a successful fund raiser for the Methodist Orphan Home. Jones jumped into larger prominence during a visit to Memphis in 1884, when he offered a special sermon, "for men only," about the well-known sins of the gender. "Hundreds of men wept like whipped children," a local newspaper reported.

In 1885 Jones went to Nashville and left the city "buzzing"; a committee of laymen and ministers from several denominations invited Jones back to lead a twenty-day revival. A "Gospel Tent" with room for 7000 went up in anticipation of the large crowds; Baptist, Methodist, and Presbyterian clergy eagerly awaited the augmentation of their numbers. Yet Sam Jones did not preach what many people expected to hear. "I will say something to you rich men of Nashville," he began one sermon. "If I had your money I would do something with it that would redound to my credit in eternity." Instead, he declared, the prosperous businessmen of the New South and their wives were too wrapped up in themselves. "Selfishness! Selfishness!" Jones chastised them. "Hell is selfishness on fire, and the great wonder to me is that some of you don't catch on fire and go straight to hell by spontaneous combustion. . . . you love money more than your souls." Under Jones's influence, many of these respectable Christians changed their ways.

Jones was hard on everyone: poor as well as rich, white as well as black, women as well as men, the clergy as well as the unchurched. Sam Jones was more than a demagogue, a cynical manipulator, a businessman selling salvation. Jones's lacerating language proved strangely comforting and appealing to many Southerners who heard the preacher tell people to blame no one but themselves for their troubles. Like the South itself, Sam Jones denounced worldliness even as he became more worldly, dreamed of a purer time in the past even as he pursued a distinctly modern ministry. As word of Jones's message spread, people begged him to come to their towns and cities. With the leverage of his rapidly growing fame and the luxury of being able to leave a place after he had insulted its leading men, Jones could speak in ways regular ministers could not. He often attacked local officials for their lassitude, especially those who drank. Jones gloried in taking Christianity out into the streets. He tried to break down the barriers between scared and secular life, even if it meant fights and hard words. He had only contempt for pale and soft ministers afraid to encounter life as it was. "We have been clamoring for forty years for a learned ministry and we have got it today and the church is deader than it ever has been in history," he told a Memphis audience. "Half of the literary preachers in this town are A.B.'s, PhD's, L.L.D.'s, D.D.'s and A.S.S.'s."

Jones spoke to black people in a language virtually no other white man used. Politicians might appeal to blacks' self-interest with patronizing language and vague promises, but Jones told blacks during a biracial meeting that if they voted for the saloon forces "you deserve to be debauched and then taken out and lynched, and it is the gang that debauches you that lynches you every pop." He harangued "you colored men out there, if there is a man on earth that ought to let whiskey alone it is the colored man. God bless you, you will need all the sobriety and manhood you can get, and whiskey cuts that grit from you every day you live. You may be as black as the ace of spades, but be a black MAN, and not a black DOG and don't vote with these whiskey devils." Jones supported Booker T. Washington, calling him "the greatest negro on earth, and a negro who leads his race and leads them right." Jones, like Washington, told black Southerners they had to be accountable for their own actions, regardless of the odds they faced. While Dwight Moody, the nation's preeminent revivalist, "sprinkled cologne over the people," one observer commented, Jones "comes along and gives them a dose of carbolic acid and rubs it in."

Jones reached the peak of his popularity in the late 1880s and 1890s, when he preached all over the country. He owned a number of businesses and an imposing home in Cartersville, Georgia, and counted some of the wealthiest men in the South among his friends. While he originally opposed disfranchisement as a sin, he changed his mind around the turn of the century. Jones died in 1906 and his memory was displaced by men such as Billy Sunday, who strode across the stage of the South and the nation in the early twentieth century.

Jones's "carbolic acid" message hardly seemed calculated to assuage the consciences of his audiences. Perhaps his listeners assumed that he was talking about someone else when he assailed those who partook of the temptations of the world. More likely, it seems, Jones spoke with the voice of the conscience of those Protestants who lived in the towns and cities of the New South. While the rich and poor, black and white, men and women all bore different kinds of burdens of conscience, Jones could touch them all. Who had not at least been tempted to play a game of cards, ride a bicycle, join in a dance, or watch a show or ballgame on Sunday? Who did not know someone who drank too much at times, spoke harshly to his wife and children, or even struck them? Who had not yearned after some of the new conveniences or luxuries in the local stores? In Sam Jones's sermons we hear the New South chastising and reassuring itself, listening to its own versions of the jeremiads that had helped ease the consciences of the New England Puritans by exposing their sins. The thousands who searched their souls as those around them sang, those who left their friends and families, tears in their eyes, to walk up the aisle to admit publicly that they had sinned, knew that Sam Jones dared say what others, making their bargains with the new order, would not admit.

The South had long nourished a tradition of popular religion that opposed any kind of reconciliation with the world, even the chastened kind preached by Sam Jones. The first evangelical churches in the region had grown directly out of a revolt against an Anglican church that had become cold, but as the children of the early Southern Baptists and Methodists spread across the South, they made their peace with slavery, missionaries, and denominational colleges. Almost immediately, however, some groups of evangelicals tried to reclaim the original impulse. In the 1830s and 1840s, an antimission movement in the Baptist church counted 900 preachers and 68,000 members. Those in the antimission churches protested against what they saw as their

denomination's unbiblical and dangerously secular impulse to support educated missionaries, a clerical elite, Sunday schools, and reform societies.
The revolt took a variety of forms over the antebellum decades, including
the formation of the Disciples of Christ, the Primitive Baptists, and a "Landmark" movement that portrayed the Baptists, and the Baptists alone, as the
direct and unbroken descendants of the first church.

Affluent churches hurried to make up lost time after the Civil War and
Reconstruction, hurried to match the standards of town churches elsewhere
in the United States. Almost immediately many white Christians grew unhappy with the direction in which their denominations were traveling. The
rural churches dominated numerically, but town ministers seemed to exert
a disproportionate influence in the denominations as a whole. Landmarkism
experienced a resurgence among the Baptists in the 1880s and 1890s, again
attacking missions and driving their opponents out of the Southern Baptist
Seminary. After this victory, the denomination, decentralized and generally
conservative in any case, witnessed relatively few desertions over the next few
decades. The Disciples of Christ experienced a deeper challenge, as those
opposed to musical instruments, a broad view of the scriptures, and titles
such as "Reverend" abandoned the Disciples to create the Church of Christ.

The most volatile conflict, though, came in the Holiness movement
within the Methodist Church. Because the Methodists worked within an ecclesiastical structure more elaborate and centralized than that of the Baptists,
the challenge to the denomination's official tenets proved far more disrup-
tive. Like the antimission impulse among the Baptists, the Methodist Holiness movement had roots deep in the denomination's history. Drawing on
the writings of John Wesley himself, antebellum Northern Methodists such
as Phoebe Palmer preached that a Christian could attain complete sanctification or "holiness." As they became understood in the New South, holiness
doctrines held that a Christian would be uneasy until he or she had received
a "second blessing," an emotional peace that came to those who had been
sanctified, who achieved holiness. A sanctified person would enjoy the "perfect love of Jesus" in a new state of grace and a more ascetic and disciplined
life.

The Northern Holiness movement, quiet during the Civil War, exploded
back into visibility in 1867 with a huge interdenominational camp meeting
in New Jersey. Throughout the 1870s and 1880s, dozens of other camp meetings followed in the North while literature poured from a growing number
of Holiness presses to eager audiences among Southern Methodists. By 1892,
over forty publications espoused Holiness doctrine. Georgia proved especially receptive; there, a large proportion—perhaps even a majority—of
Methodist ministers claimed a second blessing. The Holiness movement traveled first to Southern cities and towns, working its way into the countryside
from there. Southern Holiness began among relatively educated people

within the Methodist churches, people who had seen with their own eyes the denominational papers and Sunday school literature. They feared that the boundary between the church and the world was growing too indistinct, that the churches were too susceptible to the new biblical scholarship, fine buildings, and social pretension.

The leaders of the Methodist Church initially viewed the movement as a healthy resurgence of piety, but soon began to have second thoughts. Those church members who experienced sanctification began to press for innovations in their churches. As one Southern Methodist layman wrote in 1885, "they have changed the name of our meetings, substituting Holiness for Methodist. They preach a different doctrine . . . they sing different songs; they patronize and circulate a different literature; they have adopted radically different words of worship." In the Midwest and in Texas in the 1880s, Holiness churches began to separate from the Methodists. Evangelists, mostly from Kentucky, Iowa, and Texas, began to carry the word into more remote areas of the country, including the South. They preached a far more radical version of Holiness, insisting that adherents wear simple dress, abjure worldly amusements, and abandon coffee and pork. Some went even farther; in Texas, evangelists preached the possibility of absolute perfection and of freedom from death.

In 1894, the General Conference of the Methodist Church forced its bishops to choose between Holiness and the church hierarchy. Leaders in Georgia, especially, found themselves caught between their well-known support for the new movement and the position of the church. Atticus Greene Haygood led an attack in the denomination's periodicals and conventions against the Holiness movement. Bishops warned that the church was being eroded from within by "Holiness associations, Holiness meetings, Holiness preachers, Holiness evangelists, and Holiness property." The Methodist leadership decreed that no preacher could enter another's territory without the invitation of the regular pastor, thus undercutting the influence of itinerant Holiness evangelists. Ministers who insisted on identifying themselves as Holiness were banished to the poorest and most remote circuits; congregations that had been infected with Holiness belief were sent new, orthodox pastors to lead them out of the error.

The extermination of Holiness failed. While the Methodists reclaimed official leadership of churches and districts, devout Holiness people established camp meetings and, in one case, a liberal arts college independent of denominational control. The movement into separate congregations took place throughout the South and Midwest, as congregations large and small moved into any quarters they could find. Some managed to establish dominion over their communities and even expand, while others were persecuted and crushed by their opponents. A significant number of Holiness advocates, however, began to accept new, more radical doctrines of divine healing and a third blessing called "the fire." Instead of coming together into a unified Holiness movement, the movement splintered into new churches and new denominations.

The Methodists on Virginia's Eastern Shore confronted most of the characteristic struggles surrounding Holiness. In the late 1880s and early 1890s, the peninsula's newspapers carried accounts of the mainline Methodists' brass bands, croquet, dramas, donkey parties, bicycle races, picnics, and even balloon ascensions—all testimony to the church's easy relationship to the secular world. In a church on Chincoteague Island, however, an influential layman named Joseph B. Lynch longed for and experienced the second blessing. Lynch spread the news and soon others of the church joined him in sanctification; they petitioned the bishop to send a true "holy man of God to preach to them." Their current minister, furious, dismissed Lynch and his supporters from positions of power within the church. In 1892 they formed Christ's Sanctified Holy Church. Within a matter of months, the church was among the largest on the island.

The sanctified church, like so many others cut loose from the mainline denominations, pushed the implications of its doctrine into new territory. A woman—Sarah Collins—ministered, conducted weddings, and officiated at funerals. The church's discipline forbade marriages between sanctified and unsanctified people; any minister who performed such a marriage would be expelled and any such marriage would be void. Sanctification had divided many couples in the first place, and now the church decreed that the partner who had experienced the second blessing should separate from her or his spouse, and even children. One female member left her husband and four children; a male member abandoned his family as well.

Word soon spread that those who had left their worldly spouses were taking up with sanctified partners from the church. People on the island began to turn against the congregation; one evening eleven young men set out to persecute the transgressors. Not finding their first target, they ended up shooting into the home of another Holiness church member, killing him in his bed. The unsanctified residents of the island supported the eleven, announcing that "the wonder is that the lewd and lascivious habits of the Sanctified crowd practiced by them under the guise of religion has not led to bloodshed before." In fact, four sanctified church members—three men and one woman, including Joseph Lynch and Sarah Collins—were arraigned for "free love" and allied offenses. They were sent to jail, convicted, and fined. Soon, the church members sold their belongings at a public auction, at considerable loss, and set out to find new homes in North Carolina and elsewhere, leaving several husbands and wives behind. Three of the "saints" eventually traveled to Calcasieu Parish, Louisiana, where they inspired a Holiness movement among black residents there. The church they founded— Christ's Sanctified Holy Church Colored—flourished on its own.

The story of the Eastern Shore's experience testifies to the volatility of the Holiness movement. The sanctified people often met hostile and even violent responses, not only from the worldly but from the devout members of other churches as well. By their existence, the Holiness churches seemed to mock the piety of mainline denominations. The Holiness churches were sometimes willing to broach racial lines, even as the older denominations became more segregated. Perhaps most shocking, Christ's Sanctified Holy Church challenged dominant gender relationships, valuing faith over domestic loyalty and giving women a more prominent place.

Sects' rejection of the embodiments of status in the secular world opened them to the possibilities of female leadership. A number of women seized the opportunity—or, as they felt, were seized by God—and embarked upon bold ministries. "There were many women preachers, who did much to plant Holiness," one early memoir by a male participant in Southern Holiness stressed. "There were also bands of girl preachers who went out two and two as evangelists, one a preacher and the other a singer." Perhaps as many as a third of the Holiness preachers were women. A 1905 book, *Women Preachers*, conveyed the testimonies of ten brave souls and used scripture to defend women's right to preach. Some of the women were widows, others were single, others traveled with their husbands "two and two," while others left their husbands for extended trips.

Mary Lee Cagle was one of the ten women preachers. Born in 1864 in Alabama, Cagle felt called early in her life to preach; although she prayed that God intended her to serve abroad as a missionary, she knew He meant for her to preach in her own country. "What a struggle I had," she recalled, "I pled with God to release me from the call." While she felt "it would be so easy for me to say 'Good-bye' to loved ones and native land and pour out my life among the heathen," Cagle knew that to go out in her own country as a woman preacher would mean facing "bitter opposition, prejudice, slanderous tongues, my name cast out as evil, my motives misconstrued and to be looked upon with suspicion." She had a clear sense of her limitations: "I was reared a timid, country girl and had never been out in the world—in fact until 27 years of age, had never been outside my native county in the State of Alabama. It seemed very strange God would call me when all these things were considered." She waited, resisting, for ten years, though her Bible would often fall open to the verse that seemed to urge her on: "Be not afraid of their faces: for I am with thee to deliver thee, saith the Lord. Then the Lord put forth His hand, and touched my mouth. And the Lord said unto me, Behold, I have put My words in thy mouth." Cagle admitted that she often wished the passage could be torn from her Bible.

Cagle thought that her marriage to a Holiness evangelist, Robert Lee Harris, might be enough. Both the trials and the triumphs surrounding Holiness were even stronger than she had imagined, as an account of events in Milan, Tennessee, in 1893 revealed. "Great crowds of people from the country attend the meeting here day and night," the local newspaper reported.

(From top left, clockwise) *The Rev. Fannie McDowell Hunter, Miss Trena Platt, the Rev. Mary Lee Cagle, and the Rev. H. C. Cagle. (Nazarene Archives, Kansas City, Missouri)*

"When you see five or six people congregated on the streets now, you may be sure they are talking of religious matters." The controversy had begun the Sunday before, when a local Baptist minister preached "a strong sermon" denouncing the "mistakes of modern Holiness." The church was "crowded to overflowing, and many stood at the windows" to listen to a sermon that "bristled with scripture quotations." That evening, Robert Lee Harris responded, answering each of the Baptist's points, "plausibly if not convincingly to his large audience." The newspaper sought to quiet matters, writing off the dispute as a misunderstanding. Many had thought the Holiness people claimed to be without sin, but Harris clarified the issue, advertising himself as "not so cranky" as some of the other Holiness preachers they might have heard. Thousands of people flowed into Milan, the Baptists brought in a more formidable opponent from Kentucky, and the Memphis *Commercial* even sent a reporter. By all accounts, Harris acquitted himself well, though few minds were changed.

Harris died not long thereafter, and Mary Lee Cagle again had to confront her calling. She felt a "loosening" by God that allowed her to overcome her timidity and she set out with another woman, Fannie McDowell Hunter, into Arkansas. As in a trial, early in the trip Cagle received a request to speak before 500 penitentiary inmates. Standing before them, she fell speechless. "There were old men, young men and middle-aged," she recalled, "white men and black men, white women and black women." Finding her voice, the female preacher offered them a sermon that led several prisoners to seek conversion. From then on, Cagle would minister to the poorest and most outcast Southerners, to unwed mothers and orphans. Her Holiness crusade continued for decades.

While the doctrine of Holiness began in the Methodist church, a broader quest for a more vital religion began to work in sects and denominations that had nothing to do with Methodism. One of the first and most powerful was to become known as the Church of God. Its origins were modest and its spread gradual at first. In August of 1886, at the Barney Creek Meetinghouse near the Tennessee-North Carolina border, an elderly Baptist and large landowner named Richard G. Spurling addressed a group of local people of several denominations who had become dissatisfied with the spirituality of their churches. "As many Christians as are here present that are desirous to be free from all man-made creeds and traditions, and are willing to take the New Testament, or law of Christ, for your only rule of faith and practice," Spurling offered, "giving each other equal rights and privilege to read and interpret for yourselves as your conscience may dictate, and are willing to sit together as the church of God to transact business as the same, come forward." Only eight people accepted the radical invitation—three men and five women, representing three families. On a second invitation the next day, Spurling's son and namesake, a Baptist minister and skilled millwright, joined. The younger Spurling was to take over the new Christian Union when his father died the next month.

For the next ten years, Richard G. Spurling, Jr., climbed over the mountains on foot, visiting hollows and tiny communities, testifying and debating with other ministers, praying and weeping, but converting few. His Christian Union was dismissed as "Spurling's Church" or the "Wild Sheep Union." Then in 1896 a new set of allies appeared in the mountains. Three men bearing word of entire sanctification came to Cherokee County, North Carolina, and sparked a revival. Women outnumbered men two to one among the converts.

Local residents had tolerated Spurling but would not tolerate this new departure. Whitecaps whipped and fired guns at members of the congregation and ransacked their homes. Arsonists attempted to burn the church to the ground several times, finally resorting to dynamite. Although the congregation rebuilt the church, its members soon stood by and watched helplessly, tears streaming down their faces, as 106 men from the community gathered at noon on a Sunday to tear down the building. Those who destroyed the structure were the most prominent men in the neighborhood—ministers, deacons, a justice of the peace, and a sheriff. They pried the logs apart and carefully stacked them for burning, not willing to ignite a standing house of worship. A local court prosecuted the desecrators and would have convicted them, but the Christian Union asked for and won their clemency.

Over the next six years, the Holiness believers drifted, sometimes fragmenting over true doctrine. They changed their name to "The Holiness Church at Camp Creek." In 1903, the church welcomed a new member who was to transform it once more: A. J. Tomlinson, an itinerant agent of the American Bible Society and a mystical Quaker. Under his influence and leadership, the church began to spread throughout the mountains, preaching that this church was the only true church, that it was preparing the way for the imminent second coming of Christ. The congregation adopted foot washing and set themselves apart from other Christians. In 1907, the church moved to Cleveland, Tennessee, and took the name of the Church of God. Within three years, missionaries had helped create congregations not only in Tennessee and North Carolina, but also in Kentucky, Virginia, Georgia, Alabama, and Florida. Within the new century, the church was to expand to 114 countries and over a million members.

Black Southerners rushed to embrace the Holiness movement on their own terms. Several black congregations calling themselves the Church of God appeared in the South after 1890. The Church of the Living God, founded in Arkansas, understood Jesus to be a black man; another, the Church of God, Saints of Christ, believed blacks to be descended from the ten lost tribes of Israel. The most prominent of these new black churches, though, became the Church of God in Christ. Created in the mid-1890s, the church's doctrine was radical even in the context of Holiness: it accepted entire sanctification—a "third blessing." The congregation had been gathered by two black elders of missionary Baptist churches, C. H. Mason and C. P. Jones. Mason, the dominant of the two, had briefly attended Arkansas Baptist College but soon left, persuaded that "there was no salvation in schools or colleges." He and Jones discovered the doctrine of entire sanctification and began to promulgate the message. Despite their expulsion from the Baptist Association, Mason and Jones soon led a Holiness revival of their own in a Mississippi cotton gin house and then incorporated the new denomination in Memphis—the first Holiness church of either race to become legally chartered. Armed with this advantage, the Church of God in

Christ was able to win clergy rates on railroads and perform legal marriages. White ministers from independent Holiness congregations sought and received ordination from Mason. The Church of God in Christ was the Holiness church most receptive to musical experimentation, encouraging instruments and music related to ragtime, blues, and jazz.

The year of 1906 witnessed a transformation of Southern, and American, Holiness religion. The course of events revealed how even the most rural parts of the South were tied to processes far beyond their borders, how race relations could still take unpredictable turns. Charles Fox Parham, a charismatic, dwarfish white minister from Kansas, worked throughout the years around the turn of the century in the Midwest, spreading a gospel of Holiness and faith healing. He established a school in Topeka in 1900, where a diverse group of Holiness students sought new spiritual experiences. Those experiences came in the form of speaking in tongues, and the school became well known through the articles of a bemused press and through the testimony of believers. Parham carried his message to other towns, leaving disciples to maintain the faith while he moved on to other fields. In 1905, Parham began work in the Houston-Galveston area, receiving wide publicity when he healed a prominent woman who had been injured in a street-car accident. People flocked to Parham's Bible school outside Houston, the headquarters of the Apostolic Faith Movement.

One of the people who came to Parham's school in Texas was William J. Seymour. Born a slave in Louisiana, Seymour had taught himself to read and write. He became a waiter in Indianapolis and converted to Holiness. Quiet but magnetic, missing one eye, Seymour exerted a powerful influence on people. On his way to the West Coast, Seymour had stopped in Houston to search for relatives lost during slavery; there, he evangelized and visited a black mission. At the mission, he heard speaking in tongues for the first time, probably from the lips of Lucy Farrow, the black governess of Parham's family. Impressed, Seymour went to Parham's school to seek admittance; Parham, fearful of repercussions against his school, resisted at first but relented under Seymour's insistence, allowing his black disciple to sit alone outside the door of the classroom. The experience of speaking in tongues eluded Seymour, but at a black mission he met another woman involved in the Holiness movement, a woman whose church back in Los Angeles was in need of an associate pastor. Seymour wanted to spread the word of Parham's message to the West. After some attempt by Parham to talk Seymour into working among black Southerners instead, the leader gave the black man train fare to California and offered him his blessing.

Los Angeles was the fastest growing city in the United States, ethnically diverse and home to many religious sects, including Holiness. Worshippers expected the characteristic Pentecostal gift—speaking in tongues—to appear soon; revivals repeatedly agitated the city. When William Seymour told the congregation that brought him to Los Angeles that their earlier beliefs had been mistaken, that they had experienced no real baptism until they had spoken in tongues, they padlocked the doors against him. He turned to others to spread the message, finding that only the poorest black laundresses were willing to listen. Seymour himself, after all, had not yet received the gift and had not been able to loose the tongues of others. He sent to Parham for reinforcements, who dispatched a white woman to spread the glossolalia, the speaking in tongues, she had experienced. Seymour himself was one of the recipients and soon set out to share the gift.

Seymour rented a hall at a former African Methodist Episcopal Church on Azusa Street, a building that had become a stable, surrounded by stockyards, lumberyards, and a tombstone shop. His listeners made benches from planks stretched between nail kegs and Seymour spoke from a pulpit of packing boxes. The new gospel worked slowly at first, but word eventually spread that amazing things were happening at the Azusa Street Mission: meetings went on day and night, as worshippers not only spoke in tongues but also cast out demons, prophesied, healed one another, beheld visions, and sang songs—in harmony—that none of them had ever heard before. Everyone was welcome, and as many as twenty different nationalities received the gifts of the Pentecost, as these manifestations were called. Soon Pentecostal missionaries spread out all over the country, carrying word of the miracle of Azusa Street to the North and South, to blacks and whites, to cities and villages. While some missionaries labored in Europe, the Middle East, Africa, and China, others testified before small Southern congregations of both races. The Pentecostals ministered to anyone who would listen, ranging from brothels and chaingangs to courthouses and town squares. Women no less than men could receive and share the gifts.

Southerners in remote places saw only the gifts of the Pentecost, knowing nothing of the racial identity of the man who had sparked the movement. One white minister from Dunn, North Carolina, G. B. Cashwell, traveled to Azusa early on to receive the message firsthand. Discovering that most of the worshippers, including Seymour, were black, he almost left. But during that first session, a young black man walked up to Cashwell, placed his hands on the white man's head, and prayed for him to be baptized with the Holy Ghost. This caused "chills to go down my spine," the white minister recalled. Still struggling with his prejudices, Cashwell eventually "lost his pride" and asked Seymour and other black people present to lay their hands on him so that he could be "filled." He soon received the gift and returned to his home in North Carolina, where he converted a tobacco warehouse into a meeting place for a Pentecostal revival that would transform the Southeast. On December 31, 1906, only a few months after William Seymour had left Texas for California, the word came back to the South. Thousands of Holiness believers came to hear and left converted to the Pentecostal gospel. Cashwell traveled for three years throughout the South, winning vast numbers of converts wherever he went.

Pentecostalism worked among black Holiness believers as well. Mason and Jones of the Church of God in Christ traveled from Memphis to Los Angeles to see Seymour themselves. They returned to the South five weeks later having received the gift, only to find that a white minister, Glen A. Cook, was already spreading the message. Mason joined with Cook to transform the Church of God in Christ to Pentecostalism, while Jones led a group of Holiness believers away from Mason's congregation. The new Church of God in Christ was to grow into the largest Pentecostal organization in the United States.

During the years that marked one of the lowest points in American race relations, the Pentecostal movement remained almost uniquely open to exchange between blacks and whites. There was the usual conflict: Charles Parham rushed to claim credit for the movement Seymour inspired even as he labored to dissociate himself from Seymour personally and blacks in general. More than in any other religious or social group, though, black and white ministers and worshippers interacted with one another in the Pentecostal churches through the 1910s and into the 1920s. Many of the manifestations of the spirit in Pentecostalism, especially spirit possession, bore an obvious connection to African and African-American religious practices, and Seymour's influence was obviously central to the movement. Cashwell allowed black men to lay their hands on him and his white Southern audiences willingly listened to him after he admitted such inspiration. Religion could overcome, for a while at least, the worst parts of Southern culture.

Indeed, the Holiness and Pentecostal churches violated more of the cultural shibboleths of the New South than any other organization in that time and place. In many ways, these churches inverted the cultural values being disseminated throughout the South by towns, railroads, and advertising. The new churches stressed simplicity and locality over consumption and ever-shifting national standards. They stressed the ability of anyone, regardless of race, class, or gender, to experience the most thrilling manifestations of God's love, ignoring the distinctions that multiplied elsewhere in the New South. They drew on expressive styles of behavior being discredited and displaced among blacks as well as whites in the South.

That does not mean, though, that the Holiness and Pentecostal churches were simple reactionary movements, restoring a lost old-time religion. As their early histories make clear, these churches were profound acts of creation, of invention. They did not grow up by default, in isolation from the main currents of American life. In virtually every case, the Holiness and Pentecostal churches grew out of an interaction between movements from outside of the South and indigenous leaders who had already begun to strive toward a new vision. Whites and blacks, men and women, worked together and argued with one another to bring the new churches into being; Southerners clashed and cooperated with Northerners, Midwesterners, and Westerners.

The Holiness and Pentecostal churches were in their chaotic state of creation when the religious censuses of 1890 and 1906 were taken, so it is difficult to define their geographic points of strength. The distribution of the Church of God in 1926, however, reveals a startling pattern. That Pentecostal church was concentrated, first of all, in and around some of the towns and cities that had grown most quickly since 1880—Birmingham, Chattanooga, Knoxville, and Nashville. The church flourished, too, in the cotton mill belt of the Piedmont of the Carolinas; in the fall-line cities of Columbus, Macon, Augusta, Raleigh, and Richmond; in the smaller manufacturing towns of northeast Alabama and northwest Georgia; in the coal fields of Alabama, Tennessee, and Kentucky; in the citrus groves of Florida and the new agricultural areas of south Georgia. In other words, the churches were not located in the backwaters of the South, but in the very places that had experienced the greatest change over the preceding fifty years.

The Holiness-Pentecostal movement cannot be reduced to a reflex of economic change. The new churches were so powerful precisely because they wrestled with the problems of life on a higher plane, because they refused to accept life on the terms that secular politicians, businessmen, and landowners followed. More than the Populists, the Holiness-Pentecostal Christians rejected the dominant vocabulary of human worth, replacing it with a language of glorious struggle. Only those outside the movement could believe such a faith to be escapism, retreat, narcotic. Their faith made life more challenging, not less; it made social conflict more meaningful, not less. The early Holiness-Pentecostals, certain that the South was being subsumed in a shallow materialism, sought to eradicate its effects by beginning with their own hearts.

Chapter 10

~~~~~~

Books

Throughout the 1880s, 1890s, and 1900s, as politics and depression convulsed the region, authors of fiction sought to make sense of the South around them. They wrote less of public events than of conflicts over sexual identity, religious faith, the meaning of race, the experience of one's generation, the volatile changes in the class order, the meaning of industrialization. By and large, they did not use fiction as smokescreens for a Southern political agenda, but rather as a way to order and explore the events and forces that so affected their lives. Their explorations help us map the elusive emotional geography of the New South.

In the United States, as in Europe, the late nineteenth century saw a fascination with a literature of specificity, of exotic locales, of quaint subordinate classes. The growing suburbs and small cities of the Northeast hardly seemed the stuff of literature, and the new journals turned to the West, New England, and the South for the vicarious experience of places where life had greater depth and resonance. Readers in the Northeast were curious about these parts of their own country, especially so now that the South had been defeated, its threat removed. In fact, a large part of the appeal of this new literature was the way it domesticated everyone it discussed, translating troubling people into forms comforting to a genteel readership. By putting words into the mouths of ex-slaves, former secessionists, and mountaineers, authors could tame these outcasts, relegate them to their place in the national hierarchy of speech and manners. The detail of local color gave the illusion that a reader could understand the full context of the stories' subjects, could understand why they were so unusual, so quaint.

Southern authors saw themselves as mediators between a genteel readership and a South that often refused to conform to standards of Northern gentility. Their works sought to translate Southern experience into the molds provided by the standards of English and American literature. Southern writers wrote out of a desire to explain the South, to suggest that despite slavery and military defeat the Old South had nurtured some values worth maintaining, that despite their unusual accents people in the New South held emotions and ideals not unlike those elsewhere in the country.

Almost to a person, the people who were to emerge as the enduring authors of the New South felt distanced from the easy conventions of the region. Virtually all had discovered classic English literature at an early age, had grown to view their own lives and the lives of others from their region through the prism of another place and time. Some had grown up on the borders of the South, seeing the region's strengths and weaknesses thrown into relief in the contrasts of their own families and hometowns. Others had been precocious or sickly children, kept from others and educated by tutors in their fathers' libraries. Others had traveled outside the South at an early and impressionable age. Others were mere visitors to the particular locale with which they became identified, arriving for business or a vacation only to find their imaginations captured. Others were women who found themselves outside the usual domestic relationships because they never married or because they were widowed at an early age. Each of the authors self-consciously set out to explain a problematic New South to themselves and to a readership beyond the region.

The literature these authors produced in such profusion in the 1880s and 1890s was called "local color." The very name trivialized the work: "local" suggested that its focus was necessarily peripheral, "color" emphasized its exotic surface detail. It was a literature more complex than it seemed, riven by conflicting desires and intentions, torn by its authors' own uncertainties.

George Washington Cable of Louisiana was the first Southern author of the postwar era to achieve renown. Born in 1844, the son of a Virginia father who had moved to Indiana, freed his slaves, and married a New England woman, Cable grew up a devout Presbyterian in New Orleans. After serving in the Confederacy, Cable, twenty-one years old, returned home to help support his mother and siblings by working on a newspaper. To fill space in the paper, Cable wrote ninety columns on the life around him and on the literature of England and America. Cable, who had been an ardent supporter of the South during the Civil War, began in the 1870s to question the injustice and brutality he saw inflicted against blacks. In 1875, he publicly protested the segregation of New Orlean's public schools; rebuffed by the newspaper's editor, he saved his outrage for the fiction he began writing in his spare time during these years. Editors and readers in both North and South applauded one Cable story after another, soon gathered in his popular book *Old Creole Days* (1879).

Cable's conflicting feelings about the South became clearer in his novel *The Grandissimes* (1880), published serially in *Scribner's* in 1879. Depicting the years immediately after the Louisiana Purchase in 1803, Cable portrayed a society not unlike the South after Reconstruction, a place marked by governmental corruption, racial conflict and confusion, violence, and economic turmoil. Cable insisted, despite the pleas of his editors, on building the novel around a legend of a noble runaway slave. In that legend a towering African prince, Bras Coupé, leveled a curse on his owner's plantation. For Cable, racial guilt and anxiety, like the curse, underlay the apparently carefree society of old New Orleans. Characters negotiated across blurred lines of race and respectability, as sensitive men and women with one-eighth or one-quarter black ancestry struggled to find a place in a society divided by slavery, as dignified white men sought to find a way to maintain their honor, as an outsider sought to make sense of the tangle of families and secrets. Cable's novel was subtle and ambivalent, devoted to making palpable the difficult decisions faced by its characters, unflinching in its portrayal of the consequences of slavery and its aftermath: violence, insensitivity, deception, lassitude, sexual immorality.

Northern reviewers loved *The Grandissimes,* calling Cable "the first Southern novelist (unless we count Poe a novelist) who has made a contribution of permanent value to American literature." Southern reviews were generally favorable as well, though uncomfortable with a tone they deemed judgmental. The most forthright—indeed, ferocious—attack came in an anonymous pamphlet written by a New Orleans acquaintance of Cable's, a Creole priest. He attacked the book for Cable's "disguised puritanism, assuming the fanatical mission of radical reform and universal enlightenment," charging that the author had prostituted himself for "the prejudiced and inimical North." A wide readership in both the North and the South waited to see what Cable would write next.

Joel Chandler Harris quickly emerged in the years around 1880 to join Cable as one of the most famous Southern authors. Although the writers appeared quite different on the surface, they shared deep affinities. Cable and Harris were troubled by the South they saw and knew, even as the region exerted its strong emotional pull on both of them.

Harris, born in 1848, was young enough to escape the Civil War but old enough to remember life under the antebellum order. The illegitimate son of a seamstress and an Irish laborer who abandoned mother and child soon after the boy's birth, Harris grew up in a small town in middle Georgia.

Joel Chandler Harris, from Harper's, May 1887.

Small, red-headed, and freckled, shy and with a stammer, Harris nevertheless had what he considered a happy childhood, on warm terms both with his peers and with the black people, slave and free, of the village. His life took its decisive if unlikely turn in 1862, when the thirteen-year-old youngster applied for and became an apprentice for a newspaper published on a nearby plantation. For the next four years, Harris was to learn from Joseph Addison Turner, the plantation's owner and the newspaper's editor, both the ways of writing and an affection for plantation life. Harris's idyll was destroyed by the end of the Civil War, when the newspaper suspended operations. The young newspaperman moved from one Georgia town to the next, each time to a larger place with brighter prospects. Even as he prospered professionally, though, Harris seemed always uneasy, his doubtful origins and idiosyncratic education making him unsure of himself, doubtful of his abilities. Nevertheless, he made a name on a Savannah newspaper as a humorist and in 1875, at the age of twenty-seven, became an editor of the leading newspaper of the South, the Atlanta *Constitution.*

Harris, like many white Southern newspaper writers in the 1870s, combined editorial comment and humor by mimicking black speech and opinion. He found an especially effective mouthpiece in the person of "Remus," a fictional elderly black man who came into the offices of the *Constitution* from his wanderings in the streets of Atlanta. While the first Remus stories concerned life in the city, Harris eventually added another Remus who told tales of plantation life before the Civil War. Harris, long fascinated by the tales he heard as a youth, did not realize until he read an article in *Lippincott's* on black Southern folklore that the tales might be of interest to other whites as well. In 1879, Harris had "Uncle Remus" tell the story of "Mr. Rabbit and Mr. Fox" in the *Constitution.* Readers of the paper requested more, and soon the stories began to appear in each Sunday edition. Newspapers in the North and South reprinted the stories to great acclaim; Harris received over a thousand letters calling for a book of the tales.

In 1880, *Uncle Remus: His Songs and Sayings* won immediate critical and commercial success throughout the country and abroad. Harris ignored the inflated and stereotyped imagery of the big house and endless cotton fields; the boy and the old man who shared the tales sat in the slave's rough cabin next to the fire. The slave and the boy were equalized for the moment of the story by the black man's age and knowledge. The tales were all allegories, enacted by animals in a mythical time when they could talk, think, and scheme like people, when motives of greed, vanity, and survival lay close to the surface. The hero of the stories was "Brer Rabbit," who invariably triumphed with quick thinking and the unflinching pursuit of his self-interest.

In the characteristically modest introduction to his first book, Harris claimed that he had merely transcribed stories he had overheard, stories that revealed the thoughts of black people in a form distorted as little as possible by white concerns and language. Harris was sympathetic to Remus, eager to show that slaves had kept alive their own traditions and views of the world. "It needs no scientific investigation to show why he selects as his hero the weakest and most harmless of all animals, and brings him out victorious in contests with the bear, the wolf, and the fox," Harris commented, for surely slaves had to confront foes who possessed greater strength and advantages. While Harris thought it would be "presumptuous" to offer his own theory about the origins of the stories, "if the ethnologists should discover that they did not originate with the African, that effect should be accompanied with a good deal of persuasive eloquence." Unlike those who claimed that black Southerners had no culture whites need respect, in other words, Joel Chandler Harris portrayed himself as the humble conveyer of black stories good enough to gather and publish, good enough for whites to read to their children. Uncle Remus, for all his good nature toward his young white friend, sometimes nodded by the fire "dreaming dreams never told of." Whites could never know blacks, it seemed, as thoroughly as blacks knew whites.

Harris was no reformer out to undermine white notions of superiority. He believed blacks would do well to accept white guidance. Harris's Uncle Remus stories, though, brought ambiguity to popular postwar Southern literature at the very beginning. While the stories did not carry the political agenda of the novels of Reconstruction by Northerners such as John W. DeForest or Albion Tourgée, or the deep and comprehensive historical vision of George Washington Cable, they did subvert easy notions about black simplicity and contentment. As soon as Harris created Uncle Remus, allowed him to tell stories in which the weak could outwit the strong, in which a putatively inferior being could use others' sense of superiority as a powerful weapon, in which a black man traced out lessons for a young white boy of the planter class, Harris complicated the fictional portrayal of blacks. Remus himself might not be a threatening character, but Brer Rabbit was, the embodiment of the sauciness, deviousness, and ambition so many whites feared in the newer generations of black Southerners.

Harris himself, a bastard, a shy, homely man visitors could hardly believe was the author they so admired, a man who found his first and greatest happiness on a plantation, had reason to sympathize with Remus and Rabbit, to respect their longings and their satisfactions. Despite his identification with Henry Grady and the loudest booster paper of the New South, Harris held serious doubts about the rapacious greed he saw unleashed in the region. The money-making wolves and foxes of the nation and the region seemed to want everything for themselves, leaving nothing for the smaller and gentler beings over whom they glowered and with whom "Joe" Harris identified.

One of the most admiring readers of Harris's early tales was Mark Twain. With *The Innocents Abroad, Roughing It,* and *Tom Sawyer* already to his credit, and with a well-established presence on the lecture circuit, by the early 1880s Twain had become the most visible and successful American man of letters. Twain, reading the Uncle Remus tale of the tar baby at one of his performances, discovered its popular appeal. The veteran tried to persuade Harris to accompany him and Cable on tour; Harris, all too aware of how painful his shyness would make the performances, nevertheless gratefully accepted an invitation to meet with Twain, hoping "to drop this grinding newspaper business and write some books I have in mind." In 1881, Twain and Harris met in New Orleans, where Cable joined them. It soon became clear that Harris had never read any of his stories aloud and could not do so even for the appreciative and sympathetic audience of Twain and Cable, who read from their own works to show the Georgian how easy it really was. Harris returned to the grind of the *Constitution,* where he worked for the next eighteen years, writing his books and stories in the time the newspaper did not consume. Cable and Twain went out on the circuit alone.

Like Harris, Twain bore a problematic relationship to the South. He was the son of a Virginia father and a Kentucky mother, slaveholders in Missouri. An early recruit for the Confederacy, he soon thought better of the decision and became an expatriate in the West and then in New England. Like Harris, too, Twain came to literature through the columns of raw newspapers, where the language ran distinctly to the vernacular. Like Harris, Twain had no interest in writing sectional literature—and most certainly not Southern literature—but sought to catch the diversity and richness of America. Harris's success in the early 1880s encouraged Twain to realize that some things about the country as a whole could best be said through black Southerners. During Twain's trip down the Mississippi in 1881 to reacquaint himself with the river for a book on the subject, he discovered things about the South he felt needed to be said.

In *Tom Sawyer*, Mark Twain had painted for himself and his readers a bucolic image of the Mississippi and its Southern town of Hannibal. His return to the river appalled him. The Northern part of the Mississippi was lovely, but as soon as it came to his native Missouri everything began to decay and disintegrate. White men seemed lazy and unkempt, their houses and towns slovenly, their language coarse, their fixation on the past ludicrous. The New South presented for Twain "a solemn, depressing, pathetic spectacle. . . . There is hardly a celebrated Southern name in any of the departments of human industry except those of war, murder, the duel, repudiation, and massacre." Twain, always a man of extremes, floated by a narrow strip of the New South on a flooded river and passed virulent judgment on the entire region. The only class of people he found worthy of admiration were black Southerners, whose ironic and deflating sense of humor he admired. Twain's disgust and dismay at the New South changed his view of the Old South as well, leading him to replace his commonplace racial jokes with a view of black Southerners as the most honest and interesting people in the cursed region. He pronounced that the only Southern writers worth reading in 1882 were George Washington Cable and Joel Chandler Harris, both of whom set high standards of portraying black people.

The book Twain was working on when he met Cable and Harris turned out to be the greatest work of his career, *The Adventures of Huckleberry Finn*, published in 1884. That book is in many ways an exploration of the South, Old and New, and it bears the imprint of the specific years in which it was written, both in what it rejected and in what it accepted of the new local color literature then sweeping the nation. Twain reveled in the particularity of the Mississippi River. He depended on the "color" of the rogues and the deluded people along the river's shore. He explored the enormous distance between the South's perception of itself as a bastion of civilization and the reality of an impoverished backwater, between the rationalizations surrounding slavery and the casual brutality of the system. Twain was not through wrestling with the problems race posed for him and his country, but he would never approach the topic so directly again.

In the meantime, George Washington Cable's Southern career was being crushed. Always a man of conscience, Cable's contact with the North on his visits there after his early success gave him a clearer sense of his own society's failings. Struck by the difference between the prisons and asylums of New England and those of the South, he embarked on a campaign to improve conditions in New Orleans. Although he enjoyed some success, the scale of suffering he discovered in the South's convict lease system infuriated him. Asked to speak before a national conference on corrections, Cable publicly chastised the South for its inhumanity and its deceit. On the way to the conference, passing through Alabama, Cable watched horrified as a conductor confined a young black mother and her small child to the same segregated railroad car as nine "vile" black convicts, though there was more than enough room in the white car behind. In speeches in 1882 and 1883, Cable told Southern audiences that Southern literature, like everything else in the region, had been ruined by "that crime against heaven and humanity," slavery. It was time to send the idea of caste "back to India and Africa," time for all citizens, not just those who styled themselves "the intelligent," to rule. Even as Cable won admirers in the North, he burned his bridges in the South.

Cable's Southern reckoning was delayed by the lecture tour he took with Mark Twain in 1884. Traveling over 10,000 miles throughout North America, the two authors were billed as "The Twins of Genius." Cable said nothing to hurt Southern pride, but the next year he published an article that was to make it impossible for him to live in the South. He had long been considering what he would say, and he felt compelled to say it despite warnings from those who cared about him. This piece, "The Freedman's Case in Equity," appeared in the Century, and it contradicted what the South considered the permanent modus vivendi of the post-Reconstruction political order: home rule and constricted black rights. Cable attacked the convict lease system, segregated transportation, segregated schools, and unjust politics.

The white South—including almost all of white New Orleans—turned on Cable with a viciousness he had not anticipated. Old friends refused to acknowledge him; the newspapers carried personal attacks. He moved his family to Massachusetts, where they lived the rest of their lives. Over the next decade, Cable poured most of his energies into articles and debates over racial justice in the South. He was convinced there was a "Silent South" of whites who longed for justice as he did, who would speak up if they had a chance. Despite Cable's repeated personal encounters with such people on his tours of the South, they remained silent after he left.

Cable's departure seemed to mark a symbolic end to the first outburst of postwar Southern literature. In just a few years, important books from several writers had charted the social terrain of the South in a way other kinds of public writing could not. These writers, gifted and distanced, could say what other whites could only feel. The injustice of racial discrimination and the moral drift of the New South appeared early in the New South's history.

Competing with the honesty of Cable, Harris, and Twain, however, was a stream of popular sentimentality. Thomas Nelson Page broke into sudden prominence a few years after Cable and Harris. Because of his personal history, Page seemed qualified to speak for the vanquished Virginia aristocracy. A large Northern readership worshipful of British literature found his voice poignant and compelling. Page, born in 1853, recalled the antebellum years with the fondness of a young white master. Even the war years had been exciting and chivalric for the boy, as Page and his brother played at war and endured some of its privations. When his father returned to the plantation after the fall of Richmond, though, "it seemed like a funeral," Page recalled. "The boys were near the steps, and their mother stood on the portico with her forehead resting against a pillar. . . . It *was* a funeral—the Confederacy was dead." The young Page, scion of two of Virginia's most prominent families, was forced to tutor cousins in Kentucky to scrape together enough money for school. By 1874 he had managed to earn a law degree from the University of Virginia and went into the practice of law. He also began to write. His first published work was a poem, written in black dialect, that recalled the glorious life of the antebellum years.

This poem, and the enormously successful stories that followed, were fantasies, unbridled glorifications of a lost childhood, lost innocence, and a lost civilization. The plantation tradition of Southern literature emerged complete in Page's first major story, "Marse Chan," written in 1881 but not published until 1884. The story was told by an old slave who recounted the tragic story of two young white lovers on neighboring plantations, driven apart by their fathers' political differences. The hero Channing ("Marse Chan") went off to war heartbroken over the sundered engagement. His beloved, hearing that Channing had made a public defense of her father's name, sent a letter to the front proclaiming her love. Channing, wearing the letter over his heart, was killed. His fiancée died not long after, and the two were laid side by side in the graveyard. The old slave, certain that the lovers would be married in heaven, longed for their presence and for the good old days before the war, when black and white, male and female, had their fixed and secure places. The aged black man's view of the world allowed the tale to be told with unchecked sentimentality. White readers, North and South, wept unashamedly. While Cable was complex and problematic even when entertaining, Page was just what editors and readers had in mind. Soon, American magazines were filled with Southern fiction that celebrated the old order with the formulaic and uncritical voice of Thomas Nelson Page.

The nineties saw a reaction against sentimentality such as Page's and his many imitators'. The new wave of authors seldom wrote novels as explicitly

Kate Chopin in 1893. (Missouri Historical Society)

political as Cable's, or Page's for that matter, but they wrote novels that sought to bring the latest standards of British and American literature to bear on their experiences in the South. Their works found new narrative styles that purged their literature of much of its sentimentality, banned the knowing narrator who distanced the reader from characters depicted in dialect, and tried to deal more honestly with sexuality, race, and religious belief.

For the most part, this new work was not the product of a new generation. Most of the Southern authors to emerge around the turn of the century—Kate Chopin, Charles W. Chesnutt, James Lane Allen, Ruth McEnery Stuart—had been born in the late 1840s and 1850s, the same time as Cable, Harris, and Page. The literary careers of this second wave had been delayed by other work or, in the case of the women, family responsibilities. While the authors of the first wave met early success and relatively rapid artistic decline, those in the second wave passed long years of apprenticeship and were far more aware of the literary innovations of the late nineteenth century. Those who could remember the antebellum years, it seems, those who were jarred by the experience of the war, felt compelled to make literary sense of the massive change in the South. Those who grew up in the 1870s, on the other hand, were silent. Perhaps it was their loss of schooling or their poverty, but in any case the new generation had little to say.

Literary work had long been deemed acceptable for women in the South, a genteel way for an educated young lady to pass her time or for an unmarried woman or widow to support herself and her children. Girls and young women were often raised on literature, granted access to this kind of indirect learning while denied access to technical and professional fields. Moreover, because the largely female readership of fiction in the Gilded Age seemed fascinated with works by women, publishers willingly accepted stories written by them. Since the antebellum years, the South had produced a series of women writers; several, such as Augusta Jane Evans, E.D.E.N. Southworth, Mary Noailles Murphree, Grace King, and Amélie Rives, had achieved some fame and success between the 1850s and the 1880s.

A number of Southern women took advantage of this opportunity to become professional writers of fiction in the New South. Two of them—Kate Chopin and Ellen Glasgow—won considerable visibility late in the century. Chopin lived long enough to see her greatest book denounced and even banned, but not long enough to see that book resurrected as a classic of American literature. Glasgow, over the course of a long career, built on her fiction of the turn of the century to become a living inspiration for the Southern Renaissance of thirty years later. These authors approached the South from different angles, bringing perspectives none of their male counterparts could provide.

Kate Chopin was born in 1850 and raised in St. Louis; like that other Missouri native, Mark Twain, she developed an early identification with the South but also harbored deep reservations about the region. Chopin's childhood was hardly idyllic. Her father, a well-to-do merchant, died when Chopin was five, killed on the inaugural trip of a new railroad in which he had invested. As a twelve-year-old, Chopin tore down a United States flag Northern soldiers had tied to their front porch and suffered when her half-brother died of typhoid fever while fighting for the Confederacy. She was raised in a family of women, several of whom flouted one shibboleth or another of Southern womanhood. Chopin was educated in a convent school, and the conflict between the strong independent women in her life and the expectations of her Catholic faith apparently caused Chopin considerable doubt and anxiety.

After Chopin's marriage in 1870, she and her husband moved to New Orleans, where she bore six children in nine years. Chopin took her children each summer to the resort of Grand Isle for relaxation and to escape the city's disease. When Oscar Chopin's cotton factorage business failed in 1879, the family moved to his family's plantation in northwestern Louisiana, reputedly the site on which the plantation in *Uncle Tom's Cabin* was based. Chopin was fascinated with the life she found in the countryside. Working in her family's general store, Chopin got a chance to know virtually everyone in the community. She was a topic of some conversation, fascination, and concern in the small village: only twenty-nine years old and striking, boldly riding through the countryside in her plumed hat, day and night, or strolling through the village lifting her skirts a bit higher than absolutely necessary. Chopin continued to read the Darwin and Huxley she had long admired, but she also enjoyed the rich local life of cards, gossip, and dances.

Chopin's husband died unexpectedly in 1882, leaving the young widow to run the plantation and store. She reveled in the new economic autonomy and in the flattering attention she received from the men of the district as well. Chopin engaged in a much-discussed affair with a handsome and wealthy young planter, a rake who was unhappily married and who beat his wife. Chopin put her financial affairs in some order, though she was by no means wealthy, and moved to St. Louis to live with her mother and sisters. The move seemed the best way to resolve a situation that could not be resolved otherwise, divorce being out of the question in the Catholic community. Chopin was to return in her fiction over and over again to her years in the country, the years of her newly discovered financial, physical, and sexual independence.

Soon after Chopin's return to St. Louis, her mother died unexpectedly. Filled with grief, Chopin turned to writing as a way to master her emotions. She also soon became an integral part of the flourishing intellectual life of St. Louis, enjoying a somewhat bohemian circle whose members were skeptical of religion and sympathetic toward feminism. She admired the French writer Guy de Maupassant most of all, first discovering his work in 1888. "I read the stories and marvelled at them. Here was life, not fiction," she recalled, "for where were the plots, the old fashioned mechanism and stage trapping that in a vague, unthinking way I had fancied were essential to the art of story making." Virtually all of Chopin's important work depended upon the particular moral and physical geography of the Louisiana district so central to her own life. Reviewers and editors were troubled from the very beginning by Chopin's themes and by her refusal to offer the usual moral commentary and conclusion to her stories. She soon grew disenchanted with the literary establishment's caution and narrowness. Her stories tested one and then another boundary: divorce, miscegenation, and adultery. While some stories, such as one concerning venereal disease, were never accepted, she managed to get most of them published in major magazines such as *Vogue* and the *Century*.

Chopin did not identify with organized feminist groups or causes. Her revolt followed a less public line, juxtaposing what she saw as more honest and healthier European standards of sexual behavior with the conventions of Protestant America. The internal struggles in her fiction juxtaposed her Catholic background, lush Southern setting, and female sexuality. While she created sympathetic black and mulatto women characters, she expressed little interest in political matters of any kind, including greater justice for black people. Like most of the other writers of the second wave of postwar Southern literature, Chopin focused on personal life rather than public events. While Cable and Page set romantic heroes and heroines against a historical background, Chopin put the conflicts within her characters, using the setting to symbolize warring private emotions.

Throughout the 1890s, Chopin was considered by most readers and reviewers, to her surprise and disappointment, a talented writer of pleasant Louisiana local color. Late in the decade she turned her energies toward a novel that would encompass virtually all of her major concerns, that would again use the Louisiana setting but not be bound by it, that would bring a European eye to the way problems of sexual definition were being played out in provincial America. The result was *The Awakening,* published in 1899 to an outcry that caused the book to be pulled from library and bookstore shelves.

More complex in language and effect than any other work by a Southern writer in these years, *The Awakening* followed a plot unconventional in pacing as well as event, timed more by the rising and falling of emotion than by the driving logic of other iconoclastic novels of the day, such as Theodore Dreiser's *Sister Carrie.* Chopin's novel described a brief period in the life of Edna Pontellier, a Kentucky woman who married a businessman from New Orleans. Like Chopin, Edna spent much of each summer with her children and other women at a vacation resort on the Gulf while her husband worked in the city during the week and visited his family on the weekends. Surrounded by the tropical inducements of the resort, Edna became infatuated with a young single Creole man. Although he left to avoid scandal, Edna found herself unable to resume her customary domestic duties even when she returned to her home in New Orleans. Her confused husband sought to placate her for a while, then went on a business trip without her. While Edna's children were away in the country, she embarked on a desultory affair with a womanizer. Still dissatisfied, she moved away from her husband's home, determined to become an artist. Her original lover returned only to leave immediately, while Edna aided a friend in childbirth. Unable to resolve her conflicting feelings, Edna returned alone to the resort, where she swam naked into the sea to drown.

Willa Cather, along with virtually every other critic, attacked *The Awakening* for demanding "more romance out of life than God put into it" and for making "the passion of love . . . stand for all the emotional pleasures of life and art." It was Chopin's lack of commentary in the face of Edna's transgressions, along with the sense readers felt that Edna must in fact be a thinly disguised Chopin, that led to the book's denunciation. Women could be cold and evil in literature, could betray their natural self-sacrificial instincts, but such women had to be punished. By having Edna simply swim to her death, calmly reviewing without remorse the events and images of her life, Chopin seemed to be evading her responsibility to her readership and to literature. It is that same ambiguity, that same refusal to judge, that has made the book so fascinating to later generations of readers. There have been almost as many interpretations of *The Awakening* as there have been critics.

Contemporaries did not feel that literature should tolerate that ambiguity. It was literature's role, most thought, to make sense of the conflicting urges and impulses of life, not merely to mirror or capitulate to them. Although Chopin received many letters that lavished praise on the book and some sympathetic reviews appeared in papers as prominent as the *New York Times,* other reviewers suggested that Chopin did not know what she was doing when she cut Edna Pontellier loose from her moral moorings. One paper declared that the story "can hardly be described in language fit for publication"; it was merely "gilded dirt," nauseating. Chopin wrote a sardonic but disarming statement in response to the reviews: "Having a group of people at my disposal, I thought it might be entertaining (to myself) to throw them together and see what would happen. I never dreamed of Mrs. Pontellier making such a mess of things and working out her own damnation as she did. If I had the slightest intimation of such a thing I would have excluded her from the company. But when I found out what she was up to, the play was half over and it was then too late." Bookstores and libraries, though, were not assuaged and remained reluctant to carry such a dangerous work; *The Awakening* quickly vanished.

Although Chopin refused to complain about the treatment of her book, she wrote little afterward. The conclusion of her life would not have been out of place in a didactic novel of the sort Chopin despised. Close friends and grandchildren died, financial difficulty descended on her, her son suffered a nervous breakdown, and Chopin herself died in 1904 of a brain hemorrhage. Her reputation soon faded, until she became merely one in the perfunctory lists of minor local color writers. It was not for more than another half-century that many readers rediscovered Kate Chopin's *The Awakening,* admiring in the novel the very things that caused readers to detest it in 1899.

The role of the leading woman writer of the South fell not to Kate Chopin, then, but to a member of a new generation just beginning her career in the late 1890s: Ellen Glasgow. From the start of her writing life, this self-conscious representative of the postwar Southerner reveled in her iconoclasm. She searched for a place where young people could breathe free of the suffocating past of the South. Her search was to prove long and circuitous.

Glasgow was born in 1873, nearly a quarter of a century after Kate Chopin, but her opinions of the state of literature in America and the South mirrored those of her sophisticated Louisiana counterpart. "Something was wrong, I felt, in the mental state of the eighteen-nineties," she recalled. "I felt it, I knew it, though I could not say what it was. Ideas, like American fiction, had gone soft." Although everywhere there were aspects of American life that cried out for honest examination, "the literary mind had gone delirious over novels that dropped from the presses already mellowing before they were ripe." The South was in especially bad shape, for "an insidious sentimental tradition" ruled there. Glasgow knew that she did not stand above that sentimental tradition: "I had been brought up in the midst of it; I was part of it, or it was a part of me; I had been born with an intimate feeling for the spirit of the past, and the lingering poetry of time and place." It was Glasgow's struggle with that tradition that shaped all her early work.

Ellen Glasgow was the daughter of parents who embodied for her the conflicting ideals of the New South. Her mother was a descendant of the South's oldest aristocracy, that of the Virginia Tidewater, Episcopal and refined. Her father, on the other hand, was Scots-Irish, from the southwestern end of Virginia's Shenandoah Valley, Presbyterian and driven, an ironmaker and businessman. To Glasgow, her mother seemed fragile, emotionally and physically exhausted by her eleven children, suffering depression and insomnia after a breakdown; her father, on the other hand, seemed insensitive and uncaring, devoted only to money-making and his own satisfaction. Glasgow, at the age of seven, felt crushed and betrayed when the black woman who had taken care of the young girl left the family. From then on, Glasgow experienced an overwhelming "sense of loss, of exile in solitude, which I was to bear with me to the end." She found most of her solace in reading and writing, though she went to school only one day, disgusted and overwhelmed by the young humanity she confronted there. Alone in her room, Glasgow prayed that God would let her write books, books that would express her sense of anger at the unfairness of life, at its moral dullness.

After several years of wide reading, travel, and the writing of somewhat philosophical novels, Glasgow decided to turn to what she thought she knew best, the hidden force driving her first two novels, "modern conditions of life in Virginia." Characteristically, she set out to study the state, living for a month in Williamsburg, sneaking into the Democratic State Convention, allowing herself to be "stranded" in the mountains to discover the patterns of primitive life. Calling the book *The Voice of the People,* Glasgow portrayed the rise of a man of obscure origins, Nick Burr, through the ranks of Virginia society and politics to the governorship, only to die trying to protect a black man from a lynching. The novel bore the mark of Glasgow's determination

Ellen Glasgow in the 1890s. (University of Virginia Special Collections)

to tell the truth about the South; not only lynching but sexual immorality, political corruption among those with honored names, a sweaty and banal political convention, and a bleak portrayal of rural life marked her *Virginia.* Yet Nick Burr was still something of a conventional hero and his rise against the hypocrisy and rigidity of the Southern class order a familiar story. As with so much of the fiction of the New South, the real and compelling subject was not the central plot but the background and subordinate characters, the social order of the New South itself. For Glasgow, that order was marked by unthinking arrogance about women, the poor, and blacks, even when that arrogance came in the form of noblesse oblige. Women were able to escape from their blind prejudices no more than men. *The Voice of the People* did well, finding a temporary place on a bestseller list dominated by nostalgic historical romances.

Glasgow, unlike Chopin, did not put female characters on center stage. But after finishing a novel by Glasgow, her close friend James Branch Cabell observed, "what remains in memory is the depiction of one or another woman whose life was controlled and trammeled and distorted, if not actually wrecked, by the amenities and the higher ideals of our Virginia civilization." Glasgow's women either fought back against the outmoded chivalry of the New South and were driven out of society, or they succumbed to its dictates and fell into a sort of death in life. Older women often spoke with the voice of the Old South, urging and coercing their daughters of the New South to follow the ways of the past. A gulf separated young people born after the Civil War from those for whom everything since emancipation was denouement, anticlimax. While many young people humored their elders, and many others believed along with them in the grandeur and glory of the lost days, Glasgow rebelled in her fiction.

Most of Glasgow's themes were embodied in her book of 1904: *The Deliverance*. The book was filled with people caught in the confusion of the 1880s. The protagonist of the novel labored over the unyielding ground of his Virginia tobacco farm, trying to support five people who lived in the former overseer's house. The central figure in the household was his mother, an elderly blind woman who believed that the South had won the Civil War and that she lived in the family's colonial plantation residence. Her son and daughters sacrificed and lied so that their mother might rest easily in her delusions. Her son, illiterate despite his intelligence, burned with anger and resentment at the man he blamed for stealing his family's land. Through a complex series of love affairs, marriages, deaths, treacheries, and reconciliations, the young people managed to fight their way out of their inherited identities and suffocating pasts. They sloughed off the false identities forced on them by history and by their elders, found the strength and hope that grew out of the renewal of nature, made the brown land green again. The book explored the intersection of personal psychology with the forces of history, developed characters instead of merely shoving stock figures across a historical background. It became the second best-selling book in America in 1904.

Ellen Glasgow was to publish for four more decades, returning again and again with new tactics to understand her South, her Virginia. Just as she refused to fit the expectations of 1900, though, so did she refuse to tailor her writing to the changed expectations of the 1920s. From the viewpoint of the earlier era, her work seemed starkly realistic; from the viewpoint of the latter era, her work seemed old-fashioned. While *The Deliverance*, her best novel before 1910, was powerful and original, it seems unlikely that Glasgow's work in that period would win her a place in the literary history of the period as great as Kate Chopin achieved with *The Awakening*. Glasgow was not, as she liked to think of herself and as later historians have agreed, virtually alone in the New South in her determination to write fiction that spoke in a modern voice. Her subsequent success and memoirs foreshortened Southern literary history, ignoring those who embarked on their own quest at the turn of the century.

A number of other Southern writers achieved considerable attention at the turn of the century, jostling one another at the tops of the bestseller lists. At the time, in fact, their reputations outstripped those of other writers now remembered more clearly. Ruth McEnery Stuart of Arkansas wrote stories of middle-class women in the South in a language of quiet realism and controlled humor; her speaking tours attracted large audiences throughout the country. James Lane Allen of Kentucky wrote in a vein of bold naturalism, showing the force of nature behind human striving. His novel *The Kentucky Cardinal* was thought by one English critic to be "among the best that ever came out of America." John Fox, Jr., became the leading novelist of the Appalachian Mountains. A confidant of Theodore Roosevelt, Fox enjoyed great praise for his mountain dramas, especially *The Trail of the Lonesome Pine*. Critics and readers in England and the North in the years around 1900 were certain that Stuart, Allen, and Fox were major writers, bound to endure.

White readers and audiences North and South could not get enough of black dialect. The stories they heard from the platform and the pages of their magazines were white words put in the mouths of old black people, people who lived figuratively or literally in the past, people who, like the mountaineers, were happy in their poverty and simplicity. In 1892, Anna Julia Cooper, herself a black novelist, spoke caustically of white authors, such as William Dean Howells, who "with flippant indifference have performed a few psychological experiments on their cooks and coachmen, and with astounding egotism, and powers of generalization positively bewildering, forthwith aspire to enlighten the world with dissertations on racial traits of the Negro." Black writers of the era struggled to overcome these deeply entrenched stereotypes, just as they had struggled throughout the antebellum era and through the years of war and Reconstruction. The dominant strategy early in the New South era was to prove to genteel white readers that blacks had feelings and aspirations much like those of the most admirable whites.

Black literature changed markedly in the mid-1890s. Before that time, most black leaders and spokesmen had disdained black dialect writing as a rationalization for black subjugation, as the embodiment of black inferiority, as an insult to black Americans who had educated themselves and their children. On the other hand, white readers seemed perpetually fascinated with black dialect writing, which appeared in everything from Cable to Twain, from Harris to Chopin; dialect often conveyed black humanity and complexity, undermined easy notions of black character.

A black writer who possessed firsthand knowledge of what it meant to

Charles W. Chesnutt. (Cleveland Public Library)

live in the South and who mastered dialect emerged in Charles Waddell Chesnutt. He had been born in Cleveland, but grew up in the 1860s and 1870s in Fayetteville, North Carolina. His grandfather, a white man, acknowledged his children by his black mistress and helped Chesnutt's father get established in the grocery business after the Civil War. After his schooling the young and ambitious Chesnutt worked in the family's store, sold door-to-door, and then became a teacher near Charlotte, sending money back to his parents.

Although Chesnutt quickly rose to some prominence as an educator, marrying and beginning a family, he anguished over the stigma of his father's illegitimacy and his own mixed racial background. He felt cut off from blacks as well as whites. "I am neither fish, flesh, nor fowl—neither 'nigger,' white, nor 'buckrah,'" Chesnutt confided to his journal in 1881. "Too 'stuck-up' for the colored folks, and, of course, not recognized by the whites." Chesnutt, like so many blacks in North Carolina in these years, thought he would do better elsewhere and went on exploratory trips to the North. Convinced he would need considerably more income to support his family in the North, Chesnutt began to look for ways to make that money. He decided literature offered promise, though he reckoned his chances of success at barely "one out of a hundred." Like white authors, Chesnutt set out to gather examples of authentic folklore, especially "the ballads or hymns which the colored people sing with such fervor." He thought such songs were certain to be objects of "curiosity to people, literary people, at the North."

From the beginning, Chesnutt intended his literature to change white minds about black people. He was inspired by Albion Tourgée's *A Fool's Errand* and other novels that tried to counter the white Southern view of life in the region. Chesnutt decided that he would write to effect a "moral revolution," fighting against the "almost indefinable feeling of repulsion toward the Negro, which is common to most Americans." Rather than confront white prejudice head-on, as Cable had done, Chesnutt thought white racism had to be "mined" from underneath; whites had to be led "imperceptibly, unconsciously, step by step" into the recognition that black people possessed all the feelings and abilities of whites.

Such plans came to Chesnutt while he lived in North Carolina, but he carried them out in Ohio. He moved his family to Cleveland in the early 1880s, passed the bar examination, and established a profitable court reporting business. His concern with the South could not rest, however, and Chesnutt continued to write. "I was comparatively fresh from the South," he later told an interviewer, and "I soon found that there was a greater demand and a better market for writing along that line." It took a while to find the right voice, but he hit upon artistic and financial success in 1887 with his story "The Goophered Grapevine," published in the *Atlantic Monthly*. Over the next decade, while maintaining his court business, Chesnutt slowly polished one story after another. Readers assumed that Chesnutt was a white author; while his stories were admired and did well, Chesnutt did not become a literary celebrity. These stories were published as a book, *The Conjure Woman,* in 1899.

Chesnutt's fiction lived up to the resolve he made as a younger man, for it sought to undermine white prejudice, not attack it. The black people in his stories were not people like himself, educated, urban, financially successful; rather, they were, on the surface, black people of the sort readers expected to encounter in stories about the South. Most of the early tales were told by a former slave named Julius, who used stories of conjuring to manipulate, for his economic advantage, a Northern white couple living in the South. The stories, elegantly crafted and concise, undercut much of the plantation tradition. Chesnutt's plantation was no refuge from modern greed, but its very embodiment.

Chesnutt's narrators told chilling allegories. One young man, continually separated from his wife, wished he could always stay with her; to his surprise, she confided to him that, as a conjure woman, she possessed the power to transform him into anything he wished. They finally decided that he would take the form of a tree. For a while the stratagem worked, as the man and woman were able to see one another each evening when she turned him back into a man. One day, though, she was sent away and the master cut the tree down to make a kitchen for the house, the lumber screaming as the saw bit into the wood, the kitchen forever haunted by his groans and sighs. The conjure woman was driven mad with guilt and grief. It turned out that the wood had subsequently been used to build a black schoolhouse, which the Northern white man was going to tear down for wood to build an addition to his house; after the story, his wife would have nothing to do with the thought. Fortuitously, some black members of a church that had split over the temperance question would be able to use the building for their new congregation; Julius was among their number.

In another story, an industrious and moral slave was framed as a thief by a rival for a young woman's love. The slave was forced to wear a ham around his neck, an emblem of his guilt. Abandoned by one after another of his friends and family, he fell into madness, thinking of himself as nothing more than a piece of meat himself. He finally hanged himself by the neck. In these stories, as in others of Chesnutt's, it was the psychological toll of slavery that proved so horrifying, the psychological toll that even well-intentioned white writers sought to deny, that most dialect hid.

Chesnutt also published another collection of stories, *The Wife of His Youth and Other Stories of the Color Line,* in the same year *The Conjure Woman* came out. As the title suggested, these stories confronted his own experience more directly, exploring the irrationalities and injustices surrounding people of mixed racial backgrounds. These stories had even more of an edge than the dialect stories of the other book, exposing the hypocrisy and delusion that surrounded race mixture in the South and in the North, exposing the aspiration and achievement among postwar black and mulatto people in a way no white writer had. Encouraged by the critical success of his two collections of stories, Chesnutt gave up court reporting and became a full-time writer in 1899. He completed a novel on which he had been working for years, *The House Behind the Cedars* (1900), the story, as Chesnutt put it, "of a colored girl who passed for white."

The theme of racial mixing was a topic of considerable literary and political interest at the turn of the century. White writers repeatedly turned to miscegenation as a major theme, beginning with George Washington Cable in 1880 and in ever greater numbers as the years passed. For several of Kate Chopin's characters, the discovery of mixed blood led only to suicide or death, for the distance between white gentility and black inheritance was too great to be endured. Mark Twain, in *Pudd'nhead Wilson,* explored the irrational and destructive notion of race, showing that environment and expectation, not "blood," made all the difference. Thomas Nelson Page, on the other hand, portrayed the mulatto as the worst of both races, as the most frightening embodiment of lowered boundaries between white and black. At the time Chesnutt published *The House Behind the Cedars,* then, the "story of a colored girl who passed for white" was a charged topic.

Chesnutt's approach differed from those of white writers by dealing with racial mixing as a widespread fact with which many thousands of "black" people lived, not a curse reserved for a few damned souls or the beginning of the end of the pure Anglo-Saxons. The problem of mulattoes was not biological, but social; they were caught, like Chesnutt, between two peoples whose lives were sharply constrained by law and custom. His very first essay, "What Is a White Man?," had displayed the legal inconsistencies surrounding any definition of race. On the other hand, he told black Americans that racial mixing was their best hope of full participation in the nation's life. Chesnutt flew in the face of mounting white feeling by advocating more, not less, racial intermarriage. As a result, he did not pass judgment on the mulatto characters in his fiction, even though in his personal life he chose to be known as a black man rather than the white man he appeared to be. While *The House Behind the Cedars* thus broke with some of the conventions of the genre of race mixing, its ending—where the heroine died without consummating a relationship with a man of either race—used the easy way out, the convenient death of the "tragic mulatto." The book won some critical approval but sold poorly. Chesnutt looked for a theme that would allow him to continue his "mining" of white prejudice even as it attracted a larger audience.

He turned to the Wilmington race riot of 1898 for his next novel, *The Marrow of Tradition* (1901). Chesnutt had never lost touch with North Carolina and he watched events there in the late 1890s with anger and disgust. His purpose was straightforward: to "create sympathy for the colored people of the South in the very difficult position which they occupy." On the other hand, he knew that if he was to win the attention of white book buyers and reviewers he would have to create attractive white characters. Chesnutt saw *The Marrow of Tradition* as his chance to change the minds of white people about the spiral of events in the South. Like Cable, Twain, and Glasgow, Chesnutt thought that the major problem was the white South's unthinking adherence to the shibboleths of the past, to tradition. The South had changed deeply since emancipation, but whites refused to acknowledge that fact, insisting that the racial order of slavery would remain the racial order of freedom. Chesnutt urged people to recognize that the South was evolving, that the tides of change could not be held back with violence and brutality. The book, with its muted tones and plea for moderation combined with a rather obvious didactic structure, did not sell well or win very favorable reviews. Chesnutt—and his publishers—began to lose confidence in his literary career. He tried one more novel, about the South but focused on whites, then returned to his profitable court business, writing only sporadically through the first two decades of the new century. Black audiences were to remember Charles W. Chesnutt, but white audiences paid little attention.

Even fewer whites knew of the other important black writer of the turn of the century, Sutton Griggs, even though Griggs may have had more black readers than Chesnutt. Griggs, born in 1872 in Texas, came to Richmond in 1893 to attend a seminary. He was to go on to churches in several Southern states and to a position in the National Baptist Convention. In the years between 1899 and 1908, however, Griggs wrote five novels and published them himself. Although they emerged in quick succession, the novels followed widely divergent lines, exploring, from a number of angles, the problem of being black in the South at the turn of the century. Griggs established few literary connections—unlike Dunbar or Chesnutt—and wrote for no white publishers who might urge him toward stock conventions or white sales. Griggs, a curious amalgam of assimilationist and rebel, never resolved his positions but oscillated among them.

Griggs's fiction often turned around the maddeningly arbitrary limits faced by young black people of intelligence, education, and good will. In his first and strongest novel, *Imperium in Imperio,* disappointment and bitterness surrounded the protagonist, who was drawn into a black insurrectionary army after all his legitimate ambitions were thwarted. The novel, like most of Griggs's work, experimented with various combinations of racial and sexual identity; in one episode, the male hero passed himself off as a black maid to get the inside story from whites. So effective was the disguise that young white men tried to seduce him. The hero later became distraught when his light-skinned wife bore him a "white" child. Feeling he had nothing left to lose, the black man threw himself into the black revolution, only to betray it at the last minute, damning himself to execution. Clearly, Griggs had no plan himself, only a willingness to display his anger and frustration without the cover of dialect or sentimental plots. The farther black writers got from the conventions of the plantation tradition, the less likely they were to win a hearing from genteel readers of either race.

Sadly, the literary experimentation of Southern literature that flourished in the early 1880s and then again at the turn of the century soon faded. Only Ellen Glasgow was to keep her momentum, publishing excellent novels in 1911 and 1913. Virtually every other author fell into silence. The South continued to play an important role in the nation's popular literature, but its voice became reduced to a shrill, virtually hysterical, white scream. The literature of exploration was displaced by the vicious and bitter literature of racial hatred.

Thomas Dixon was the leading figure in the new reaction. One of the most successful of the many thousands of white Southern émigrés in the late nineteenth century, Dixon went to Johns Hopkins with Woodrow Wilson, became an actor, then a lawyer and state legislator in North Carolina, then a minister in Boston and New York (preaching the social gospel), then an accomplished speaker on the lecture circuit. Dixon's life changed in 1901, when he happened to see a stage production of *Uncle Tom's Cabin*. Outraged, he sat down to write a novel in response. In a mere sixty days, Dixon completed *The Leopard's Spots*, which he then sent unrevised to Walter Hines Page, an outspoken Southern émigré himself who had helped writers such as Glasgow. Page, overwhelmed by the book, accurately predicted its fate: published in 1902, the novel eventually sold nearly a million copies. Unlike the novels of ambivalence and uncertainty that came out of the South in the 1890s, *The Leopard's Spots* spoke with the fire of conviction and race hatred. Dixon followed it with *The Clansman* (1906), soon to provide the script for another Southern émigré's powerful meditation on his homeland, D. W. Griffith's *Birth of a Nation*. Those books and that film provided white Southerners a way to have what they wanted most: a clear conscience, a way back into the national mythology of innocence, a way to see the violence against Reconstruction and the continuation of lynching as means to racial and national redemption.

Through the 1910s Southern literature seemed in retreat. The South even disappeared from the bestseller lists, with Ellen Glasgow's appearance in 1916 marking the region's only presence. In 1915, H. L. Mencken, a young newspaperman from Baltimore, leveled a brutal assessment of the South's culture: "In that whole region, an area three times as large as either France or Germany, there is not a single symphony orchestra, nor a single picture worth looking at, nor a single public building or monument of the first rank, nor a single factory devoted to the making of beautiful things, nor a single poet, novelist, historian, musician, painter or sculptor whose reputation extends beyond his own country." Mencken blamed "Puritanism" for the South's barrenness, which he was later to liken to the Sahara.

The desert metaphor was all wrong, a Southern critic sympathetic to Mencken responded. The South was, in fact, a cultural jungle. If Mencken would only plunge into Southern literature he could "wander for years, encountering daily such a profusion of strange and incredible growths as could proceed from none but an enormously rich soil." The South was "not sterile. On the contrary, it is altogether too luxuriant"—not the Sahara, but the Congo. The South produced not symphony halls, but juke joints, holiness churches, and country dances. American culture proved richer for the imbalance.

Chapter 11

~~~~~~

Voices

Most Southerners preferred singing, playing, and dancing to reading and writing. Whether at opera houses or medicine shows, barrelhouses or singing schools, music attracted people of every description. The ledger books of Southern stores were filled with entries marking the sale of fiddle, guitar, and banjo strings, or the sale of the instruments themselves, many for less than a dollar. Cheap banjos were mass-produced in the 1880s, guitars in the 1890s. The banjo increasingly became identified with white musicians in the mountains, where it had not been especially important before. Associated for generations with black musicians, by the late nineteenth century the banjo had become eclipsed as the instrument of choice among young black people, replaced by organs, pianos, accordions, guitars, and brass instruments. Pianos appeared throughout the South, in black and white churches, in juke joints, and in the homes of the genteel.

Students of both races were eager to learn formal music. Instructors taught classical music and voice throughout the towns and cities of the South. Bouncy popular music filled parlors, stages, tents, and streets; every town of any size had an "opera house" and traveling performers brought shows of variable talent to their stages. Novelty acts, troupes of Alpine singers, Hawaiian steel guitarists, and the leading popular performers of the day came through Southern towns, large and small. As a result, Southerners knew the latest songs. In 1893, a young South Carolina girl, her aunt reported with mixed feelings, spent much of one day "singing 'ta-ra-ra-boom-

Black men with a guitar in southwest Virginia. (University of Virginia Special Collections)

de-ay' at the top of her shrill little voice." The song's nonsense lyrics masked its bawdy origins in a brothel; the checkered past of the tune did not prevent it from becoming one of the first "hits" throughout the English-speaking world. The most popular song in America in the 1890s—"After the Ball"— was repeated so much in the South that it became tiresome; a writer in a Louisiana paper announced in 1895 that singing the song should be "specially prohibited" over the town's new telephone system.

Sentimental songs, so-called "parlor songs," proliferated. Like the mass-produced literature of the day, sheet music for songs filled with sadness, death, Mother, and Home went for the easy tear and catch in the throat. Such sheet music rolled off the presses in editions numbering in the hundreds of thousands, often decorated with evocative color prints. The pianos and organs of the South played the sad tunes prominent in the amateur entertainments that flourished across the region.

Some of the most widespread songs at the turn of the century were "coon songs." These songs, popular on stages from New York to New Orleans to San Francisco, were parodies of black language, styles, and aspirations. Some idea of their tone can be gathered from their titles: "All Coons Look Alike to Me," "Mammy's Little Pickaninny Boy," "My Coal Black Lady," "You'se Just a Little Nigger, Still You'se Mine, All Mine." Between 1896 and 1900, at least 600 coon songs were published, with several of the most popular tunes written by black men. Some songs adopted a newly fashionable syncopation, while others followed the sentimental tradition of the parlor songs. The performers were both black and white, male and female.

The coon songs, and many other forms besides, were played out in the enormously popular minstrel shows of the South. Before the Civil War, minstrel shows had been the rage in the North, staged almost entirely by white men hidden behind blackface. After emancipation, Northern audiences curious about real black people were eager to attend minstrel shows where blacks performed; if the men on stage were former slaves, so much the better. The novelty of even authentic blacks began to wane in the North by the 1880s, but in the South these black minstrel shows, usually under white management, offered the greatest opportunity for black musicians and singers to make a living with their skills. "It goes without saying that minstrels were a disreputable lot in the eyes of upper-crust Negroes," one minstrel recalled, "but it was also true that the best composers, the singers, the musicians, the speakers, the stage performers—the minstrel shows got them all." The minstrel shows, always on the lookout for new material, brought a steady infusion of the latest songs from vaudeville, Tin Pan Alley, and ragtime to the South.

The songs soon became part of the repertoire of a large, loose network of performers in the region, ranging from those who sang at carnivals and circuses to blind singers who worked the streets of larger cities. The boundary between folk and commercial song was blurred from the very beginning.

Not only did songwriters build upon themes, words, and tunes of music with anonymous "folk" origins, but singers picked up songs of unknown beginnings from one another that had been written in Northern cities. For example, before 1910 one of the earliest students of black music collected a version of the song "I Got Mine," originally composed in Tin Pan Alley in 1901. The song turned up again over the next decade in Alabama and Georgia, sung by a black guitar player, an elderly black male cook, a black road working camp, and a black minstrel show. The song had been made a part of a black folk tradition, its origins a matter of no concern.

The genealogy of Southern music is tangled. There is no way to separate out the strands, to establish firm chronologies in the era before mechanical recordings. But it seems likely that Southern music did not begin as the naive outpourings of the folk and then become more sophisticated and commercialized as it evolved. To the contrary, Southern music seems to have become more distinctly "Southern," more specifically regional, as the decades of the New South era passed, as older styles and newer fashions mixed and cohered, as musicians of both races learned from one another.

That process had been going on for generations, of course, as black plantation musicians learned to play European music and as whites copied black musicians, down to the burnt-cork imitations of African-American skin color. The currents of black music remained strong, played surreptitiously in the slave quarters, sung without accompaniment in the fields, incorporated into work songs with disguised meanings. The African origins of black music were most obvious in religious songs, where the congregation combined the most important aspects of African music: polyrhythms, call and response, improvisation, rough and slurred voice textures, falsetto. A ritual called the "ring shout" helped carry such musical preferences intact from one generation to the next. Worshippers gathered in a circle, their arms extended and their shoulders hunched, moving counterclockwise without crossing their feet. Other worshippers standing against the walls created a complex rhythm of clapping and stamping. Worshippers answered the preacher's cries until religious ecstasy seized the dancers.

Increased diffusion and accelerated musical invention began soon after the end of slavery. Part of the exchange became institutionalized as early as 1871, when the Fisk Jubilee Singers embarked on highly publicized and well-attended concert tours to collect money for the new Fisk University in Nashville. Though advertised as authentic "negro spirituals," the songs the Jubilee Singers performed bore the mark of white choral styles. Singing before either all-black or all-white audiences, singing popular songs of diverse origins, the Jubilee Singers found their greatest success in songs identified with the slave era—much to the dismay of some of the young singers, who prided themselves on their distance from slavery. The "spirituals" became popular among whites, published in books with arrangements by whites, converted to European standards and preferences. Black colleges continued to use singing groups as instruments of fund-raising and publicity for decades, giving whites a chance to hear "real" black music in an atmosphere of refinement and good will.

A form of black music closer to the preferences of the poorer black majority—"patting juba," or simply "pats"—soon proved to be even more popular than the spirituals. Participants beat their palms on various parts of their bodies, creating complicated rhythms. Musicians accompanied this patting with syncopated playing on fiddles or banjos. As early as 1874, "Civil Rights Juba" appeared in print and was followed a few years later by "Rag Baby Jig"; both tried to translate the syncopation of black music, the stress on the weaker beat, into white musical notation. Throughout the 1880s, black string bands played syncopated music, finding that audiences of both races responded enthusiastically to the exciting rhythm.

In the 1890s, this "ragged" music became a national sensation, driven by the determination and talents of Scott Joplin. Born in 1868 in Texarkana, Joplin learned the banjo from his mother and more genteel forms from his father, who had played European parlor and dance music for his masters as a plantation musician. Although Joplin's father abandoned the family, the youngster's obvious talent led educated members of the black community to help with music lessons. His mother, working as a maid, saved enough money for an old piano, an increasingly popular instrument. Joplin began his professional life as an itinerant musician, one of the many crisscrossing eastern Texas. Along with other black musicians, Joplin began to translate the banjo syncopation to the piano in the late 1880s. By the time he was sixteen, Joplin had his own band; by the time he was twenty, he had decided on St. Louis as his base for travels into the North and the Midwest. In 1897, Joplin, along with others, began to write down "ragtime" music for publication, but his white publisher, uncertain of the market, took two years to release it. In 1899, Joplin composed "Maple Leaf Rag," named for a black social club in Sedalia. The song soon became nationally famous, partly through the aggressive marketing efforts of the Sedalia piano dealer who bought the rights.

Over the next few years, people throughout America heard ragtime. White players and publishers appropriated the music, watering it down and blending it into less challenging forms such as the "coon song." Brass bands, black and white, prided themselves on being able to play what passed for ragtime. Audiences expected a band that played marches and overtures to produce, on demand, a coon song or a version of ragtime mass-produced for brass bands by large publishing houses. Even John Philip Sousa's band played ragtime.

Such blurring of musical boundaries was common. No musician, black or white, was expected to play only one style. The early life of W. C. Handy, the self-professed "father of the blues," revealed the complex exchanges. Handy was born in 1873 in Florence, Alabama, firmly within the postwar generation of black Southerners and firmly within the genteel tradition. His family once traded a gallon of milk for a copy of *Poor Richard's Almanac* and made sure they always kept enough cash on hand to contribute a nickel for Sunday school and a dime for the church collection. Handy's life took an unexpected turn, however, when a trumpet player performed at his church with a Baptist choir from Birmingham. The boy longed for an instrument and eventually saved enough money to buy a guitar from a local store. His father was outraged, Handy recalled. " 'A box,' he gasped, while my mother stood frozen. 'A guitar! One of the devil's playthings. Take it away. . . . Whatever possessed you to bring a sinful thing like that into our Christian home? Take it back where it came from. You hear? Get!' " Handy was forced to exchange the instrument for a new Webster's Unabridged Dictionary.

Other musical opportunities continued to appear, though. Handy's parents relented enough to allow him to take vocal lessons, unaccompanied by instruments, and in this way he learned to read music. The arrival in Florence of Jim Turner, a well-traveled black violin player, allowed Handy to glimpse another world. Turner had been to Beale Street in Memphis, "where life was a song from dawn to dawn. He described the darktown dandies and high-brown belles" and planted in Handy a "seed of discontent." The seed grew, as the youngster bought an archaic cornet from a member of a white circus band stranded in Florence, taught himself to play, and secretly joined a band and a minstrel show. Meanwhile, Handy had stayed near the head of his class, sang in the AME choir, and served as a political campaign speaker. He left Florence in 1892 to teach school in Birmingham, but found that work in the city's steel mills paid considerably more.

Handy was not unhappy with his situation, but the depression of 1893 cost him his job. He drifted through the Midwest and Upper South, looking for work. He had his best luck with music, heading a brass band in Indiana. His break came in 1896, when a minstrel troupe invited him to join; Handy, ambitious as well as talented, steadily worked his way up, taking on increasing responsibility in the company. The band members covered vast areas of the country, risking their lives in several Texas towns where "authentic" minstrel shows were not appreciated, traveling to Cuba in 1899, and eventually working their way to northern Alabama. He was constantly on the lookout for new styles and techniques he could incorporate into his show. In a few years, a major discovery would come that would make Handy famous, but in the meantime he was merely another black musician on the road.

W. C. Handy was not the only black youth at the turn of the century who combined formal training with a taste for popular music and the rewards it brought. In New Orleans, the largest city in the South, a young mulatto named Ferdinand Pechet grew up in a French-speaking household in the late 1880s and early 1890s, listening to classical music, trying out the instruments in the house—guitar, drums, piano, trombone—and beginning lessons at the age of six. His mother, raising him with the help of her mother and sisters, had no desire for her son to become a musician, but the temptations were just too strong in New Orleans. Unknown to his family, by the time Pechet was a teenager he was playing piano in the tenderloin district where prostitutes plied their trade. He made more money than he could have imagined and dressed the part. Pechet's mother died when he was fourteen and his grandmother discovered the boy's money-making efforts; she put him out on the streets. Pechet changed his last name to Morton, perhaps the name of his father. The youngster traveled to Biloxi and Meridian, where he played in a whorehouse run by a white woman until locals, suspecting sexual liaisons, threatened a lynching.

The New Orleans to which "Ferd" Morton returned at the turn of the century, with its ethnic variety, complex racial code, and large number of musicians, concentrated the musical diversity of the New South. Secret societies flourished among people of all races, and each held a steady round of dances, parties, parades, and wakes. Marching bands and funeral processions influenced one another; French, Spanish, Caribbean, African, and English music jostled and mixed. While pianists such as Ferd Morton worked in bordellos—he became known as "Jelly Roll," a sexual allusion—bands played for dances in ballrooms, saloons, clubs, and parks. Bands mixed brass instruments with guitar, fiddles, and banjos. The line between white and black music remained indistinct, as a wide range of styles influenced one another and as white musicians as well as black performed the latest songs. Relatively affluent and trained black "creoles" mixed with poorer and musically rougher blacks from the country, clarinets mixed with trumpets, "clean" European styles mixed with "dirty" African-American embellishments. Bands pulled wagons into the streets during the day, playing their music for free to advertise their paid performances in the evening. They competed with one another, sometimes good-naturedly, sometimes viciously. "If you couldn't blow a man down with your horn," one musician remembered, "at least you could use it to hit him alongside the head."

Some of this music began to sound like what later generations would know as jazz. Even as they played the most fashionable waltzes or quadrilles for white dances, black musicians infused the music with distinctly African-American styles. The form of the song did not constrain black musicians, for the forms could change on the spot to reflect the musicians' or the audience's preferences. The fashions of the day came and went, but the underlying unities of black music remained, especially complex rhythms. Marches faded, and ragtime rose and fell, but all along musicians turned toward polyrhythms, call and response, improvisation, the imitation of the human voice by instruments, and the accent on notes not emphasized by Western music. From an early age, future musicians heard distinctively African-American music in church, in the tunes their parents sang, in the work songs of cotton pickers or dock hands, in the banjo music played by older musicians, and in the ragtime and plantation ditties performed on the minstrel stage. These musicians self-consciously highlighted African-American elements when they played new music, emphasizing certain harmonies, rhythms, and textures while de-emphasizing European elements.

Black music in New Orleans in the 1890s and early 1900s, then, had begun to sound like jazz but was not yet a coherent style. A key figure in the crystallization of the music later to be known as jazz was Charles "Buddy" Bolden, the "King." Born in New Orleans in 1877, close to the railroad depot, Bolden was of the postwar generation, attending school and taking formal lessons on the cornet. Yet Bolden was old enough to have heard the black musicians who played African drums and other instruments in the city's Congo Square up through the early 1880s, directly conveying African styles. Bolden picked up further African-American influences at the barbershops of his neighborhood, where men played guitars and fiddles while waiting for work, and at the Baptist church he attended, where clapping and perhaps an occasional piano accompanied the hymns. Bolden put together his own band early on, combining a bass, guitar, clarinet, cornet, and sometimes a violin. This band, unlike the traditional brass bands of the city, played dances and parties rather than marches. Unlike the piano "professors," such dance bands did not play at bordellos, where dancing was not the preferred physical activity. Bolden's band and others often played at parks, picnics, advertising wagons, and Masonic halls.

Bolden was an ambitious showman, determined to become the most famous musician in New Orleans. As a result, he was always on the lookout for the latest thing, something to set him and his band apart from the many competitors in the city. By the late 1890s, Bolden had begun to play his cornet "wide-open," speeding up the tempo and "ragging" familiar hymns and other popular songs. He was not the first to experiment with different rhythms—piano players and marching bands had been playing ragtime for several years—but he was the first to put the new rhythms into the context of a dance band. While earlier dance bands had featured the fiddle, guitar, and banjo, Bolden relegated those string instruments to the rhythm section, featuring the brass instruments instead.

Bolden, in his early twenties at the time and with players as young as sixteen in the band, often "faked" a passage in a popular song, throwing in attention-getting embellishments in place of the written music. At first, some listeners of both races who were steeped in the European styles found Bolden's experiments distasteful, but younger blacks responded with enthusiasm. Bolden, working as a plasterer in his day job, began to build a following. He and his band soon "had the whole of New Orleans real crazy and running wild behind it," Bunk Johnson recalled. Johnson considered Bolden's band "the first band to play jazz" because it contained the largest stretches of improvisation, "head" music, "faking" it. "And King Bolden was one fine-lookin' brown-skin man, tall and slender and a terror with the ladies. He was the greatest ragtime cornet player, with a round keen tone. He could execute like hell and play in any key. He had a *head*, Buddy did!" Another jazzman

Buddy Bolden in the mid-1890s, reprinted from Marquis, In Search of Buddy Bolden.

remembered seeing Bolden's band for the first time, at Odd Fellows Hall: "It was plenty rough. You paid fifteen cents and walked in. The band, six of them was sitting on a low stand. They had their hats on and were resting, pretty sleepy. All of a sudden, Buddy stomps, knocks on the floor with his trumpet to give the beat and they all sit up straight." Soon the crowd was screaming for more. "I'd never heard anything like that before. I'd played 'legitimate' stuff. But this, it was something that pulled me in." Bolden played loud, but specialized in slow numbers, "dragging" the beat, leaving more room for embellishment. His signature tune was "Funky Butt," a sort of novelty piece with improvised words, often with overt anatomical references, often containing put-downs. One place where Bolden played became known as "Funky Butt Hall." In the early 1900s, King Bolden ruled New Orleans. He was famous for the loudness of his horn and the heat of his music, characteristics admired by black audiences especially.

Bolden worried, though, that other bands were stealing his ideas, that he constantly needed new angles, new audiences; he started having intense headaches, drinking far too much, and becoming violent. "That fellow studied too hard—always trying to think up something to bring out," a contemporary recalled. "He could hear you play something and keep it in his head—then go home and think up parts." The alcohol and the competition wore on Bolden, whose behavior became more erratic and extreme. He lost jobs and his money. The only time Bolden made it into the white newspapers was during these hard days, when they blandly mentioned that a deluded colored musician, convinced his mother was poisoning him, attacked her with a water pitcher. In 1907, the King was sent to a mental hospital, where he lived until his death in 1931. He peacefully wandered through the ward, ritualistically touching each post at least once in his tour of the building. The only record of his music that remained were the memories of those present at the birth of jazz.

In the years around 1900, then, Southern black music was evolving rapidly, forms blurring and bending, experimentation becoming the expectation. Genteel dances became ragged tunes; hymns became secular songs; commercial hits became folk ditties. The music was so diverse and changing so quickly that it was not codified into fixed forms, its notes transcribed to paper and disseminated through the channels of the marketplace. Key figures worked on their own in these early years, generally unknown to one another.

While the musical exchange went on fastest in the cities of the Mississippi River from St. Louis to New Orleans, it also reached into the small-town and rural South. Black songsters traveled throughout the region making their living by playing a wide range of songs, eager to learn a new tune, willing to share what they had learned. When W. C. Handy went to the Mississippi Delta in the 1890s he confronted "the blind singers and footloose bards that were forever coming and going. Usually the fellows were destitute. Some came sauntering down the railroad tracks, others dropped from freight cars, while still others caught rides on the big road and entered town on the top of cotton bales." They tended to gather at the railroad station. "There, surrounded by crowds of country folks, they would pour out their hearts in song while the audience ate fish and bread, chewed sugar cane, dipped snuff while waiting for the trains to carry them down the line." The songsters earned money by selling songs they had written, some working the trains, some going from church to church.

When these songsters came to town, they often joined with local players and singers to swap songs and to show off. In this way, their repertoires constantly grew and diversified. The musicians, especially those who won the coveted jobs of playing at dances, eagerly combined many kinds of music. The most successful musicians were those who could shift among sad ballads, quick-stepping minstrel ditties, old-time fiddle tunes, waltzes, quadrilles, and ragtime. Black musicians played for audiences of both races and prided themselves on their ability to play in any popular style. A new song was a valued possession, a catchy new style or novelty something worth working up.

The lumber camps of the lower South proved especially receptive to itinerant musicians. One of the buildings in virtually every camp was the "barrelhouse," "honky tonk," or "juke joint." The structure, like all the other buildings in such a camp, was merely a large box or boxcar brought in on the railroad by the lumber company. With few diversions available for their workers in the remote and isolated camps, the management used the barrelhouse as a lure to prospective laborers, a source of additional income, and a place to allow hard-drinking lumber men to gamble, dance, and patronize prostitutes. "They shoot craps, dice, drink whisky, dance, every modern devilment you can do," one musician explained, "the barrelhouse is where it's at." The barrelhouses, known for their violence, usually spared the musicians. The musicians were approved by, even paid by, the bosses, who provided meals and a place to sleep; if their music met the approval of their audience, they might win tips, more often than not in the form of free drinks.

The piano, provided by the lumber companies, was perfect for the barrelhouse, loud and percussive, durable and versatile. While almost all of these early barrelhouse players remain in obscurity, Eubie Blake, later to become a jazz great himself, recalled seeing a 300-pound pioneer named William Turk as early as 1896: "He had a left hand like God. He didn't even know what key he was playing in, but he played them all. He would play the ragtime stride bass, but it bothered him because his stomach got in the way of his arm, so he used a walking bass instead." Blake remembered how Turk "would play one note with his right hand and at the same time four with his left. We called it 'sixteen'—they call it boogie-woogie now."

The barrelhouse piano players worked circuits of towns and camps in Texas and Louisiana, developing unique styles and followings. The sources of the barrelhouse style were complex and diverse. Like the other instrument gaining favor among black musicians in the late nineteenth century—the guitar—people admired the piano for its ability to convey the cadences of the railroad, both the rhythmic rumble of the wheels and the high-pitched ring of the bells. The barrelhouse style probably owed something to the church music evolving in these years, also based on the piano and also drawn to railroad imagery.

Despite any musical affinity with the churches, the barrelhouse player occupied a place near the bottom of the black musical hierarchy. Unlike those musicians who traveled with a fiddle or guitar, who often included religious music in their repertoires or even specialized in hymns, the barrelhouse piano player played for the roughest kind of secular audience in the roughest kind of places. Even the more exclusive bordellos would have nothing to do with such crude music, good mainly for the most overtly sexual kinds of dancing. "When you listen to what I'm playing, you got to see in your mind all them gals out there swinging their butts and getting the means excited. Otherwise you ain't got the music rightly understood," one early Texas player, "Fud" Shaw, recalled. "I could sit there and throw my hands down and make them gals do anything. I told them when to shake it, and when to hold back ('Squat low, mama, let your daddy see . . . you got something keeps on worrying me.') That's what this music is for." Other musicians considered barrelhouse musically crude as well, monotonous and inflexible, indicative of the player's inability to tackle more demanding forms. When barrelhouse players came to a town such as New Orleans, they were relegated to the alleys and dives. Yet the barrelhouse style soon became a part of the repertoire of the more sophisticated piano players, one more attention-getting technique, one more exciting kind of dance music with an insistent beat.

Charles Peabody, a white archaeologist from Harvard University, came to supervise black workers as they excavated a burial mound in Coahoma County, Mississippi, in 1901 and 1902. As he put it in the folk language of academic life, "our ears were beset with an abundance of ethnological material in song." The workers sang as they dug, alternating between hymns and ragtime, especially a song known as "Goo-goo Eyes." Peabody was surprised at their choice of material and a bit disappointed: "Undoubtedly picked up from passing theatrical troupes, the 'ragtime' sung for us quite inverted the supposed theory of its origin," having passed from professionals to the folk rather than the other way around. Other songs, though, work songs, were improvisational and rhythmic, drawing on established themes but otherwise tailored to suit the occasion. Peabody recognized social commentary in these songs, whether it was directed at sheriffs, slavery, the heat, or Peabody himself. "One evening when my companion and I were playing a game of mumble-the-peg, our final occupation before closing work," a worker sang loud enough for the boss to hear: "I'm so tired I'm most dead, Sittin' up there playing mumblely-peg." The men could not, or would not, sing well on demand, and turned in a dispirited performance of "Goo-goo Eyes" for Peabody's wife.

What struck Peabody most was a kind of music, sung solo, that fit none of the other categories. As a nearby black farmer followed his mule for fifteen hours, he sang tunes that "melted into strains of apparently genuine African music, sometimes with words, sometimes without. Long phrases there were without apparent measured rhythm, singularly hard to copy in notes." This singing was clearly distinct from the hymns and the ragtime, though the plowman could skillfully slide from one form to the next. Peabody heard such singing again one evening as a black mother sang her baby to sleep. "Her song was to me quite impossible to copy, weird in interval and strange in rhythm; peculiarly beautiful."

This singing—unaccompanied, improvisational, fluid—was clearly related to the "field hollers" that black working people had sung for generations. The hollers echoed the vocal techniques heard in the ring shout: the guttural, the slurs, the roughness, the falsetto, the tones between major and minor thirds and sevenths. Like the work songs, these field hollers carried African styles from one generation to the next, from one place to the next. Much more than ragtime, the slower pacing of the field hollers and work songs left room for great experimentation and inflection.

The blues used parts of the field hollers and work songs but drew on ballads for their organization, chord progressions, and lyrical content. The ballads were narratives, stories about real or mythical characters, written and sold by the itinerant singers of both races who rode the rails of the New South. The ballads might concern an event such as a train wreck or flood, a particularly spectacular crime (such as "Frankie and Johnnie"), or a hero (such as John Henry). The lyrics were often elaborate, carrying the story forward in time and moral. Yet some songsters, finding the ballads too constraining, began in the 1890s to perform songs called "jump-ups." These tunes were accompanied by guitar, like ballads, but repeated nonlinear, often unconnected lyrics over strummed accompaniment. Such lyrics left much more space for improvisation than the ballads, and their simple rhyme scheme made it easy to think of lines on the spot.

The guitars which spread so quickly in this era proved especially suited to ballads and jump-ups, filling in the space around the words far more effectively than a banjo or fiddle. The guitars also had the virtue of being able to mimic an instrument that had remained popular for generations in African and African-American culture. Known in the South as the "didley bow" or "jitterbug," this instrument consisted of a wire stretched taut along the side of a building. The player, often a child, plucked the wire with one hand while sliding a stone, bottle, or some other smooth and hard object against it, creating a sort of wavering, crying sound. The guitar, black musicians soon discovered, could be made to do the same thing in a far more satisfying way, as a bottleneck or knife slid up and down the neck produced a wide range of effects.

W. C. Handy, traveling the music circuits throughout the Mississippi Valley, thought he had heard just about every kind of popular music, black or white. In 1903, though, he heard something different, something he had not confronted before in his travels from Alabama to Chicago to Cuba and back, something he had not heard in the town places where they played ragtime or even barrelhouse. Handy had come to the Mississippi Delta to lead a band in the town of Clarksdale, where a black bank cashier and clarinet player had recruited him. Handy's nine-man band performed throughout the Delta, playing for "affairs of every description." He traveled the Delta's railroads with such regularity that he "could call every flag stop, water tower and pig path" along the way with his eyes closed. "Then one night in Tutwiler, as I nodded in the railroad station while waiting for a train that had been delayed nine hours, life suddenly took me by the shoulder and wakened me with a start."

"A lean, loose-jointed Negro had commenced plunking a guitar beside me while I slept. His clothes were rags; his feet peeped out of his shoes." Handy listened, amazed, as the guitarist "pressed a knife on the strings of the guitar," making them slur and buzz. The singer repeated a single line three times—"Goin' where the Southern cross' the Dog"—as he played "the weirdest music I had ever heard." Handy asked the player what the words meant. "He rolled his eyes, showing a trace of mild amusement." The player explained that he was going to Moorhead, where the Southern Railroad crossed the Yazoo Delta Line, known colloquially as the Yellow Dog, or just the Dog. "That was not unusual," Handy recalled. "Southern Negroes sang about everything. Trains, steamboats, steam whistles, sledge hammers, fast women, mean bosses, stubborn mules," and they accompanied themselves with anything that would make a "musical sound or rhythmical effect, anything from a harmonica to a washboard."

Despite the appeal, novelty, and power of this music, Handy approached such "low folk forms" with "a certain fear and trembling." Handy was schooled in the "music of the modern world," schooled to believe that simple repetition could not be adequate, that music not written down was inferior, that something so raw would not attract the public. He found out to the contrary one night in Cleveland, Mississippi.

"I was leading the orchestra in a dance program when someone sent up an odd request," Handy recalled. "Would we play some of 'our native music,' the note asked. This baffled me. The men in this group could not 'fake' and 'sell it' like minstrel men. They were all musicians who bowed strictly to the authority of printed notes. So we played for our anonymous fan an old-time Southern melody, a melody more sophisticated than native." Soon after finishing this attempt at meeting the desires of the audience, a second request came up to the bandstand. "Would we object if a local colored band played a few dances? Object! That was funny. What hornblower would object to a time-out and a smoke—on pay?" So Handy's band slipped off the stage and made room for a "long-legged chocolate boy" and his band: "a battered guitar, a mandolin and worn-out bass. The music they made was pretty well in keeping with their looks." The music they began seemed to Handy to have "no very clear beginning and certainly no ending at all. The strumming attained a disturbing monotony, but on and on it went, a kind of stuff that has long been associated with cane rows and levee camps. Thump-thump-thump went their feet on the floor. Their eyes rolled. Their shoulders swayed. And through it all that little agonizing strain persisted. It was not really annoying or unpleasant. Perhaps 'haunting' is a better word."

Straining to see the bandstand, Handy was flabbergasted to discover that "a rain of silver dollars began to fall around the outlandish, stomping feet. The dancers went wild. Dollars, quarters, halves—the shower grew heavier." In fact, "there before the boys lay more money than my nine musicians were being paid for the entire engagement." The epiphany was not long in coming: "Then I saw the beauty of primitive music. They had the stuff the people wanted. It touched the spot. Their music wanted polishing, but it contained the essence. Folks would pay money for it." Despite the music's power, however, Handy wondered whether "anybody besides small town rounders and their running mates would go for it."

Handy returned to Clarksdale to orchestrate several "local tunes," translating the "weird" and "haunting" "native" music into notes for his polished band to play. The popularity of the group increased "by leaps and bounds," though the offers did tend to come from "less respectable places." The band would not hesitate to go where the money was, and the biggest money came from a Clarksdale bordello called the "New World," near the railroad, where were gathered "lush octoroons and quadroons from Louisiana, soft cream-colored fancy gals from Mississippi towns." While the Baptist and Methodist black families living nearby clearly disapproved of the events inside, especially the overt interracial sex, Handy and his group, "hired to play music rather than to discuss morals, . . . kept their mouths shut." Not only did "big shot" white officials wink at the New World, but the musicians were also induced to play at such a place because "these rouge-tinted girls, wearing silk stockings and short skirts, bobbing their soft hair and smoking cigarets," were wonderful clients, especially when important white men were the guests. The New World demanded "appropriate music. This led us to arrange and play tunes that had never been written down and seldom sung outside the environment of the oldest profession. Boogie-house music, it was called." Handy first heard the songs "thumped out" on Dopy McKnight's piano, then "took them up, arranged orchestrations and played them to the wild approval of the richly scented yellow gals and their company."

Handy and his band moved freely among every facet of Delta society. "Contacts made in these shady precincts often led to jobs in chaste great houses of the rich and well-to-do," and the band also played on the main street of Clarksdale each week, winning the favor of the whites with more conventional music. The politics of such a situation were complicated, for even though the band played for Southern white Democratic race-baiters at political barbecues, Handy also secretly sold copies of Northern black newspapers such as the *Chicago Defender* and the *Indianapolis Freeman*. The band would play "Dixie" for the white crowds and then ridicule the claptrap they heard from the demagogue's podium. "We could laugh and we could make rhythm. What better armor could you ask?" Handy was making more money than he had ever seen, with the Delta enjoying the peak of its prosperity. "In those days they had a way of opening every new store in the Delta with a big free dance. And it was our fortune to come along at a time when country stores were popping open like cotton blossoms." Handy soon became known in nearby Memphis, playing with his twenty-piece band for large audiences of blacks at a place called Dixie Park, polishing the blend of popular and "native" music. In 1909, Handy and his band were hired to play for mayoral candidate E. H. Crump. The song Handy wrote tried to capture the "weird melody in much the same mood as the one that had been strummed on the guitar at Tutwiler" six years earlier.

Handy was honest about the origins of the song. While the melody was his, the twelve-bar, three-line form was "already used by Negro roustabouts, honky-tonk piano players, wanderers and others of their underprivileged but undaunted class from Missouri to the Gulf, and had become a common medium through which any such individual might express his personal feelings in a sort of musical soliloquy." Handy's innovation "was to introduce this, the 'blues' form to the general public." He tried to put into notes the "flatted" thirds and sevenths of the music, suggestive of "the typical slurs of the Negro voice," that became known as the "blue notes." They played the new song, "Mr. Crump," from a wagon in the streets of Memphis and those who listened, white and black, could not get enough. The band's business took off and Handy, changing the name of the song to "Memphis Blues," sought to publish it. Because no commercial publisher would consider such a song, Handy published it himself. The edition did poorly, though, and he sold the rights for a hundred dollars to a white man in Memphis, who took the song to New York. It became an enormous success in 1912, but Handy was to get little from the song for decades. He wrote other hits thereafter, including one of the most popular published blues of all time, "St. Louis Blues."

Because W. C. Handy was able to translate the blues into a form accessible to a large audience, he deserves a large place in the history of American music. Handy admitted, though, that he was only the adopted "father of the blues." This "weird" and "haunting" music was beginning to surface throughout the lower Mississippi Valley in the years around the turn of the century. Handy was not the only, or even the earliest, professional performer to pick up the form. Gertrude "Ma" Rainey, who traveled with a black tent show singing vaudeville and minstrel songs, confronted the blues in 1902 in a small Missouri town. Rainey heard a young girl singing a "strange and poignant" song about being left by her lover. Struck by its power and novelty, Rainey and her band began working the tune into their show, to enthusiastic response. She began looking for, and finding, similar songs, but they were not then known as "blues."

All the diverse elements of what was to become known as the blues were present, then, around the turn of the century. Field hollers, hymns, and work songs, along with ring shouts and preaching, offered vocal styles. Ballads offered an adaptable structure. Jump-ups offered a flexible approach to lyrics, a way to build improvisation into a song more structured than a field holler. The pats and ragtime offered complex rhythms. Guitars offered a kind of accompaniment that suited singing, versatile enough to be strummed for a satisfying and loud rhythm, played with a slide that could drag out long notes, or picked to bring out a sort of ragtime sound.

With so many elements so widespread in the South, it is impossible to identify the first blues or the first blues singer. Music that sounded something like the blues had been around since slavery. But the form that became known as "the" blues—guitar-based, with lyrics usually sung in an AAB pattern, improvisational, often solo—had not come together until early in the twentieth century. It differed from ballads both in its accompaniment, which was strummed and relatively subdued in the ballads but picked and slid in the blues, and in its lyric structure. In the blues, lyrics did not build in the linear way of the ballad, but rather in a looser way, by association. The singer would choose a general theme—trouble in love, sexual dealings, and traveling were the most important—and then comment on the theme with a series of verses, obliquely connected. The verses could be imported from one song to the next or made up on the spot. The lyrics worked more in the style of modern poetry than in the style of European folk songs, creating a mood through the juxtaposition of discrete and even contradictory images rather than by telling a straightforward story with a straightforward moral.

Given its widespread and diverse origins, it is not surprising that something like the blues appeared in various guises in the South in the early twentieth century. In the older southeastern states of Virginia and Georgia, the blues were relatively melodic and bore stronger resemblances to ballads or ragtime than they did farther west. In East Texas, the rhythms were deemphasized in favor of stylized instrumental flourishes that echoed the vocal lines. In the southern parts of Texas and Louisiana the blues were played on the barrelhouse piano as well as the guitar. The blues took on their most influential form in the Mississippi Delta, though, partly because migrants carried that version of the Mississippi blues to Chicago and the other cities of the Midwest in the years around World War I. The Delta blues tended to favor rhythm over melody, building rhythms while leaving room for embellishment, especially slide work.

The most famous figure in that Mississippi blues was Charley Patton. Like Buddy Bolden, Patton has been the object of considerable fascination

Charley Patton. (Courtesy of Yazoo Records)

and considerable myth-making. Even more than jazz, early blues has been surrounded with an aura of mystery and misinformation, but Patton's early years are beginning to come into focus. Patton came from a small town halfway between Jackson and Vicksburg, Mississippi; he was born some time between 1887 and 1891, ten years later than Morton and Bolden. The son of a farm worker and part-time preacher, Patton was small and light-skinned; his hair was "fine," wavy and parted; to at least one black acquaintance he looked "Mexican," to others he looked more like an "Indian." Like so many other black families in the 1880s and 1890s, Patton's family moved to the Mississippi Delta, about a hundred miles to the north. They took up on the immense, forty-square-mile plantation of Will Dockery, near the Sunflower River, where over 500 black laborers cleared new land for cotton.

Dockery, college-educated and progressive, knew and cared nothing about Charley Patton and the music being created on his plantation. Patton was not much of a worker, too small and too preoccupied. He focused his energies instead on music. Patton could hear all kinds of music in the Delta, from ballads to ragtime, white dance numbers to Tin Pan Alley fads, minstrel tunes to waltzes. Chances are, too, that Patton heard early versions of the blues. Despite claims that Patton invented the blues, his age alone—only about ten years old at the turn of the century—suggests that he arrived on the scene when the blues had already begun to take shape. Patton did, though, make the blues more original and more entertaining. By 1906, only a few years after Handy, Rainey, and Peabody had overheard individual blacks singing the blues to entertain themselves, Charley Patton was becoming well known throughout the Delta as someone who could use the blues to entertain an audience with impressive guitar playing and exciting vocals.

While a plowman, laundress, or mother sang in private places, the young Charley Patton sang in the Delta's barrelhouses. Like their counterparts in the lumber camps, the barrelhouses of the plantation districts were often owned by whites, run by blacks, and ignored by sheriffs who had been paid to look the other way. The barrelhouses appeared near each town's railroad depot and thus attracted people from many miles distant; they were often painted green so that new, and perhaps illiterate, customers could easily find their way to their doors. Gambling, drinking, and dancing were the favored activities, and the music had to fit.

In such a boisterous place, a musician had to play loud and had to lay down a heavy beat for the dancers. The guitar blues, with its repetitive bass lines, piercing high slides, and staccato bursts, could do very well in the barrelhouses. The structured but loose lyrical techniques could allow the singer to compose lyrics on the spur of the moment to fit the situation. A song could be carried for a long time, verses added on as needed. Songs could be strung together, one blurring into the next, as long as the rhythm continued. Unlike the plantation "frolics" still going on during these years, where the music was driven by a fiddle and featured distinctly old-fashioned styles, the barrelhouses thrived on novelty. Charley Patton became so well known partly because he "clowned" with his guitar, playing it between his legs and behind his back, showing off.

The context of Patton's music helps account for its form. His blues were designed for the barrelhouse, for a loud and paying audience. They were not introspective pieces created for the porch of a sharecropper's shack, but extroverted tunes built for appeal and durability. Patton played the blues in a strenuous and sophisticated way. He used the guitar, and his voice, as rhythm instruments. While the guitar accented one beat, his voice would accent another or cut across the expected rhythm; he would strike the body of his guitar or suspend a vocal line, creating a complicated set of competing rhythms. His lyrics were not songs of overt protest but, like most blues, fixed on his personal exploits, real and imagined, as a lover and traveler. His lyrics said little about work, little about a boss, but they did talk in respectful terms of sheriffs and jails. His blues were not the sad songs of stereotype, but songs defiant in their tone and exuberance, in their hedonism and celebration of freedom.

Patton's blues, later labeled "country blues" to distinguish them from the blues of Chicago and St. Louis, were thus quite sophisticated. Growing up not on remote plantations but in crossroads barrelhouses, played not in isolation but at medicine shows and picnics where hundreds of people of both races gathered, played not to express private grievances but to facilitate public jubilation, these blues were hardly the products of an isolated folk. Despite the apparent simplicity demanded by one man playing one guitar, the blues combined elements of ballads, field hollers, work songs, jump-ups, the didley bow, and ragtime. In some ways, the early blues were more innovative than early jazz, deviating more from customary instrumentation, musical notation, and venue than the dance bands of Buddy Bolden.

The earliest blues singers navigated a complicated social terrain as well. They were not simple exponents of black male hell-raising and sexuality, poets of secular alienation and embitterment. A man such as Charley Patton played songs besides the blues, ranging from what was to become known as "hillbilly" music to religious songs. Just as Patton might play for a white audience, so might he play for black audiences more restrained than those in the barrelhouses. A picnic, fair, or party demanded a broader repertoire than the intense dance music of the blues. Many of the people at a party Saturday night went to church the next morning. Black sermons and blues songs bore considerable stylistic similarities, as both labored to create a sense of tension and release, as the words of both worked more by association and improvisation than by linear progression, as the voices of the leaders beckoned with a wide range of textures. The blues and the church spoke in a common African-American vernacular, lowering the boundary between secular and religious music. The one steadily influenced the other, inspired the other.

The music of white Southerners seemed far removed from the exciting new black music. White music was known for its "old-time" flavor, for the preservation of styles, diction, and themes that seemed far removed from the modern age, for its evocation and longing for a lost world. Yet white popular music, too, flourished in the New South, diversifying and spreading. Tent shows, minstrels, sheet music, and mass-produced instruments had their effects among whites no less than blacks, in the mountains just as in the lowlands. Railroad towns and coal camps in the upper South, like plantation districts and lumber camps in the lower South, witnessed the congregation of new musicians, ideas, and styles.

The earliest student of mountain music admitted, to his disappointment, that "in the Southern Highlands one finds the traditional song rudely jostled by the extensively diffused, and more modern type, each vying with the other for persistence." Josiah Combs, a Kentucky native who became a scholar and wrote about the mountains from the vantage point of France, bemoaned the way the subjects of the "traditional" song—"lords, kings, princes, 'ladies of high degree,' " jarred with the heroes of the "more modern type." In the newer songs, the central characters bore a more American appearance: "the outlaw, the pioneer, the railroader, the adventurer, the soldier." Many of the same characters intrigued white and black Southerners alike.

Just as Southern black musicians constantly remade the music they heard, so did Southern white musicians. The sentimental parlor songs that poured out of Tin Pan Alley in these years had an immediate appeal in the South, where the sad lyrics and music resonated with evangelical religion. The older ballads brought to the South by British settlers recounted tragic events in a relatively detached voice, telling of distant happenings in the third person. The sentimental parlor songs of the Gilded Age, on the other hand, spoke of the loss of children and mothers in an intimate language and music that proved comforting to the people of the time. Although these parlor songs were written by and for Northern middle-class audiences, Southerners quickly made them their own, simplifying the music, changing the key, altering names to fit a more familiar context. Songs that came to be known as mainstays of "country" music—such as "Wildwood Flower" or "Little Rosewood Casket"—began as parlor songs.

Similarly, while young people might neglect the ballads their grandparents had sung, they still turned to the ballad form to describe events in their own lives. Balladeers, professional and otherwise, were quick to memorialize a train wreck, a notorious crime, a mine disaster, or labor's struggles. While the introduction of organs, guitars, banjos, or pianos displaced fiddle-based "folk" music among some families, the new instruments could also encourage the revival of older songs as people tried to come up with music to play on their new purchases. Josiah Combs acknowledged that many of the folk songs he recorded had been taken "from the singing of young people in communities into which the organ had been introduced. This instrument seems, for a time, to have given a new impetus to the singing of folk-songs. Of course, the players, nearly always girls, played by ear . . . because there was no music for the songs."

Country music, as the amalgam of ballads, folk songs, parlor songs, and other popular music was eventually to become known later in the twentieth century, bred its own version of W. C. Handy, Jelly Roll Morton, and Charley Patton. The person who was able to crystallize and commercialize a broadly popular yet distinctive style of music was John Carson of Georgia. Born in north Georgia in the early 1870s, at about the same time as Handy and Morton, Carson's early life was more obscure than those of the black musicians. While the usual legends abound, it is clear only that Carson worked on the railroad as a youth, testified to by a newspaper account of a waterboy named John Carson who accidentally shot himself in the leg in 1886. Carson married during the hard times of 1894 and quickly fathered three children. No matter what work he followed, Carson's real passion was his fiddle and his music.

In his early twenties, Carson played mainly at rural dances in his native north Georgia. Such dances shaped country music just as barrelhouses shaped black music. Played before an audience that was more participatory than passive, the music at such dances had to be flexible and attention-getting. A fiddler, the mainstay of early country music, might play alone or might be accompanied by a banjo. In either case, another participant might help by striking the strings of the fiddle with two straws, knitting needles, or sticks—"fiddlesticks"—adding rhythm to the fiddler's tunes. Often, the musicians would sit in the doorway between two rooms so that the number of dancers could be multiplied, with one musician calling out the dance. The dancers slid their feet rather than picking them up, and the host sometimes sprinkled bran or sugar on the floor to make the sliding easier. Not infrequently, a bucket of whiskey helped everyone dance better. A good fiddler was an asset to any rural community, but even a good fiddler could not make any real money; it was an avocation, not a calling. Even with farming and fiddling, John Carson could not make a satisfying living.

With another child on the way in 1900, Carson and his wife clambered into a covered wagon to try out a mill village near Atlanta. Carson's father and brothers already worked there, in the Exposition Mill, housed in a building erected for the Cotton Exposition of 1881. Carson worked twelve hours a day in the mill then went to play his fiddle in the poolrooms of Decatur Street, famous for its racial mixing and debauchery. Nothing dramatic happened to Carson for years, as the number of children multiplied and the family moved from one company house to another. It was not until 1913 that Carson's music made much of an impact.

In that year, the cotton mill where the Carsons worked went on strike and he turned to music to feed his family, passing the hat in the poolrooms or playing in the streets. Carson also took advantage of another opportunity: commercial fiddlers' contests in the city's auditorium. Such contests had been around since the colonial era and had enlivened fairs and Fourth of July celebrations in Atlanta since the 1870s. The contest attained a new visibility in 1913. The big-city papers made a point of exploiting the supposed rusticity of the players (even those, like Carson, who had lived in the city for years), exaggerating their isolation and ignorance, playing up their country ways for all they were worth. Apparently they were worth something, for 6000 people packed into the auditorium for several days for the "Old Fiddlers' Convention." In a pattern that was to mark country music throughout the twentieth century, archaism was invented or played up so it could be sold. Performers clowned for the papers and the audiences, using in-group humor about poor whites much as black minstrels told nigger jokes. One of Carson's bands, for example, called itself the "Lickskillet Orchestra," advertising its supposed hunger and poverty, its distance from any real orchestra. Like Buddy Bolden, Fiddlin' John Carson—as he quickly became known—prospered because he could play loudly, because he was entertaining, and because he was hard-working.

Carson did well in the conventions, but there was no real money even for the winners. He achieved far more visibility when he wrote a ballad about the 1913 murder of Mary Phagan, a young white factory worker whose death unleashed enormous interest, anti-Semitism, and violence among white laboring people in Atlanta and far beyond. The tune for Carson's song was lifted from an earlier ballad about the assassin of President James Garfield, "Charles Guiteau," which in turn was similar to an earlier American ballad whose origins were probably Irish. Carson's song, sold as a popular broadside, stressed the sentimental aspects of Phagan's murder, referring to death as sleep, avoiding any direct reference to sex, and dwelling on heaven. Carson's ballad combined with his newspaper coverage during the fiddlers' convention to make him well known when early radio and recording entrepreneurs came to the South in the early 1920s looking for people to record, hoping to sell the hillbilly music Carson represented.

The early record-business people made other discoveries, too, as they tried to find authentic voices that other hillbillies would recognize and—paradoxically, given their supposed isolation and poverty—buy. One of the most successful was Uncle Dave Macon, born, like John Carson, in the early 1870s. Like Carson, too, Macon had strong ties to the urban South. His parents ran a boarding house in Nashville that served theatrical people, and so Macon from his earliest days was surrounded by the music, stories, and personalities of performers. Macon, like Carson, married and settled down, running the Macon Midway Mule and Wagon Transportation Company in a small middle Tennessee town. He played constantly, but not for a living; the story had it that he charged only once, to put an arrogant farmer in his place. As it turned out, a talent scout happened to be at that party in 1918, "discovered" Macon, and sent him to Birmingham, where his musical career took off. Macon's style was more vaudeville and minstrel than folk, since he had mastered repartee and a wide array of playing styles. To a wide audience, though, he embodied the good old days. From the very beginning, "country" music had to walk a fine line between novelty and tradition, sounding old-fashioned even as it constantly adapted to changing times.

Even with the ferment in jazz, blues, and country styles, religious music was the most widespread form of popular music in the South at the turn of the century, exerting a strong and steady influence among both races. Since well before the Civil War, Southerners at camp meetings had sung hymns from hymnals variously labeled "shape note," "sacred harp," or "fasola." Singing school masters traveled throughout the region selling books, teaching people how to read music, and leading singing classes. Many of the lyrics reflected their origins in eighteenth-century England hymns, with a strong emphasis on the depravity of man and the overwhelming strength of God. Southerners were drawn to such a view of the world and made the hymns their own, compiling books as early as the 1840s for Southern audiences, selecting those hymns with proven appeal in the region.

The post-Civil War years found no diminution of the tradition. If anything, the experience of defeat and the loss of so many loved ones made the shape-note hymns even more powerful. To white Southerners, Christians seemed pilgrims in a hostile world, a place where the rich enjoyed their temporary dominion, where the blessed were also the poor and the despised. Like the parlor songs, the hymns evoked home as the best of all worldly places, the one refuge from the cares of the world, the place where "precious father, loving mother" would always rest in Christian memory.

The phrase "gospel music" was first widely used after 1875, when a book called *Gospel Hymns and Sacred Tunes* appeared in the North. The South was an early participant in the movement, as the Ruebush-Kieffer Company, founded in 1866 in Virginia's Shenandoah Valley, popularized a shape-note system based on seven rather than the older four-note scheme. Kieffer founded the South's first normal singing school in 1874 to train teachers who fanned out all over the region; he also started a periodical called *The Musical Million* and published seven-note songbooks for the teachers to carry with them. Advertisements praised the songbooks as especially suitable for extended "special singings." The music bore strong similarities to its secular contemporaries. It was simplified, optimistic, rhythmic, sentimental. Some gospel songs written in the North—such as "Bringing in the Sheaves" and "What a Friend We Have in Jesus"—became especially associated with the South. Other songs—such as "Onward, Christian Soldiers" and "Keep on the Firing Line"—were propelled by the martial imagery of Protestant missionaries.

The song leaders who accompanied major evangelists accelerated the spread of gospel music. Leaders such as Ira Sankey, Dwight L. Moody's companion, disseminated their songs through appearances and books. No evangelist was as popular in the South as Sam Jones, whose song leader was an energetic man with a name to match: Edwin Othello Excell. Preparing the way for Jone's message of tears and redemption, Excell led choirs of up to 400 voices in stirring hymns. He won a reputation as the best song leader among the many who traveled across the nation in the Gilded Age. Excell wrote songs of his own in the 1880s and early 1890s, filling books that sold nearly half a million copies every year until World War I.

Gospel music was both folk and commercial from its beginnings. During the 1890s, a teenaged graduate of one of the ten-day-long schools of the Ruebush-Kieffer Company, James D. Vaughan, established a quartet with his three younger brothers in Tennessee. Vaughan took the quartet to singings and church meetings, demonstrating his abilities as a music teacher and singer, drumming up business. His was apparently the first gospel quartet, later a key institution in recorded and popular gospel music. Hungry for even greater training, Vaughan traveled to Roanoke, to one of the normal schools where future "professors" of music were taught. Meanwhile, Vaughan began collecting music of his own as he taught school in Tennessee and Texas. In 1902, he sold books out of the county office building in Tennessee where his brother-in-law was register of deeds; by 1910, after a series of new editions, Vaughan was selling 60,000 copies a year. He soon built a major publishing house. Other firms, such as those of A. J. Showalter of Georgia, Eureka Music of Arkansas, E. T. Hildebrand of Tennessee, and Trio Music of Texas, became competitors of Vaughan, selling enormous quantities of books in their own right.

Josiah Combs, in his hapless quest for pure unadulterated folk in the Southern mountains, was appalled at the effect of the singing schools. "The 'singing-school' master, or 'perfessor,' has put in his appearance in the Southern Highlands, as well as elsewhere over the rural sections of America. Upon his arrival he carried no brief for the folk-song, but instead, a huge tuning-fork," Combs sneered. The singing master might even be a Highlander himself, and in any case "he turns up his nose at Highland music, which is 'old-fashioned,' out of date, and 'not in books.'" Not only did the professor hold the folk songs in disdain, but he was incapable of teaching the older songs if he tried: "His stock-in-trade usually consists of the simplest tunes, those of the hymn books used by churches in the lowlands and in Highland towns." What Combs could not see was that the shape-note hymns were themselves quickly converted into "folk" songs, music that identified members of an area with one another, that signified the times when people became a community. The songs became so well known that a singing leader could merely call out a song's number and people would know it by heart, not needing to open the book. The folk were not overly concerned about the origins of the music, but rather with the way it resonated in their lives.

The flood of new Christian music flowed into complex channels, offering additional testimony to the rapid social and doctrinal differentiation of Southern religion. Because the book publishers strove to please a diverse audience rather than a central ecclesiastical body, they combined songs with divergent theological emphases. The book companies often accepted unsolicited hymns, regardless of the donor's denomination. As a result, a song book might celebrate doctrines ranging from the most conventional Christian virtues to speaking in tongues, foot washing, and divine healing.

The new shape-note gospel music was soon adopted by the dissident religious groups in the South, who seized on the music as their own and experimented with its possibilities. In congregations scattered across the region, people were eager for a more vital religion and for a music suitable to its stirring message. These congregations were unembarrassed by emotion,

by testifying in music. Such congregations outlawed no kind of musical instrument; even guitars were welcome. The new churches quickly adopted
James D. Vaughan's quartet style of singing and a strongly rhythmic piano
to go with it. A. J. Showalter's "Leaning on the Everlasting Arms" became
one of the most popular songs of the new congregations, with its catchy
chorus and driving rhythm.

The music of the South, then, like so much else in the region, was an elaborate dance between old and new, Southern and national, black and white,
secular and sacred. Those tensions have remained at the heart of the blues,
jazz, country, and even gospel music for the generations since, constantly
driving each form. Southern culture has continually reinvented itself, continually replenished itself from its own contradictions.

Chapter 12

Twentieth Century Limited

In the years around the turn of the century the South appeared to reconcile and converge with the rest of the country. Sports brought North and South together in friendly competition, the Spanish-American War created a new sense of nationalism, and veterans of the Civil War joined in peaceful celebration. Underlying all these reunions, however, were powerful forces pulling the other way. Violence, suppression of dissent, and resentment testified to the deep ferment in the New South as it entered the twentieth century.

By the 1890s a new group of Southern intellectuals had come of age. Born, in large part, in the country, raised in religious and hard-working families, these young men saw in intellectual work their best chance at making the South what it could be. Unlike their parents, these young intellectuals channeled their energies into secular rather than religious causes. They had been impressed by their parents' moral certainty and purpose, but the young men focused their certainty on issues of history, literature, politics, race relations, and education. They were cosmopolitan men, often educated in Germany and in the North, but full of love and concern—and often despair—for their native South. They thought the region's only hope lay in progress driven by economic growth, sectional reconciliation, and educational enlightenment.

The South had long produced men and women who declared themselves writers and intellectuals, but the young thinkers of the turn of the century enjoyed positions in professorships, editorial chairs, and advisory boards unavailable to most of their predecessors. While the leading intellectuals of the antebellum years had labored to create a uniquely Southern philosophy, the new scholars worked to bring the South into the national and international mainstream. Instead of writing tracts in lonely studies, these men pronounced their ideas from platforms and in quarterly journals. They institutionalized and legitimated critical thinking about important parts of Southern life, offering something new to the South: a nonpartisan and informed debate over issues of widespread concern. They were not radicals eager to challenge fundamental racial mores or class relations, but they did possess a critical cast of mind and the courage to call attention to at least some of the South's many problems.

Ironically, young Southerners who went North for historical training found a distinctly pro-Southern intellectual environment. Herbert Baxter Adams at Johns Hopkins and William A. Dunning at Columbia bred a generation of scholars who used the latest techniques of Germanic scholarship to "discover" that Southern slavery had been benign and that Reconstruction had been unjust. Out of Adams's seminars came men of prominence such as Woodrow Wilson, along with scholars who were to dominate Southern historiography throughout the early twentieth century. At the turn of the century, leading white scholars saw in slavery an attractive solution to the "race problem" and in Reconstruction the dangers of an overly zealous national government. Young Southern historians enjoyed the luxury of simultaneous loyalty to their homeland and a position in the scholarly vanguard.

Yet these scholars found themselves in conflict with the South to which they returned. Their belief in economic development, sectional reconciliation, and racial moderation—articles of faith on campuses in Baltimore and New York—caused them problems in the South. The beginning professors often found willing students and supportive colleagues, but they confronted vitriolic critics beyond the walls of the college, critics who had no appreciation for academic freedom, who had developed no taste for friendly criticism by some upstart infected with Yankee notions.

One of the first scholarly critics of the New South met the harshest response. In 1888, William P. Trent, a Virginian, came to the University of the South, in Sewanee, Tennessee, with the warm endorsement of Professor Adams at Hopkins, under whom Trent was completing his doctoral dissertation. Full of energy and fire, Trent did not plan to stay long. He quickly became an important figure at Sewanee, however, and in 1892 founded the *Sewanee Review*, the postwar South's first literary and historical journal. The *Review* modeled itself on the best English examples and intended itself for a national audience and purpose; by and large, its ideals and articles were genteel and improving rather than reformist.

Trent gained the eye of a Northern editor, Charles Dudley Warner, who visited Sewanee to give a talk. The editor, long on the lookout for someone to write a biography of William Gilmore Simms, the antebellum South's leading author, decided that the twenty-eight-year-old Trent was just the man for the job. Simms's friends and family had been aghast at Warner's first choice—George Washington Cable—and thought that Trent, though unknown, would be fine. Trent threw himself into the work, turning out an enormous biography in a couple of years while teaching a heavy course load.

Trent accepted Simms's belief that Charleston snobs had disdained the antebellum author and his work because of his plebian origins. Accordingly, the biographer portrayed pre-Civil War Southern society with a harshness quite unusual for the New South, characterizing it as decadent, primitive, emotional, feudalistic, irrational, a nightmare, "a life that choked all thought and investigation that did not tend to conserve existing institutions and opinions." Southern critics savaged Trent for selling his birthright in hopes of gaining Northern praise. His family was snubbed, fellow professors refused to stand beside him, former teachers denounced him, and the board of trustees at Sewanee was rumored to be considering his dismissal. Trent weathered the storm, however, and his book quickly became an inspiration to other young men of similar backgrounds and ambition. It now seemed possible, if one had the courage, to write about the South without falling into sentimentality and apology. Yet the South lost Trent, as it was to lose so many of its thoughtful sons and daughters: in 1900, Columbia University called him north and Trent, feeling that he could never advance at Sewanee and that no other Southern institution would touch him, went.

Ten years passed between Trent's notorious biography of Simms and the next outburst over Southern scholarship. In 1902, Andrew Sledd of Emory College suddenly became a target. Like Trent, Sledd was a Virginian who had gone north for graduate school; he had a master's degree from Harvard. An ordained minister, Sledd had recently married the daughter of a former president of the college, a powerful bishop; the young man seemed positioned for a successful career at the Methodist school. Although influential whites in the denomination had begun to take a more active stance toward helping black orphanages and colleges, people were surprised and appalled when Sledd published an article in the *Atlantic Monthly* denouncing the white South for its attacks on blacks' "inalienable rights." Probing the recent and highly publicized Georgia lynching of Sam Hose, coolly evaluating the white South's usual explanations, Sledd concluded that "the radical difficulty is not with the negro, but with the white man." He blamed the irrational white lower classes for the rampant violence, dismissing the talk of rape as mere excuse.

At first, Sledd's bold article met only silence. Then Rebecca Latimer Felton, a firebrand and independent for thirty years (and a bitter enemy of Emory's leadership), attacked Sledd in the Atlanta *Constitution* for his betrayal of Southern womanhood. She pulled no punches: "Pass him on! Keep him moving! He does not belong in this part of the country. It is bad enough to be taxed to death to educate negroes and defend one's home from criminal assault, from arson and burglary, but it is simply atrocious to fatten or feed a creature who stoops to the defamation of the southern people only to find access to liberal checks in a partisan magazine." Other papers and other writers picked up the attack and the Emory administration buckled under the pressure; the faculty offered no help. "I want to get away; I feel alien and wronged," Sledd wrote to his influential father-in-law. "I am cramped and stunted by the atmosphere that prevails. I had thought to be able to bring about a better state of things; but the people and the College will have none of it. Emory College needs regeneration. I had hoped its time had come. But I now believe that I was wrong in such a hope." Emory accepted Sledd's resignation but, guiltily, gave him an extra thousand dollars to pursue his doctorate at Yale.

Faculty at another Southern Methodist college, Trinity in North Carolina, watched the Sledd case uneasily. "The only hope of freedom is in the colleges of the church, and these have been marked for slaughter," the president of Trinity wrote Sledd's father-in-law. "Well, Trinity shall be free tho' all the Bishops, preachers, politicians, and wild women on earth decree otherwise, and I will get out only when shipped out, and then I will leave the church on record for a crime, the stench of which will never cease to rise to heaven." Trinity's president would soon have the opportunity to back up his words with actions, for his college was about to be thrown into even greater turmoil than Emory had endured.

At the center of the storm stood John Spencer Bassett. A native of North Carolina, a graduate of Trinity and then of Hopkins, a pioneering scholar of the state's history and a respected teacher, Bassett built a strong reputation. Bassett, like so many of his young compatriots, had little appreciation for the Democratic machines newly triumphant in the South; he had been particularly disgusted with the white supremacy campaign that wracked North Carolina. "We are crowing down here like children because we have settled the negro question," Bassett wrote to Herbert Adams in the wake of the 1898 election. "We don't see that we have not settled it by half. At best we have only postponed it." The young historian thought "the negro has acted admirably. Vilified, abused, denounced as the unclean thing, he has kept his peace; he has been patient. He has borne what no other people in history have borne."

In 1901 the thirty-five-year-old Bassett founded the *South Atlantic Quarterly,* a journal more concerned with current social concerns than was Trent's *Sewanee Review.* The quarterly soon printed searching essays written by some of the South's new generation, espousing the academy's ideals of openness and enlightened progress, gently chastising the South for its provincial sensitivity to criticism. In a series of articles, Bassett attacked the South's "reign of passion" and the lingering influence of the plantation ideal. Emboldened, in 1903 Bassett wrote an article intended to startle, "Stirring Up the Fires of Race Antipathy." His critique of the Democrats' use of racial fear was a theme he had struck before, but this time he went farther in criticizing segregation and disfranchisement: "The 'place' of every man in American life is such as his virtues and capacities may enable him to take," Bassett proclaimed. "Not even a black skin and a flat nose can justify caste in this country." In a phrase that provoked special virulence, Bassett characterized Booker T. Washington as "the greatest man, save General Lee, born in the South in a hundred years." Bassett predicted that black Southerners would not endure their subjugation forever, that a day of conflict and reckoning would come.

As in the Sledd case, it required the attention of newspapers to create a full-blown controversy out of an article with an otherwise small readership. Josephus Daniels, editor of the powerful Raleigh *News and Observer,* major protagonist in the white supremacy campaign, and bitter opponent of the Republican, monopolistic, and Trinity-supporting Duke family, launched a crusade against Bassett—or "bASSett," as he subtly put it. Other newspapers, especially from the eastern part of the state, jumped on the bandwagon, calling Bassett a "nigger lover." The Trinity board of trustees, pressured to fire Bassett, met to consider the issue. The president of the college, John C. Kilgo, bravely stood up to the onslaught, talking with Bassett and defending him before the board; twelve faculty members wrote letters of resignation to take effect if Bassett were fired; current and former students eloquently supported the professor. No one defended what he had said, but they did defend his right to say it—however misguided they considered such ideas to be. The board voted to keep Bassett, who remained quiet though unrepentant and contemptuous of his tormentors. Three years later, though, persuaded that another generation would pass before the South "will be ready for the scholar or writer of serious books," Bassett took a job at Smith College in Massachusetts, another exile from the New South.

As in so much else, then, the turn of the century found Southern colleges awkwardly pinned between the weight of the past and the pull of the future. Some of the men, some of the institutions, and some of the ideas were in place to create a relatively independent intellectual class in the South. Men of enlightened thought and good will worked in classrooms scattered across the South, trying to live up to ideals of scholarly honesty. They taught students receptive to those ideals and they encouraged one another in their break from the past. Yet beyond the walls of the colleges other white Southerners awaited, determined to strike down any dissident voice, no matter how restrained or scholarly its tones. Fires were kindled in the South of the turn of the century, only to fall victim to the chill of reaction. The fires would continue to smolder, though, waiting for another generation to stoke them back into flames.

Sports became established in the 1890s as the embodiment of everything new, youthful, and wholesome in the United States. Men turned to baseball, boxing, calisthenics, and swimming as evidence of their fashionable health-fulness; women took up bicycling, tennis, and golf. The South eagerly embraced each of these sports, finding that they fit well with a longstanding Southern fascination with physical display and competition. Southerners, recognizing that they had begun a bit late, tried to make up for lost time.

Sports quickly assumed an important place in the public culture of the region, appealing to people in town and countryside, in coal mining districts and in textile villages, to women and to men. Boxing matches and baseball scores were widespread topics of conversation and wagering early in the history of the post-Reconstruction South. For a while in the 1880s black men boxed white men and black baseball teams played against white ones. Those days quickly came to an end, though, when whites decided that victories for blacks on the playing field or in the boxing ring seemed to violate the racial order being so carefully constructed in other parts of life. Sports, segregated by race and gender and, increasingly, class, became a place for the social order to be buttressed, not challenged, a place for the white South to show the rest of the country what it could do.

The new game of football seemed especially suited for this role, capturing the South's imagination in the late 1890s. The game began at Northern colleges, migrated to Southern colleges, then slowly worked its way into the region's high schools, where interest built quickly and never flagged. The first college game in the country was played in 1869, and by 1877 Washington and Lee College and Virginia Military Institute had locked in combat. The game gained little momentum in the 1880s, remaining a curiosity and a casual sport, but then burst upon the collegiate scene in the early 1890s. By the turn of the century, college football had become a major spectacle in the South, generating interest far beyond the scattered campuses of the region and attracting crowds numbering 10,000. Coaches of Southern football helped create some of the sport's enduring innovations. In 1895, John Heisman of Auburn began using offensive guards to block for running backs and the South pioneered in adapting the forward pass into a powerful offensive weapon. Schools such as the University of the South and Vanderbilt achieved status as football powers early on, along with universities such as Alabama and Clemson soon to become traditional powers in the region and nation.

The student paper of the University of Virginia celebrated football players for their "coolness, as well as courage, quick wits, readiness of resource and all manliness of soul." Football's greater risks and greater need for teamwork seemed to build character in a way baseball, now bearing the contempt of cozy familiarity, did not. The appeal, and the threat, of football lay close to the surface. "It beats baseball all to pieces for excitement," Oliver Bond wrote in his diary after a game between Furman and South Carolina College in 1892. "One of the college fellows got his leg broken—a fracture of the tibia, I believe." A Baptist newspaper from Richmond presented an inadvertent advertisement for football in its denunciation of the game, "that dirtily clad, bare and frowsy headed, rough-and-tumble, shoving, pushing, crushing, pounding, kicking, ground-wallowing, mixed-up mass of players, of whom any might come out with broken limbs, or be left on the ground writhing with ruptured vitals."

Athletics, subordinated for generations to debating societies and fraternities, became the center of student life on many campuses in the South. Schools across the South adopted school colors, college yells, and mascots in the 1890s to help identify their teams. One reporter described Virginia's cheer as a "Wah Who Wah" compared with which the " 'rebel yell' was a summer zephyr to a cyclone." The comparison was apt. Ironically, it was the South's adoption of a Northern game that provided a vehicle for the reassertion of state and regional pride, as teams adopted the colors of the Confederacy and the imprimatur of legendary figures from the South's past. As in so much else, modern innovations did not so much dilute Southern identity as give it new, sharper, focus.

News of the escalation of tensions with Spain dominated the front page in the South and the nation in the 1890s. A conflict that had been growing ever since the end of an unsuccessful attempt by Cuba to gain its independence from Spain, a conflict waged during the South's Reconstruction years, broke out anew. Both black and white Southerners looked on the Caribbean crisis with considerable interest. Black Americans viewed the struggle of the Cubans as a struggle analogous to their own, a struggle for the freedom of colored peoples. A mulatto general, Antonio Maceo, captured the hearts and minds of blacks in the United States; his fight against the Spanish General Valeriano Weyler inspired black editors to urge United States intervention in Cuba. Black leaders, along with many other Americans, expected President McKinley to take quick action against the Spanish in Cuba. While some whites dreamed of a new American empire, blacks wanted to further the cause of liberty, to urge the world toward greater justice for others than "Anglo-Saxons."

The sinking of the *Maine* at the beginning of 1898 forced McKinley and the nation into action. Many black leaders saw a great opportunity as America prepared to go to war. Booker T. Washington, his strength and visibility growing in these years, proclaimed himself willing to take responsibility for recruiting "at least ten thousand loyal, brave, strong black men in the south who crave an opportunity to show their loyalty to our land and would gladly take this method of showing their gratitude for the lives laid down and the sacrifices made that the Negro might have his freedom and his rights." Across the country, black people saw in the war a chance to claim their rightful place in America, a chance to display their patriotism and their manliness in the tradition of Crispus Attucks.

Other black spokesmen denigrated such notions as wishful thinking.

Widespread militarization would only put more guns into the hands of the men who were lynching black men, some charged. Others denied that they owed the United States anything, for the country had steadfastly refused to recognize their humanity or citizenship. Others argued that instead of fighting for the freedom of Cubans, Americans should be fighting for the freedom of Southern blacks. The war would be only another excuse for whites to ignore the flagrant injustice and brutality in their own backyard, an excuse for the United States to get its share of the imperialist spoils being grabbed by the European powers.

The white South divided as well. Some Southern businessmen, especially cotton manufacturers, believed that overseas markets offered the South its best chance of avoiding colonial status itself within its own country; in their eyes, the war might be a useful step in gaining those markets. On the other hand, Southern congressmen often voted to check what they saw as dangerous tendencies toward centralized military power, whether the plans emanated from Republicans or from Democrats. Few Southern districts benefited economically from the expansion of the Navy, and peacetime military spending flew in the face of Southern Democratic ideals of frugality and small government. The Populists, too, denounced military spending and spoke little about expanding overseas markets. The South, despite its bellicose reputation, appeared no more militaristic than the rest of the nation in the 1890s.

Sectional reconciliation marked a prominent theme in the rhetoric early in the war, and those who identified with national values showed the greatest enthusiasm for the impending conflict. "Nothing short of an archaelogical society will be able to locate Mason and Dixon's line after this," a Detroit newspaper exulted. Someone concocted a song entitled "Battle Hymn," sung to the tune of "Dixie," with the stirring revised chorus of "Look away, look away, look away, freedom calls." Those white Southerners who enlisted in the war tended to be those tied closest to the towns and newspapers of the South, virtually identical to their Northern counterparts in age, marital status, occupations, and geographic mobility. Farmers, on the other hand, were underrepresented, as were those who lived in economically depressed areas.

Southerners assumed prominent positions in the United States forces, including generalships, and thrilled to the sight of young Southern men in the uniform of the nation. As a young girl, Evelyn Scott watched, fascinated, as troops drilled in the streets of her hometown, excited that "the Spanish yoke was about to be lifted. And by southerners! By *Clarksville* boys!" As if orchestrated from on high to bring white Northerners and white Southerners together, the first soldier killed in the Spanish-American War was a white Southerner, Worth Bagley of North Carolina. Newspapers north and south vied with one another to describe the sectional symbolism of Bagley's death. The New York *Tribune* announced the common theme: "The South furnishes

Men of the Tenth Cavalry in Huntsville, Alabama, 1898. (Huntsville Public Library)

the first sacrifice of this war. There is no north and no south after that, we are all Worth Bagley's countrymen.''

Black men who had enlisted in the military service long before 1898 had little choice in the matter of whether to fight in Cuba. Black soldiers had been among the most visible of the United States troops assigned to "pacify" the American West in the decades since the Civil War. While they remained under white officers and sequestered in remote outposts in the West, these "Buffalo soldiers," as the natives of the plains called them, had attained high reputations as fighting men. The threatening conflict against Cuba led the Army to pull these soldiers from the West to the South. Indeed, these black men were among the very first to be mobilized in 1898, since white military leaders assumed that blacks' physiognomy suited them to fight in the tropics. Patriotic crowds of both races cheered the black soldiers during the first part of their trip from Utah and Montana. As soon as they crossed over into the South in Kentucky and Tennessee, however, they met only silence. Black supporters were kept from the train; whites merely stared, glowered. "It mattered not if we were soldiers of the United States," one sergeant wrote, "we were 'niggers' as they called us and treated us with contempt.''

In June, black soldiers played key roles in the first battles on Cuban soil, winning 26 certificates of merit and 5 congressional Medals of Honor. Poems to their honor filled the black press; even white soldiers confessed that their black compatriots had served heroically. Their success and their glory fueled the desire of other blacks to join them for the planned assault on Havana.

Despite the reservations of some black spokesmen and the opposition of Southern whites who feared the massing of black troops, black men rushed to fill the black regiments. Even with obstacles thrown in their way, more than 10,000 black men enlisted in the volunteer ranks by the end of the summer.

The white citizens and newspapers of the places where black troops were stationed made it clear from the beginning that these black men, soldiers or not, would have to stay in their place. The black soldiers made it just as clear that they would tolerate nothing less than equality. The soldiers were able to see the new world of segregation with a perspective no white could bring, able to challenge that world in a way no individual Southern black could dare. The New South they described was harrowing.

The trouble began even before the first black troops left for Cuba. Both white and black regiments had been brought to Tampa, where they were stationed for a month. One group of Ohio volunteers got drunk and set out "to have some fun." One soldier grabbed a two-year-old black boy from his mother, spanking him with one hand while holding him with the other—a feat much enjoyed by his comrades. Then they used the boy for a target to display their marksmanship, seeing how close they could come with their bullets. The soldier who put a shot through the infant's sleeve took the prize. Finished with their shooting practice, they handed the boy back to his mother, who had been forced to watch, hysterical. Hearing of the episode, black soldiers from two regiments tore into the city, venting their anger and their frustration on white bars, cafes, and brothels that had refused to serve black soldiers. The police could not stop them, so a white regiment from Georgia was brought in to restore order. They did so by seriously wounding at least 27 black soldiers, while four whites also became casualties.

Black soldiers from the North wrote back home to tell of the scenes they confronted in the South. C. W. Cordin related how black soldiers had cut down a tree used for lynching in Macon. He had heard from more than a dozen "reliable citizens" that a man lynched from that tree had had his genitals cut off, "put into a bottle and pickled with alcohol. It was kept in Hurley's saloon on Avenue Street (in a prominent place) until a few weeks ago, but was hid away since on account of the presence of the soldiers." White Southerners, for all their bluster and occasional bloodshed, soon discovered that the black soldiers were not going to fall into the world of segregation easily. Soldiers refused to ride in the special segregated cars attached to Macon's streetcars. Conductors killed three soldiers in three separate conflicts for insisting on riding in the front, but the black troops never consented to the humiliation of separate cars.

The war against the Spanish, which so many black Americans thought might be a turning point in race relations in this country, in fact accelerated the decline, the loss of civility, the increase in bloodshed, the white arrogance. The long and bloody fight against the Filipinos that followed the defeat of the Spanish eroded American race relations even farther, the insurgents in the Philippines identified as "niggers" by the white soldiers sent to quell them, racializing America's first great moment in the sun of international attention. The war enlisted the North as an even more active partner in the subjugation of black Americans, bringing Southern and Northern whites into contact with one another to discover that they had grown more alike than they had expected. The war also brought blacks and whites of all regions into contact. They discovered, much to the disgust of the whites and much to the dismay of the blacks, that they were even farther apart than they had imagined.

The years of reconciliation at the turn of the century saw the peak of the Cult of the Confederacy. The United Confederate Veterans organized in 1889; somewhere between a fourth and a third of all living veterans joined, with men of all classes enlisting in its ranks. By 1895, the United Daughters of the Confederacy had formed. Towns across the South, often following the lead of the UCV or the UDC, raised funds for the erection of monuments. While early postwar monuments were located in cemeteries, the new monuments went up in the center of town; funeral urns and obelisks gave way to statues of solitary Confederate soldiers, vigilant forever as they faced to the north.

The Lost Cause was not simple evidence of Southern distinctiveness, Southern intransigence, but was also ironic evidence that the South marched in step with the rest of the country. The Gilded Age was the great era of organization in the United States, the time when nearly 500 social clubs and orders of every sort were established, enrolling six million Americans. History and genealogy provided the basis for many groups, such as the Daughters of the American Revolution. The Grand Army of the Republic attracted half of all veterans of the Union army, a considerably higher percentage than its Southern counterpart could claim.

The men behind the United Confederate Veterans came from town, from business backgrounds. They were not famous veterans, but rather from the rank and file, men who had become insurance agents or accountants after Appomattox, men looking for a new avenue to prosperity and pride. The Confederate statues were monuments not only to the past but also to the thoroughly commercialized present. While the Muldoon Company of Louisville turned out middle-aged soldiers bearing mustaches and thick girths, the Frank Teich Company of Llano, Texas, specialized in thin, young, and beardless Confederates. The firm that dominated the market, though, was the McNeel Marble Company of Marietta. While its craftsmanship did not surpass that of its competitors, its sales force did. Representatives of McNeel Marble crisscrossed the South, visiting United Daughters of the Confederacy chapters, offering advice on fund-raising. While the Georgia company manufactured the bases for its statues, the monuments themselves were

Confederate veterans marching in front of the Equitable Building and Trust, Atlanta, 1898. (Atlanta Historical Society)

carved in Italy. The salesmen encouraged veterans' chapters to vie for the largest statues, seeking precedence over competing towns in statuary and patriotism as in everything else.

The South erected impressive monuments during the peak years between 1885 and 1912. Some 9000 whites of all ages, occupations, and genders dragged, by rope and hand, a new statue of Robert E. Lee to its site in Richmond in 1890. Over 100,000 people came to the unveiling three weeks later, the largest ceremony attendant to any Confederate monument. The region's natives revered Decoration Day, when they carried spring flowers to the graves of the soldiers killed decades earlier. For generations, it was a time of unity, when young and old, male and female, felt a part of the larger lost cause. Nevertheless, even this ceremony could evoke worries about the South's fading ardor for its fallen generation. One Alabama newspaper felt it had to chide the town's citizens into decorating the cemetery. The paper urged the local militia into action. "It will only take a few hours on Friday evening to visit the cemetery, fire a salute over the bones of the dead, and let the children and others scatter a few flowers on the mound that covers them," the paper wrote, not making the prospect sound very inspiring. "Some one may be selected to tell the young people who may be there something of the deeds of valor performed by their fathers and grandfathers 30 years ago, and why the day is observed, etc." By the 1890s, there was a widespread sense that the stories of the "deeds of valor" needed to be formalized, institutionalized, because the veterans were passing from the scene. Despite the monuments and the sporadic parades, the veterans of the Civil War, as one put it, came "down from a different age." They seemed lost in the New South.

Southern race relations remained unstable, malleable, even after disfranchisement and segregation. Those relations constituted a complex environment of symbols over which no one person had much control and through which everyone had to navigate. Though the negotiations between whites and blacks were unequal, they were never completely scripted or contained. It was this open-endedness, this persistent buzz and confusion of human interaction, that kept some Southern whites worried and uncomfortable, that made others bloodthirsty and vengeful.

The economic and class conditions of black Southerners in the late 1890s and early 1900s were marked by sharply contrasting tendencies, each of which strained race relations in a different way. The black community seemed divided between a relatively successful property-holding or educated class on the one hand and an increasingly dispossessed working class on the other. Some black workers threatened white jobs even as others seemed perpetually underemployed. Whites found it hard to find domestic workers and distrusted the help they did find. To whites, many blacks seemed too satisfied with themselves, too confident with the trappings of the new order, too well spoken and too well dressed. Yet those blacks seemed unable to control other blacks, unable to persuade them that cooperation with whites was the best strategy. Most whites found reasons to fear, detest, or distrust most black people among whom they lived.

By later standards, virtually every white Southerner was racist. No matter how well intentioned whites might be, they believed that blacks were fundamentally different from themselves in intelligence and character. The most respected scientific thought of the age encouraged whites in this belief; the magazines and newspapers of the late nineteenth and early twentieth century were filled with a new assertion of Anglo-Saxon superiority, a self-consciousness of the hierarchy of races around the world, a heightened disdain of black aspiration and dignity. Unlike the years of the antebellum era or Reconstruction, there was virtually no school of thought outside the South to prod whites in the region into more egalitarian ways of thinking. Those Southerners who went to universities in New England, or Europe for that matter, heard their prejudices confirmed and given scientific vocabulary. The newly respectable racialism of Social Darwinism, early anthropology, and imperialism led whites to expect black deterioration. White Southerners drew comfort from the tone and content of dominant racial thinking even as they became increasingly uncomfortable with the black people in their midst.

Once segregation began, moreover, there was no logical place for it to stop. If railroad cars were segregated, why not railroad stations, even ticket windows? If jails were segregated, why not courtrooms, even the Bibles on which witnesses swore? If Bibles, why not schoolbooks, even when they being were stored over the summer? The new parks, playgrounds, swimming pools, schools, and hospitals of the Progressive era were segregated as a matter of course. Whites touted segregation as a way to ensure social peace, to reduce conflict in public places, to make sure that blacks received at least some social services. The newer a place or institution, the more certain it was to be segregated. The sanctity of the growing system of segregation had to be ensured. Any breach came to seem to whites a breach in the natural order. New generations of whites became squeamish about black people in ways their grandparents could never have imagined—or afforded.

Ironically, segregation appeared in so many guises in the New South that it created considerable confusion and ambiguity. There was less room for personal bargains that individual whites and blacks might strike with one another, less room for white nonconformity. When she was about eight years old, in 1905, Katherine DuPre Lumpkin happened to see, unintentionally, her father beat the family's cook, a small black woman. Lumpkin "began to be self-conscious about the many signs and symbols of my race position that had been battering against my consciousness since virtual infancy." As soon as the young girl could read, she "would carefully spell out the notices in public places. I wished to be certain we were where we ought to be." The railroads, by this time, were no problem, and neither were theaters; the rules of segregation were clear in both places. The streetcars, though, were another story altogether. "Here too were the signs—'White' at the forward end, 'Colored' at the rear. But no distinct dividing line, no wall or rail between. How many seats we occupied depended upon our needs. Sometimes conductors must come and shift things around in the twilight zone between."

The streetcars, in fact, created a "twilight zone" of race relations in towns and cities across the South. While the railroads had been the crucial battlegrounds of segregation in the 1880s and 1890s, in the 1900s the critical struggles were fought on the streetcars. The question was not whether blacks could ride without restrictions, but whether black passengers were to be relegated to separate cars or to separate sections within cars with white passengers. Custom could not decide, for blacks refused to bow before anything other than a sternly enforced law. Like the railroad companies, the streetcar companies had no interest in running separate cars. As an attorney for an Augusta street railway company explained in 1900, "Travel is not uniform. Congestion at times is inevitable. The hauling of empty cars is ex-

Marietta and Broad streets in Atlanta, 1901. (Atlanta Historical Society)

pensive." White public pressure led to a compromise: the cars would be integrated, with the sort of sliding and invisible line between the races which caused so much confusion for Katherine Lumpkin.

The conductors on the cars "might handle the delicate rearrangement quietly by just a tap on the shoulder and a thumb pointing back—this to a Negro," Lumpkin recalled. They might be "surly or even belligerent, speak in a loud rough voice so all could hear—'Move back.' A little white girl would rather stand, however much she knew it was her right to be seated in place of Negroes, than have this loud-voiced notoriety." The little girl would rather stand than "have a fleeting glimpse of the still, dark figures in the rear of the car, which seemed to stare so expressionlessly into space."

Not all whites were as sensitive as Lumpkin, of course, and the streetcars witnessed everything from embarrassment to lynching. The streetcar segregation inconvenienced whites as well as blacks, and whites often refused to sit in their assigned places. Conductors forced to decide a person's race at a glance often made mistakes; whites visiting from out of town often did not know how to navigate the ambiguous terrain; white working men returning from dirty jobs sometimes chose to sit in the black section rather than among white women. The conductors sorting through the confusion frequently found themselves in altercations, lawsuits, and fistfights. "Street-car relationships are, therefore, symbolic of the new conditions" in race relations throughout the South, Ray Stannard Baker observed in 1908. Although there was a color line "neither race knows just where it is. Indeed, it can hardly be definitely drawn in many relationships, because it is constantly changing. This uncertainty is a fertile source of friction and bitterness."

Black Southerners constantly fought back in ways large and small, overt and covert. They boycotted the streetcars in virtually every city where they were segregated, refusing to ride separate cars. They boycotted newspapers that referred to black children as "coons." They refused to patronize stores that treated black customers shabbily. They fought against disfranchisement with all the resources they could command. They held public meetings and conventions; they organized campaigns against the suffrage referenda; they sent petitions and protests to the legislatures; they listened as the few remaining black legislators spoke out against the new laws; they launched suits to challenge the voting restrictions. Some individual blacks continued to vote throughout the South, overcoming the restrictions against their voting with significant property accumulation, higher education, the good will of a white sponsor, a willingness to vote Democratic, the help of a Republican machine, or sheer grit and nerve.

A black strategy contrary to that of Booker T. Washington began to evolve. The man who was to emerge as the voice of opposition to Washington, W. E. B. DuBois, had been born in Massachusetts in 1868 and awarded a Ph.D. from Harvard in 1895. Coming to the South to teach at Atlanta University in 1897, he was to stay for the next thirteen years. "Here I found myself," DuBois was to recall. "I lost most of my mannerisms. I grew broadly human, made my closest and most holy friendships . . . [and] became widely acquainted with the real condition of my people."

DuBois launched a series of studies and yearly conferences on black life at Atlanta University and by 1900 was recognized as the leading student of black America. Booker T. Washington, by this time the head of the powerful "Tuskegee machine," was working behind the scenes to fight disfranchisement in Louisiana and Alabama and spending thousands of dollars to fight segregation. Washington had only praise and encouragement for the young DuBois. Not only did both men believe in the necessity of black pride, education, and entrepreneurship, but both were also willing to settle for strict property and literacy requirements that would disfranchise poor and illiterate black men while preserving the vote for more privileged blacks.

On the other hand, DuBois grew increasingly critical of Washington's overweening power among blacks, his ability to make or break a young career, his virtual monopoly of white aid. DuBois, along with other blacks, thought Washington did irreparable harm with his denunciation of higher education for black people. As the years passed and the racial situation in the South grew worse, it also began to seem that Washington's 1895 plea for fairness had fallen on deaf ears, that the time had come for more assertive action. Washington tried to pull DuBois to his side with several job offers, but DuBois had already begun to formulate an alternative vision. In 1903, DuBois published his classic work, *The Souls of Black Folk*. DuBois's book was immediately perceived as the manifesto of a new black strategy. In an essay entitled "Of Mr. Booker T. Washington and Others," DuBois praised Washington but argued that the Atlanta Compromise lost sight of the higher aims of life: "So far as Mr. Washington apologizes for injustice, North or South, does not rightly value the privilege and duty of voting, belittles the emasculating effects of caste distinctions," DuBois wrote, " . . . we must unceasingly and firmly oppose them."

Washington, whose autobiography, *Up from Slavery,* had achieved widespread acclaim and sales only a few years earlier, fought back with all the powerful weapons he could marshall: informants, newspapers, hostile reviewers, advertisers, potential employers. DuBois retaliated by creating an alternative to the Tuskegee Machine in 1905, a group of 59 like-minded blacks who called themselves the Niagara Movement. The movement, despite constant pressure from Washington, continued to grow in numbers and influence. "We will not be satisfied to take one jot or tittle less than our full manhood rights," the Niagara Address of 1906 declared. "We claim for ourselves every single right that belongs to a freeborn American, political, civil, and social; and until we get these rights we will never cease to protest and assail the ears of America."

The year of 1906 witnessed two events that suggested just how long the ears of white America would have to be assailed before they would hear. In Brownsville, Texas, 167 black soldiers, several of them recipients of the Congressional Medal of Honor, were summarily tried and dishonorably discharged after a racial incident in the town, punished for their unwillingness or inability to surrender the perpetrators. President Theodore Roosevelt, brusquely rebuffing Booker T. Washington's appeals for fairness, alienated black Americans even farther from the Republican party. If years of honorable military service to the United States seemed to account for so little, what would?

In Atlanta, the symbolic heart of the New South, the very embodiment of everything modern and hopeful, a race riot culminated the racial bitterness of the preceding three decades. The riot unleashed all the forces of New South violence. An eighteen-month campaign for statewide disfranchisement—Georgia was by this time the only Southern state without such restrictions—saw all the worst aspects of race relations dragged onto the front pages of competing newspapers. Those campaigning for prohibition, the focus of interracial cooperation in Atlanta twenty years earlier, talked of liquor laced with cocaine and bottles labeled with pictures of naked white women.

Accounts of black rape, murder, degeneration, and insolence filled columns of newspapers competing with one another for attention. "Bad niggers," the paper alleged, were flowing into Atlanta from the countryside, their past crimes unknown, their proclivities toward vice unchecked. Reconstruction was recycled for the growing number of readers too young to remember, and a play based on Thomas Dixon's *The Clansman* gave an especially lurid lesson. Conflicts on streetcars and other public conveyances were trumped up into portentous events. Prurient discussions of black sexuality titillated readers and inflamed susceptible white imaginations. The police raided "dives" considered the heart of black sexual deviancy.

On the hot evening of Saturday, September 22, a white man mounted a dry-goods box on Decatur Street, the "vice district" of the city, waving an extra edition of an Atlanta paper that screamed, "THIRD ASSAULT." "Are WHITE men going to stand for this?" he asked. The crowd began to respond, "No! Save our Women!" "Kill the niggers!" The mayor and the police commissioner called for restraint, but were hooted down; the fire chief rushed to Decatur Street and turned six hoses on the crowd. The mob pushed into other areas nearby, assaulting any blacks they happened to come upon; blacks fought back the best they could, but were badly outnumbered. One hardware store sold $16,000 worth of firearms to white men at the same time police disarmed black citizens. By eleven o'clock that evening, more than 10,000 white men, many of them carrying guns, marched through the city searching out blacks. The police made a few gestures at containing the violence, and several took heroic stands, but most did nothing. The mob broke into one black business after another, assaulting, killing black people, male or female, who happened to be inside. One black man was tortured to death, then had his fingers and toes cut off; the crowd fought to gain bloody souvenirs. Other black victims were piled at the base of Henry Grady's statue in perverse homage. The mob trapped streetcars, indiscriminately attacking any black person unlucky enough to be on board. The riot convulsed for two more days, reaching eventually into the black college district of the city. While the death toll was uncertain, about 25 blacks and one white were killed, dozens more wounded.

The Atlanta riot culminated virtually all of the changes in economy, culture, politics, public behavior, and violence that characterized Southern race relations in the 1890s and 1900s. The fulfillment of widely held white fantasies, the riot solved nothing. Whites felt no more secure; race relations seemed no more settled. Leaders began backing from the event, explaining it away, pushing it on to lower-class white scapegoats, enacting reforms in the police, organizing interracial leagues, leading interracial prayer meetings. The Atlanta of 1906 was not the New South progressive white Southerners wanted to advertise, not the New South they wanted to live in, not the New South they wanted the new generation to inherit. But it was all those things nevertheless.

History did not stop in 1906, of course, nor in any other year. The same patterns that marked the South at the turn of the century were to mark it for generations to come. For decade after decade, Southerners have negotiated between home and a longing to be a part of something larger. For decade after decade, Southerners of both races have eagerly sought the promise of America, knowing that they remain, in ways subtle and profound, a people set apart by their past.

Guide to Further Reading

The book from which this narrative was drawn, *The Promise of the New South: Life after Reconstruction* (New York: Oxford Univ. Press, 1992) contains documentation for all the topics discussed here, including tables and maps as well as references to newspapers, manuscript collections, and memoirs. This guide focuses on the most accessible and important of the secondary accounts of the era. The New South has been the subject of intense study and debate over the last several decades and so the literature is large and rich.

The starting point for understanding the New South is the work of C. Vann Woodward. His powerful biography, *Tom Watson: Agrarian Rebel* (New York: Macmillan, 1938), laid out most of the themes Woodward was to develop in later works and that have preoccupied historians of the society ever since. Woodward's *Origins of the New South, 1877–1913* (Baton Rouge: Louisiana State Univ. Press, 1951) was a stirring overview that focused on economic and political history. The "Critical Essay on Sources" by Charles B. Dew published in the 1971 edition of *Origins* is an exhaustive introduction to the literature up to that point. For more recent surveys, see the essays by LaWanda Cox, Harold D. Woodman, and Richard L. Watson, Jr., in John B. Boles and Evelyn Thomas Nolen, eds., *Interpreting Southern History: Historiographical Essays in Honor of Sanford W. Higginbotham* (Baton Rouge: Louisiana State Univ. Press, 1987), and Howard N. Rabinowitz, *The First New South, 1865–1920* (Arlington Heights, Ill.: Harlan Davidson, 1992). Compelling interpretations of the New South appear in Paul M. Gaston, *The New South*

Creed: A Study in Southern Mythmaking (New York: Alfred Knopf, 1970), Lacy K. Ford, "Rednecks and Merchants: Economic Development and Social Tensions in the South Carolina Upcountry, 1865–1900," *Journal of American History* 71 (Sept. 1984): 294–318, Paul Escott, *Many Excellent People: Power and Privilege in North Carolina, 1850–1900* (Chapel Hill: Univ. of North Carolina Press, 1985), and I. A. Newby, *Plain Folk in the New South: Social Change and Cultural Persistence, 1880–1915* (Baton Rouge: Louisiana State Univ. Press, 1989).

Many historians have focused on the troubling economic history of the New South. The key books on the history of the rural economy are Thomas D. Clark, *Pills, Petticoats, and Plows: The Southern Country Store* (Indianapolis: Bobbs-Merrill, 1944), Harold D. Woodman, *King Cotton and His Retainers: Financing and Marketing the Cotton Crop of the South, 1800–1925* (Lexington: Univ. of Kentucky Press, 1968), Roger Ransom and Richard Sutch, *One Kind of Freedom: The Economic Consequences of Emancipation* (Cambridge, Eng.: Cambridge Univ. Press, 1977), Jonathan M. Wiener, *Social Origins of the New South: Alabama, 1860–1885* (Baton Rouge: Louisiana State Univ. Press, 1978), Steven Hahn, *The Roots of Southern Populism: The Transformation of the Georgia Upcountry, 1850–1890* (New York: Oxford Univ. Press, 1982), Gilbert Fite, *Cotton Fields No More: Southern Agriculture, 1865–1890* (Lexington: Univ. Press of Kentucky, 1984), Pete Daniel, *Breaking the Land: The Transformation of Cotton, Tobacco and Rice Cultures Since 1880* (Urbana: Univ. of Illinois Press, 1985), and Gavin Wright, *Old South, New South: Revolutions in the Southern Economy Since the Civil War* (New York: Basic Books, 1986), the key reinterpretation since Woodward.

On industrial development in general, see James C. Cobb, *Industrialization and Southern Society, 1877–1984* (Lexington: Univ. Press of Kentucky, 1984). The most important studies of the textile industry, which include some of the best books written on the New South, are David L. Carlton, *Mill and Town in South Carolina: 1880–1920* (Baton Rouge: Louisiana State Univ. Press, 1980), Jacqueline Hall, James Leloudis, Robert Korstad, Mary Murphy, Lu Ann Jones, and Christopher B. Daly, *Like a Family: The Making of a Southern Cotton Mill World* (Chapel Hill: Univ. of North Carolina Press, 1987), Allen Tullos, *Habits of Industry: White Culture and the Transformation of the Carolina Piedmont* (Chapel Hill: Univ. of North Carolina Press, 1989), and Douglas Flamming, *Creating the Modern South: Millhands and Managers in Dalton, Georgia, 1884–1984* (Chapel Hill: Univ. of North Carolina Press, 1992).

On Appalachian development, see David Alan Corbin, *Life, Work, and Rebellion in the Coal Fields: The Southern West Virginia Mines, 1880–1920* (Urbana: Univ. of Illinois Press, 1981), Ronald D. Eller, *Miners, Millhands, and Mountaineers: Industrialization of the Appalachian South, 1880–1930* (Knoxville: Univ. of Tennessee Press, 1982), Altina L. Waller, *Feud: Hatfields, McCoys, and Social Change in Appalachia, 1860–1900* (Chapel Hill: Univ. of North Carolina Press, 1988), and Crandall Shifflett, *Coal Towns: Life, Work, and Culture in*

Company Towns of Southern Appalachia, 1880–1960 (Knoxville: Univ. of Tennessee Press, 1991). On lumbering, see Robert S. Maxwell and Robert D. Baker, *Sawdust Empire: The Texas Lumber Industry, 1830–1940* (College Station: Texas A & M Univ. Press, 1983).

On rural life, some fascinating studies include Robert K. Gilmore, *Ozark Baptizings, Hangings, and Other Diversions: Theatrical Folkways of Rural Missouri, 1885–1910* (Norman: Univ. of Oklahoma Press, 1984), a work with broader implications than its title might suggest, and Sydney Nathans, " 'Gotta Mind to Move, a Mind to Settle Down': Afro-Americans and the Plantation Frontier," in William Cooper, Michael F. Holt, and John McCardell, eds., *A Master's Due: Essays in Honor of David Herbert Donald* (Baton Rouge: Louisiana State Univ. Press, 1985), Orville Vernon Burton, *In My Father's House Are Many Mansions: Family and Community in Edgefield County, South Carolina* (Chapel Hill: Univ. of North Carolina Press, 1985), Jacqueline Jones, *Labor of Love, Labor of Sorrow: Black Women, Work, and the Family from Slavery to the Present* (New York: Basic Books, 1985), and Durwood Dunn, *Cades Cove: The Life and Death of a Southern Appalachian Community, 1818–1937* (Knoxville: Univ. of Tennessee Press, 1988).

Historians have not given much attention to town life, but there is a rich literature on cities, including Walter B. Weare, *Black Business in the New South: A Social History of the North Carolina Mutual Life Insurance Company* (Urbana: Univ. of Illinois Press, 1973), Howard N. Rabinowitz, "Continuity and Change: Southern Urban Development, 1860–1900," in Blaine A. Brownell and David R. Goldfield, eds., *The City in Southern History: The Growth of Urban Civilization in the South* (Port Washington, N.Y.: Kennikat Press, 1977), David R. Goldfield, *Cotton Fields and Skyscrapers: Southern City and Region, 1607–1980* (Baton Rouge: Louisiana State Univ. Press, 1982), James Michael Russell, *Atlanta, 1847–1890: City Building in the Old South and the New* (Baton Rouge: Louisiana State Univ. Press, 1988), and Don H. Doyle, *New Men, New Cities, New South: Atlanta, Nashville, Charleston, Mobile, 1860–1910* (Chapel Hill: Univ of North Carolina Press, 1990).

The political history of the New South began with Reconstruction, the best account of which is Eric Foner, *Reconstruction: America's Unfinished Revolution, 1863–1877* (New York, Harper and Row, 1988); an interpretation of an especially important topic appears in Mark W. Summers, *Railroads, Reconstruction, and the Gospel of Prosperity: Aid Under the Radical Republicans, 1865–1877* (Princeton: Princeton Univ. Press, 1984). The end of Reconstruction is analyzed well in Michael Perman, *The Road to Redemption: Southern Politics, 1869–1879* (Chapel Hill: Univ. of North Carolina Press, 1984). Southern charges of a discriminatory federal government are given some credence in Richard Franklin Bensel, *Yankee Leviathan: The Origins of Central State Authority in America, 1859–1877* (Cambridge, Eng.: Cambridge Univ. Press, 1990). A sophisticated and stimulating overview appears in Steven Hahn, "Class and State in Postemancipation Societies: Southern Planters in

Comparative Perspective," *American Historical Review* 95 (Feb. 1990): 75–98. Few historians have explored what the state governments actually did; an exception is the fine book by Peter Wallenstein, *From Slave South to New South: Public Policy in Nineteenth-Century Georgia* (Chapel Hill: Univ. of North Carolina Press, 1987). Studies of particular and important facets of Southern politics include J. Morgan Kousser, *The Shaping of Southern Politics: Suffrage Restriction and the Establishment of the One-Party South, 1880–1910* (New Haven: Yale Univ. Press, 1974), Gordon B. McKinney, *Southern Mountain Republicans, 1865–1900: Politics and the Appalachian Community* (Chapel Hill: Univ. of North Carolina Press, 1978), and Bess Beatty, *A Revolution Gone Backwards: The Black Response to National Politics, 1876–1896* (Westport, Conn.: Greenwood, 1987). A rare challenge to Woodward's interpretation of the Redeemers appears in James Tice Moore, "Redeemers Reconsidered: Change and Continuity in the Democratic South, 1870–1900," *Journal of Southern History* 44 (August 1978): 357–78. Two thorough treatments of Southern progressivism are Dewey W. Grantham, *Southern Progressivism: The Reconciliation of Progress and Tradition* (Knoxville: Univ. of Tennessee Press, 1983), and William A. Link, *The Paradox of Southern Progressivism, 1880–1930* (Chapel Hill: Univ. of North Carolina Press, 1993).

Many of the best works on political history are state studies. Important ones include Francis Butler Simkins, *Pitchfork Ben Tillman, South Carolinian* (Baton Rouge: Louisiana State Univ. Press, 1944), Albert D. Kirwan, *Revolt of the Rednecks: Mississippi Politics, 1876–1925* (Lexington: Univ. of Kentucky Press, 1951), Allen W. Moger, *Virginia: From Bourbonism to Byrd* (Charlottesville: Univ. of Virginia Press, 1968), William I. Hair, *Bourbonism and Agrarian Protest: Louisiana Politics, 1877–1900* (Baton Rouge: Louisiana State Univ. Press, 1969), Sheldon Hackney, *From Populism to Progressivism in Alabama* (Princeton: Princeton Univ. Press, 1969), William Warren Rogers, *The One-Gallused Rebellion: Agrarianism in Alabama, 1865–1896* (Baton Rouge: Louisiana State Univ. Press, 1970), Alwyn Barr, *Reconstruction to Reform: Texas Politics, 1876–1906* (Austin: Univ. of Texas Press, 1971), Roger L. Hart, *Redeemers, Bourbons, and Populists: Tennessee, 1870–1896* (Baton Rouge: Louisiana State Univ. Press, 1975), Edward C. Williamson, *Florida Politics in the Gilded Age, 1877–1893* (Gainesville: Univ. Press of Florida, 1976), Eric Anderson, *Race and Politics in North Carolina, 1872–1901: The Black Second* (Baton Rouge: Louisiana State Univ. Press, 1981), and Raymond Arsenault, *Wild Ass of the Ozarks: Jeff Davis and the Social Bases of Southern Politics, 1888–1913* (Philadelphia: Temple Univ. Press, 1984), an especially imaginative interpretation.

Populism has created one of the most vibrant fields of Southern historical debate. In addition to the Woodward and Hahn books mentioned above, see Theodore Saloutos, *Farmer Movements in the South, 1865–1933* (Berkeley: Univ. of California Press, 1960), William F. Holmes, "Demise of the Colored Farmers' Alliance," *Journal of Southern History* 41 (1975): 187–200, Robert C.

McMath, Jr., *Populist Vanguard: A History of the Southern Farmers' Alliance* (Chapel Hill: Univ of North Carolina Press, 1975), Lawrence Goodwyn, *Democratic Promise: The Populist Moment in America* (New York: Oxford Univ. Press, 1976), Michael Schwartz, *Radical Protest and Social Structure: The Southern Farmers' Alliance and Cotton Tenancy, 1880–1890* (New York: Academic, 1976), Gerald H. Gaither, *Blacks and the Populist Revolt: Ballots and Bigotry in the "New South"* (University: Univ. of Alabama Press, 1977), Bruce Palmer, *"Man Over Money": The Southern Populist Critique of American Capitalism* (Chapel Hill: Univ. of North Carolina Press, 1980), William F. Holmes, "The Southern Farmers' Alliance and the Georgia Senatorial Election of 1890," *Journal of Southern History* 50 (May 1984): 195–224, and Barton C. Shaw, *The Wool-Hat Boys: A History of the Populist Party in Georgia, 1892 to 1910* (Baton Rouge: Louisiana State Univ. Press, 1984).

Relations between blacks and whites have, understandably, long been of great interest. Good places to start are C. Vann Woodward, *The Strange Career of Jim Crow* (3d ed., New York: Oxford Univ. Press, 1974), and Howard N. Rabinowitz, "More Than the Woodward Thesis: Assessing *The Strange Career of Jim Crow*," *Journal of American History* 75 (Dec. 1988): 842–56. The rich discussion of the topic includes August Meier, *Negro Thought in America, 1880–1915: Racial Ideologies in the Age of Booker T. Washington* (Ann Arbor: Univ. of Michigan Press, 1963), Frenise A. Logan, *The Negro in North Carolina, 1876–1894* (Chapel Hill: Univ. of North Carolina Press, 1964), George M. Fredrickson, *The Black Image in the White Mind: The Debate on Afro-American Character and Destiny, 1817–1914* (New York: Harper and Row, 1971), Judith Stein, " 'Of Mr. Booker T. Washington and Others': The Political Economy of Racism in the United States," *Science and Society* 38 (Winter 1974–5): 422–63, Willard B. Gatewood, Jr., *Black Americans and the White Man's Burden, 1898–1903* (Urban: Univ. of Illinois Press, 1975), Joseph H. Cartwright, *The Triumph of Jim Crow: Tennessee Race Relations in the 1880s* (Knoxville: Univ. of Tennessee Press, 1976), Howard N. Rabinowitz, *Race Relations in the Urban South, 1865–1890* (New York: Oxford Univ. Press, 1978), John W. Cell, *The Highest Stage of White Supremacy: The Origins of Segregation in South Africa and the American South* (New York: Cambridge Univ. Press, 1982), Barbara J. Fields, "Ideology and Race in American History," in J. Morgan Kousser and James M. McPherson, eds., *Region, Race, and Reconstruction: Essays in Honor of C. Vann Woodward* (New York: Oxford Univ. Press, 1982), Joel Williamson, *The Crucible of Race: Black-White Relations in the American South Since Emancipation* (New York: Oxford Univ. Press, 1984), Leon Litwack, " 'Blues Falling Down like Hail': The Ordeal of Black Freedom," in Robert H. Abzug and Stephen E. Maizlish, eds., *New Perspectives on Race and Slavery in America: Essays in Honor of Kenneth M. Stampp* (Lexington: Univ. of Kentucky Press, 1986), and Neil R. McMillen, *Dark Journey: Black Mississippians in the Age of Jim Crow* (Urbana: Univ. of Illinois Press, 1989).

Two superb biographies of the most prominent black leaders of this era are Louis R. Harlan, *Booker T. Washington: The Making of a Black Leader, 1856–1901* (New York: Oxford Univ. Press, 1972), and David Levering Lewis, *W. E. B. DuBois, 1868–1919: Biography of a Race* (New York: Henry Holt, 1993).

A number of scholars have tried to understand the rampant violence of the New South. Among them are Edward L. Ayers, *Vengeance and Justice: Crime and Punishment in the Nineteenth-Century American South* (New York: Oxford Univ. Press, 1984), George Wright, *Racial Violence in Kentucky, 1865–1940: Lynchings, Mob Rule, and "Legal Lynchings"* (Baton Rouge: Louisiana State Univ. Press, 1990), William Cohen, *At Freedom's Edge: Black Mobility and the Southern White Quest for Racial Control, 1861–1915* (Baton Rouge: Louisiana State Univ. Press, 1991), and W. Fitzhugh Brundage, *Lynching in the New South: Georgia and Virginia, 1880–1930* (Urbana: Univ. of Illinois Press, 1993).

On education and intellectual life in the South, see Bruce Clayton, *The Savage Ideal: Intolerance and Intellectual Leadership in the South, 1890–1914* (Baltimore: Johns Hopkins Univ. Press, 1972), William A. Link, *A Hard Country and a Lonely Place: Schools in Rural Virginia, 1870–1920* (Chapel Hill: Univ. of North Carolina Press, 1986), James D. Anderson, *The Education of Blacks in the South, 1860–1935* (Chapel Hill: Univ. of North Carolina Press, 1988), and Robert A. Margo, *Race and Schooling in the South, 1880–1950: An Economic History* (Chicago: Univ. of Chicago Press, 1991).

Southern women's history is just now coming into its own, following the pioneering series of articles on the suffrage by Antoinette Elizabeth Taylor, including "The Woman Suffrage Movement in Mississippi, 1890–1920," *Journal of Mississippi History* 30 (Feb. 1968): 1–11, the graceful interpretation by Anne Firor Scott, *The Southern Lady: From Pedestal to Politics, 1830–1930* (Chicago: Univ. of Chicago Press, 1970), and Paul E. Fuller, *Laura Clay and the Woman's Rights Movement* (Lexington: Univ. Press of Kentucky, 1975). A fine synthesis appears in Marjorie Spruill Wheeler, *New Women of the New South: The Leaders of the Woman Suffrage Movement in the Southern States* (New York: Oxford Univ. Press, 1993). There remains much to be done on other facets of the history of women, black and white, in the South.

Southern religion is another topic that could use additional work, though useful studies include Hunter Dickinson Farish, *The Circuit-Rider Dismounts: A Social History of Southern Methodism, 1865–1900* (Richmond: Dietz Press, 1938), Charles W. Conn, *Like a Mighty Army Moves the Church of God, 1886–1955* (Cleveland, Tenn.: Church of God Publishing House, 1955), Rufus B. Spain, *At Ease in Zion: A Social History of Southern Baptists* (Nashville: Vanderbilt Univ. Press, 1967), Vinson Synan, *The Holiness-Pentecostal Movement in the United States* (Grand Rapids: Eerdmans, 1971), Frederick A. Bode, *Protestantism and the New South: North Carolina Baptists and Methodists in Political Crisis, 1894–1903* (Charlottesville: Univ. Press of Virginia, 1975), Robert Mapes Anderson, *Vision of the Disinherited: The Making of American Pentecostalism* (New York: Oxford Univ. Press, 1979), David Edwin Harrell, Jr., "The Evolution of Plain-Folk Religion in the South, 1835–1920," in Samuel S. Hill, ed., *Varieties of Southern Religious Experience* (Baton Rouge: Louisiana State Univ. Press, 1988), and Mickey Crews, *The Church of God: A Social History* (Knoxville: Univ. of Tennessee Press, 1990). A study that stands out for its originality and breadth is Ted Ownby, *Subduing Satan: Religion, Recreation, and Manhood in the Rural South, 1865–1920* (Chapel Hill: Univ. of North Carolina Press, 1990).

Southern literature has been the object of considerable thought and talent. Useful overviews of particular facets of that literature include J. V. Ridgely, *Nineteenth-Century Southern Literature* (Lexington: Univ. of Kentucky Press, 1980), Wayne Mixon, *Southern Writers and the New South Movement, 1865–1913* (Chapel Hill: Univ. of North Carolina Press, 1980), Anne Goodwyn Jones, *Tomorrow Is Another Day: The Woman Writer in the South, 1859–1936* (Baton Rouge: Louisiana State Univ. Press, 1981), and Dickson D. Bruce, Jr., *Black American Writing from the Nadir: The Evolution of a Literary Tradition, 1877–1915* (Baton Rouge: Louisiana State Univ. Press, 1989). Most work in the field has focused on individual writers. The best of those include Arlin Turner, *George W. Cable: A Biography* (Baton Rouge: Louisiana State Univ. Press, 1966), Louis D. Rubin, Jr., *George Washington Cable: The Life and Times of a Southern Heretic* (New York: Pegasus, 1969), Paul M. Cousins, *Joel Chandler Harris: A Biography* (Baton Rouge: Louisiana State Univ. Press, 1968), Arthur G. Pettit, *Mark Twain and the South* (Lexington: Univ. Press of Kentucky, 1974), Per Seyersted, *Kate Chopin: A Critical Biography* (Baton Rouge: Louisiana State Univ. Press, 1969), Emily Toth, *Kate Chopin* (New York: William Morrow, 1990), J. R. Raper, *Without Shelter: The Early Career of Ellen Glasgow* (Baton Rouge: Louisiana State Univ. Press, 1971), and William L. Andrews, *The Literary Career of Charles W. Chesnutt* (Baton Rouge: Louisiana State Univ. Press, 1980). Two works that have especially influenced my own are Helen Taylor, *Gender, Race, and Region in the Writings of Grace King, Ruth McEnery Stuart, and Kate Chopin* (Baton Rouge: Louisiana State Univ. Press, 1989), and Anna Shannon Elfenbein, *Women on the Color Line: Evolving Stereotypes and the Writings of George Washington Cable, Grace King, and Kate Chopin* (Charlottesville: Univ. Press of Virginia, 1989).

Southern music, fittingly enough, has been lovingly studied. Good places to begin are Lawrence W. Levine, *Black Culture and Black Consciousness: Afro-American Folk Thought from Slavery to Freedom* (New York: Oxford Univ. Press, 1977), Paul Oliver, *Songsters and Saints: Vocal Traditions on Race Records* (Cambridge, Eng.: Cambridge Univ. Press, 1984), Bill Malone, *Country Music, U.S.A.* (Austin: Univ. of Texas Press, 1985), and W. C. Handy, *Father of the Blues: An Autobiography* (1941; rpt., New York: Collier, 1970). More specialized works that offer compelling accounts are Gunther Schuller, *Early Jazz: Its Roots and Musical Development* (New York: Oxford Univ. Press, 1968), Donald M. Marquis, *In Search of Buddy Bolden: First Man of Jazz* (Baton Rouge: Louisiana State Univ. Press, 1978), Peter J. Silvester, *A Left Hand like God: A*

Study of Boogie-Woogie (New York: Quartet Books, 1988), Robert Palmer, *Deep Blues* (New York: Viking Press, 1981), Stephen Calt and Gayle Wardlow, *King of the Delta Blues: The Life and Music of Charlie Patton* (Newton, N.J.: Rock Chapel Press, 1988), and Gene Wiggins, *Fiddlin' Georgia Crazy: Fiddlin' John Carson, His Real World, and the World of His Songs* (Urbana: Univ. of Illinois Press, 1987).

The years of reconciliation between white Southerners and white Northerners are well covered in Gaines Foster, *Ghosts of the Confederacy: Defeat, the Lost Cause, and the Emergence of the New South* (New York: Oxford Univ. Press, 1987), and Nina Silber, *The Romance of Reunion: Northerners and the South, 1865–1900* (Chapel Hill: Univ. of North Carolina Press, 1993).

Despite this small mountain of scholarship we have not begun to exhaust the complexities and contradictions of the New South.

Index

CPSIA information can be obtained
at www.ICGtesting.com
Printed in the USA
FFOW02n1504131215
19441FF